Re-Framing Educational Politics for Social Justice

Catherine Marshall

University of North Carolina, Chapel Hill

Cynthia Gerstl-Pepin

University of Vermont

PEARSON

Boston • New York • San Francisco
Mexico City • Montreal • Toronto • London • Madrid • Munich • Paris
Hong Kong • Singapore • Tokyo • Cape Town • Sydney

Senior Editor: Arnis Burvikovs
Editorial Assistant: Kelly Hopkins
Marketing Manager: Tara Whorf
Editorial-Production Administrator: Annette Joseph
Editorial-Production Service: Colophon
Electronic Composition: Publishers' Design and Production Services, Inc.
Composition Buyer: Linda Cox
Manufacturing Buyer: Andrew Turso
Cover Administrator: Kristina Mose-Libon
Cover Designer: Jennifer Hart

For related titles and support materials, visit our online catalog at www.ablongman.com.

Between the time website information is gathered and then published, it is not unusual for some sites to have closed. Also, the transcription of URLs can result in typographical errors. The publisher would appreciate notification where these errors occur so that they may be corrected in subsequent editions.

Library of Congress Cataloging-in-Publication Data

Marshall, Catherine
　　Re-framing educational politics for social justice / Catherine Marshall, Cynthia Gerstl-Pepin.
　　　p.　cm.
　　Includes bibliographical references and index.
　　ISBN 0-205-37142-6 (alk. paper)
　　　1. Politics and education—United States.　2. Critical pedagogy—United States.　3. Social justice—United States.　I. Title: Re-framing educational politics for social justice.
II. Gerstl-Pepin, Cynthia I.　III. Title.

LC78.M228 2004
379.73—dc22
　　　　　　　　　　　　　　　　　　　　　　　　　　　　2004054436

Printed in the United States of America

10 9 8 7 6 5 4 3 2 1 HAM 09 08 07 06 05 04

To the leaders who will re-frame schooling for all children
and
To Catherine's grandchildren, Kim, Andrea, Peter, Stevie, Breanna, and Stephanie
and
To Cindy's sons, Ethan and Reid.

You spark our desire to make a difference in the lives of all children.

Contents

Foreword

Politics of education texts have for many years told us that the myth of "apolitical" education is long dead (Wirt and Kirst, 1972). But if the "apolitical myth" of education has been vanquished, then why do we continue to believe that in the study of educational politics we can and should remain neutral, unbiased observers? Why do we teach our students *about* politics without ever addressing how to *do* politics? This text, *Re-Framing Educational Politics for Social Justice*, by Catherine Marshall and Cynthia Gerstl-Pepin, challenges this assumption and revives discussion of the purposes of our field. This text diverges from previous politics of education textbooks in two fundamental ways: It acknowledges the forgotten importance of advocacy in the politics of education, and in so doing it illuminates the covert role of power in sustaining traditional norms of practice both within the field and within our schools.

Many authors have traced the development of the field of politics of education, identifying shortcomings and recommending improvements (Boyd, 1988; Cibulka, 1995; Johnson, 2003; Layton, 1982; Mitchell, 1990; Scribner & Englert, 1977; Wong, 1995). Absent from these discussions is acknowledgment that, over time, our field has moved toward portraying itself as increasingly neutral and objective. In an essay on the future of our field, Hawley (1977) stated that "if systematic scholarship has little to say to those who would bring about change, then a potentially significant source of political power, namely knowledge, is in effect neutralized" (p. 320). Despite this early call for engagement, today our field is characterized as a critical yet conservative discipline—critical of institutions but cautious about proposing changes (Peterson, 1995). Borrowing from Wildavsky's (1979) work, the field has focused on speaking truth and studying power but has failed to "speak truth to power." Few educational politics scholars believe their task extends to improving the systems that they study.

This text both implicitly and explicitly questions the appropriateness of couching research on the politics of education only in terms of "contributing to the discipline." Instead, the authors push us to frame our studies of politics in terms of how they contribute to the development of a more just society. In arguing that research on the politics of education—unlike art, music, and literature—cannot rest on its intrinsic value, they also push us to question the worth of our current pedagogical practices in the field. If our research should be judged by its contribution to social justice, should not our teaching of politics also be judged not by whether our students can identify different political process theories but by whether those students will participate in the process in ways that improve the lives of children?

In addressing both impact and advocacy, Marshall and Gerstl-Pepin also confront the implicit conceptions of power that are often overlooked by the field. The politics of education field has exhibited a preoccupation with overt manifestations of power, at the expense of studying the structures and conceptualizations of power that disguise, suppress, and silence marginal populations. As Johnson has suggested (2003), this excessive preoccupation with overt conceptualizations of power has not only perpetuated "blind spots in the field" but has also encouraged an unwillingness to acknowledge alternative explanations for political phenomena. Earlier inattention to these competing conceptualizations, and to their implications regarding underlying social, political, and ethical doctrines, has led to silences that obscure both important normative issues and desirable options for social improvement.

Our traditional understandings of politics have kept us from questioning the forces that shape and constrain both schools and our broader culture. More importantly, Marshall and Gerstl-Pepin suggest, our traditional understandings of politics and power have kept us from acting against those forces. While this book represents a departure for our field, the authors acknowledge older frameworks and the roles they have played, and still play, in understanding political phenomena. They do not dismiss these theories as irrelevant but instead push readers to understand each theory's inherent limitations and assumptions, what each includes and excludes, and what actions each encourages and discourages.

This text rightly asks us, as researchers and students of the politics of education, to become engaged, and in doing so to expand our understanding of both power and politics. The further development of our field and the attainment of socially just goals require direct action.

V. Darleen Opfer

References

William L. Boyd (1988). Policy Analysis, Educational Policy and Management: Through a Glass Darkly. In Norman J. Boyan (Ed.), *Handbook of Research on Educational Administration*. New York: Longman Press.

James G. Cibulka (1995). Policy Analysis and the Study of the Politics of Education. In Jay D. Scribner and Donald H. Layton (Eds.), *The Study of Educational Politics*. Washington, DC: Falmer Press, pp. 105–126.

Willis D. Hawley (1977). If Schools Are for Learning, the Study of the Politics of Education is Just Beginning. In Jay Scribner (Ed.), *The Politics of Education: The Seventy-Sixth Yearbook of the National Society for the Study of Education, Part II*. Chicago: University of Chicago Press, pp. 319–334.

Bob L. Johnson (2003). Those nagging headaches: Perennial issues and tensions in the politics of education field. *Educational Administration Quarterly, 39*(1), 41–67.

Donald H. Layton (1982). The Emergence of the Politics of Education as a Field of Study. In H. L. Gray (Ed.), *The Management of Educational Institutions*. Lewes, UK: Falmer Press, pp. 109–126.

Douglas E. Mitchell (1990). Education Politics for the New Century: Past Issues and Future Directions. In Douglas E. Mitchell and Margaret R. Goertz (Eds.), *Education Politics for the New Century*. London: Falmer Press, pp. 153–167.

Paul E. Peterson (1995). Foreword, Study of Educational Politics. In Jay D. Scribner and Donald H. Layton (Eds.), *The Study of Educational Politics*. Washington, DC: Falmer Press, pp. ixx–xiv.

Jay D. Scribner and Richard M. Englert (1977). The Politics of Education: An Introduction. In Jay Scribner (Ed.), *The Politics of Education: The Seventy-Sixth Yearbook of the National Society for the Study of Education, Part II*. Chicago: University of Chicago Press, pp. 1–29.

Aaron Wildavsky (1979). *Speaking Truth to Power: The Art and Craft of Policy Analysis*. Boston: Little, Brown and Company.

Frederick M. Wirt and Michael W. Kirst (1972). *The Political Web of American Schools*. Boston: Little, Brown and Company.

Kenneth K. Wong (1995). Politics of Education: From Political Science to Interdisciplinary Inquiry. In Jay D. Scribner and Donald H. Layton (Eds.), *The Study of Educational Politics*. Washington, DC: Falmer Press, pp. 21–38.

Preface

"Oh, that's rich!" or "What a tough topic!" are the kinds of response we received when we mentioned we were writing a book on educational politics. We wanted to write a book that delved into the nitty gritty of understanding educational politics and challenged our readers to think about themselves as political actors. We believed that there is much need for a book that goes beyond critique and challenges readers to imagine new possibilities for understanding and influencing educational politics.

The politics of education is a discipline that is unique to the field of education and as such has struggled over defining itself (Scribner & Layton, 1995), particularly with respect to (1) establishing what is distinct about educational politics without overrelying on related fields such as political science and economics; (2) keeping politics of educational studies, which focus on processes and power dynamics, from being lost, given the preponderance of policy studies and policy analysis that tend to focus on outcomes; and (3) addressing the challenges to include political issues raised by oppressed and excluded groups. By borrowing so much from other fields, educational politics has missed poignant and pressing educational realities. By developing research agendas that focus on the central arenas of power, the politics of the marginalized have been missing from many political analyses. By focusing attention on the power of elites, educators received deceptive messages about the potential power they have in influencing their own field. The politics of education can be a depressing topic of study (as when the field-based graduate student says, "I hate politics—it just gets in the way of doing what's right for kids."). Politics of education ultimately teaches educators to recognize power and learn how to compromise, survive, and cooperate in a system of dominance.

In this book, we acknowledge and use traditional perspectives, but our analysis is not limited to political science–, economic-, or organizational theory–based strategies used for understanding educational politics and policy. These perspectives tend to reinforce assumptions that educators have little power over the decisions that dictate and constrain their work. They fail to incorporate the lived realities, the emotions, the altruistic motivations, the cultural intricacies, the policy-generated dilemmas, and the issues (and children) that educators see falling through political cracks. They do little to help and empower educators to think differently and creatively about the power systems and policies with which they deal daily. They do little to provide models and methods for politically astute leadership in which educators can take charge, re-frame, and create new ways of looking at the realities that politicians do not see when they make educational policy.

Our book leaps across disciplines to use sociocultural and critical lenses to identify theories and methodologies that uncover cultural dominance, oppression, and silencing.

Rather than remaining mired in critique, we then identify strategies (and success stories) for educators and researchers to envision alternative policy approaches aimed at improving education. We concocted challenging end-of-chapter exercises that build skills and dispositions for political analysis. Some are more oriented toward research and some toward action. We challenge you, the reader, to become a policy advocate who conducts research and engages in politics in order to re-vision and re-frame policies in ways that offer viable alternatives.

Stories gleaned from people encountered in our own practice and research and from our combined twenty-seven years of teaching in educational administration leave us rich and grateful and able to ground this book in reality. Thanks go to our numerous students and colleagues who have desired information on how to be policy advocates and to our editor Arnie Burvikovs. Thanks also go to Anita Alpenfels, Amy Anderson, Gary Anderson, Pat Forgione, Carolyn Herrington, David Holdzkom, Catherine Lugg, Torch Lytle, Craig Pepin, Peggy Placier, Darlene Opfer, and Gerry Sroufe. Finally, thanks to our reviewers: Margaret Grogan, University of Missouri–Columbia; Larry Hughes, University of Houston; Betty Malen, University of Maryland; and Anthony Normore, Florida International University, who helped us focus, tighten, lighten, and deepen our writing. We are fortunate, indeed, to have been able to find such generous scholars who cared enough about our getting it right!

Part I

Re-visioning Educational Politics

To make a difference, we must find new ways to analyze education policies and to work in and around political forces and arenas of power. Traditional frameworks, though, help us understand how powerful elites work the system, how their values shape the ways of talking about education, and how those values and the talk are transformed into the policies aimed at fixing schooling. These traditional ways of analyzing politics and policy, however, often do not encompass the passions, needs, and voices of educators nor those of a range of marginalized groups. New models, modes of analysis, and ways of viewing education politics are emerging to embrace the everyday lived realities of schooling. They offer hope, as they provide frameworks that validate political activities of non-elites and that seek out alternative visions and stories about how schooling should and could be.

Chapters 1 and 2 of this section identify theories that are useful for understanding the actions and processes in powerful political arenas. They also identify a range of concepts for identifying types of policies and for analyzing the processes that occur as policies are implemented in education systems. To be able to work with the usual ways of "doing" politics and policy, one must have this information.

To move beyond those dominant forces, one must recognize and critique the limits, constraints, and disempowering, exclusionary practices of politics-as-usual. Critique-talk and grumbling are not enough, though. To be able to powerfully and effectively lead education systems, roadmaps are needed. Chapter 3 demonstrates the functioning of "politics of knowledge," that is, how we are swayed to define education policy issues in line with the values and views promoted by people with powerful voices. Chapter 3 then examines theories and methodologies that can be used to envision democratic, inclusive, and collaborative approaches to politics and policy. We offer the Politics from Margin to Center model as a hopeful re-visioning and re-framing of traditional approaches to policy and politics presented in Chapters 1 and 2. The first three chapters, taken together, lay the groundwork for the book, which seeks to inspire educational leaders to be effective policy advocates who seek to include marginalized voices.

1

Frameworks for Puzzles in Politics and Policy

Guiding Questions _____

- What role does power play in educational politics and policy?
- How are policy and politics intertwined?
- How can one make sense of the confusion of characters, cultural processes, and values conflicts in arenas where policy is formulated?
- What are ways to frame and analyze the realities of partisan politics?
- What is missing in the framing of education policy?

Education policy and politics often can leave us frustrated, angry, and puzzled. Did you ever hear, "I hate the way politics gets in the way of what we're trying to do for kids!" or "I feel *so* betrayed by that #$%! bureaucrat who cut the budget again!" or "How did they ever come up with *that* idea?" To many educators, the source of their work challenges is politics. *Politics* is often considered a dirty word, and politicians are people to avoid, except when you need certain policies, programs, or budgets passed. For many, education politics is mean fighting rather than studious debate over issues affecting children. Or, conversely, politics is falsely polite debate that never gets at the deeper needs and avoids real conflicts and never gets anywhere. How confusing and frustrating!

Politics and policy are inseparable. Policy is made in arenas with complex struggles for power. In policy making, actors try to get the values, needs, and goals of their constituents and their political parties to be the winners, to be embedded in policy. So, policy created from politics is confusing. This chapter begins to provide frameworks for making sense of this intertwining of policy and politics.

FIGURE 1.1   *Policy Puzzles*

Copyright 2003, Tribune Media Services, Inc. Reprinted with permission.

Educators sometimes think about policy in terms of its good intentions. For example, some policies give specific rights to parents whose children have special needs, and other policies are aimed at strengthening teachers' pensions. While policies can seem rational and well intentioned, aimed at bettering society, they also can be harmful. Having the ability to interpret policy puzzles analytically gives an educational leader a great deal of power over frustrating political situations. Figure 1.1 illustrates just one such frustrating incongruity. The ability to interpret political puzzles can also help us chuckle and cope with policy paradox.

What Is Politics? What Is Policy?

The study of education politics emphasizes the dynamics of how power operates in educational decision making. Studies often focus on the particulars of one policy-making arena (e.g., a state legislature) or on one policy (e.g., in-school suspension policies created by a school board). In order to understand educational politics, though, it is important to understand *power,* the ability of a group, individual, or structure to exercise control or authority. Collins (2000) suggests that power relations are unequal and operate on an array of levels. These power relations include overt and covert exertions of control and domination, including individual experiences of prejudice and bias and structural forms of power (such as policies, organizational structures, or legislation). Policies are a form of structural power that operates through a "constellation of organized practices in employment, government, education, law, business, and housing that work to maintain an unequal and unjust distribution of resources" (Collins, 2000, p. 301). While policies operate as a form of structural power, the force they exert can be felt on an individual level by teachers, students, staff, administrators, and parents. Conversely, individuals and groups can form coalitions to resist and rebel against unequal power relations. The Civil Rights Movement and the Women's Movement are two examples of how power can be resisted and redefined.

Understanding how this type of power operates in educational policy and politics requires asking questions about who gets what, when, and how. It requires focusing on the authoritative allocation of values (Easton, 1965a), that is, on the legitimized decision making about the values that will shape programs and budgets. Analysis and study of politics reveals, explains, and even helps predict who will get what, laying bare the conflicts of both the values and the arenas where policies are developed and determined by political actors, processes, and structures. Thus, politics is conflict, culminating in powerful forces allocating values, determining who gets what. Policy, then, is the result of politics, the result of that allocation of values; policy is what governments choose to do. Analyzing policy entails focusing more on the content of policy, asking questions about the type or content of policy and about how and whether it is working as intended.

To analyze politics, one must identify power issues and actors' motivations. As Stone (1997) says, "Politicians always have at least two goals. First is a policy goal—whatever program or proposal they would like to see accomplished or defeated, whatever problem they would like to see solved. . . . [Secondly,] politicians always want to preserve their power, or gain enough power to be able to accomplish their policy goals" (p. 2). Whether the politician is a presidential candidate, the local school superintendent, or even the teacher who always gathers people together in the teachers' lounge, this statement holds true. Looking at political actors *is* looking at policy; looking at policy *is* looking back at the effects and outcomes of political actors' exertions.

Usually, when we speak of politics, we are referring to those conflicts that occur in and around government arenas such as boards and legislatures. But conflicts of values occur, and powerful forces prevail, in informal interactions that take place in offices, corridors, and classrooms. All of this is the exercise of power, to get people to do things they would not otherwise do, in overt ways, as in rules and laws, and in covert ways, as when powerful norms and understandings direct behaviors. Thus, one must look beyond such hegemonic centers as legislatures, and one must look beyond such formal acts as votes and lobbying. One must search for the array of subtle strategies used to keep power and to exclude challengers. One must also search for the strategies used by challengers to raise often-silenced and ignored voices and needs.

In this book, Chapters 1 and 2 emphasize the frameworks for understanding power dynamics in formal arenas of power and for analyzing the policies produced therein. Chapter 3, however, critiques these traditional lenses and provides alternative theories and methods that encompass the often-silenced voices, the politics from the margin. With these three chapters in mind, the remaining chapters focus on the different levels of politics, applying both the traditional and the challenging frameworks, each ending with examples of politics-done-differently, or re-visioned and re-framed. By the last chapter, the presentation of policy advocacy will make good sense for educators as powerful and effective strategists on the way to taking charge, with a sense of agency and an ability to interrupt and challenge.

Chapter 1 now begins by providing tried and true methods of focusing on politicians and policy as they intertwine in formal arenas of power. First, we present Lived Realities, which are down-to-earth stories or vignettes, and then we provide conceptual frameworks that will help make sense of the situations in the stories and in everyday events of education politics.

Analyzing Behaviors and Arenas in Policy Formulation

Legislatures and school boards are the accepted locations, and elected executives such as presidents, chairs, and governors have legitimized power for producing policy. Both locations and people are empowered by elections and appointments, and they have formal proceedings. Yet looking at policy arenas can be confusing, as the following Lived Realities illustrates. The need for frameworks, theories, and models for making sense of the behaviors and events becomes more noticeable. Concepts and theories presented throughout this chapter will provide lenses for understanding this Lived Realities.

Lived Realities: Is It Politics, Policy, or Drama?

The goings-on were so dramatic—less like education policy analysis and more like theater! Here are the scenes, the actors, and the events: Wilson Riles was the elected State Superintendent of Schools in California in the 1970s. He was elected partly on the promise of his Early Childhood Education program (ECE), saying it would prevent huge problems by giving all kids an early start at school success. But when the Legislature approved funds for ECE, they demanded immediate evaluations. When the evaluations were a bit shaky in showing huge returns for ECE, Riles went into action. He had his own staff conduct the evaluations, and then attacked the critics of his appointed evaluators. He bused in numbers of parents (dubbed the "Mamas in the Audience") to sit in the legislative hearings on ECE, and testify about how great it was. He attacked legislators who questioned ECE, with high drama, saying, "You people who would cut back ECE are like those who, to see whether a budding peach tree is healthy, would kill it by pulling up its roots to take a look." Was this pure manipulation? Good policy? Or a power play?

The *audience* and *symbolic politics* frameworks explained later in the chapter could help make sense of the "Is It Politics, Policy, or Drama?" example. This approach highlights how politicians use symbolism such as "killing budding peach trees" to support their favored policies.

Studies of the politics of education encompass power arrangements and values conflicts, whether they occur in and around governmental bodies or individual's bodies. Traditionally, the focus of these studies has been on boards, legislatures, and their activities. In recent years, though, studies of the politics of education include consideration of more subtle forms of power and ideological conflicts. In the past, this field has relied on political sci-

TABLE 1.1 *Lenses for Understanding Organized Rationality*

Organized Rationality Lenses	Focus
Political and Bureaucratic Structures	Examines the organizational and political structures in political systems to understand the functions, responsibilities, lines of communication, and the timetables and regulations constraining issues related to policy
Rational Choice	Searches to identify what makes a policy choice logically preferable to other possibilities
Systems Model	Examines local, state, or federal policy-making environments as producing *inputs*—demands and supports entering the political system, which, in turn, produces decisions and actions as *outputs*
Stages of Activity	Examines the policy process as *functional stages of activity* from issue definition through decision enactment. The model recognizes that there will be alternative and competing proposals.

ence, economics, and sociology, while many in education pretended that education and politics were separate. We know this separation is fantasy. To be powerful actors involved in shaping directions for schools, we know that we need ways to understand politics. The concepts and theories presented in this chapter are lenses for viewing scenes from the vignettes and examples from our own experiences. Some frameworks emphasize structure, organization, and rationality. Some emphasize the culture of policy arenas. Some emphasize the realities of partisan politics. Table 1.1 presents a diagram of frameworks for understanding organized rationality.

Organized Rationality

Looking at the hustle and bustle of political action, we search for order and structure. Several frameworks, borrowed from looking at the familiar organizational charts and rules for churches, businesses, and the like, help create that order. In making sense of politics, one can identify structure, rules for behavior and decision making, and organizational and communication channels, and identify a degree of organized rationality that can govern choices.

Political and Bureaucratic Structures. Why does a school superintendent spend a great deal of time explaining school programs to a restaurant owner who happens to be a school board member? Why did your representative in the General Assembly vote against funding for paraprofessionals? Why does the Director for Research and Evaluation speak so cautiously, hedge, and qualify her statements, even though the data in her reports quite clearly show poor results for that pilot program? There is some organizational system guiding this behavior. The organizational hierarchy provides a common mode for analysis: To understand any system, one must learn a great deal from an organizational chart providing the structure, the functions, the responsibilities, the lines of communication, and the timetables and regulations constraining the tasks at hand. Such a chart provides some clues to explain the behavior of individuals who work within the structures.

We were all taught about the structure of our governance: the layers of federal, state, and local control, and the separations of the legislative, judicial, and executive powers. Such structures are useful as starters but present political puzzles, too. Many political conflicts ensue as one part of this seemingly neat and orderly structure conflicts with or attempts to take power from another part. The eighth-grade lessons in civics about balance of power are not enough for analyzing such conflicts. Desegregation is the most obvious example of such an education puzzle. When, in *Brown vs. the Board of Education,* the Supreme Court justices decreed that the practice of separate school systems for Blacks could not continue, the justices were asserting federal power. The court had an obligation to take away state and local district officials' discretion when they violated the equal protection clause in the constitutional amendments.

A great deal of policy and political activity is about nothing but establishing or changing the structure of control. For example, when the Pennsylvania legislature passed the Regulatory Review Act to review the regulations created by state agencies, they were creating a policy to tighten their control. Legislators thought that the Department of Education was, in effect, remaking policy as it managed and evaluated education programs. Political parties create another organization, with hierarchies and rules. Responsibility to political parties will affect many actions.

Understanding structures provides a start in helping to diagram who is in charge, who reports to whom, who has specific tasks, whose tasks are interrelated, who must give the go-ahead before there is action, where resources come from, how they are approved, and who must communicate with whom. Although these are organizational and structural frameworks, much that is political emanates from them.

Comparing Outcomes: Rational Choice and Actor-Centered Institutionalism.
Political scientists who study education policy have tended to examine policy via a lens of *rational choice theory* (e.g., Chubb & Moe, 1990; Schneider & Ingram, 1997). This perspective has three central tenets: (1) Humans are rational beings, (2) humans' behavior is influenced by institutional regulations, and (3) humans seek to change institutional rules in order to influence others' actions. Given this set of assumptions, policy approaches using this framework seek an understanding as to why certain decisions are made and why certain policies are promoted over others. Rational actors then go through steps, defining goals, developing alternatives, evaluating the alternatives, and then choosing the alternative most likely to attain the goal. It is always interesting to think about what we mean by *rational.* One rational actor's choice for a certain policy decision might be based on a review of research and a set of recommendations from a policy analyst who has examined a range of alternatives for improving schooling. But a different kind of rationality might include political factors such as how many constituents will be pleased and will vote in the next election based on this choice.

Systems Models.   Looking for a simplified model to understand policy systems? Easton (1965) developed a model from theory that could encompass policy making generally,

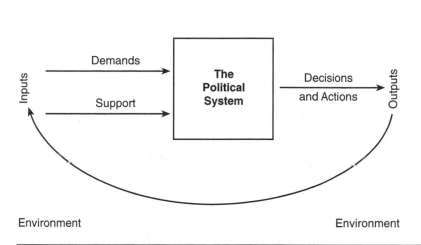

FIGURE 1.2   *A Simplified Model of a Political System*

Source: From Easton, David. (1965). *A Systems Analysis of Political Life.* Chicago: University of Chicago Press. Reprinted by permission of David Easton.

whether it was local, state, or federal, and whether it was policy for education, health, transportation, or banking.

Figure 1.2 pictures the local, state, or federal policy-making environments as producing *inputs*—demands and supports entering the political system—which, in turn, produce decisions and actions as *outputs.* Policies, then, are outputs from the political system. These outputs are applied to the environment (e.g., as policy directives) and may come back as new inputs through a feedback loop. For example, demands from business leaders for high school graduates with better computer, math, and reading skills constitute a demand from the environment. These demands are processed through the political system, which produces outputs such as high-stakes testing policies. Later, when educators and parents feel that the testing policies harmed their children's opportunities, their discomfort might be mobilized into a new political input. They might create a demand for different testing policy, and support political candidates who promise to get the policy system to alter the testing.

Refinements of Easton's model highlight details that add depth to our understanding of the Systems Model. Figure 1.3 shows how Milstein and Jennings (1973) call attention to the role orientation, needs, and group affiliation of actor groups, and to aspects of the institutional structure *within* the policy system. Such a model calls attention to the people in policy arenas and serves to highlight the influences on the actors, such as legislators, lobbyists, bureaucrats, and analysts, as they take their parts in policy making. When they are making speeches, casting votes, producing recommendations, or, for example, considering budgets for state-subsidized driver education, these actors are behaving in response to their reward systems and role orientations. They are calculating how their situation in the system will be affected by their speech or their vote. Thus, they, and the proposed policy, are walk-

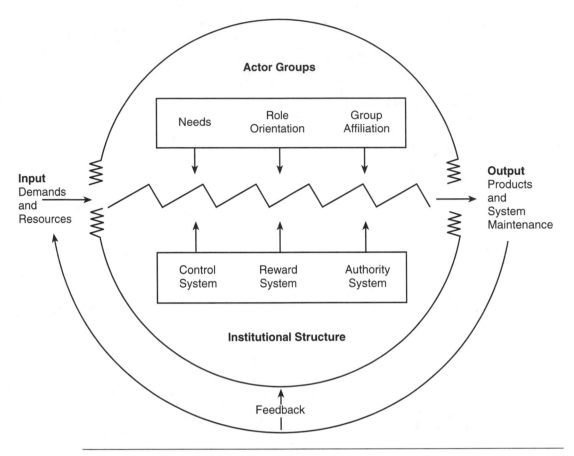

FIGURE 1.3   *Dynamics of the Thruput Process*

Source: From Mike M. Milstein. *Educational Policy-Making and the State Legislature.* Copyright © 1973 by Praeger Publishers. Reproduced with permission of Greenwood Publishing Group, Inc., Westport, CT.

ing the jagged and precarious line through the policy arena. Their sense of themselves and their mission, role, behavior, and place in the policy arena therefore affects the course of events for policies moving into and through the policy-making process.

Stages of Activity.   To identify more about activities in policy arenas, detailed models of stages provide guidance for observers and for people trying to accomplish policy goals. In Figure 1.4, note how the authors (Campbell & Mazzoni, 1976) provide several levels of detail. They call attention to "functional stages of activity"; potential policies move from issue definition through to decision enactment. Their model recognizes that there will be alternative and competing proposals. For example, to address the problems of teen-aged drivers, there might be several alternative proposals (e.g., private driver education vouchers, change driving age to 18, etc.). In the section entitled Influence Relationships, their model high-

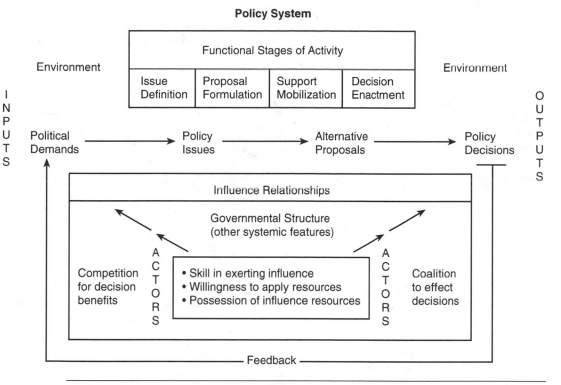

FIGURE 1.4   *EGP System and Influence Concepts*

Source: From Roald F. Campbell and Tim L. Mazzoni, Jr. *State Policy Making for the Public Schools,* copyright 1976 by McCutchan Publishing Corporation, Richmond, California. Used by permission of the publisher.

lights realities. The model points out actors' skill and willingness to work on driver educa-tion, and the "competition for decision benefits" as policy makers try to get the benefits and credit for themselves and their constituents. Thus, driver education subsidies may be com-peting with AIDS education for the same dollars. Finally, Figure 1.4 calls attention to the ways coalition building affects decision making.

When we seek the order and structure in political processes, it is useful to identify structures, hierarchies, and stages. Politics then seems less chaotic and more predictable. However, by focusing on structures, one may miss power dynamics and cultural processes underlying the formal organization. Woodrow Wilson, the scholar who described the for-mal organization of Congress, encountered huge challenges in getting Congress to approve the Treaty of Versailles, because of details and confusions emanating from, for example, party caucuses and special interests: "Special interests from steel and coal to tourism and mushrooms, [and] . . . party structures . . . then come the fifty state delegations . . . aug-mented by staff organizations, press assistants' clubs . . . [so that one should] approach Congress as an anthropological endeavor" (Weatherford, 1981, pp. 19–20).

Cultural Processes in Policy Arenas

Looking at politics culturally means identifying the behaviors, norms, and understandings that people share, and that shape the events that occur. Table 1.2 presents a diagram for understanding cultural processes in policy arenas.

TABLE 1.2 *Lenses for Understanding Cultural Processes in Policy Arenas*

Cultural Process Lenses	Focus
Values and Value Shifts	Seeks to identify the values of dominant actors in the policy-making process, and whether values shift when key actors change.
Policy Streams	Provides a way of understanding how certain issues get on the policy agenda. Suggests that policy opportunities around an issue occur when separate streams come together around an issue to form a *policy window,* an opening, in which a problem is recognized and a policy solution is seen as viable, making the political climate ripe for change.
Policy Communities	Examines how agencies, politicians, political parties, interest groups, their leaders and staff, policy advocates, and scholars in universities or research institutes form *policy communities* in which they develop shared understandings in framing policies
Assumptive Worlds	Shows how, in policy-making arenas, policy actors learn unstated rules of the game—*assumptive worlds*—about unwritten rules and undefined understandings about roles
Hierarchies of Power and Circles of Influence	Examines key policy actors and assesses their relative power to influence any particular education policy issue; considers whether their power and interests shift over time, and as the context changes and issues shift
Policy Makers' Role Orientations	Focuses on policy makers' different orientations to their roles. For example, some operate as delegates, bound to follow their constituency's instructions, while others are trustees, entrusted to make good decisions.
Political Culture	Views policy and politics through a cultural lens, examining political culture as the collective agreements about how politicians should behave, about what government is for, and about how politics should be
Symbolic Policy Action	Examines how policy makers use symbolic language to mobilize audiences and constituencies for action; focuses on the audience attending to the issue or conflict, assuming that mobilizing activities will tell a great deal about the politics
Policy Logics	Identifies the rationales presented to buttress mobilization of a political agenda or policy
Political Socialization	Focuses on the ways education policies and structures aim to shape children to fit into national political and social values
Policy Issue Networks	Examines the network relationships among groups in the policy-making process
The Arena Model	Focuses on the decision sites through which power is exercised to initiate, formulate, and enact policy. The model suggests that most of us never see the subsystem—a small and stable group of committee-based legislators, bureaucrats, and interest group representatives—who dominate the education policy agenda.

Values and Values Shifts.　When education policy is formulated and set into policy mandates and regulations, these seemingly concrete artifacts are, in fact, merely temporary, vague, ambiguous agreements. They represent a compromise in chronic values conflicts among those who would try to shape education systems. Scholars seek to identify the dominant values driving policy choices and also to trace the shifts among these values.

By analyzing policy thrusts over decades, we can see policy shifts among the basic values—efficiency, equity, quality, and choice/democracy (Garms, Guthrie, & Pierce, 1978; Marshall, 1991; Marshall, Mitchell, & Wirt, 1989). *Efficiency,* emphasizing organization and management that increased productivity, was a dominant value in the years of early development of the profession of school administration and, thus, in the structuring of the profession and assumptions about schooling (Callahan, 1962; Tyack & Hansot, 1982). The 1960s and 1970s incorporated values of *equity,* with mandates for school desegregation, for equalizing access for children with disabilities, and for gender equity. However, the election of Ronald Reagan, then George Bush, in the 1980s inaugurated a new key value dominating policy making—*quality,* often called excellence (Clark & Astuto, 1986).

Quality values were emphasized in reform reports (e.g., *A Nation at Risk*) that alarmed policy makers and citizens, providing momentum for federal and state policies that rewarded higher performance of schools and districts. Policy makers and administrators were clamoring to be at the front of, and in control of, agendas that had *excellence* and *quality* as their bywords. State policymakers rushed to demonstrate their abilities to manage the problems with policies, raising minimum standards for students' coursework curricula and creating incentives for educators to raise their training, certification, and performance (e.g., career ladders). At the same time, the value of choice—whether for individual decisions over personal issues or for giving citizens electoral choice in a participatory democracy—has always been symbolically potent.

Education *choice* is evidenced in such examples as giving states and local districts more discretion and flexibility. Additional examples of choice include the movement toward providing parental choice through voucher experiments, tuition tax credits, and increased parental voice (e.g., in site-based decision making). Therefore, the identification of the values of dominant actors, and the shifts in both those values and the policy actors, is a promising analysis strategy. In Chapter 7 we demonstrate the utility of this framework of values shifts by focusing on the major shifts that occurred when Ronald Reagan was elected president. But this *values shift* approach to political analysis is useful for analyzing all levels of governance. Further, by understanding and tracking dominant values, one can be more effective in critiquing them and articulating alternative values.

Ideas and Issues Emerging from the Policy Stream.　Some policy ideas are not even acknowledged, much less considered viable options, if they do not click with prevailing ideology and culture. It matters whether the option has *value acceptability,* or how a given idea fits with national culture or ideology. Some ideas and problems languish in doldrums of inactivity before getting policy action. Policy streams and policy windows provide useful ways to view these phenomena.

In his influential work, *Agendas, Alternatives, and Public Policies,* Kingdon (1984) examined the process by which policy issues get on the public agenda. In trying to understand how policies get adopted, he imagines the wide range of policy possibilities in the "policy stream" in which ideas are constantly floating around in a kind of "policy primeval soup" (Kingdon, 1984, p. 21).

What activates the idea and needs in this primeval soup to the extent that there might be policy action? Political players recognize and identify problems, create proposals for policy changes, and engage in political maneuvering, such as election campaigns and lobbying. Kingdon identifies three processes in government agenda setting: problems, policies, and politics.

1. Problem recognition. The process by which an issue is identified as in need of a policy solution
2. Policy proposal formation and revision. The process through which information about the problem, the need, the ways to address the need are consolidated for formulation of new policy or a revised policy proposal is developed
3. Politics. The process through which key players recognize the political viability of the problem and then use their positions of influence the political process in favor of an issue

These three parallel processes may co-occur as independent streams of problems, policies, and politics flowing along with little interconnection. But when conditions are right in all three streams, the window opens for policy action. When streams converge, a *policy window* occurs. There is an opening in which a problem is recognized and a policy solution is seen as viable, making the political climate ripe for change. Kingdon argues that interconnections between the streams in which policy opportunities occur are key to understanding agenda and policy change. See Figure 1.5 for a schematic of these three streams coming together to open a policy window.

Historical and current occurrences in education politics are clarified with this model. Think, for example, of the pre-Sputnik U.S. federal education politics: some sense that federal leadership and funding of innovation was needed for education and studies, and proposals existed. Thus, two streams were flowing: The problem was recognized and proposals were available. The window opened wide, though with the third stream converging in the political crisis of Cold War competition with Russia. Similarly, one can view the publication of *A Nation at Risk* (NCEE, 1983) as a device that opened windows in the 1980s. The policy stream–policy window model can be useful for analyzing all levels of education policy formulation. The model is applied in more detail in Chapter 7.

Policy Communities.   Looking at policy arenas as cultures provides useful lenses. Sociologists and political scientists identify community power structures and power elites in towns and in legislatures (Mills, 1956; Hunter, 1953). Looking at governmental power elites and community power structures, one can see, and study how, among the agencies, politicians, political parties, interest groups and their leaders and staff, policy advocates, and "experts" in universities or research institutes who interact regularly, that there develop, inevitably, shared understandings and norms and shared ways of framing policies.[1]

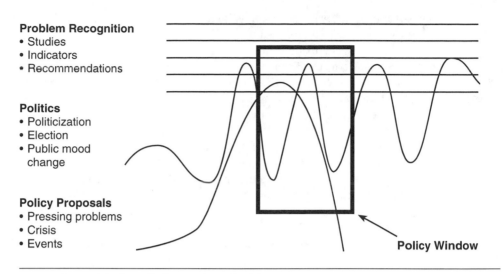

Problem Recognition
- Studies
- Indicators
- Recommendations

Politics
- Politicization
- Election
- Public mood change

Policy Proposals
- Pressing problems
- Crisis
- Events

Policy Window

FIGURE 1.5   *A Policy Window*
A policy window is an opening for policy action. Three streams from policy, problems, and politics come together, creating the opening. The three streams converge when problems are recognized and policy proposals are refined and there is a change in the politics. When policy windows open, policy action can occur.

A *policy community* is a network of policy professionals and advocates that cluster around a specific area of governmental action. They may collude to make policy with little outside input. Look at policy communities and you will note their characteristics: conservatism versus innovation, cooperation versus conflict, authoritarian versus democratic government, political culture, party systems, state structure, hierarchies and hierarchical attitudes, their intolerances and biases, and their mannerisms, such as tolerance for dispute (Campbell et al., 1989).

In this perspective, notice how "patterns of speech, written language, internal interaction . . . architectural settings, office accouterment, personal life styles . . . organizational stories, ceremonial rites of passage, logos and nomenclatures, and models of heroes and villains" (Goodsell, 1990, p. 496) are the sources of data used to understand a policy community.

Assumptive Worlds.   In policy-making arenas, policy actors have learned unstated rules of the game—assumptive worlds—about unwritten rules and undefined understandings about roles (Marshall, Mitchell, & Wirt, 1989). Newcomers learn, by trial and error and from mentors, that there are things you just *don't* do; there are understandings about how certain people should be treated and spoken to. Scholars have applied assumptive worlds in analyzing state and micropolitics (e.g., school-level politics) (LaMagdaleine, 1992; Marshall & Mitchell, 1991; Sacken & Medina, 1990), revealing insiders' understandings of the roles they must play and the behaviors they must follow to keep their power (formal or informal) in their policy arena; this constitutes the actors' cognitive map of their arena, which guides and constrains their initiatives and their values.

They know, for example, that only certain actors have the Right and Responsibility to Initiate—and when someone violates these assumptions, others are quite willing to undermine the one who takes initiative "improperly." So, when the state superintendent takes initiative instead of the governor, or when state Department of Education bureaucrats do something that is seen by legislators as too much initiative or too much like lobbying, they will feel the wrath.

Policy actors know, too, that they will have trouble introducing policies that trample on powerful interests. This principle arises when recognizably powerful interests are directly threatened. For example, policy proposals that might hurt a state's big city are often deemed unacceptable. Similarly, actors know that they take huge risks in introducing policy debates that diverge from the prevailing dominant values. Political insiders learn to work with tricks and constraints. In maneuvering to build coalitions within any political system, some ways of doing so are acceptable ("tricks"), while others are not. They learn that information or research is only good if it has sponsorship of key policy actors, and that outside expertise that could challenge the power base of the dominant knowledge is not welcome and can easily be dismissed as irrelevant. Special conditions, like limits on budgets or state cultural views of the value of education, affect policy making. For example, in the 1980s many West Virginians had mixed emotions about the value of higher education because it usually resulted in upward mobility out of their state. On the other hand, in Wisconsin, education is expected of citizens as the key to self-enhancement, including state-supported higher education. In Chapter 6, we present more descriptions of the assumptive worlds of state policy actors.

Hierarchies of Power and Circles of Influence.   People in formal positions of authority *and* people with expertise and vested interest vie for power to be *the* shapers of policy that interests them. This perspective examines the relative power and influence of policy groups for education decision making and organizes them into a model for understanding their hierarchical relationship to each other: Inner Circle, Near Circle, Far Circle, Sometime Players, and Often Forgotten Players (Marshall, Mitchell, & Wirt, 1989). When identifying these key actors and then assessing their relative power to influence any particular education policy issue, we must keep in mind that their power and interest shifts over time and as the context changes and issues shift. Figure 1.6 presents a diagram portraying the groups' relative closeness to centers of power and influence.

This approach, identifying circles of power and influence among actors, may be useful for studying, for example, local policy making for special education, or even the less formalized power and influence on site-based committees or among school faculties. Assume that anyone or any group with a vested interest—whether economic, partisan, ideological, or professional—will become actors. Seek to understand the motivations and beliefs of actors; assess the resources of actors; identify the arena and its rules (assumptive worlds). Note the political strategies they use—for example, cooptation, compromise, rhetoric, heuristics (gaining advantage by manipulating the circumstances of political choice), manipulating the agenda, refusing to consider options and calling for a study, deciding in what order to consider options. Further strategies include mobilizing other polit-

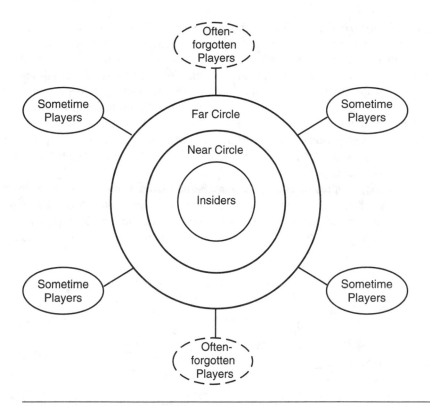

FIGURE 1.6 *The Subculture of State Education Policymakers: A Model of Power and Influence in Education Policy Making*

Source: From Marshall, C., Mitchell, D., and Wirt, F. (1989). *Culture and Education Policy in the American States.* London: Falmer Press. Reprinted by permission of the publisher.

ical actors (so it would be costly for others to block your proposal) and sophisticated voting (by not voting your preference at some stage in order to achieve a better final outcome). These are behaviors known by insiders to be useful tricks of the trade in political arenas.

Policy Makers' Role Orientations.   Policy makers have different orientations to their roles: Some are delegates, bound to follow their constituency's instructions, and some are trustees, entrusted to make good decisions. Some see themselves as true representatives (Eulau & Wahlke, 1978). Some refer to their ward or district often as they take a stand or vote, while some see themselves representing the whole state or the whole nation. The question sometimes arises about who rules whom, or when constituents can demand certain behaviors from their representatives and make it clear that electoral punishment will ensue from the "wrong" choices. It is important to note that these orientations are modified by many circumstances, such as political party demands and the particular interests of a policy maker. A schoolteacher-turned-politician, for example, might demonstrate voting behaviors that reflect her interest, biases, and expertise as an educator, whether or not it pleases her party or her district constituents.

Political Culture.   Politicians work with understandings of the political culture of their state or region. Political cultures are collective agreements about how politicians should behave, about what government is for, and about how politics should be. The settling and migration patterns of immigrant populations in the United States resulted in different political cultures for different regions of the country (Elazar, 1984). As people migrated to the United States, they brought some of those cultural assumptions to the geographic areas of settlement and in-country migration. Figure 1.7 shows Elazar's (1984) geographic distribution of the three political cultures, Moralistic (M), Individualistic (I), and Traditionalistic (T). Of course, some states are a mix, as, for example, Missouri, labeled IT, is Individualistic and Traditionalistic.

The main source of political culture is the assumptions of settlers of the region or state. Early settler and immigrants carried with them, embedded in their traditions and their laws, tacit cultural senses. Many came from monarchies and feudal systems in England and France and brought vestiges of those systems with them. Thus, they set up Traditionalistic

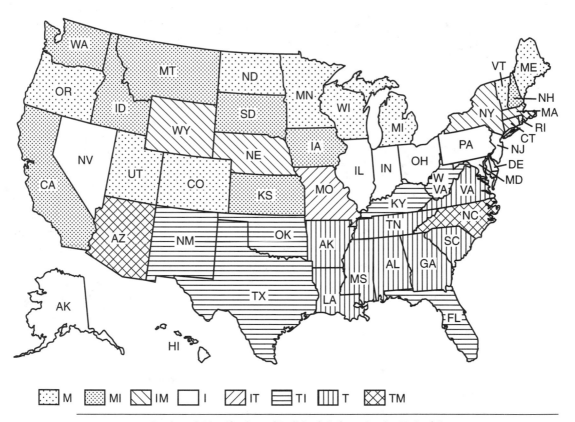

FIGURE 1.7   *Regional Distribution of Political Culture in the United States*

Source: Fig. 5.4, p. 135 from *American Federalism: A View from the States,* 3rd ed. by Daniel J. Elazar. Copyright © 1984 by Harper & Row, Publishers, Inc. Reprinted by permission of Pearson Education, Inc.

political cultures, which assumed, for example, that certain people inherit the right to govern. People whose ancestors settled New England states sometime brought anti-monarchy sentiments and set up governance and bureaucratic structures with political culture understandings that government, politicians, and bureaucrats will and should promote the public interest, with their Moralistic political cultural underpinnings. In contrast, Individualistic political cultures (particularly the Middle Atlantic States) viewed government, politicians, and bureaucratic agencies quite differently: Government was to ensure that an individual's competitive efforts could prevail in an orderly public arena.

The political culture affects the judgments about what is right and proper governmental and political activity and who should take part in it. One must identify the political culture to understand "appropriate" assumptions. Trying to function with Individualistic political culture assumptions, for example, in a Moralistic or Traditionalistic political culture would be frustrating and ineffective, as one would bump into cultural barriers and fall into cultural chasms. Elazar's theory is useful even as new populations alter the demographics of a region or state. Cultural patterns are altered only slightly. The assumptions brought from early migratory and settlement patterns are only slowly altered by new populations and new assumptions, because the cultural traditions have become embedded in political, government, and bureaucratic systems. Thus, immigration to Texas, California, and Florida, for example, does bring new demands, but the political culture is slow to change. The dominant views about the purpose of government and bureaucracy stay the same.

Symbolic Policy Action. Much policy activity centers on identifying problems, drawing attention through performances and spectacles, naming and labeling, and creating potent, grand, conspicuous symbols and catchy phrases for great-sounding solutions. Policy talk is sometimes banal and full of pomp and politeness and ceremony but still has political salience, for "whatever is ceremonial or banal strengthens reassuring beliefs regardless of their validity and discourages skeptical inquiry about disturbing issues" (Edelman, 1977, p. 3). Terms like *world class standards, ghetto riots, strict accountability, welfare cheat, national security, paperwork,* and *red tape* can sway emotions connected to issues such as school quality, race, poverty, the national budget, innovation, and equity policy. Such terms can be used to collect, condense, and shape opinions so forcefully that alternative views sound irrelevant or unsound. Legal, professional language and bureaucratic procedure language seem to convey reassurance of control and status. Politicians employ rhetoric to marshal support for political programs. They refer to unobservable or generalized people, and assert statistics that shape political support or opposition. The terms become symbols, useful for mobilizing audiences and constituencies for action. *Bully pulpit* is a term used to denote the power words that convey an almost moral message and, at the same time, are delivered from on high, as, for example, from the powerful position of President or Secretary of Education. Ronald Reagan's Secretary of Education, William Bennett, when promoting character education and urging schools to compete to be schools of excellence, was known for turning the bully pulpit into an effective political tool.

Symbolic policy action occurs, too, when rituals, ceremonies, and words are *all* that happens (Edelman, 1988; Anderson, 1990). When political platforms, promises, and even laws and programs are passed and approved, they are not necessarily real or substantive. When there is no money, no regulation, no designation of time frames, no assignment of tasks and responsibility for implementation, the policy may be symbolic or a token. It gives the impression that something is going to be done to fix a problem, and it provides the opportunity for the use of rhetoric as a political tool. These observations are useful for observing political talk and behavior and asking about the emotional weight of phrases and the substance of policy proposals. To push forward their agendas, policy actors choose words, phrases, and the best arenas for presenting their rhetoric. They also choose words to denigrate the opposition's ideas and needs in a discourse of derision (Malen, 1994). A recent example of such derision is Rush Limbaugh's calling Senator Robert Byrd's speeches "Byrd-droppings."

Politicians work to get audiences filled with like-minded people who will help sway the action to meet their purposes. In observing policy activity, our attention is usually centered on those who are manipulating those symbols in political talk. By focusing on the audience—that is, the target of the words and performance—we see who is there listening and wonder why they are there, why they were assembled, and who will gain from this assembly. One wonders what happened beforehand to mobilize this audience and get their attention, and, conversely, who is *not* there and why. What happened to ensure that certain people would not attend (Schattschneider, 1960)?

Policy Logics.   Arguments articulated to justify political action and momentum for a certain policy choice appeal to constituents and decision makers when those arguments make sense and fit with their values and needs. The bases of policy formulation, the logics, models, or frameworks, as well as standards of how to judge and criticize policy-making performance (Rein, 1983; Anderson, 1978) build the assumptions. Attention should be paid to the rationale and the normative standards evident in policy development and analysis, as they carry both explanatory and evaluative potential. Rationales for policy postulate expected behavior but also state an evaluative presumption (Anderson, 1978). Thus, to make sense of and to identify the overall direction of policy and political processes, we must uncover these rationales, evaluations, standards, and assumptions about the goals or purposes for education. Some people believe that schools should focus on preparing citizens (democratic equality), while others believe schools are for preparing people for the workplace (social efficiency). Others look for schools to prepare children to compete well in order to move up in the world (social mobility) (Labaree, 1997). Many political debates have, at their root, conflicting logics about the goals for schooling and competing views of policy problems. Current debates over school reform, including the challenge the school voucher advocates make, asserting that public schooling meet goals, hinge on such competing views. So debaters have very different values and evaluations of public schooling (Boyd, 2000). Presidents' State of the Union addresses and governors' State of the State addresses often contain policy logics as they justify proposals for programs and spending for education. Reading the following excerpt from Bill Clinton's 1994 State of the Union address reveals policy logics connecting school initiatives with the needs of the economy. Its proposals for Congress to act on school choice and for Goals 2000 are crafted to appeal to business interests and also to traditions for grass roots initiatives. After addressing needs related to fair housing, civil rights, creating jobs, and providing better medical care, the President said,

> We can do all of these things . . . we also must give our people the education, training, and skills they need to seize the opportunities of tomorrow.
>
> We must set tough, world-class academic and occupational standards for all of our children—and give our teachers and students the tools to meet them. Our Goals 2000 proposal will empower individual school districts to experiment with ideas like chartering their schools to be run by private corporations, public school choice—so long as we measure every school by one high standard: Are our children learning what they need to know to compete and win in this new economy? Goals 2000 links world-class standards to grass roots reforms, Congress should pass it without delay.
>
> Our school-to-work initiative will for the first time link school to the world of work, and will provide at least one year of apprenticeship beyond high school. After all, most of the people we're counting on to build our economic future do not graduate from college. It's time to stop ignoring them and start empowering them. (Goals 2000, 1994)

Policy logics and values are dripping from each phrase. They can powerfully shape public policy when delivered from such a bully pulpit as a State of the Union address.

Political Socialization.   Support of education policy proposals often depends on arguments about schools as instruments of socialization. This is the most common policy logic justifying public education policy. People often assume that a major reason to have free and accessible public schooling is to prepare and socialize children to be "good" citizens and to pledge allegiance to a common culture and national agenda. When policy makers specify the content of curriculum—for example, for civics, history, social studies, and government—they are using education policy as a way to create the citizens they desire. They are conveying messages about the need to be educated voters, a sense of affiliation with one's national heritage, and the belief that participation, working hard, and support of the political system will help make their country strong for the benefit of everyone. Naturally, this is an area of great political debate, as people do not agree on what is the right preparation or the right goal for that socialization. Is it to prepare children to be ardent challengers and critical thinkers, or is it to prepare them to be ardent patriots, willing to defend their government and way of life? Policy makers do not write details of curriculum or the textbooks, but they do make policy about how many units of American history, for example, a high school student must have. Their power and ways of framing issues result in policies affecting schools' selection of materials, units for study, and amount of time devoted to any topic.

Policies direct curriculum and materials. Research shows that Black American youths' attitudes and knowledge and desire to participate in politics were raised by such coursework but, interestingly, according to Wirt and Kirst (1992), "Repeated research finds that the impact of high school civics classes on white middle class high school student is minimal" (p. 63). Social studies teachers, in particular, see their curriculum and materials affected by political debates about whether students know enough about the Bill of Rights, jury trials, international relations, constitutional government, and democracy. All educators are affected by public sentiment about schools. Educators hear and feel public expectations for their responsibility to teach about morality, truth, justice, patriotism, integrity, manners, tolerance, and respect—and also about diversity, empathy, and self-esteem. Debates over which of these are correct expectations reveal how schooling is, in essence, about making classroom living laboratories for democracy (Awbrey, 1995; Banks & Banks, 1997). Still, Apple says, "There is a complicated politics . . . in which dominant groups are attempting to redefine what we actually mean by democracy, equality, and the common good" (1997, p. 168).

Political struggles over textbooks, classroom materials development and review policies, and curriculum and testing policies are the most likely contexts for these struggles.

Another common policy logic for public education comes from human capital theory. Assuming that people are great contributors to the resources and capacities of a country, this theory influences schools to develop children's skills for contributing to the economic development; as they learn skills, they learn attitudes for citizenship, morality, and public life. Thus, students should be socialized in work ethics and in a concern that their futures and labors will strengthen their country's development.

Teachers learn in teacher training and induction that they are key socializing agents for our children. In their own professional socialization they learn that they are role models and that their dress, demeanor, lifestyle, and political values must reflect the preferred values of their society (or at least that they must hide any that veer from the norm).

All such policies, written or unwritten, reflect strong dominant values, but they are continuously contested in political settings at all levels of education—from the classroom, hallways, and parking lots of schools, to the state boards, to even the international comparisons of education productivity. Differences in basic assumptions about the purpose and values to be conveyed through schooling show up in conflicts over issues such as dress codes or girls' and boys' proper behavior, as much as they do in Character Education curricula, mock legislatures, and civics units on voting.

Policy Issue Networks.   Relationships among groups that constitute the policy-making process can be identified through network analysis. This approach views interest groups as mediators in democratic government (Rhodes & Marsh, 1992). In other words, it helps address questions such as how people gain representation and whether the system is pluralistic, elitist, or somewhere in between. *Network theory* points out that the existence of a group to defend or promote an interest does not constitute meaningful representation of that interest unless it is accompanied by actual influence in the policy-making process. Tightly integrated relationships between traditional groups and policy makers effectively shut out these new voices from the process. Further, the procedural inclusion of citizens' groups without effective power or influence maintains an illusion of fairness and equity that subverts subsequent attempts to protest these groups' lack of input and to mobilize effective opposition.

Dominant networks exercise control over distribution of authority, money, legitimacy, information, organization, and the rules of the game (Saward, 1992). Issue networks usually have large numbers of participants due to their openness to membership. These groups have varying levels of resources and compete with one another to influence the policy process (Rhodes & Marsh, 1992).

The Arena Model.   What happens as legislative initiatives are brought to a policy arena? Focusing on the decision sites through which power is exercised to initiate, formulate, and enact policy helps highlight characteristics of policy maneuvering. According to the arena model, there are four primary arenas: the subsystem, macro, leadership, and commission arenas (Mazzoni, 1991).

Most of us never see the *subsystem,* which is a small and stable group of committee-based legislators, bureaucrats, and interest group representatives who dominate the education policy agenda. They are sometimes called the "iron triangle." Media coverage is scant and policies are formulated within the status quo limits; there is a bias toward interests already represented at the bargaining table. Members of the subsystem are not interested in major policy changes; incremental changes and system maintenance predominate. Members may conflict but usually over short-run differences. Discussions and debates are behind the scenes, concealed and quiet or privatized, with only a few people involved (Schattsneider, 1960).

However, when policy actors are attempting major policy innovation, they move the action to other arenas, thus inviting other actors and dynamics. If they act in the *macro* arena, they engage in the more visible, ideological, and accessible dynamics of politics. In this arena, policy makers can manipulate symbols in a dramatic and open fashion in order to garner public opinion in favor of a particular agenda. They may actively spread the word to involve widened audiences, thus socializing the conflict or issue, bringing it into macro arena policy making that is more visible and contentious. Top-level officials promote and publicize policy positions. "Basic social cleavages and philosophic differences" (Mazzoni, 1991, p.117) find political voice, and givens are challenged. Media campaigns, front-stage appeals, and high drama attract broad attention. In macro arenas, "Widely shared, stylized political myths are likely to triumph over sophisticated, subtle analyses" (Hildegartner & Bosk, 1988, p. 623; Edelman, 1977). Newly energized participants crowd the arena; the conflict is socialized, with wide audiences. Ideological confrontation and momentum—these are conditions that make possible nonincremental and redistributive policy proposals. Effective strategies are first "meeting opposition head on and overcoming it . . . (then) slipping an initiative by as a side issue or non-issue" (Polsby, 1984, p. 159, as referenced in Mazzoni, p. 118).

Two other arenas exist: the leadership arena (stable group of elites, usually executive and legislative leaders, who forge alliances without inviting participation of outsiders) and the commission arena (temporary, appointed group of prominent people with diverse interests, selected by top leadership, often to represent a wide array of stakeholders and given temporary power to recommend policy action) (Mazzoni, 1991). Policy actors may, at times, place their agendas into one of these arenas in order to engage different power arrangements. Figure 1.8 displays the conditions that cause arena shifts and resulting opportunity for a different kind of politics and policy innovation.

It is useful, analytically, to identify the arena being used to push a policy proposal. It is also useful to note when a proposal is shifted, to be placed in a different arena. When or what makes the arena shift happen? External pressures like public interest groups, crises, the circulation of policy entrepreneurs, and newly available resources can enable arena shifts. Revenue shortfalls can also cause arena shifts, creating such a crisis that structural change is called for—politicians have powerful motivations to search for alternatives. As

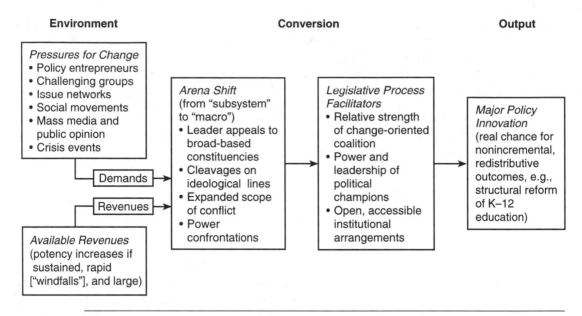

FIGURE 1.8   *A Model of Political Initiation of Policy Innovation*

Source: Mazzoni, T.L. (1991). Analyzing state school policy making: An arena model. *Educational Evaluation and Policy Analysis,* 13(2), 115–138. Copyright 1991 by the American Research Association. Reprinted by permission of the publisher.

Mazzoni did with the story of Minnesota's school choice policy (to be discussed in Chapter 6), one can use these cultural lenses to make sense of puzzling education policy and politics events. The lenses do call attention to power dynamics.

Realities of Partisan Politics

The taken-for-granted, everyday understandings about education politics usefully guide analysis and help guide one's involvement in political action. Sometimes they are so commonplace that we do not notice, for example, the way certain policy logics prevail, the way we assume that school should prepare children for citizenship, that we assume government is set up to be representative, the ways that elections, stakeholders, interest groups, deals, and even corruption affect education politics. We must be cautious, though. Being complacent about such common understandings leaves them unexamined, when, in fact, as frameworks they usefully remind us of underlying issues and controversies that will, and should, recur. Table 1.3 presents lenses for understanding the realities of partisan politics.

Electoral Politics

Political parties articulate values stances and position statements, select and support candidates, and, within legislative and executive partisan politics, direct their members on how

TABLE 1.3 *Lenses for Understanding Partisan Politics*

Partisan Politics Lenses	Focus
Electoral Politics	Identifies the connections between partisan platform assertions, election results, and directions for education policy
Stakeholder Salience	Focuses on the degree to which policy makers give priority to groups' ideas and needs because of the urgency, the legitimacy, and the power of the group and their need
Pluralism, Interest Groups, Representation	Examines which interests are represented in the policy-making process and seeks to understand how they gain access and influence and whether, and how, politics represent the people
Advocacy Coalitions	Identifies coalitions and social movement activism for reform centered on common values and beliefs, which become social capital
Bargaining, Wheelin' and Dealin', Corruption	Acknowledges a range of modes of operating to make deals to gain power and for political benefit, legally and illegally, and use power to dispense access, positions, and money

to vote. Currently, in Congress and legislatures, education policy proposals are drawing more and more attention, although they are often presented as part and parcel of proposals for buttressing the economy. In local school board elections, voters and candidates focus more on education issues, often ignoring political party influences. Still, at all levels, candidates for office know they must, through their talk and actions, appeal to the needs and values of the people who vote. They must talk about the goals, strategies, and structures for schooling in ways that shape or fit with many voters' sense of what is right and good. The candidate or the incumbent who talks and acts, for example, in favor of "the basics" and about wanting schools to teach children to respect elders, to be punctual and honest, and to believe in God will appeal to different voters than the candidate/incumbent with visions for interdisciplinary curricula and pedagogies for critical thinking. Often embedded in candidates' and voters' assumptions are fundamental beliefs about the purpose of schooling. For example, we can search for the differences between the candidate or party more in favor of schooling for citizenship and for vocational preparation and the ones more in favor of schooling for lifelong, creative, emancipatory, critical thinkers. Although the lines are fuzzy, the party platform for vouchers and tuition tax credits is more likely to be Republican, and the platform that clearly provides the most benefits for public school teachers and defends public schools as providers of equal opportunity is more likely to be Democrat.

Election campaigns, speeches, platforms, promises, campaign contributions, and political action committees (PACs) all build on and collect symbols, images, and values that influence the way people vote. The winning party and candidates' values and strategies are supposed to reflect the majority, the dominant values. In the democratic ideal, the public is given a mandate that reflects the articulated values, ideas, and strategies of the winners.

Many factors complicate this simple picture. Political parties' powers have waned as interest group coalitions and as individual candidates sway electoral politics more and more, but parties retain great capacity for affecting policy debate and decisions (Heineman, Bluhm, Peterson, & Kearney, 1997). When voters query "What have you done for me lately?," incumbents hold onto their positions by highlighting the results they have produced. The result is increasing orientation of elected officials toward "errand-running and constituency service and away from developing a coherent policy orientation" (Heineman et al., 1997, p. 107). Further, the power of PACs from associations ranging from the American Association of Retired People, the American Education Research Association, the American Federation of Teachers, the American Federation of Trial Lawyers, to the National Rifle Association and hundreds of others, can shape policy promises. Deals, trade-offs and compromises, and pork barrel politics shape policy realties. The habit of making incremental policy, based on past policy, restrains innovative policy possibilities. Nevertheless, some election politics signify real values shifts when voters seemingly agree with platforms and candidates whose platforms and promises are clearly different from the status quo.

Stakeholder Salience

For education policy, who gets the most influence and when and why? By figuring this out, the education leader can have useful information both for policy analysis and for acting strategically. Stakeholders—groups who will be affected or who affect the action, decisions, policies, practices, or goals—have some degree of legitimacy, power, and sense of urgency regarding the policy issue (McDaniel & Miskel, 2002). With the proliferation of groups competing for attention in policy arenas, it is useful to identify the *salience* of groups, that is, the degree to which policy makers give priority to a group's claims. McDaniel and Miskel (2002) classified stakeholder types and their salience, as demonstrated in Table 1.4.

We are least familiar with the nonstakeholders who, though usually ignored, can play important roles when an educational issue shifts to affect them. The demanding, discretionary, and dormant stakeholders have some potential to exert significant influence, but they remain passive because they cannot or choose not to act. McDaniel and Miskel (2002) give the example of the corporate CEO who might have power through economic resources but whose claim is perceived by policy makers as inappropriate or nonurgent. We are most familiar with the remaining types—those who are most active in the policy environment and who have a high probability of exerting influence on policy issues. A state teachers association with established lobbying mechanisms is a dominant stakeholder, but policy makers might not always see their claims as urgent. Dangerous stakeholders—less legitimate, more marginal groups whose loud and urgent actions are unpredictable—sometimes get the cold shoulder from policy makers. With their high salience, definitive stakeholders make explicit and recognized claims and are highly respected by policy makers. Applying these categories to a case study of policy makers, including the Business Roundtable group in Michigan in the 1990s, proved to be a way of demonstrating the shifts in salience of the Roundtable's claims for education reform initiatives through the decade in the McDaniel &

TABLE 1.4   *Stakeholder Typology and Salience*

Stakeholder Class	Power	Legitimacy	Urgency	Level of Salience
Nonstakeholder	Low	Low	Low	Very Low
Demanding	Low	Low	High	Low
Discretionary	Low	High	Low	—
Dormant	High	Low	Low	—
Dangerous	High	Low	High	Moderate
Dependent	Low	High	High	—
Dominant	High	High	Low	—
Definitive	High	High	High	Very High

Source: From J. McDaniel and C. Miskell. Stakeholder Salience: Business and Educational Policy, *Teachers College Record,* vol. 104, no. 2, pp. 325–356, 2002. Used by permission.

Miskel (2002) study and, in turn, can have tremendous explanatory power in analysis of educational policy arenas.

Pluralism, Representation, and Interest Groups

Focusing on the behaviors and relationships of lobbyists as they represent their constituents' interests provides a powerful lens for understanding politics. This phenomenon can be viewed as illustrative of pluralism and representative democracy, as interest groups constitute linkage institutions that act as transfer agents between policy makers and the public (Dahl, 1961; Wirt & Kirst, 1992). The interests and desires of their publics are communicated to policy makers through these groups. Teachers associations; administrators associations; school board associations; and associations representing reading specialists, researchers, and professors; representing folks who want to limit property taxes; representing home-schooling—all may be present, with their conflicting needs and values, working to have policies to meet their desires. Pluralist theories of democracy hold that groups will form out of common interests held by people in society, thus allowing for all sides of an issue to be represented in the process of policy making (Truman, 1951). However, it has been noted that, in the universe of all interest groups, "the heavenly chorus sings with a strong upper class accent" (Schattschneider, 1960, p. 35).

Critics of pluralistic theory, however, note that groups do not form spontaneously. Instead, they need entrepreneurs and some material incentive for people to participate (Moe, 1980; Olson, 1965). The "free rider problem," in which people do not join a group because that group will represent their interests regardless of their actions, presents a distinct obstacle to group formation. Though groups can overcome this problem through psychological or social benefits to membership, the system still appears weighted in favor of economic interests (Moe, 1980). In the subfield of special education policy, legislative reforms attempted to remedy this situation by requiring broader participation by all relevant interests.

A study of interest group activity at the national level reveals evidence that people join and get involved in mobilizing tactics of interest groups for ideological reasons, not just as rational choices for economic benefit (Opfer, 2001a).

Analysis of interest groups lends insight into questions about the representativeness of government, about how well all interests are represented. Debates over pluralism revolve around whether or not all interests have groups to represent them. There exists a kind of subgovernment of interest group actors who specialize in one policy domain (e.g., insurance, education) with, as Cibulka (2001a) says, "a tendency for a few powerful interests to dominate policy making for their narrow ends to the exclusion of the interests of broader segments of society that lack comparable power" (p. 14).

Advocacy Coalitions

Coalitions form and are maintained often over long periods of time. They work together for common goals and have some degree of commonality of beliefs. Coalitions may include some formal interest groups, such as the PTA or the School Board Association, but are more likely to be coalitions of activists with affiliations in social movements or of people holding certain institutional positions (Sabatier & Jenkins-Smith, 1993). Thus, the glue holding them together is values and beliefs rather than interests, or passion, spirit, and principle rather than the gain to be made by working the political scene. Advocacy coalitions work both within and outside policy agencies, and their instruments include persuading through testimony, obtaining media publicity, providing research reports, publicizing agency performance gaps, offering inducements such as bribes or promises of future employment, changing the personnel who make decisions, conducting systematic reviews of agencies, pursuing litigation, pursuing major changes in budgets, and changing public opinion. Their membership may be fluid and amorphous, evolving over time as these reform movements themselves evolve.

Such advocacy coalitions have existed over the decades of legislative and judicial politics for desegregation (Cooper, Fusarelli, & Randall, 2004). Similarly, advocacy coalitions for passage and enforcement of Title IX have included women's groups, professionals in state and local departments of education, and teacher unions (Marshall, 2002). Commonality of values is transformed into a kind of social capital, available for a powerful moral force and available to be coalesced into coordinated political stands. Figure 1.9 displays the activities of political advocacy coalitions. Such a framework is useful for identifying who's who and why and how they work together. It is also useful for anyone who is planning strategies to work in coalitions to advance their own favorite values, needs, and programs.

Bargaining, Wheelin' and Dealin', and Corruption

In a pluralist system, where many powerful actors have a vote, or even blocs of votes, proposals do not become law unless they get approval from many interested groups. As a result, few major reform proposals are successful, and when they are, deals must be made. Also, one must remember that political activity includes political tactics used to get things done. Politicians often care more about being able to show their constituents how well they

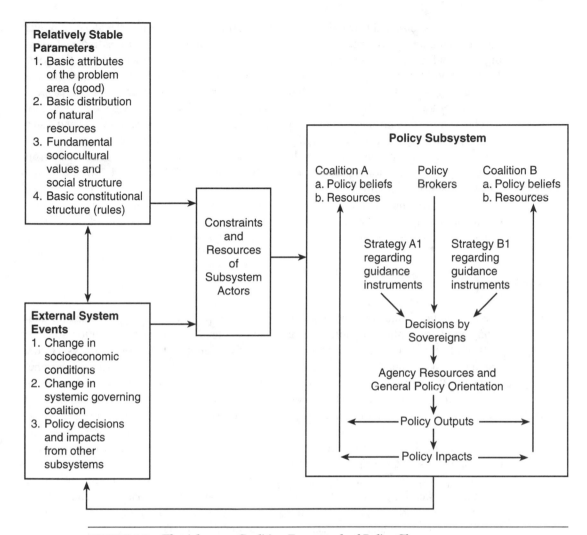

FIGURE 1.9   *The Advocacy Coalition Framework of Policy Charge*

Source: From P. A. Sabatier and H. C. Jenkins-Smith. *Policy Change and Learning: An Advocacy Coalition Approach.* Copyright 1993 by Westview Press. Used by permission.

obtain benefits for them than about the particular vote or issue. "Pork barrel" or "earmarks," for example, in which congressmen "bring home the bacon," refers to the last-minute items attached to appropriations bills to get special projects assisting ones' home district or pet project. Terms like *in bed with* and phrases such as *scratch my back and I'll scratch yours* allude to the quiet deals made to compromise, agree to, or ally with something or someone just to get help and votes for something else you want. This kind of terminology is used in everyday parlance and by journalists far more often than scholars' research-based terms about politics.

People who say, "I hate politics" often are defining politics as the illegal use of power for personal gain. When school board members or legislators use their position to, for example, push forward their underqualified relatives for business contracts or education jobs, this is a kind of detested politics. When the Buildings and Grounds Director uses the district's crew and bricks and mortar for building the porch on his summer cottage, those people may get away with stealing because of their power. When congresspersons' votes on voucher funding are influenced after they spend a great deal of time being wined and dined by companies offering private schooling, this kind of greed gives politics a bad name. Reformers try to prevent this brand of politics. In the early 1900s Progressive era, the effort was to separate educational politics from "dirty city politics." In recent decades, constant scrutiny and coverage of educational politics by the media and the demand for increased public access to school board deliberations are attempts to prevent "dirty politics" from affecting schooling. The lenses focusing on political realities point out power, particularly how power produces results and how power is used in negotiations.

Choosing a Lens

The conceptual frameworks presented in this chapter provide an array of lenses for analyzing and participating in political arenas. Each is a lens that draws attention to particular parts of the arena or particular behaviors (and tends to ignore others). In his analysis of decision making surrounding the Cuban Missile Crisis, Allison (1971) demonstrated this phenomenon: When using one particular organizational theoretical framework, one focuses on certain actors, certain data, and thus comes up with a certain analysis, whereas a different framework and focus yield a different story. In their presentation, Bolman and Deal (1997) point to the viability of the political frame for highlighting power, conflict, competition, and advocacy, but show that other frames highlight rather different aspects of organizations. None of the stories are wrong, just different, because the theory, model, and concepts draw attention differently. By identifying the theories or frameworks being used, one can be much more effective in recognizing biases, critiquing, and seeing what is there and what is missing. Particularly, one can begin to ask how each lens provides tools for accessing political arenas and whether lenses can incorporate missing voices.

Missing Voices and Issues and the Need to Take a Stand

The concepts presented so far are very useful for understanding how powerful people behave and what happens in centers of power. They give us hypotheses that might help us understand who has power, how they keep it, and how to analyze the behavior of legislators or school board members. They help us understand why it is so confusing to move from one region in the country to another. They help us plan for the supports and gauge the timing of a policy window to push forward an agenda. But this pertains to the power centers and those with access to power. Something is missing. Educators and many of the pressing issues affecting learning and the abilities of children and their families to thrive are often not represented well in these powerful arenas. Thus, focusing on arenas of power provides analyses that leave educators frustrated when policy makers ignore reports or pay attention to one particular constituency.

Political analysis, too often, is the study of the influentials, that is, those who get more of what there is to get—deference, income, safety—without addressing "the reality that disproportionate numbers of women, minorities and working-class persons fall into the category of the uninfluentials and are thus defined out of politics (save as those over whom influence is exerted)" (Elshtain, 1997, p. 26). When we focus on the activities of organized interests and arenas of power, we fail to recognize that some things are *made* into nonissues as the outcome of political processes, which skew results toward those who have access to the arenas. According to Elshtain (1997), "Power is implicated in eliminating certain areas for explicit political consideration" (p. 28).

The Need for a Focus on Education Realities

The most frequent refrain in educators' lounges is, "Those politicians make policy, but they just don't know what it's like in real schools!" Educators' sense of powerlessness and anger is multiplied by their lack of connection to the decision-making arenas that create the policies and programs that affect their work demands. Myriad groups and individuals, similarly, feel anger and frustration over policies and programs they cannot accept. Whether it is in the failed campaign against the bond issue by an organized antitax group with a network of alliances, or in the tears of a single parent who is unable to attend PTA meetings and senses that this harms her child's chances for success, lots of people see themselves as disconnected from the centers of power.

Many of the previously mentioned conceptual approaches leave these experiences out of the picture. Even school leaders feel powerless and angry when they must convince staffs and communities to accept policies they know will not work well. And when school leaders are called on to demonstrate their abilities to work with community groups, to exercise democratic leadership, and to be inclusive, they need models and concepts that connect the arenas of power with the range of less powerful groups and individuals. New models and concepts are needed to include that anger, frustration, and powerlessness. As important, we need new ways of thinking about and focusing on the outsiders as true participants in policy processes, not as outsiders, so that the boundaries between insiders and outsiders are permeable. When this is achieved, policies will be more attuned to realities in and around schools.

Lastly, we need to question what more is needed, beyond the theories outlined in this chapter, for addressing the needs of children and families, for addressing teaching and learning, for addressing the particular kinds of people attracted to education careers. In other words, we need to examine how well these theories get at some of the fundamental debates in education (Stout, Tallerico, & Paredes-Scribner, 1995), as the following questions exemplify:

Who should go to school?
What should be the purposes of schooling?
What should children be taught?

How should they be taught?
Who should decide issues of school direction and policy?
Who should pay for schools?

Because all aspects of current schooling practices, problems, and policy proposals are in some way dependent on the economic and political history, frameworks are needed to help make that context visible. Lenses are needed for focusing on the ways that trends such as those in economic, banking, industry, immigration, industry, highways, labor unions, population control, juvenile justice, and minority access have shaped the challenges facing schools over decades, even centuries (Anyon, 1997).

Similarly, we need to face the persistence of historical patterns of neglect and unequal outcomes in schooling. The persistent rhetoric in educational politics is about caring for our children because they are the future and because through their access to public education, we promote democracy. But political analysis needs to incorporate power that is unseen and even unintentional—power that creates consequences and outcomes simply because a particular class, group, or sex has a position within a set of social structures and arrangements. They derive benefits and privileges—and those social structures and arrangements developed historically (Elshtain, 1997; Anyon, 1997).

Analysis is needed that examines and seeks to understand what happens outside these arenas of power—politics from the outside-in and the connections and disconnections between insiders and outsiders. Educators need to find ways to understand the needs of marginal groups, to incorporate the passions that we bring in the desire to make education right and good for children, and to search for and present alternative views of what is right and good. Further, many of the theories and frameworks in this chapter treat policy making as just something to describe empirically and neutrally. From this perspective, subjective preferences and values are seen as personal and irrational, and thus are not appropriate for public arenas, public policy, public debate, and public analysis.

For educators to be empowered and enabled to take charge of the directions for education policy, we need analytic frameworks and methodologies that help us incorporate personal insights, values, and passions that are so much a part of what happens in schooling. Further, we need political analysis and political strategies that guide the way for our taking a stand as policy advocates. The political frameworks and the people in power, those in the center of the arenas for formulating the policies that educators must implement, sometimes miss these understandings, passions, and needs.

Frameworks are needed that incorporate the power of ideas and emotion. Noting the community, public, and group-ness aspects of politics, Stone (1997) says that politics is not just about competition: Power "operates through influence, cooperation, and loyalty. It is based also on the strategic control of information. And finally, it is a resource that obeys the laws of passion rather than the laws of nature" (p. 32). Change occurs "through interaction of mutually defining ideas and alliances. Ideas about politics shape political alliances . . . [which] in turn shape the ideas people espouse and seek to implement . . . ideas and portrayals [are] key forms of power in policymaking" (p. 32). People do not get as excited and ready to fight according to rational models of behavior or according to economic market logics nearly as much as they do over ideas. According to Stone, "The passion in politics comes from conflicting senses of fairness, justice, rightness, and goodness" (p. 34).

Traditionally, economic and political frameworks for understanding educational politics are most commonly used. But if politics is really about conflicting ideologies and values, and is carried out through talk and symbols manipulation, then we need different frameworks (Ball, 1990b). In Figure 1.10, Stephen Ball points out that, when we acknowledge values and ideologies as the focus of politics of education, we are shifting to different frameworks. So, along with the theories that recognize that every policy direction is a representation of values and ideology, theories and methodologies are needed that are powerful guides for re-framing policy logics to incorporate values and a sense of what is good. Thus, we end this chapter by recognizing the need for alternatives in framing politics of education.

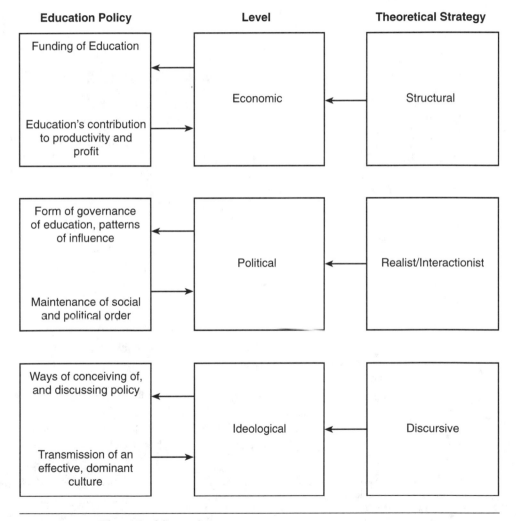

FIGURE 1.10 *Theoretical Strategies*

Source: From S. Ball. *Politics and Policy Making in Education: Explorations in Policy Sociology.* Copyright 1990 by Routledge Publishers. Used by permission.

Summary

Once one accepts that politics cannot be avoided, the array of frameworks for analyzing political arenas can provide ways to make sense of the action. Frameworks, theories, concepts, and models can be applied to understand how politicians view their roles, how policy windows open, why audiences are large or small, why there are stages of policy activity, and so on. However, this traditional focus on the actions of the powerful in their arenas of power does not fit with the everyday lives and passions of educators. Further, they do not provide the insights needed for propelling educators to shape their own politics for schooling. More is needed.

Exercises for Critically Analyzing Politics and Policy

1. Here is a range of definitions of politics, policy, and government which are either attributed to philosophers and political theorists or are everyday sayings. Think about your own observations and choose the definitions that best fit your experiences. Think also about the way you *wish* things worked. Then prepare an argument, backed up by your observations, to persuade others that your chosen definitions are the correct ones.

Definitions of Politics

Easton—Authoritative allocation of values

Schattschneider—Politics is the mobilization of bias.

Lowi—The exercise of the only form of legitimate coercion

Laswell—The determination of who gets what when where and how

Lasswell—The study of the influential

C. Wright Mills—Politics is a matter of turning personal issues into public problems.

Marx and Engels—Government is a committee of the ruling class.

Jean-Jacques Rousseau (used by Thomas Jefferson and James Madison)—Politics is the means by which needs and inequities are addressed; and, the realization of the general will and the common good.

Ben and Peters—The making of moral rules

Then there is an array of everyday common usage definitions of politics, such as

"The art of obtaining money of the rich and the votes of the poor, on the pretext of protecting one from the other."

"The art of preventing people from meddling in their own affairs."

"The art a politician adopts in approaching every problem with an open mouth."

"Using power to get more power and money."

Definitions of Policy

Mann—Policy is what governments do.

Marshall, Mitchell, and Wirt—Temporary agreement over fundamental conflicts

Elmore—The dominant pattern of practice

Definitions of Government

"Government as the pursuit of justice."

"Government as the pursuit of order."

John Locke—government as the pursuit of individual liberties

2. With a partner, attend a meeting where education policy is the main topic—it may be a university faculty senate, a local school board, a school site council meeting, or a legislative education committee meeting. Sit separately, for an hour afterwards, and decide which of the models, theories, and approaches to analysis

discussed in this chapter are the most useful for making sense of what you observed. Write some notes and then discuss with your partner what you each decided, noting similarities and differences. Follow-up exercise: Look up the original sources cited in Chapter 1 and read the relevant original literature. Then write a paper summarizing the original source and demonstrating how it helps to frame or analyze your observation.

3. Draw your own original picture of an educational policy system. Borrow from any models presented in this chapter, but make sure to place yourself, your neighbors, your education colleagues, and some students in the picture. Then write a paragraph or two about how you feel (e.g., powerful, dominated, scared, determined, "a player," skilled, silenced, naïve, sad, etc.) as you examine what you have drawn. Discuss what you need to know to be able to make sense of this and to do something about it.

4. Through political socialization teachers and students learn political lessons from pledging allegiance, from assemblies, from the employment system in schools, and even from the nods of approval and disapproval in classrooms and faculty meetings. Make a list of at least ten lessons teachers and students learn from the informal curriculum (e.g., bulletin boards, interactions in hallways, lunch rooms and locker rooms, and allocations of resources to different teachers).

5. Have a classroom debate about the purpose of schooling, about goals to be accomplished by sending children to schools. Have students choose and defend the "correct answer," the one in which they believe:

- We educate our children so they can
   a. have skills and aptitudes to get good jobs;
   b. get into a good college, marry well, and move upward in class and/or socioeconomic status;
   c. be knowledgeable enough to understand and participate in the nation's success as citizens and voters;
   d. be critically attuned to the nation's socioeconomic, cultural, and political struggles to participate as activist and reformer citizens;
   e. be well-rounded, confident, individuals who can take care of themselves;
   f. be ethical, caring, emotionally intelligent people who make contributions to community life;
   g. be steeped in the culture and traditions of the nation and prepared to fill the roles appropriate for them;
   h. explore and develop identities;
   i. have maximal exposure to literature, arts, and life experiences so they can pursue enriched intellectual lives;
   j. be critical thinkers;
   k. be lifelong learners;
   l. speak and write in the dominant language;
   m. learn just enough chemistry to make lifesaving drugs but not enough to make bombs;
   n. learn about institutional racism, sexism, and corporate greed and governmental oppression and be inspired to attack and overthrow such forces;
   o. become empowered, liberated people who will use their talents to make a better world;
   p. be good parents and role models;
   q. etc.
- Schools are the places we send our children because there they can
   a. have the chance to be great athletes;
   b. socialize with other children;
   c. be kept out of competing with adults in the labor market;
   d. be supervised while parents work;
   e. have a *system* in which professionals and resources are provided to educate them;
   f. most efficiently manage the largest number of functions listed above;
   g. etc.
- Free access to schools should be provided
   a. for those with the most potential to increase the nation's productivity;
   b. for all boys;

    c. for all children whose parents can subsidize the costs of clothing, tuition, and transportation;

    d. for all children from ages 6 to 10 and, after that, for the exceptionally talented;

    e. for all children from ages 4 to 16, except those with handicaps;

    f. for all children who are white and middle class;

    g. etc.

Note

1. We also see (but less often study) patterns of family names, connections, race, and gender and class dominance.

2

The Politics of Policy Implementation and Analysis

Guiding Questions _____

- How are problems defined for policy making in political arenas?
- What are the structures and cultural process affecting education policy?
- What types of policy exist?
- What are the politics of policy implementation?
- What are policy analysis traditions?
- What is missing from traditions for education policy analysis?

"Typically, governments enact policy with an eye to solving some problem or ideal" (Cibulka, 1995, p. 106). The phrase *public policy* is often defined as what governments choose to do. The phrase covers a range of public activities, including departmental and agency projects and programs, and bureaucratic reforms. Thus, *policy* can refer to a federal government directive or an educational public policy such as "No Child Left Behind." The word *policy* is used sometimes as well to refer to unofficial, nongovernmental, informal, even inadvertent practices that powerfully shape behaviors and outcomes. Unofficial policy can be the unstated patterns of behavior and attitudes that have consequences, such as the guidance counselor's doubt and hesitation to support the college aspirations of students from low-income families. It can cover instances in which a public policy (e.g., a curriculum directive) is undermined by the informal, unofficial practices of teachers who often remake the curriculum to fit their sense of what works. To confuse matters more, public policy can be what governments choose to ignore! The choice to ignore an issue or problem can be a powerful policy action. While this can be very confusing, frameworks for making sense of policy do provide some order to this confusion.

In Chapter 1 we identified ways of looking at who acts and what happens in the political arenas where powerful forces make policy. These perspectives provided a way to understand policy origins and actors; how values, ideas, and biases move onto the governmental agenda; and the momentum of forces that shape and alter the ideas as they moved through political arenas.

Chapter 2 provides frameworks for identifying the way a problem definition shapes policy, ways to identify different kinds of policies, and the mechanisms that are built into policy to make people take it seriously and follow directions. A later section of this chapter presents what we know about policy implementation, providing ways to look at how educators and schools respond, and the intended and the unanticipated outcomes of policy. Finally, this chapter introduces policy studies and policy analysis to delineate how each is used in politics. From such insights, one can develop skills for sorting through policy complexities and for recognizing the political choices behind any policy. One can then focus on the power and values behind any policy direction, pointing to the political beneficiaries and losers.

The following Lived Realities presents the kind of policy puzzle that an educational leader might encounter tomorrow or next year. Insights into realities about the politics of policy will enhance leaders' abilities to take control of schooling,

Lived Realities: So What Is School Improvement?

George's assigned task for the Education Commission of the States was to compare the policy directions for school reform in the fifty states. The Commission cautioned him with tales of outraged state superintendents' reactions to old-fashioned, simplistic, input-output analyses that just compared things like dollars and test scores. So George now had huge piles of white papers, legislation, regulations, and evaluations in response to his requests to each state for information. But how should he start? If he started with the names given to reforms, they were all for "Good Schools," "School Improvement," "Better Start," and the like. The assumptions about how policies would fix schools were embedded and hidden throughout the documents. Besides, each document had policies-within-policies. For example, North Dakota's Improving Our Schools Act was comprehensive, with policies for teacher quality, curriculum redesign, access to computers, and a special focus on at-risk students. George thought, "This is similar to my home state's School Improvement Plan, so I'll try a comparison." The experiment was going well until he encountered the superficially comparable at-risk programs. He just couldn't, in good conscience, ignore the evidence that North Dakota viewed and defined *at risk* very differently from the way his state defined it. With a deadline, George was tempted to shove his doubt under the rug and proceed with a faulty comparison. But what *would* be a good way to compare state initiatives?

This Lived Reality can be unpacked using theory, concepts, and frameworks based on research and analysis of the various kinds of policies and their effects. When George was searching for ways to compare policies, he could have used scholars' comparative work on political culture (presented in Chapter 1). He could have benefited from having a set of categories of policy mechanisms to compare his own state's policies with those of North

TABLE 2.1 *Overarching Approaches to Studying Policy*

Structural	Focuses on aspects of the policy framing
Cultural	Identifies what happens when policies meet educational cultures
Policy Studies and Analysis	Provides information to inform policy makers about predefined policy

Dakota; then he could have understood how the politics within each state had an impact on definitions of *at risk.* Frameworks for studying policy (presented now in Chapter 2) can provide roadmaps for policy planners, policy implementers, analysts, and critics who want to understand what went well and what went wrong with best-laid plans. From there, they can work on the political strategies required to move policy in desired directions, including the voices of marginals and constructing policies in ways that fit with realities of schools.

The *structural,* or the use of structures and stages for planning policy, are presented first. Even though politics and policy are never straightforward and linear, it is still useful to find and label structures and stages, such as the *problem definition stage.* For analytic purposes, it is sometimes useful to use *stage theory* to try to identify the political forces in the stages for policy. Supposing for the moment that the policy world were structured and linear, we could identify the kind of problem definition, the policy type, and the policy instruments. We would see what model of implementation was chosen to move the policy into practice. We would see what mechanisms or policy levers were used to support or demand change and how schools responded. Finally, we would look at *outcomes* to ask what were the effects or results, intended and unintended, of the policy, both on students and on other parts of the education system (Levin, 2000).

These structural approaches are also useful for policy planning, as we can identify policy types and the choice of policy instruments. However, all of these structural approaches lead to the need for *cultural processes* approaches. As policies are implemented, they are greatly affected by organizational and political cultures. A third overarching approach is *policy studies and analysis.*

This chapter provides frameworks for understanding policy: the structures and stages, the cultural processes affecting policy implementation, and then the various approaches to policy studies and analysis, as outlined in Table 2.1.

The Structures of Policy and Policy Planning

In searching for something concrete and tangible in political settings, we sometimes find policies that can be seen and held in our hands! A written statute, code, regulation, or directive is a tangible product of political processes. We can even track and identify aspects and variables of the policy's structure that reveal aspects of its origin, its goals, its intentions about reform, its instruments, its preparation for building consensus and anticipating resistance, and its mechanisms and instruments for attaining goals. Table 2.2 presents a diagram outlining the structural lenses for understanding policy.

TABLE 2.2   *Structural Lenses for Understanding Policy*

Structural Lenses	Focus
Problem Definition and Constraints	Looks at how an issue is set up, as it is identified and named, given the tendency to satisfice and to add on and given constraints
Policy Types	Recognizes variables in the structure of a policy
Basic Goals, Values, and Logics	Focuses on the policy purpose
Redistributive or Developmental?	Identifies whether the policy is a small add-on or whether it takes from some to give to others
Degree of Consensus	Focuses on whether attention was given to obtaining consent
Radical and Incremental Reforms	Focuses on whether this is a small alteration or a very basic change in the whole structure and purpose
Backlash?	Recognizes the likelihood of resistance and plans for it, combining radical change with gradual change
Values, Moral Legitimacy, and Token Policy	Assesses the degree to which the policy encompasses the values and true intentions of policy makers and implementers
The Logic of Classification and Policy Mechanisms	Examines the mechanisms used in policy for shaping education
Policy Instruments	Identifies the instruments inserted in policy for implementation; to get to the goal
Rules, Facts, Rights, and Powers	Delineates the structures for implementing a policy
Administrative Structure Variables	Examines elements of the administrative support for assuring policy implementation

Problem Definition

Policies are never generated *tabula rasa,* from a blank slate, as if nothing had previously been in place or tried out. First, as ideas are generated, decision makers' definitions of the problem to be solved are constrained by realities like limited time, limited resources, and the need to move on from, for example, considering this education problem to this afternoon's consideration of a transportation problem. So, instead of generating all the information needed, all the concerns of a full range of potential stakeholders, and all the possible options to get to a fully satisfactory proposal, decisions are made by compromising. This whole process has been dubbed "satisficing" (Cohen, March, & Olsen, 1972). The proposal is usually some version of adding on or altering the current way of doing things, so most policy making is for small, successive adjustments, and thus incremental change (Lindblom, 1959). According to Heineman and colleagues (1997), "Pressed for time and information, policymakers cannot defer decisions, and it makes good sense for them to focus on specific incremental changes from current policy. Thus, cautious, politically wise administrators can retain a tentative stance and need not stray far from the known parameters of policy (p. 124).

First, the *problem definition* (e.g., test scores are declining) happens in highly politicized contexts. Media attention, powerful actors' use of the bully pulpit to shape opinion, and partisan politics are usually a part of the context when a problem is defined. Still, marshalling the facts, indicators, and comparisons, and searching for causes can include rational, systematic analysis. It also includes normative judgments as political actors' values shape the definitions. Thus, a policy analyst may present data on student course taking in a straightforward manner, shaping the problem definitions. But policy actors' views about "kids today"—about how things ought to be or about how teachers' behaviors must be directed—are values-based normative judgments that affect problem definitions in political arenas. Second, the resources available and the constraints to action, often interconnected, affect choice of policy instrument. Policy actors may simply mandate a change; they may choose to offer inducements and rewards. Policy actors may decide that policy to build capacity is needed or that system changing is needed (see page 48 for more detail on this). As they decide on a type of policy, they are working with some knowledge of the fact that these kinds of resources and constraints exist:

1. The Institutional Context (authority among policy actors, the structure of existing agencies, some of which have capacity-building capacities and some don't)
2. Governmental Capacities. The capacity to use an instrument (e.g., personnel with expertise using that instrument, ability to monitor compliance, to impose sanctions); also capacity across targets, among local systems, to get near-uniform responses
3. Fiscal Resources. Fiscal slack is needed to experiment with these instruments to offset the opportunity costs of enacting new policies. Where resources are not available or taxable, policy makers may choose the least costly instrument.
4. Political Support and Opposition. Where other policy makers and organized interests have preferences for certain instruments, they can manipulate elite and public opinion in favor of their choice. Inducements require the least level of political support; mandates must garner higher levels. Their potential for capacity building isn't visible to any but the beneficiaries, so political coalition support is not likely. System changing is often controversial because it veers from widely held beliefs and promotes radical departures; system changing requires very strong political support through coalitions.
5. Information. Political intelligence about preferences and constituencies; strategic information about the target's capacity and probable response; and analytic information about the technical requirements of instruments and how they will work under different conditions. (One can make bad choices, such as setting inefficient reward schedules, and inducements that are too weak or too strong. Little is known about which inducements work to motivate actions other than changes in economic behavior, so policy goals, such as better teaching or stopping sexual harassment, are difficult to gauge. Similarly, gaps in information about system changing and capacity building make these instruments risky or costly.)
6. Past Policy Instrument Choices. The cumulative effects of past instrument choices influence what the public wants and expects. The electorate judges policy actors' per-

formance on their making "correct" choices. The budgetary effects of past choices may have committed monies in ways that limit current policy instrument choices. So, for example, a new reform policy needs to negotiate the sparse resources left over after the previous policy's expense and the lost human resources caused by fed-up veterans leaving the school.

7. The Political Legacy of Past Policy Choices. The cumulative effects of the politics of past policy affect receptiveness to new policy. So, a new attempt to shape school reform needs to anticipate the local regard that any new policy would be viewed with because of recent policy history. Veteran educators, recalling reforms of the past that lasted only two years, or were unfunded, may simply say, "I'll wait and see if they mean it this time before I buy in and get burned again."

Thus, the reasons for choosing a policy instrument are also interesting. It is useful to include the following kinds of questions in analyzing policy: What factors shape policy actors' instrument choices? Are certain instruments typically used? Are certain leadership strategies used to advance certain instruments? Do policy instruments interact with targets (e.g., teachers, students) as hypothesized? Do organizational and political contexts affect implementation for some policy instruments more than others (McDonnell & Elmore, 1991)?

Policy Types

Most policies aim at some sort of change or reform. When someone asks, "What sort of policy *is* this?" it is helpful to know some ways of sorting and categorizing. The frameworks we present next can provide some guidance.

Basic Goals, Values, and Logics.   One can usefully analyze education politics, as shown in Chapter 1, by identifying the conflicts among policy actors, which are usually over basic goals, values, and logics for schooling. "Schools are responsible . . . for the moral and technical socialization of young people," as Boyd (2000, p. 266) says, but how, to what extent, why, and even where that should happen is an area of huge, unrelenting debate. Key questions to ask about a policy are what goals and values are being pursued and what policy logics are presented to shape powerful actors to support a policy? If this policy is implemented, ask what directions will it take schools and what are the convincing arguments used to gain acceptance of those directions.

Examining the fundamental direction or purpose of a chosen policy can reveal a great deal about the goals, values, and logics being pursued. Recall from Chapter 1 the ways in which dominant cultural values are shaped into policy logics during political deliberation. Arguments articulated to justify political action and momentum for a certain policy choice appeal to constituents and decision makers when those arguments make sense and fit with their values and needs. The bases of policy formulation, the logics, models or frameworks, as well as standards of how to judge and criticize policy-making performance (Rein, 1983; Anderson, 1978), build the assumptions. As explained in Chapter 1, the political articulation of policy logics are seen in the connections and purposes stated to promote their passage. Recall Clinton's State of the Union Address, asserting that to "seize the opportunities of tomorrow" we must have policies for tough, world-class academic and occupational standards for all of our children, for empowering individual school districts to experiment with ideas like public school choice—with the ultimate goal that children will know how to compete and win in this new economy. Such policy logic juxtaposes economic success for our children with choice for school districts and for parents, laying the groundwork and opening minds to consider new policy directions.

Redistributive or Developmental? Sometimes policy makers attempt to make huge and fundamental structural alterations in education systems, and sometimes they decide to work toward gradual change. Developmental programs are those in which most governments are involved anyway (e.g., transportation, education), so government initiatives tinker with the current system, making small changes, tending to reinforce local initiatives and provide extra resources, especially when there are new requirements. These get implemented fairly quickly with relatively little contention.

Redistributive programs (e.g., special education, compensatory education) require that those working at the local school level engage in activities that require special services to certain designated clients but not others. Even as such policies are formulated, they provoke controversy; they are often resented, viewed as taking away from some to give to others. For example, when policy makers discuss state formulae for funding local education, proposals giving disproportionately more funds to poor districts are resisted. Initial implementation is contentious, but eventually redistributive policies are implemented in compliance with legislative intent. "Initial grandiose redistributive program goals get tailored through a mutual adaptation process" (Odden, 1991b, p. 7) that produces a workable program, with the development of internal professional expertise writing the rules and regulations to define the program, to administer it, and to discover classroom practices for use in program delivery. Clearly, policy planners need to consider whether the structures for implementation have been adequately planned to build support and consensus among the people on whom they are depending to carry out the policy.

Policy Consensus. Where the organization's members are in agreement about a policy's goals, it will be implemented. Where the changes in routines and rules are minor, the policies will be obeyed readily. But low consensus for major change results in resistance to policies; implementation is problematic. These ideas, displayed in Figure 2.1 (Van Meter & Van Horn, 1975, p. 460), may be useful for understanding, planning, and predicting change, as acceptance of change depends on how radically the system will be altered. A policy analyst examines the degree of consensus and the degree of change required to see the effects of policies.

Radical and Incremental Reforms. Does the policy demand radical change? In the rare instances in which radical change is proposed in policy, fundamental values shifts must be enacted and implemented. Further, the structural requirements for getting them adopted and implemented cannot be according to standard operating procedures. For a local example, the "schools without walls program" was a way that some districts radically attempted to alter the structural arrangements of teacher, student, and curricular relationships. Policies conveyed through schooling to ameliorate racism, classism, and sexism are usually per-

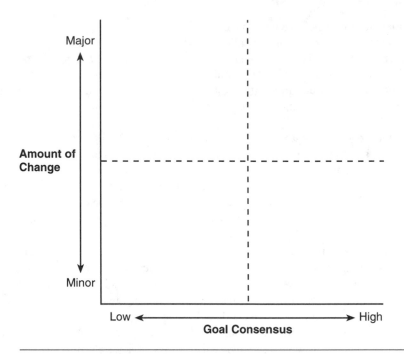

FIGURE 2.1 *Dimensions of Policy Affecting Implementation*

Source: From D. S. Van Meter and C. E. Van Horn. The Policy Implementation Process: A Conceptual Framework, *Administration and Society,* vol. 4, no. 4, pp. 445–488, copyright © 1975 by Sage Publications. Reprinted by Permission of Sage Publications.

ceived as radical. For a national example, court- and federal marshal–enforced desegregation has been a radical attack on racist practices in schooling.

Backlash must be expected when policy redistributes privilege. Gaine's (1989) analysis and recommendations on anticipating backlash help us recognize that even when one uses the dominant values and language, the policies may encounter what she calls "orchestrated backlash" (p. 35). For such policies to be implemented, educational leaders must predict resistance and plan for it, constantly seeking allies; being prepared to deal with the media; giving endless, patient explanation; advertising success; and avoiding the isolation of individuals or individual schools that can be "picked off one by one" (p. 35). Strategic policy activity in these circumstances includes, says Gaine, assessing the power base of those pressing for change, avoiding backlash, and providing for continuous development, because the policy is never "done." Thus, backlash can be managed with continuous policy development, maintaining the legitimacy of the policy, which continues long after securing the policy passage.

Anticipating Backlash.   Does the policy anticipate the resistance? Because radical change is seldom proposed, let alone implemented, without fierce resistance, it is useful to think about combining radical with gradual reform. In his analysis of the results of radical reforms under school choice initiatives, Hess (2002) calls radical changes the "bulldozer approach," aiming to wipe away the existing system to build a new, consumer-approved approach. In contrast, the "pickax approach" to reform is a picking away at specific aspects of the system in order ultimately to bring about systemic reform. The picking-away approach may work where resistance is low. There are times when radical change is called for, especially when powerful cultural patterns, ensconced in institutions' bureaucratic, hierarchical practices, prevent schools from making changes for more equitable practices. As Rorrer (2002) says, "In many areas of the country, a district's legitimacy within its community and within the larger institutional environment depends upon its ability to disrupt previous organizational norms, rules and structures that perpetuated inequality in learning opportunities and outcomes" (p. 1). To take on the task of disrupting institutional inequities requires leaders to use their abilities to "shape the taken-for-granted assumptions, norms, policies and structures . . . and behave strategically . . . to systematically deinstitutionalize inequity and build the district's capacity for equity" (p. 2). Figure 2.2 presents the model applying punctuated equilibrium to the challenge for leaders to disrupt inequity and create a reconstructed district.

During the *reproduction stage,* taken-for-granted assumptions, policies, and practices perpetuate inequity (e.g., with tracking and differential resource allocation). But the *recognition stage* disrupts the assumptions and creates tensions and instability, creating dissonance and challenging institutional legitimacy. *Reconstruction stages* prompt reexamination of inequity, with leaders acting with a sense of agency, with heightened community expectation, and with district leaders deliberately attracting attention to inequity, creating a culture of equity coupled with excellence and integrating calculated processes for achiev-

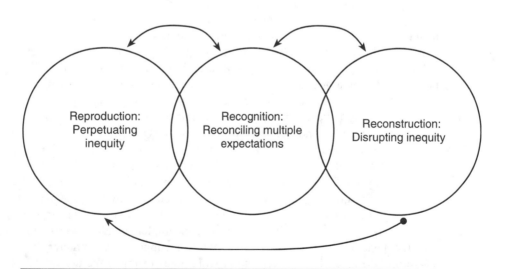

FIGURE 2.2 *Leadership for Equity Framework*

Source: From A. Rorrer. Educational Leadership and Institutional Capacity for Equality. *The UCEA Review,* vol. 43, no. 3, pp. 1–5. Used by permission of the University Council for Educational Administration.

ing equitable outcomes. The leader is a thorn in the side instead of being the protector of the old "way of doing things" (Rorrer, 2002, pp. 2–3). As opposed to tinkering and incrementalism, punctuated equilibrium allows a district to combine peaceful incrementalism with jarring change.

Figure 2.2 displays the dynamics of change when a leader recognizes the systems' reproduction of inequities and supports their recognition. This disrupts the system, increasing dissonance and discomfort. But, at the same time, by leading a process of acknowledging different expectations and allowing alternatives, the leader can then build toward reconstruction, with alterations to end inequities accepted and part of a new *status quo*. Change happens without the full effects of backlash, because the momentum accrued from the initial disruption can be used to institutionalize new equitable scripts. This avoids disenfranchising constituents who could otherwise abandon schools for alternatives (Baumgartner & Jones, 2002). Thus, radical change can happen with leaders who consciously and deliberately jar the system yet provide for maintenance of equilibrium. Where gradual change is too slow, and where and cultural values and powerful institutional backlash will obstruct change, punctuated equilibrium provides politically astute guidance.

Values, Moral Legitimacy, and Token Policy.   Is the policy real? Is it meant to be implemented? Policy is formulated within the framework of the prevailing theory (often an unarticulated theory-in-use) and its assumptions about the problem, and therefore the appropriate mechanisms and supports for solving it (Lindblom & Cohen, 1979). All officially enacted policies have legal legitimacy, which is the authority of the governing body from which they came (unless challenged in court). Not all policies have *moral legitimacy,* however (Habermas, 1975). When a policy conflicts with the ideological assumptions, values, and needs of powerful people, it may be passed into law and have legal legitimacy, but it probably is a *token* or symbolic action, not meant to do anything more than give the appearance of responding to a demand or need. It may never be funded, codified, or implemented as law or regulation. Without moral legitimacy, without dominant values driving it, without politicians and the leaders in schools feeling a sense that the policy direction is valuable and right, the token policy will result in token implementation. Minogue (1983) has said, "Nothing gets done which is unacceptable to dominant or influential political groups, which may be defined to include the 'bureaucratic leadership' group" (p. 73).

Policy is formulated within the context of policy makers' sense of what is appropriate, necessary, and valued, and their sense of the constraints on their options. Myths, beliefs, traditions—the ways things have always been done—provide the main architecture of policy makers' assumptive worlds (as explained in Chapter 1) affecting policy formulation (Raab, 1982; Young, 1977). These elements also affect implementation: Policies that fit this structure will get the attention of school administrators and their involvement in implementation.

Any examination of policy implementation must include an analysis of the value system of the people entrusted with administering the implementation, because their values affect the level of resource allocation, political support, and monitoring that occurs. Therefore, the analysis of policy and program must examine the prevailing assumptions about the problem of formulators and implementers, the traditional solutions, and the salience and valuing of those groups affected by the problem.

The Logic of Classification and Policy Mechanisms. What policy mechanisms are used? One can identify policy types by focusing on the mechanisms chosen to be embedded in the policy. Attempting to address a problem or improve programs for education, policy makers choose which aspects of education they can manipulate. When policy communities conceptualize, mobilize, and set up implementation strategies for education policy, they choose from these mechanisms:

1. School finance
2. School personnel training and certification
3. Testing and student assessment
4. School program definition
5. School organization and governance
6. Developing and regulating curriculum materials
7. School buildings and facilities standards and regulations

This classification of the policy mechanisms provides another analytic framework for identifying policy purposes. It was developed from a study with cross-state comparisons, done in the 1980s in the United States by Marshall, Mitchell, and Wirt (1989). The *program definition* mechanism may be chosen by policy makers wanting higher standards. They make decisions about how many semesters of state history or a foreign language are required, or whether physical education is needed two or five days per week. But *buildings and facilities standards* policy mechanisms are chosen for safety in school construction or to set minimum sizes for libraries, computer labs, and bathrooms. If the policy goal is to achieve equity in school leadership, the policy mechanism focused on might be *standards and certification of personnel.* This policy might support women's and minority candidates' ability to be certified in a way that increases their access to administrative positions. In Chapter 6 we present more about this classification system as it displays policy directions in states.

This sort of policy mechanisms classification can be used to analyze policy making in states and in local districts. Thus, the classifications may provide an organizer for the profusion, confusion, and complexity of local policy, as the analyst tries to predict how policy will be implemented. Using the classifications, we can identify the patterns in policy choices, noting which are most used and most neglected or which seem to work and which do not. Analysts wishing to compare, for example, the education reform policies in different countries or states might begin by comparing their recent reforms in personnel, student testing, or governance, which would help identify trends. Similarly, policy makers can use the classification system as a reminder of mechanisms they have not tapped in their efforts to reform schooling.

Policy Instruments. One can identify the instruments or tools used to translate substantive policy goals into concrete actions by classifying them as mandates, inducements, capacity building, and/or system changing. From this classification, one can identify the strengths and weaknesses of any chosen instrument for meeting a policy goal. Policy instruments are outlined in Table 2.3 (McDonnell & Elmore, 1991).

TABLE 2.3 *Policy Instruments: Assumptions and Consequences*

	Assumptions	Consequences
Mandates	Actions required regardless of capacity; good in its own right	Coercion required
	Action would not occur with desired frequency or consistency without rule	Create uniformity, reduce variation
		Policy contains information necessary for compliance
		Adversarial relations between initiators, targets
		Minimum standards
Inducements	Valued good would not be produced with desired frequency or consistency in absence of additional money	Capacity exists; money needed to mobilize it
		As tolerable range of variation narrows, oversight costs increase
	Individuals, agencies vary in capacity to produce; money elicits performance	Most likely to work when capacity exists
Capacity building	Knowledge, skill competence required to produce future value; or	Capacity does not exist; investment needed to mobilize it
	Capacity good in its own right or instrumental to other purposes	Tangible present benefits serve as proxies for future, intangible benefits
System changing	Existing institutions, existing incentives cannot produce desired results	Institutional factors incite action; provokes defensive response
	Changing distribution of authority changes what is produced	New institutions raise new problems of mandates, inducements, capacities

Source: From L. M. McDonnell and R. F. Elmore. Getting the Job Done: Alternative Policy Instruments. *Educational Evaluation and Policy Analysis,* vol. 9, no. 2, pp. 133–152, 1987. Copyright 1987 by the American Educational Research Association. Reproduced with permission of the publisher.

Policy makers seldom think about the range of instruments; they assume mandates are the cheapest, and they choose inducements (e.g., grants in aid) when there is relative consensus that the change is needed. Officials also lack knowledge about the comparative costs, the dynamics, and the fit of an instrument to an environment. Choices may be made with cost–benefit analysis in mind, or with constituent advantage in mind.

These instruments have positive and negative consequences. For example, adequate resources are essential, but money incentives may encourage opportunistic implementation. Rewards may create alliances, even collusion between the givers and the implementers (Stone, 1997). Threats of punishment (e.g., legal action or funds withdrawal) are cheaper than support but may result in hardening the resistance of those responsible for implementing policy or take resources away from the individuals who need them the most. Yearly monitoring is less expensive than evaluation but may result in paper compliance only. Training and consultant support is costly and sometimes rejected by the organization, just as a body rejects foreign tissue. Evaluation is expensive and often misses unanticipated consequences and organizational context issues by narrowly focusing on policy intent. The selection of appropriate positive, negative incentives and supports requires sensitivity to what motivates people in a particular site. The mechanisms that will effectively enable and assure implementation (and their obverse—barriers to implementation) are often locally defined and quite variable.

Rules, Facts, Rights, and Power.   Another way of classifying policy is derived from Stone's (1997) outline of instruments for structuring implementation. She included inducements, but she listed these instruments as well: *rules, facts, rights,* and *powers. Rules* impose obligations and duties. They are "indirect commands that work over time" (Stone, 1997, p. 283) and are made by legislation, administrative agencies, courts, and state and national constitutions. They vary: Some are precise, some are vague and ambiguous, and some are flexible, leaving discretion to those who implement policy. Some are symbolic, while others are monitored and enforced. *Facts,* considered to be information, can also be known as rhetoric, propaganda, and even less complimentary words. (Naming and labels are politically loaded policy instruments.) Fact making can be done through the findings of reportedly objective and scientificly controlled experiments, and also through claims of certified professional experts, based on their clinical and practical experience. Conversely, another policy strategy is withholding facts (e.g., providing only the evidence that serves to promote a policy). *Rights* govern relationships and coordinate behavior, so they can be used as policy instruments. They are often normative and also may be enforced (or not) through court action. Administrative law, grievance procedures, and contracts help substantiate the policy instruments of rights. Rights work directly through litigation, indirectly mobilizing new political alliances and laying the basis for dramatization of society's internal rules and its categories. The example of disputes over whether immigrants have the right to public education, which is a dispute about society's rules for membership rights, is instructive (Stone, 1997).

Altering *powers,* making a change in *who* makes a decision, is another policy instrument. It entails taking power from one entity and shifting some of it to other entities, or changing the size or the membership of the decision-making body. When states and school districts alter the voting precincts to make boards and legislatures more representative, they are using the power policy instrument. When a president asserts in the election campaign that he will close down the Department of Education and leave education policy decisions to individual states, he is presenting rhetoric about altering powers. A seemingly uninteresting and rational proposal, for example, to create a review board for legislators' information about the state school board's activities, gives and takes away power. Political actors, noticing this, get quite excited over proposals to alter powers, especially where theirs are affected.

Elements in Administrative Structure Variables.   A straightforward way to identify elements in a policy is simply by asking questions about whether the policy has administrative structures built in to give it "teeth," so that it can be taken seriously and implemented. These five variables of administrative structure include political support, stability of policy, fiscal support, management, and policy/administrative support, and are outlined as follows:

1. *Political Support.* Political support both within and outside the school system (district and school site) is essential for assuring implementation of any policies that demand change. Policies with mild enforcement, scant resources, haphazard monitoring, sparse expertise, and low priority are not likely to be implemented. So, the policies must have insider and outsider advocates for substantive implementation. This is particularly true for equity policies (Adkinson, 1982).

2. *Stability of Policy.* Schools are vulnerable to demands from federal, state, and local political systems. Such demands are often short-lived, however, as the pressing issue of one year fades, as politicians fade, or as funds and priorities shift. School people are wary of policies, programs, and funds that come as fads and then disappear.

3. *Fiscal Support.* The level and adequacy of support of any particular aspect of a school program are difficult to estimate and assess. In education, obtaining adequate funding is notoriously difficult.

4. *Management.* Change in organizations requires the attention of management and provision for organizational support, such as additional planning time, resources, consultants, flexibility in schedules and job descriptions, and exemptions from meeting other pressing goals.

5. *Policy/Administrative Support.* School boards (and state and federal policies) create general and, in some cases, specific policies regarding instruction, classroom procedures, minimum requirements and expectations for staff, or time allotted for instructional areas. Administrators have the task of translating these policies into regulations, communicating and interpreting policies so that the programs and people they manage will conform. Policies are frequently formulated with inadequate information as to how they will interact with other policies and programs when administered.

Using this simple outline, a policy analyst can ask questions that help untangle the complex of political, organizational, personal, and cultural factors affecting policies and programs. They are useful for assessing whether political actors, when constructing the policy, really mean for it to be implemented.

Cultural Processes of Policy Implementation

Policies, once formulated in those legitimated arenas, direct school district officials and educators to do their work in certain ways or to spend money for certain programs. *So* much happens, though, between the formulation and the implementation! Professional and organizational cultures and political realities remake policies. Read the Lived Realities on the next page and then see whether the ensuing models and theories help to analyze what happens in policy implementation.

Organizational and political cultures at multiple levels of education systems affect what happens to a policy during its implementation. By acknowledging the slippery organizational processes that affect programs and policy implementation, we can reduce the frustration and plan policy that has greater chances for implementation and for desired outcomes. The literature on implementation of change guides us to questions about administrative issues as intervening variables in changes. From this literature we can generate

Lived Realities: This Needs to Be Done by Tomorrow?

Mr. Gaines was quite surprised to learn that, along with the usual load of fifth grade students, he had two students with special portfolios—Robert and Leticia. Robert's portfolio described an array of special arrangements for handling his attention deficit disorder. Leticia's portfolio provided a list of instructional strategies to avoid or to supplement to help Leticia learn in spite of her physical disabilities. As a fully qualified, certified, and experienced teacher, Mr. Gaines was expected to know immediately how to manage this very new situation—by tomorrow, the beginning of the school year. However, he'd had no special education training, no prior knowledge, no new resources, and no sense of where to go for assistance! The portfolios looked rather legalistic—full of behavioral objectives for these two students. Despite his lack of training, time, and resources, Mr. Gaines would be held immediately accountable for making sense of the new policy.

guiding hypotheses, informed guesses that will serve as levers for analyzing the processes observed in school settings, where implementation of any equity policy must take place. What happens in implementation? There is policy slippage, due to opportunistic adoption; loose coupling; the activities of street level bureaucrats; and organizational processes of attention and interpretation. From the literature on change, on implementation, on administrative structure, and on norms, attitudes, and values, we can create cultural lenses that enable us to build a set of questions about implementation. Table 2.4 presents a diagram of the lenses for understanding cultural processes.

Implementation Realities

In policy planning, as mentioned in the previous section, the choice of instruments and mechanisms can be structured with the purpose of controlling the organizational and political responses to policy. Mechanisms that are chosen to ensure implementation can have positive and negative consequences. For example, adequate resources are essential, but money incentives may encourage opportunistic implementation. Threats of punishment (by legal action, funds withdrawal) are cheaper than support, but they may result in hurting the students by hurting their school system. Yearly monitoring is less expensive than evaluation but may result in paper compliance only. Training and consultant support is costly and sometimes rejected by the organization. Evaluation is expensive and often misses unanticipated consequences and organizational context issues by narrowly focusing on policy intent. The selection of appropriate positive or negative incentives and supports requires sensitivity to what motivates people in a particular site.

In the previous section, we mentioned an array of policy instruments (mandates, inducements, capacity building, and system changing). We also mentioned rights, power, and information. With these insights, one can look at the dynamics and politics of policy formulation, whereby actors choose one or several of these instruments. But all the policy structuring in the world cannot totally prevent the cultural dynamics that affect implementation.

TABLE 2.4   *Lenses for Understanding Cultural Processes*

Cultural Lenses	Focus
Implementation Realities	Focuses on the instruments for implementation to question whether they actually fit with realities
Policy Slippage and Mutation	Recognizes that people resist and alter policies and programs
Loose Coupling	Looks at how educational organizations' communications and monitoring systems are not well connected, so implementation will be unreliable
Street-level Bureaucrats	Looks at the point of actual delivery of services, when people make decisions about just how much they can deliver, given constrained resources
Mutual Adaptation and Opportunistic Adoption	Sees how people will adopt policy, given money incentives, but will keep the changes if they can alter them to fit their realities
Organizational Processes of Attention and Interpretation	Focuses on the way the local district receives and translates policy directives
The Lowerarchy	Recognizes the power of teachers as policy brokers
Analyzing the Match between Goals and Instruments	Raises questions about the fit between the policy instruments and policy goals
Unintended Consequences	Acknowledges that policy planning does not anticipate all positive and negative outcomes

Policy Slippage and Mutation

The ideal policy would be designed in a vacuum, without the messy involvement of organizational and professional cultures. The ideal policy or program is one that has been formulated with (1) the right definition of the problem and good information about all the areas touched on by the policy; (2) the right causal model chosen for solving the problem; (3) appropriate regulation, procedures, resources, technology, and incentives for carrying out the policy; (4) appropriate authority for implementation (legal, expert, formal, and informal authority); and (5) goals agreement on all levels affected by the policy. Clearly, this ideal is never achieved. People might err, thinking, for example, that single-family structures cause school violence and character education will cure it, thus choosing a wrong, overly simplistic causal model. Further, policies and programs for complex organizations like schools are rife with conflicting goals, wrong assumptions about subsystems, under-developed technology, and incentives at cross-purposes, shifting definitions of the problem. Poor decision-making processes result in choosing the wrong device or procedure, creating unanticipated consequences, waste, resistance—in short, *policy slippage.*

   A great deal of educators' energies goes toward responding to policy made to affect them; often their response is resistance or creating mutations of the original policy form. *Mutation* occurs, especially, when policy is formulated with little thought about implementation, regarding it as a mere technicality (Pressman & Wildavsky, 1984). The legislator who believes, for example, that schools will be fine as soon as her character education bill is passed, pays little attention to details about the needed curriculum development and about the tendency of teachers to keep their current curriculum as is. As a result, the character education policy mutates, surviving, as it is adapted to implementers' needs.

Loose Coupling

Policies and programs are often devised with the assumption that there is a tight and rational organizational structure at the implementation level, with consensus on policies (or at least acceptance of policy writ from above), a hierarchy of command, communication, regular inspection and monitoring, and evaluation to ensure implementation. School systems are *loosely coupled,* however (Weick, 1976). Although the strength of system coupling may vary cross-nationally, it is often the case that events, activities, functions, and substructures of schools are only weakly and infrequently related. Each element maintains its own identity and active independence, despite organizational interdependence and policies for coordination and standardization. Loose coupling defeats some policy efforts. However, it persists as a functional organizational phenomenon that allows schools to be responsive, adaptive, and flexible to their diverse environments. It also allows an increased sense of staff efficacy by increasing "self-determination of the actors" (pp. 7–8).

Most policy implementation involves a network of bureaucracies and subsystems that alternately compete, cooperate, and ignore each other. The coordination, monitoring, and communication of the ideal rational bureaucracy is not the reality of school systems. Thus, policies to tighten the loose coupling can certainly disrupt and upset but not necessarily fix the system. The looseness of organizational culture enables resistances and avoidance of such tightening. A look at current ongoing negotiations over policies for testing and monitoring progress demonstrates ways this looseness functions. Waivers of all sorts are granted as concrete evidence of loose coupling. Less concrete and probably more numerous are the unrecognized and not-asked-for exceptions that teachers, parents, students, and district officials simply take, without asking permission.

Street-Level Bureaucrats

Studies of implementation have demonstrated how policies conceived at the federal and state levels can have widely unintended impacts when carried out at the local level (Pressman & Wildavsky, 1973; Weatherly & Lipsky, 1977). According to Weatherley and Lipsky (1977), public employees, when they interact with the public, making decisions on their own initiative and creating routines for their work, are *street-level bureaucrats.* Where they have discretion in how they carry out their work, where personnel and organizational resources are chronically scarce, they find ways to accommodate policy and public demands. In their analysis of the implementation of Massachusetts' special education law, Weatherley and Lipsky found that school street-level bureaucrats remade policy by (1) setting priorities, (2) limiting and controlling clientele, (3) rationing services, and (4) modifying goals. This helped to explain the variations in implementation of special education policies. Teachers, wanting to avoid filling out forms, failed to refer students who did need to be evaluated; principals dissuaded parents from asking for a core evaluation; central administrators asked principals and specialists to cut back on the number of costly referrals;

teachers used the referral system to "dump" kids with behavioral problems; and parents' and principal's referrals were processed more quickly than those from teachers. So, a law that was intended to create a uniform, fair, and equitable process showed wide variation in outcomes and unanticipated negative consequences. Practitioners responsible for policy implementation had substantial discretion when performing their work, and these street-level bureaucrats found ways to accommodate and reconcile the demands placed on them with the realities of limited resources. We could expect that street-level bureaucrats would do the same with other policies and programs. Street-level bureaucrats can be at any level of the organization's implementation processes. In fact, teachers themselves are policy brokers, not merely policy implementers.

Mutual Adaptation and Opportunistic Adoption

In their analysis of implementation of federal change policies, Berman and McLaughlin (1978) asked what happens to local change projects when the federal funding stops. They found that three different modes of implementation occurred: *opportunistic, adoption,* and *mutual adaptation.* The first two modes did not result in enduring change. (*Opportunistic* implies that districts take the money but make few enduring changes; *adoption* implies token compliance.) Mutual adaptation was, however, a response that supported sustained change. Mutual adaptation is a process by which the project or policy is adapted to the reality of its institutional setting, while, at the same time, school people adapt their practices in response to project goals. Mutual adaptation was found when effective strategies were used *in concert,* such as concrete, teacher-specific training; classroom assistance from project or district staff; teacher observation of similar projects in other places; regular project meetings; teacher participation in project decisions; local materials development; and principal participation in training. Ineffective implementation strategies included outside consultants, one-shot training, packaged management approaches, formal evaluation, and comprehensive, complex projects. The authors concluded that if the goal is continuation, implementation should be by mutual adaptation and should result in having the project or policy incorporated into the ongoing activities, budgeting, administration, and staffing of the school system. It must become an expected, ordinary part of the culture of the school.

Later studies of policy implementation were more nuanced. One study started by recognizing the policy type (redistributive), then analyzing the implementation of Title I, then showing that skilled implementers, given time to cope with complexity and resistance, could succeed (Peterson, Rabe, & Wong, 1986). Studies of heightened standards policies for high school graduation showed that local districts had, in many cases, met or exceeded the requirements before the new laws were passed (Center for Policy Research in Education, 1989).

Organizational Processes of Attention and Interpretation

Policies and programs would be more successfully implemented if there were conceptual clarity (if it were clear what is to be done and why), external political support, and ways to get people to *want* to change. (Standard operating procedure is so much easier!) Sproull (1981) examined site properties, such as top management support, incentive systems, and bureaucratic obstacles, to understand organizational response to policy. Here the research question was, "How do organizational members make meaning out of policy or program directives?" Possible local responses to policy include the following:

- Ignoring policy—This occurs when the policy intent does not fit with the cognitive or values systems of those receiving the directive.
- Developing a simplified and particularly local version
- Invoking standard response repertoires (e.g., forming a committee, a retreat, a study group, or assigning it to an assistant)
- Deciding which local structure applies (deciding if the budget, curriculum, PTA, or other committees are appropriate; deciding how this policy relates to others, and if this policy has priority over existing policies)

Thus, the choice from this *response repertoire* gave some indication of a district's meaning making. So, to explore local response to policy, one must examine the *organizational processes of attention and interpretation,* chosen response repertoires, and communication channels, which all interact in a fluid, ongoing, dynamic process that affects policy outcomes.

Organizational participants' goals are ambiguous, and their attention is constrained by the need to attend to preexisting work flows and immediate demands. Policy analysts must examine the school context to see how organizational attention is captured, how organizational meaning is constructed, the organizational meaning of the response repertoires invoked, and the process by which behavioral directives or guides for action are conveyed from a central office. This examination, in context, reveals the local organizational meaning being laid on the policy or program. Different organizational meanings result in different implementation outcomes.

The Lowerarchy

In policy implementation, the power of subordinates is considerable. The existing beliefs and capacities of practitioners shape the way they perceive a policy and affect how a policy is played out. As McLaughlin (1987) says, "Change is ultimately the problem of the smallest unit . . . and what actually is delivered or provided under the aegis of a policy depends upon the individual at the end of the line" (p. 175). These people can slow and blunt policy by controlling their organization's response and productivity through subtle and overt actions, such as slow-downs, grousing, insubordination, and absenteeism. The reasons for this resistance may be numerous, such as resentment of top-down decision making or rejection of a policy or program that conflicts with immediate local concerns.

Often anger and resentment are condensed around a particular event, person, activity, or tangible object that has become a symbol representing deep emotions. For example, people have strong feelings associated with words like *busing, paperwork,* and *testing.* These words pull together or condense complex emotional reactions and are therefore weighty negative symbols. They represent all the bundled-together bad feelings that many people hold toward certain education policy directions. Policies, and the rhetoric and promotion of them, can generate such feelings and thereby create tremendous resistance from the very people who are supposed to be implementing them. Even a policy that fits with practitioners' beliefs will have outcomes determined by the *lowerarchy*. For example, teachers' responses to policies for increasing teacher retention will be transformed through the individual teacher's interpretation and response.

Analyzing the Match between Goals and Instruments

When formulating policy and trying to predict or understand the effects of policies, one can calculate likely directions. This chapter demonstrated earlier how to identify policy types. With that in mind, think about the utility of first identifying the type and then analyzing the match between policy type and the instrument used for implementation. Often, from that, we can predict the policy's effectiveness. For example, federal policies for gender equity have been primarily mandates, which must be actively enforced. But districts have eroded and avoided gender equity mandates that had little enforcement. As a result, changes and outcomes are irregularly implemented and one result is the very slow emergence of outcomes in schools and universities. Further, the goals of gender equity are redistributive: to open access and redistribute benefits, supports, and successes to women. Mandates are inadequate to meet these redistributive goals. The goals themselves demand policy instruments for system-changing policy requiring current beneficiaries to give up some benefits and authority (Odden, 1991c) as these are redistributed more equitably. Thus, the redistributive policy goals and the use of unenforced mandates are a mismatch of goals and policy instrument—a poor framework for gender equity policy. This example of analyzing the match of policy type, goals, and instruments can be used to guide analysis of a wide range of education policies.

Unintended Consequences

Education policy challenges have "tangled webs of problems with symptoms, sources, and 'solutions' that are neither readily apparent nor reliably addressed by policy provisions" (Malen & Knapp, 1997, p. 419). Further, it would be irrational to expect a rational process, given the forces affecting both the formulation and the implementation of policy. Conceived in a politicized context, policies often have ambiguous and conflicting goals because they must address multiple needs and interests. As Gillon (2000) explains, "Some legislation passes in the heat of public passion with little opportunity for careful thought" (p. 26). Thus, it is difficult to ascertain and pin down specific policy intentions and goals at their source. Ambitious social policies are often tripped up by what Milton Freidman calls "the invisible foot" (Friedman, as cited in Gillon, 2000, p. 26).

Unanticipated consequences can be positive. When President Roosevelt and Congress passed a bill giving World War II veterans free college tuition, they were really trying to stave off the threat of thousands of unemployed and angry veterans. The G.I. Bill changed American higher education forever and catapulted millions of families into the educated professional classes.

Unanticipated negative consequences get more attention. They often occur when the implementation has not been, or could not be, predicted, planned, funded, monitored, or controlled. The most obvious example in education is desegregation policy, which aims to create equity and harmony when Black and White students attend the same schools. Desegregation, however, has resulted as well in eroding financial and political support and "White flight" from urban and public schools. One should expect to encounter unanticipated consequences often when policies are constructed with inadequate attention to the complex cultural systems in which, and through which, they will be implemented.

Summarizing with a Positive Note

Trying to understand the cultural processes affecting implementation with terms like *policy slippage* and *opportunistic adoption* leaves one frustrated. How can school reform be directed in an effective way? Are tightening the coupling and increased surveillance and accountability the only recourse for those who wish to implement change? If not, what is? A current project in Maine, which one local education reformer labeled "a post-NCLB example" of viable school improvement, respects educators' cultural processes and builds from them. It also shows a policy alternative—the embedding of comprehensive rather than high-stakes measures of students' mastery of standards (Hamann & Lane, 2002, 2003). The implementation strategies in Maine's "Promising Futures" program (which combine state resources, federal Comprehensive School Reform program dollars, and a $10 million grant) demonstrate policy adaptation to avoid the prospect of educators' resistance. Hamann and Lane's (2003) strategies include the following:

- Policy customization: waivers and cooptation of federal policy to meet Maine's needs
- Policy reconciliation: alignment of the timing of implementation with state requirements for drafting state policy contracts
- Adjusting policy in relation to grassroots feedback: changing the list of required Promising Futures core practices
- Adjusting policy through group reflection: adaptation of mid-course review visit protocol
- Adjusting policy through formative evaluation feedback: emphasis on the salience of the "lateral exchange of information" (i.e., between practitioners from different sites)
- Converting practice to policy through communication: storytelling
- Working with the persona/identity of the policy intermediaries: recognizing practitioner-to-practitioner and Mainer-to-Mainer sensibilities

State- and school-level educators' face-to-face coconstruction of policy alterations, incorporating stories of their own meaning making, made Promising Futures implementable in a context in which, normally, blockage, slippage, and opportunism could have prevailed (Hamann & Lane, 2002, 2003; McNeil, 2003). Policy makers and implementers can take note of these lessons. Disgruntled and resistant recipients of top-down policy may take note as well of the lessons and hints for exercising one's voice through coconstruction and adaptation.

Politics of Education, Policy Studies, and Policy Analysis

The politics of education is a young field, identified by studies that focus on power. Those who study the politics of education delight in identifying the power dynamics and values conflicts in and around education issues, whether they happen in the formal legislative arenas or in the informal interactions among schoolchildren vying for valuable resources such as teacher praise or access to the computer. The *politics of education,* then, is inquiry into the basic nature of power and values surrounding education. Such inquiry may use a particular program or policy as an excuse to inquire into power arrangements. A politics of education study of school board decision making about sexual harassment policy is an inquiry into how certain voices and needs dominate in school politics, not so much about the policy itself. In contrast, often, *policy studies* and *policy analysis* are approaches that focus on a particular program or policy in order to inquire about its utility, effects, and outcomes. Policy studies and policy analysis are used once we accept the predefined parameters of an issue as it was determined in a political arena. Powerful policy actors have defined a problem (e.g., teacher retention, drop-outs, parental choice, school-to-work transition), and those definitions, to a large extent, become the focus for study and analysis. Table 2.5 presents a diagram of these lenses for understanding policy.

Policy Studies

Studying legislators' voting behavior and political parties, as in political science, or tracking the settlement patterns of immigrants, as in demography, or the relative ranking of

TABLE 2.5 *Lenses for Understanding Policy*

Politics of Education, Policy Studies, and Policy Analysis Lenses	Focus
Policy Studies	Studies the processes of making policy
Rationality and Quantitative Data	Recognizes policy makers' preferences for quantitative analysis
Backward and Forward Mapping	Focuses on the locations for the planned policy outcomes, and then on all the levels from there to the policy source
Policy Analysis	Aims at providing timely and useful information on a particular, defined policy question
Measuring Inputs and Outputs	Measures resources that support schooling and outcomes of schooling
Cost–Benefit Analysis	Provides policy makers with measurements of the relative benefits and outputs they should get for any funding they approve

states in their expenditures for maternal and child health, as in economics—these endeavors and fields provide useful basic information, but they do little to identify ways to solve complex problems like poverty, discrimination, and achievement gaps. Policy studies, however, do focus on problems as they are or are not affected by policies. Cibulka (1995) stated, "Those who study policy have an interest in addressing social problems by generating policy-relevant knowledge" (p. 107). Thus, *policy studies aim to explore a problem in such a way as to inform the choices being considered and debated by relevant actors.* When researchers in universities and think tanks do basic policy studies, they are interested in the assumptions behind why policy is created and adopted, and they examine a policy's effects on its intended outcomes. For example, Weatherly and Lipsky's (1977) study of special education policy identified how site-level policy implementers (which they call "street level bureaucrats") may choose to ignore certain policy provisions if they do not fit with local needs.

The Role of Rationality and Quantitative Data. Policy studies arose out of assumptions that the methodological tools of the social sciences (namely statistical analyses) could be used to aid political decision making. These studies generally fall into two categories: *basic* and *applied* research, as noted in Table 2.6 (Cibulka, 1995, p. 107). Basic research is typically conducted in university settings; the goal of the research is to gain either deeper understanding, explanation, or prediction of policy outcomes. Applied research, in contrast, can also be conducted in a university setting but is more likely to be conducted by a private research organization or public agency. These types of policy studies tend to be evaluative and focus on determining the effectiveness of a policy or whether it achieves its intended goals. In both of these approaches, quantitative methodology is preferred.

There are several reasons for this propensity for quantitative research that are related to the seemingly objective nature of statistical methods. First, policy studies arose out of the field of political science, and positioned itself as a scientific field seeking to minimize the subjective influence of the researchers. Although statistical researchers acknowledge philosophically that their work constantly struggles with researcher bias and does not necessarily represent Truth about the relative effectiveness of a given policy, this type of research is viewed as credible and useful. Because politics and policy making are highly charged po-

TABLE 2.6 *Types of Policy Analysis*

Dimension	Basic (Academic) Policy Analysis	Applied Policy Analysis
Aspect of policy that is of interest	Determinants, adoption, implementation, content, and impact	Content and impact
Aim	Understanding, explanation, and prediction	Evaluation, change, justification, and prediction
Actors	Researchers in universities or think tanks	Consulting firms, interest groups, and government analysts

Source: From J. G. Cibulka, Policy Analysis and the Study of the Politics of Education. In J. D. Scribner and D. H (eds.), *The Study of Educational Politics,* pp. 105–125. Copyright 1995 by Falmer Press. Used by permission.

litical activities, research that appears rational, and thus free of subjective bias, carries more weight in battles over ideology. Additionally, policy makers are often faced with limited resources and must make decisions about which policies to fund and which to cut. Summative data designed to assess the relative worth of policies can be used to make value judgments about policies. Studies in this vein "focus on technical efficiency, cost–benefit analysis (CBA), and other efforts such as output measures, per unit cost estimates, client satisfaction surveys, statistical testing, and decision trees" (Clemons & McBeth, 2001, p. viii). Their numerical measures hold symbolic power, which is useful in political debates.

Although quantitative methodology has been favored, it has a somewhat limited ability to actually inform politically nuanced decision making. Quantitative research can be used to determine whether a policy is effective, but it cannot necessarily explain why. The Head Start story illustrates many points about policy research caught up in political contexts. Head Start, which dates back to 1964 and has undergone numerous evaluations, is now seen as a highly successful program. What makes Head Start unique is that it seeks to address early childhood education for families and children living in poverty by empowering and supporting parents via education and employment. Parents who participate in the program are asked to be active participants in their child's classroom and in the decision-making process of the child care center their child attends. They are also give preference for jobs that become available in their child's center (White, 2001).

In 1987, legislation extended Head Start by adding the Comprehensive Child Development Program (CCDP), which created model child care centers that were to provide comprehensive services for families in poverty. The program was evaluated after one year by a private research agency and was determined to be ineffective (St. Pierre, Goodson, Layzer, & Bernstein, 1994). Gilliam, Ripple, Zigler, and Leiter (2000) reviewed the evaluation and consequently identified several limitations of the study. First, they argued that the evaluation was conducted too soon after implementation, so the program did not really have time to take effect. Additionally, the study design depended on students being randomly assigned to groups, and they were not, which called the research design into question. Further, it appeared that the program was not fully implemented (Gilliam et al., 2000). The evaluation was not actually measuring the effectiveness of the model, so the research agency could not really determine that the model was ineffective. What this example shows is the complicated nature of policy analysis. Political pressures to decide quickly on the effectiveness of a policy rushed the evaluation. As a result, that phase of Head Start was terminated. Still, we see that just because a study is quantitative does not necessarily mean that is a quality study.

In many instances, the popularity of a program makes politicians ignore negative evaluation findings. D.A.R.E. (Drug Abuse Resistance Education) has not proven its positive effects with children but is still "a runaway best seller" (Mann & Shakeshaft, 2003, p. 20). Research that is more qualitatively based (involving more open-ended data, such as interviews and observations) relies heavily on the researchers and their subjective interpretation of policy. Qualitative approaches to policy studies is an emerging field, although relatively underused in large-scale evaluations. In Chapter 3 we discuss this emerging field and the complexity of values and ideologies that undergird research studies as much as they do politics and policy.

Backward and Forward Mapping. Backward mapping is a policy analysis approach that begins with a concrete description of the desired specific behavior or outcome at the lowest level of the implementation process. The analyst then works backwards, asking what abilities and resources are needed by each organizational unit along the implementation path. Such mapping can identify "veto points" (Pressman & Wildavsky, 1973, p. 102), the influence of politics within the implementation chain (Barrett & Hill, 1984), and the varieties of acceptance behavior of implementers (Fullan, 1991). Backward mapping is a bottom-up approach to policy design (Elmore, 1979–1980). As education leaders plan policy, this approach helps identify the behavior that needs to change, and the intervention that could alter that behavior. Backward mapping could be used, for example, to analyze what happens at each stage and level of implementation of special education policies in a district. It could be used to place "fixers" (Bardach, 1978) or *consiglieres* (Firestone, 1989b) who can intervene to find what is needed (e.g., money, personnel, political support) to facilitate implementation and who can monitor progress.

For example, Capper (1988) mapped backward from the observation of the children who are recipients of equity policies (in special education in rural districts), then examined the administrative, curricular, facilities, testing, and other policy systems to understand what happened to policy intentions as they worked their way through education systems. A more recent international example mapped backward a major reform in India, finding "serious resentment . . . at the state level of centrally sponsored schemes of this sort" (Dyer, 1999, p. 56) and "six years after inception of the policy . . . limited and patchy progress in implementation" (p. 52). Teachers thought that the innovation would be "a threat to their delicately balanced patterns of work" (p. 54). Figure 2.3 displays one way to apply backward mapping.

**Backward Mapping from
Outcome Back to Policy**

Student behavior

Teacher behavior

Attitudes of teachers toward policy and effects
on individuals and organizational culture

Attitudes of administrators toward policy

Professional norms

Site policy

District policy

State policy

Court decisions

Federal policy

FIGURE 2.3 *Backward Mapping from Outcomes Back to Policy*

Source: From C. A. Capper, Students with Severe Disabilities in Public Schools: Policy in Practice. Doctoral dissertation. Nashville, Tennessee, Vanderbilt University. 1988. Used with permission.

We can use backward mapping for policy studies and also for implementation analysis. It is a powerful strategy for structuring policy and planning to make implementation more effective through turning it around into forward mapping. *Forward mapping* acknowledges the top-down nature of decision making (Bardach, 1978). For planning, this approach creates and critiques scenarios, generating what would happen at each implementation stage and level to get to policy outcomes. The scenarios help analysts imagine how those who must be involved in implementation might think and act, including the worst-case scenario. They also involve visualizing which people might have motivations to undermine the policy (Weimer & Vining, 1989, p. 402).

Policy Analysis.   Methods have been devised for pulling apart policies to look at their characteristics and to understand what will happen when they are implemented. *Policy analysis* is meant to be immediately useful, and is honed to address the questions being generated on the spot in political debates. Policy analysts are usually trained in public policy or administration and are employed in institutes, think tanks, or as legislative staffers.

Policy analysts' roles vary. Some think of themselves as objective technicians. They let their clients or bosses define the values, issues, and trade-offs, then step aside and let the analysis speak for itself. Some do what they can to advance clients' positions, believing that they should be their client's advocate and that their analysis really gives definitive answers. Others, as issues advocates, believe that analysis should be used to promote their views of the good society (Cibulka, 1995).

What is the purpose of the questions that policy analysts ask? Some questions are asked to identify the costs, benefits, and other repercussions of potential policy choices. They are sometimes asked in order to predict what would happen, given different alternatives. They are often asked to evaluate the outcomes and effects of the policies and the programs for education. The methods, models, and theories of policy analysts can help us make sense of policies that seem to go in many directions.

Measuring Inputs and Outputs.   By looking at the ingredients put into schooling and the products of schools, we can see trends such as whether school funding is increasing or whether Maine has a greater percentage of its students graduating from high school than does Montana. *Education Week* and the U.S. Department of Education are fond of collecting measurable data on what each state invests in education (e.g., teachers paid at a level for masters degrees, percentage of students with free lunch, per pupil expenditures) and outputs (e.g., students with good SAT scores, dropouts, students who go on to postsecondary education). Such data are used to make conclusions about the efforts being made in Michigan, Alabama, or New Mexico, and the results achieved. Similarly, in this accountability era, districts and schools are having their outputs, their students' measurable achievements, published in local newspapers. Sometimes administrators' careers are jeopardized by these assessments. State superintendents can be furious, making public protests when these approaches to analysis make them look bad: "But you don't account for our ESL populations!" or "You can't compare my school to Elm Grove where housing prices start at $300,000!"

The most commonly used measure of input is funding for schooling. Figure 2.4 provides an example of how inputs are measured. How would we use such an input analysis

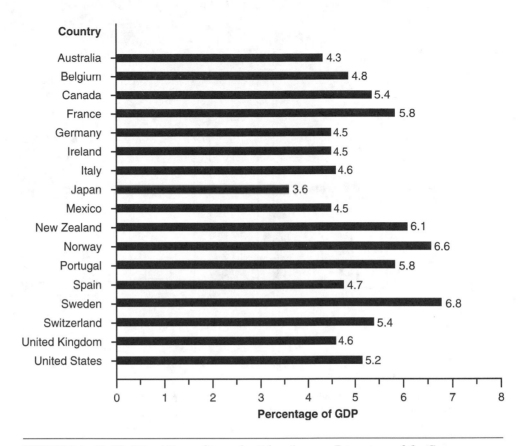

FIGURE 2.4 *Public Direct Expenditures for Education as a Percentage of the Gross Domestic Product: Selected Countries, 1997*

Source: From Digest of Education Statistics Tables and Figures, National Center for Education, U.S. Department of Education. Retrieved November 24, 2003 from http://nces.ed.gov/programs/digest/d01/fig29.asp.

for political battles over education policy directions? Figure 2.5 is an example of an analysis of an output, showing the increase in school enrollments in world regions. Enrollment increases are outcome measures. However, identifying, measuring, and analyzing connections of inputs that might have led to the outcomes would be nearly impossible!

Cost–Benefit Analysis.   Starting with the premise that projects and policies should produce societal benefits, a cost–benefit analysis aims to assess whether the benefits are greater than the costs. Further, when policy makers can choose among several projects or policy directions, cost–benefit analysis should help them choose (Peters, 1999). Such an approach assumes that we can agree on the benefits we want, and whether the costs are too much for a given benefit, using economic measures. With concrete choices, such as highways and dams, this is difficult. It is all the more difficult with issues for which we must measure the

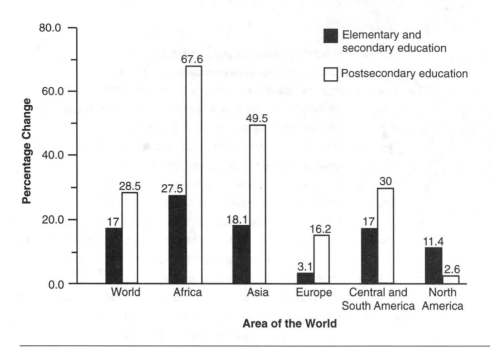

FIGURE 2.5 *Percentage Charge in Enrollment, by Area of the World and Level of Education: 1990 to 1997*

Source: From Digest of Education Statistics Tables and Figures, National Center for Education, U.S. Department of Education. Retrieved November 24, 2003 from http://nces.ed.gov/programs/digest/d00/fig28.asp.

value (e.g., highly qualified teachers) and determine what benefit is valuable. Very quickly, we move into ethical and moral questions in which "policy analysis has as much to do with the 'should' questions as with the 'can' questions" (Peters, 1999, p. 437). Now we move beyond questions of what has economic value for society and into "softer" values.

The frameworks presented in this chapter can (1) provide a handle, a way of seeing the elements of the policies that direct educators' work; (2) help identify the ways things go right and go wrong as policies are implemented; and (3) provide a view of the tools for policy analysis. This perspective enhances educators' sense of control over the policy environment in which they live, but can love, or democracy, or fun be analyzed?

Beyond Traditional Policies and Analyses

So much meaningful human activity just does not fit into structured lines, boxes, or identified patterns and theories. Indeed, radical and revolutionary or simply creative actions cannot happen within the confines of traditional structures. Imagining and doing politics differently therefore requires identifying new pictures, concepts, models, and theories to understand politics and policy. We need theories that help us move beyond the traditionally structured and accepted centers of power, beyond the behaviors and interests of elites, and beyond the issues defined at the center. Policy analysis, in the sense of pulling apart a policy problem to measure its parts, will not always work any more than pulling apart and identifying the elements of fun will enable people to make fun. More importantly, policy analysis, when it focuses on a policy problem defined by people at the center, will leave out the concerns, fears, and needs of outsiders. So the traditions and structures of policy analysis and political science that framed earlier studies are constrained and limited. Important aspects about schooling are missing. Participants in schools and policymakers are also puzzled and anxious when policies do not address key issues.

The Limits of Traditional Policy Analysis

"Policy is more like an endless game of Monopoly than a bicycle repair," says Stone (1997, p. 259). Policies and the problems they address are continuously evolving, with new players and new moves, but most policy analysis and evaluation ignores this Monopoly game. Policy analysis, as a discipline, has emphasized evaluation of policy effects and implementation analyses, where the positivist, functionalist, and pluralist assumptions go largely unchallenged (McLaughlin, 1987). Much has been "technicist and uncritical in approach" (Taylor, Rizvi, Lingard, & Henry, 1997, p. 40) and has been insensitive to theoretical issues. Policy analysis is generally based on certain assumptions: that policy can be studied in an analytical framework; that economics-based methods, such as cost–benefit or decision analysis, are reliable; and that there is a desire to improve government decision making and performance. There is a tendency to favor a theoretical "blind empiricism" (Raab, 1994) and mindless studies of effects and outcomes. These seldom provide insights about what worked, what never was considered, what policy/program ideas prevailed and why, and what contributed to their passage, acceptance, implementation, and effects. Ball (1990b) talks of "policy sociology," with scholars using varied methods and subjects to study the relationship between processes and product, between motive and action (p. 23), an approach that views policy as a "half-written text" (Ball, 1990, p. 185).

Traditional policy analysis has not looked at culture or at values. But education conveys culture and is value-laden in every sense of the words. Cultural values are instilled through schooling. Policy debates and conflicts are conflicts of culture and values. Policies result when certain cultural values win. Traditional policy analysis has not incorporated the plentiful evidence that minority cultural values, voices, and needs have not prevailed or that alternative viewpoints are pushed aside in policy arenas. It is difficult to articulate alternative narratives about, for example, teachers' idealism, or the value of instilling in children a love of learning, or the losses to democracy from re-segregated classrooms in such a way that these narratives fit into a cost–benefit analytic approach. But how do you place a child's life opportunities in a cost–benefit analysis?

The analyst often receives a problem definition determined by those who hold power. When powerful business and industry interests influence education policy questions, they may be focusing on education as training for work (Boyles, 1999; House, 1998). In such analyses, teachers are regarded as line workers, not as transformative intellectuals, and children are sorted by their test scores. Such a policy analysis angers educators and undermines their efforts to describe education realities in policy arenas. It is persuasive, though, and as Abowitz (1999) says, "Administrators, teachers and parents consume the notion that America's best interests are synonymous with the interest of big business. Hence the language of standards, national curricula, testing, global competitiveness, and world-class education has snowballed" (p. 169), and policy makers' logics are framed, uncritically, with such dominant logics.

Chapter 3 begins the exploration of theories, concepts, and models and methodologies for incorporating the missing dynamics.

Exercises for Critically Analyzing Policy Implementation and Analysis

1. Choose an education public policy that was recently enacted in your state. Interview three people who are responsible for implementing the policy. Ask them whether they are implementing the policy completely, incrementally, or not all (and be sure to ask them their reasons for doing so). Compile the results in class and match the interview responses with the concepts in this chapter. Are there any responses that do not fit? If so, what would you call them and how would you construct systematic research to explore the phenomenon?

2. Title IX is a 1972 federal policy with variable, questionable, and very slow implementation. Use the theories and analytic approaches in this chapter, applying them to the implementation of gender equity policy in your school district. Or obtain research reports by others who look at gender equity policy nationally and critique their theories and analytic approaches. How do they help us understand what has and has not happened, for example, from Title IX's intentions? Remember, you are examining administrative and organizational processes in programs that are often perceived as redistributive, as serving a specific population, aimed at achieving equity goals in schooling. Therefore, while you examine areas of the administrative context in traditional areas like decision making, resource allocation, and so on, you may need to use an exploratory approach to discover the ways in which administration functions in implementing special programs

for girls, with an equity goal, focusing on a neglected and disadvantaged population, with redistributive purposes. Critique the utility of the frameworks from this chapter and then devise a new, more useful exploratory model for analyzing gender equity policy.

3. Choose a policy with which you are familiar and use the following list of Questions to Ask When Analyzing a Social Policy or Government Program Using Traditional Lenses.[1]

Questions to Ask When Analyzing a Social Policy or Government Program Using Traditional Lenses

The Problem

What are the issues in society or in the economy that the program, policy, or legislation seeks to address? Describe the nature, seriousness, complexity, principal causes (assumed/real), and principal consequences (assumed/real) of the problem.

Problem Legitimization: The Political Context

How and why is the problem translated into a political issue—i.e., judicial decision, policy statement, legislation, and a government program? Why do you think the problem was defined the way it was? Does the problem have a social history—i.e., have there been prior efforts to act on the problem? What are the principal actors, groups, or organizations pressing for in terms of government action? How powerful are program opponents? What arguments and techniques do they employ? What coalitions are formed, if any? How widespread is support for or opposition to the program? What expectations about the program have been expressed by key decision makers and program implementers—i.e., what is their initial prediction of success?

Type of Program

What kind of function is performed—education, defense, welfare, health, etc.? Is the program primarily regulatory, self-regulatory, distributive, or redistributive? What kind of technology, if any, has been selected for the program? Does the technology match program goals? Match program policy strategy?

Program Goals

What are the announced and what are the real or hidden goals? How clear and specific are they? Do they conflict? How easily can goals be translated into quantifiable, readily gathered measures of performance? How ambitious are goals, given the current economic environment? What degree of confusion is there among the major actors who will be looking at program implementation (e.g., legislators, bureaucrats, practitioners, auditors, supporters, or the public)?

Time Dimension

How long does the program run? At what point is it reasonable to make an informed evaluation of program performance? To what extent do program goals, methods, tactics, or performance criteria change over time?

Program Resources

Are program resources—money, technical assistance, personnel—commensurate with program goals? How are funds allocated (e.g., via competitive grants, entitlement criteria, specific formulas)? How secure are program resources perceived to be? What is the mix of remunerative, coercive, and normative appeals? What is their capacity and will to use power, influence, and authority for program objectives?

Program Implementation

Does the program operate through executive, judicial, regulatory, or service agencies? How many levels of government does the program operate through, financially and administratively? What is the degree of overlap, confusion, and conflict among the various agencies formally charged with program implementation—e.g., incentives, knowledge, capacity, authority? Are the necessary programmatic, financial, and bureaucratic supports available to program implementers?

Actual Performance: Output

What indicators? Over what time period? How reliable are data sources? How valid are indicators in terms of broad program goals? What has been the cost of output in terms of dollar expenditures, administrative and staff time and energy, loss or gain in levels of support by relevant groups?

Actual Performance: Outcomes

Some questions as above plus: What is the relationship between program outputs and expected program outcomes? How many other factors—lying beyond the control of program administrators or even the government generally—affect outcomes and output indicators (i.e., "program externalities")? How plausible is it that a given change in program output could have a significant and sustained effect on solving the problem—or program outcomes? Who lost, who gained? How much, how widespread, how direct or indirect was the benefit?

Political Feedback

How controversial is the program, once started, in terms of its goals, use of resources, organizational features, output and impact? What are the issues being debated by program supporters and opponents once the program is underway? To what degree is the debate ideological or to what degree is it based on actual program performance? What impact does public (or specific) group response to the program have on the subsequent viability of the program—e.g., does it survive? What channel does feedback take?

Explanation of Performance Gaps

To what extent are gaps or failures due to *politics* (e.g., important political interests attacked the program or undermined its implementation), *administration* (e.g., administrative agencies involved were too expensive, bungling, competitive, duplicative, improperly staffed, ignorant, self-centered, corrupt, indifferent), *finance* (too little or too much money spent), *incentives* (wrong mix of positive and negative incentives to obtain program goals) *theory* (nature and causes of the problem wrongly analyzed), or the *theory linking pro-*

gram itself (too massive, too complex, too politically explosive, too elusive for government action, nonexistent or incorrectly specified).

Evaluation Studies

Has the program been evaluated? If so, by whom? What are the major assumptions and biases of the evaluators? What quantity and quality of data used in carrying out the study? What kind of research design was used? What are the major findings and recommendations? What role did evaluation studies play in gathering or disseminating the information used to expand, contract, modify, or terminate a program?

Note

1. First developed for UCLA class, Dr. Milbray McLaughlin.

3

Alternative Visions for Advocacy Politics

Guiding Questions

- What role do values and personal experience play in how policy is formulated, interpreted, and implemented?
- How can theory be used to frame politics and policy so that the realities of children, parents, and educators are incorporated and social justice issues are central?
- What counts as knowledge in the study of politics and policy?
- How can policy studies be re-visioned and re-framed?

Traditional approaches to politics are useful for understanding power and conflicts and how policy is formulated at the center of education policy making. Yet the approaches outlined in the previous chapters represent a limited understanding of politics and policy in that they often focus on the values and actions of powerful elites, insiders, and interest groups. On the other hand, the individuals most affected by policy, such as teachers, students, parents, administrators, school staff, and communities, have not been central to these studies. They do not question the dominance of political actors who define issues. Nor do they examine critically the extent to which politics-as-usual leads to education policies that reinforce or contribute to social inequities. In this chapter we examine emerging theoretical lenses that examine and address social issues. Readers who are current or future leaders, policy makers, and analysts will be instrumental in implementing, creating, and evaluating policy, and therefore need ways to assess how values and experiences affect the formulation, interpretation, and implementation of policy. Emerging theories offer ways to frame politics. They raise important questions about dominance, values, and challenges and the roles they play in the policy process, and offer lenses for understanding politics differently.

Theories that question and continually seek to understand oppressive practices can provide a way to focus the attention of scholars, policy makers, and educators on equity and social justice concerns, and broaden how to understand *policy problems* (see Chapter 1 for an overview on policy logics and Chapter 2 for an overview on how policy problems are defined). These theories question assumptions concerning what educational problems are and how to fix them. When observing policy makers' *shifting arenas* (see arena shift framework in Chapter 1, Figure 1.8), one needs ways to question the reasons for the shift and critique the value this shift might promote. *Theory*—for example, *feminist theory,* which values the perspectives of women—is useful for critiquing the political focus on test scores and for promoting school policies that place as much emphasis on creating nurturing environments (for students and staff) structured around caring relationships (Noddings, 1992) as on test scores. In Hillary Clinton's book, *It Takes a Village* (1996), she argues that children need to be nurtured for their unique abilities. Senator Clinton would be shifting policy logics, values, and arenas if she promoted her views about whole-community approaches to child-rearing in congressional debates.

Theory can be used to highlight teacher, student, and staff concerns and to envision possibilities for change. A new theory can provide a way to conceptualize how inequitable power relationships function by highlighting how discrimination such as sexism, racism, or homophobia creates inequities.

Theoretical strands, such as critical race, postcolonial, and feminism, suggest that it is problematic to assume that research can be objective. Specifically, they argue that selecting what to focus on and even framing questions is shaped by the researcher's values and subjectivity (Lather, 1991; Scheurich & Young, 1997; Smith, 1999). Numerous scholars have argued that research cannot be assumed to be value-neutral; nor can it make claims about representing so-called truth or validity (Lather, 1993). In the world of politics, though, few worry about subjectivity and researcher values in educational politics and policy research. Most research that policy makers deem legitimate operates under the guise of objectivity, as pointed out in Chapter 2. This chapter identifies the problematic aspects of what is traditionally thought to be the legitimatized research on politics and policy. It then presents the possibility of constructing policy research that is openly subjective and politically strategic in purpose. In doing so, this chapter demonstrates ways that policy and politics studies can look beyond elite policy makers to encompass the experiences of marginalized and disenfranchised groups. As the political cartoon in Figure 3.1 illustrates, with deep irony, the usual ways of doing politics and studying politics do little to resolve persistent inequities.

This chapter shows how, too often, seemingly rational and objective policy discussions fail to connect to realities—to the range of educators', families', and students' needs. Policy debates are often constrained and exclusive, and so the less powerful groups' voices are minimized. As White patriarchal values elevate rational research and policy makers venerate seemingly objective measures, emotional issues are relegated to the private sphere. Further, the activist politics of those working to create a different story and to challenge the dominant story are not included as real politics. So this chapter suggests some ways to look at policy and politics that strategically support a more inclusive conception of democracy aimed at social justice.

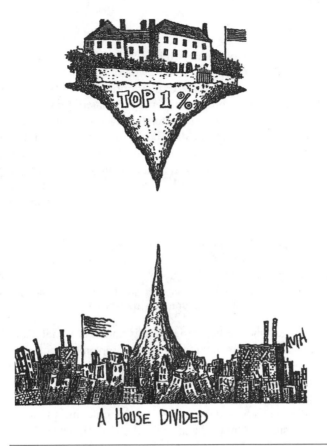

FIGURE 3.1   Politics Must Face the Inequities in Schooling

Source: AUTH © 1997 The Philadelphia Inquirer. Reprinted with permission of UNIVERSAL PRESS SYNDICATE. All rights reserved.

First, we define what we mean by *social justice,* and examine the power and politics behind the framing of policy discourse and what counts as knowledge in these arenas. Further, we demonstrate the power play behind asserting and demanding objective, rational policy discourses, showing how they privilege certain normative definitions of educational problems over others. Because policy research can in turn reinforce these distinctions, we go on to examine what counts as knowledge in the analysis of politics and policy.

To embrace democratic, egalitarian politics, one must not solely critique power politics. Democracy can be viewed as a work-in-progress, a concept that is fluid and constantly changing and that and can be strategically defined around egalitarian values, building on the work of strategic democratic theorists (Mouffe, 1992; Mouffe & LeClau, 1985). We conclude by building on this conception of democracy, providing an example of how analysts of politics and policy might reframe the dominant standard stories to encompass the realities of children, families, and educators, and discourse that supports social justice.

Defining Social Justice

Traditional visions of justice center on gaining rights for individuals. In contrast, our vision of *social justice* is relational and distributive. First, we draw from Young's (1990) notion of relational justice. Young argues that notions of distributive justice, as represented by the work of Rawls (1971), tend to focus on the portioning of material goods in society (e.g., jobs, resources, income). This focus, she argues, "tends to ignore the social structure and institutional context that often help determine distributive patterns" (p. 15). For Young, social justice in our democratic society means attending to not only how goods are distributed, but also how issues of domination and oppression (e.g., institutional racism and patriarchy) affect this process. Young (1990) suggests that a more nuanced understanding of social justice is needed, one that values individual differences and is attentive to the process by which goods are distributed in a society:

> The ideal of the just society as eliminating group differences is both unrealistic and unde-sirable. Instead justice in a group-differentiated society demands social equality of groups, and mutual recognition and affirmation of group differences. Attending to group-specific needs and providing for group representation both promotes that social equality and pro-vides the recognition that undermines cultural imperialism. (p. 191)

Examinations of policy and politics vested in this notion of social justice would en-deavor to show how the process of policy formation and implementation can exclude and potentially harm the very individuals they purport to help, at all levels of school politics.

Over the years numerous policies have intended to promote distributive notions of so-cial justice. For example, the policies that resulted from the landmark *Brown vs. the Board of Education* (1954) decision focused on achieving the outcome of racially balanced schools rather than addressing institutional and societal racism (Lipman, 1998). This focus on redistribution has not improved the racial and economic gap that exists between White middle- and upper-class students and students of color. Despite elaborate policy structures, many policies are constructed without relational, social justice perspective, and are dis-connected from the realities of embedded institutional and cultural forms of discrimination experienced by the many individuals who populate public schools. The perplexing effects of desegregation policies are just one example of the multitudes of untapped issues. Keep this in mind throughout the following overview of the power dynamics of policy framing.

Who Frames Policy?

Who has power to control the knowledge and frame the policy issues for education? What are the power dynamics and discourses? In this section, we first examine how a simplistic analysis of the policy makers who formulate educational policy reveals a seemingly homogeneous group of elite, White males in the majority. Then, we suggest that this quan-titative analysis does not really explain how policy can be oppressive, and that the knowl-edge produced by these policy-making communities is constrained. We assert that these restricted ranges of problem definitions and solutions are often reinforced, rather than chal-lenged by a widened re-visioning of politics and policy research.

TABLE 3.1 *Education Policy Makers*

	% Female	% Minority	% with K–12 Educational Background
School Superintendents[a]	13.1[c]	3.7[d]	Most
Professorate[b]	35.0	13.0	Most
School Boards[a]	40.0	10.5	—
School Principals[e]	42.0	17.0	All
Governors	2.5	2.5	8.0
U.S. House of Representatives Committee on Education and the Workforce[f]	43.0	16.2	16.0
U.S. Senate Health, Education, Labor, and Pensions Committee[g]	6.0	4.0	11.0

[a]*American Association of School Administrators*, Superintendents: Status and Views, 27(9).

[b]Digest of American Statistics Online, 2001.

[c]*American School Board Journal,* ABSJ Supplement Education Vital Signs, A12–13, December 1999.

[d]The Principal Magazine Online, Profiling the Principalship: New 2000–2001 Salary Statistics, 2001.

[e]Project VoteSmart Online, 2001.

[f]U.S. House of Representatives Committee on Education and the Workforce Online, 2001.

[g]U.S. Senate Health, Education, Labor and Pensions Committee Online, 2001.

On a surface level, Table 3.1 shows that women and especially minorities are underrepresented in the superintendency, the professoriate,[1] school boards, and principalships, and in politics at the state and national levels. In addition, women and minorities are underrepresented in teacher and administrator association leadership. Details provide insights: In the National Education Association, with more than 70 percent female membership, the three executive officers are men, the executive committee is two-thirds male, and the Board of Directors from the states are about two-thirds male.

Further, the professionals who manage schools have been shaped, to some degree, by scholars of educational administration who conduct the bulk of education policy and politics research. Although the numbers of women and minorities in the profession have increased, this cosmetic change has not necessarily challenged dominant practice. In their continuing study of the professoriate, McCarthy and Kuh (1997) found that a "major shift toward hiring more women appeared to have occurred in the mid to late 1980s" (p. 196), especially in research institutions, although only 8 percent of veteran faculty were women. Although minority representation had increased substantially since 1972, the hiring of people of color seemed to have slowed since 1994. These survey data found that new faculty were satisfied with their roles as scholars but were "somewhat complacent about problems facing educational leadership units" (p. 243), and fit into the "culture of congeniality"

(p. 251), suppressing their calls for radical reform. The increase in female faculty had not altered "the attitudes and the nature of activities that had dominated the . . . professoriate" (p. 255). Additionally, McCarthy and Kuh found that the increase in faculty of color did not significantly alter faculty attitudes or activities in either 1986 or 1994, "[indicating a] homogenization of beliefs" (p. 259). It is clear that focusing on increasing women and minority representation has not necessarily challenged previously accepted patriarchal and culturally oppressive assumptions.

Numbers alone miss deeper questions, such as how cultural assumptions elevate and legitimate one value over another, as in the priority of quality-oriented policies above equity concerns. Policy communities, mentioned in Chapter 1, hold to tacit rules and can shape decision making and limit policy options. Certain values cannot be promoted and certain policy actors' behaviors are constrained. One study, for example, suggests that minorities only become less constrained in their behavior when their representation in a group reaches 15 percent (Kanter, 1977). Another shows that even though feminist political ideals should prevent women's values from being subsumed by the dominant male culture, feminist respondents in their study "were no more likely to serve on . . . committees [that have an influence on legislation related to women and family issues]" (Dolan & Ford, 1995, p. 101). Political traditions, bureaucratic assumptions, and professional cultures may preclude an alternative framing of policy issues even when previously marginalized groups are better represented (Ferguson, 1984). In a multimethod study of how gendered orientations might shape legislation, Kathlene (1990) demonstrated the need to study the legislative processes, committee dynamics, and discourse as much as the question of how many women are in legislatures. Just focusing on the representation of women and minorities in the education policy-making process overlooks how institutional forms of discrimination such as tacit cultural rules and structures may affect the process.

What Counts as Knowledge at the Center of Politics?

When policy challenges arise, who decides their legitimacy? Who decides how problems should be framed and determines which facts are relevant? In this section we suggest that the solutions that generally prevail are based on dominant assumptions about epistemology, that is, what counts as valuable knowledge. These dominant assumptions can be conceptualized as hegemonic in the sense that they operate "as an 'organizing principle' or world view (or combination of worldviews) that is diffused by agencies of ideological control and socialization into every area of daily life" (Boggs, 1976, as cited by Weiler, 1988, p. 14). For example, the desire for research that is seen as rational and objective elevates quantifiable data such as test scores as a determinant of a "good school" while ignoring issues such as a student's sense of belonging and minimizing the racial and socioeconomic bias in the construction of tests.

The policy makers in legislatures, commissions, bureaucratic agencies, boards, superintendencies, principalships, editorial boards, deanships, and program leadership usually follow the rules of the game and utilize discourse that reflects the dominant values of insiders in arenas of power. Analyses of test score data form the bulk of policy research that policy makers consider valid. As noted in Chapter 1, certain policy logics are shared in policy communities and those that veer astray are subject to a discourse of derision. In their study of state legislators, Marshall, Mitchell, and Wirt (1989) describe the social arrangements: how the *assumptive worlds* of policy makers tell them how to behave, who is expected to initiate policy, what values are acceptable, what interests must be respected, and what policy options are logical. As a result, some values, ideas, and interests are never initiated or pushed, and policy options are constrained and limited by social arrangements. In policy communities, insiders communicate information among themselves; they glean ideas about how to manage issues through networking among consultants, lobbyists, and their counterparts in other states (Reyes, Wagstaff, & Fusarelli, 1999; Wirt & Kirst, 1992).

The assumptions of powerful insiders continuously determine what is relevant for policy attention. This hegemonic discourse "tends to shape policy across state sites, that is, a unifying or metadiscourse based on a set of organizing principles . . . constructs the public interest in terms of the interests and worldview of dominant groups" (Carlson, 1993, p. 151). Alternative ways of viewing policy issues are marginalized, co-opted, or elicit token responses in the discourse,[2] containing both the audience and the focus of debate (Schattschneider, 1960).

The Politics of Hostile Data: The Trouble with Objectivity Claims. More often than not, in elite policy-making arenas, quantitative approaches to policy analysis are considered legitimate because they seem objective (Greenstone & Peterson, 1983). With media and constituents raising alarms, and with elections on the horizon, politicians love the promises of immediate solutions, and technocratic definitions of school improvement such as class size reduction, standards, and the achievement gap dominate. These approaches focus on schools and teachers without addressing the value-based, cultural context in which education policies are formulated and implemented. The contextual or historical understanding of social inequities is not central to these analyses, unlike more naturalistic forms of inquiry (Gewirtz, 1998). They appear more like controlled experiments, and thus are perceived to be more scientific. Nonpositivistic approaches (mostly qualitative) to policy analysis, in contrast, are often delegitimized; these findings tend to be bound up in context, tentative, and entangled with researcher subjectivity (Gerstl-Pepin & Gunzenhauser, 2002). They acknowledge researchers' subjectivity, so they are perceived as being openly ideological or "soft," compared with "hard" quantitative data.

Whether the methodology is qualitative or quantitative, though, policy research runs the risk of being politicized, depending on the prevailing values of those in power. When data do not fit current policy goals, they can be treated as "hostile data," that is, data that contradict current policy goals. As stated by Dery (1990), "Politicians or administrators reject data that do not coincide with behavior they are unwilling to change" (p. xi). One recent example demonstrates powerful forces determining the "goodness" of knowledge: In 2002 an internal memo from the Department of Education (DOE), "Criteria and Process for Removing Old Content from www.ed.gov," came to the attention of several professional associations, including the American Educational Research Association and the American Library Association. The memo established criteria for removing research documents off the DOE website that did "not reflect the priorities, philosophies, or goals of the present administration" (American Educational Research Association, 2002b). Thus, any research that did not reflect the administration's priorities was in danger of removal from the website.

The potency in hegemony is that its power is often hidden. For example, concerns about class or racial bias in standardized test scores are minimized in accountability discourses, which elevate standardized test scores above other methods of assessment. We need different analytic lenses to identify whether, where, how, and by whom the problem is framed (e.g., asking whether teachers' or students' views on standardized test scores were elicited).

Hegemonic policy discourses, such as those for high-stakes accountability, create a normalized view of children, schools, and the right and proper directions to take them with leadership, policy, and research. The language used assumes that lower income families are deficient, and creates the grounds for policy action (Griffith, 1992)—"People use speech as a power tool . . . [and] privileged speakers' truths (and policy analyses) prevail" (Marshall, 1997a, p. 7). Moreover, a "discourse of derision" (Ball, 1990b, p. 18) can be used to displace or debunk alternative truths. Language in policy discourse is power-laden and ideological in nature, and can silence alternative ways of framing issues (Edelman, 1979). For example, the practice of referring to students as being "at risk" continues to dominate the discourse, despite attempts to highlight the derogatory assumptions within the use of the term that labels children as deficient (Swadener & Lubeck, 1995). Social realities, such as poverty and family structure, that define these students as deficient are considered problems, yet top-down policy discussions assume these problems will somehow be fixed by technological tinkering with test scores or fewer bodies in a classroom. Policy makers' legitimacy depends on their ability to define problems as temporary and fixable aberrations.

Any data that contradict prevailing norms or values are at risk of being viewed as "hostile." Further, some realities revealed in data go unnoticed. Sometimes maintaining legitimacy for a policy necessitates minimizing research that might highlight racism layered with sexism, such as data that document the "fact" that large numbers of African American male students are slotted into special education. There is no established arena in which educators can call attention to the ways in which schools reinforce such patterns. Issues become non-events, voices are silenced. For example, in their analysis of the impact of education reform on equity practices, Sadker, Sadker, and Steindam (1989) speak of the "national blind spot" around issues of the persistent differences of women's and minorities' economic attainments. They describe the way schools present a "model of economic inequality, with too few women and minorities in positions of leadership" (p. 47).[3] The policy focusing in dominant arenas minimizes such issues and reinforces the legitimacy of dominant policy foci.

Power is enacted in dynamics in curricula and school sites where, by controlling knowledge, those in charge can convince children, families, and researchers to accept existing power relations in society and in schools themselves: "Schools can be used to control others by distributing knowledge that builds allegiance to ruling elites" (Spring, 1998, p. 32). For example, through their schooling, girls and women may learn to accept patriarchal leadership; members of marginal groups may be socialized to learn to accept their underclass status and economic exploitation as normative.

Some issues seem to remain invisible to those who hold power and make decisions. The crisis of child poverty, with the U.S. rate holding steady at about 20 percent (highest by far among industrialized countries), is not at the center of policy arenas. As Bracey (1999) says, "The affluent eye is watching the Dow Jones, not the poverty rate" (p. 2).[4] Our critique of power arrangements shows the need to move policy analysis towards a reframing that shifts policy questions. A re-visioned policy analysis that strategically supports an egalitarian conception of democracy would endeavor to uncover and highlight issues missed by traditional policy analysis. Specifically, the grounding for conceptualizing research and action can come from a researcher's or a leader's passionate desire for social justice. The purpose of this type of leadership stance and research, then, is to examine whether the policy formulation, implementation, and outcomes processes inhibit democratic processes and oppress or marginalize certain groups, perspectives, and ways of framing policy issues, with an eye toward re-visioning. In the next section we examine how strategic democratic theory provides a way to conceptualize this type of research, and how policy analysis can be used to reframe traditional discourses and political activity.

But first, we present the following Lived Realities, which provides an example of how well-intended policies often can have unintended consequences that can be damaging to students. This vignette provides an example of how a lived reality can be damaged by seemingly objective policies. It serves to remind us why new approaches are needed and that it is important to care about theory for re-visioned and re-framed politics and policy.

Lived Realities: The Face of Failure

Jonathan is a sparkling seventh grader with curly red hair and freckles. He is an energetic boy diagnosed with severe dyslexia. Because his ability to read is severely limited, his Individual Education Plan (IEP) stipulates that any test he takes should be read to him. The state's accountability policy, however, mandates that every child must take the standardized test unassisted. Jonathan's teacher, Ms. Williams, knows that Jonathan will fail the test without her reading it to him. She dreads the testing day. Jonathan's mind is highly developed, and he can do complex problems—he just has difficulty reading quickly. If he fails the test, he is required to take summer school in order to be promoted to the next grade. When testing day arrives, Ms. Williams' worst fears are realized. She tells Jonathan he will have thirty minutes to complete the test and tells him just to do his best. He looks at the test and attempts to do the first problem, which takes him ten minutes. Ms. Williams notices him put his head down on his desk and start to cry. By the time he has calmed down, he has five minutes remaining on the test and summer school is looming.

Policy makers and politicians often make educational policies in arenas far removed from the lived realities of the individuals, like Jonathan, who are most affected by them. A policy mandating that all students must take a statewide test without assistance sounds good in positivist theory, but what of the unanticipated consequences for students like Jonathan? Theory grounded in the experiences of individuals at which policies are targeted hold promise for exposing submerged issues in education, such as Jonathan's pain, and provide additional lenses with which to analyze policy problems.

Theories for Re-visioning and Re-framing Policies

For politics and policy to recognize frequently submerged issues, powerful critiques and so-cial movements are afoot. Influenced by social, historical, and cultural changes growing out of social movements for civil rights, women, Chicano students, and rights for gays and les-bians, new visions of politics, political activism, and knowledge have emerged. An increas-ing number of scholars use postmodern theoretical perspectives, which acknowledge that subjectivities are embedded into all analyses of policy issues, even in the questions and re-search designs. Although the term *postmodernism* is in wide use to describe current theoreti-cal shifts, it encompasses both a particular theoretical perspective (Bauman, 1992) and a historical shift in how we view the world. Rather than get caught up in ongoing debates defin-ing what postmodernism is or isn't (Ebert, 1991), this chapter focuses on how these theoreti-cal debates, discoveries, and perspectives can be used to re-frame and re-vision politics and policy research. Theoretical shifts have raised important questions about how *power,* the ex-ertion of symbolic and physical force, operates in social relationships, cultural understanding, language, and organizational and social structures, influencing the educational policy process.

These new theories expose how the needs and values of certain segments of the pop-ulation are seldom promoted unless powerful policy makers view them as important. Dom-inant values leave little room for alternative viewpoints on issues such as teen pregnancy, sexual harassment, and the gendered and racist nature of administration. (See Dillard, 1995; Laible, 1997; and Pillow, 1997 for critiques of such policy discussions.) In the policy-making and implementation process, without open discussion or a historical understanding of the roots of these suppressed issues, it is difficult to articulate such viewpoints or to cre-ate a strategy to change them. Unreflective policy researchers and policy makers often un-knowingly elevate their own values as the unquestioned norm. Of particular note, feminist, critical race, and sexuality theorists have exposed how tacit value systems based on elite, heterosexual, White male experiences have often shaped how we view educational prob-lems. These theories highlight how the very language of policy making and the processes surrounding its formulation and implementation can be oppressive (Ball, 1990b; Carlson, 1993; Marshall, 1997a). These perspectives seek to show how policies assumed to be eq-uitable can actually reinforce discriminatory practices. *Cultural production, strategic democracy,* and *social capital* theory seek to uncover the potential of human agency. The-ory needs to be connected to lived experience, lest it homogenize the human experience. Table 3.2 provides an overview of these theoretical perspectives. In the following sections, we discuss these theories in greater detail.

The theoretical strands listed in Table 3.2 are examples of frameworks that can be used for examining politics in a way that strategically encompasses marginalized groups. They can assist with exposing the interlocking nature of oppressive relationships in the hegemonic center of policy making and provide a way to re-frame and re-vision policy questions.

Feminist Perspectives

Feminist insights acknowledge that the values traditionally associated with women—for example, caring, collaboration, and nurturance—are devalued in society. These perspec-

TABLE 3.2 *Theories for Re-framing*

Theoretical Framework	Purpose
Feminism	Acknowledges the existence of patriarchy, which privileges male norms such as objectivity and marginalizes feminine concerns such as emotions and caring. These perspectives demonstrate how arrangements of political structures, legal systems, and hierarchies and curricula in schools exclude the realities of gendered existences and the legitimacy of subjective needs.
Critical Race	Conceptualizes whiteness (an elite, heterosexual, White male worldview) as an oppressive force in a society that marginalizes women, ethnic groups, homosexuals, the poor, and anyone not fitting the normative assumptions
Heterosexism	Suggests that heterosexist knowledge claims have reinforced a binary (only male-female) understanding of what constitutes gender/sex. These perspectives seek to expose oppression related to sexual orientation or nontraditional determinations of gender or sex.
Cultural Production and Cultural Capital	Breaks from deterministic Marxian theories in which actors have no agency. Cultural production theory builds on the notion of "cultural capital," the idea that wealth is not linked exclusively to material possessions such as money but also includes cultural forms such as education, dress, and speech. Central to this perspective is the notion that these cultural constructions are continually produced within social and material contexts. Cultural production replaces a conceptualization of culture as a static, unchanging body of knowledge transmitted between generations.
Democratic	Asserts that democracy can be conceived in meritocratic (individual achievement) or egalitarian terms (promoting equity) or some variation of these. This framework conceptualizes democracy as a way to understand and critique social structures, organizations, and processes.
Social Capital	Provides a way to study the formation of social movements and how they can energize groups, communities, and networks to achieve some common good

tives place women's concerns at the center of analysis and seek to uncover institutional and cultural forms of gender discrimination. These analyses go beyond blame-the-victim approaches (e.g., saying, "Oh, women just don't have the motivation for tough leadership positions") to the identification of barriers. They demand critical reexamination of intimate relationships as well as national policies. For example, feminist work on "caring" highlighted how human relationships and emotions are central to teaching and learning processes (see especially Gilligan, 1982, and Noddings, 1984). Noddings challenges education policy makers and researchers to envision policy-making processes in which concerns for the emotional and intellectual needs of students, teachers, and administrators are just as important as test scores. Such perspectives expand the visions and purposes of policy making.

We begin to see the plight of those women and minority representatives (shown in Table 3.1) who are in power positions but are overpowered. *Patriarchy, the gender regime,* and *the gender order* are terms that evoke the power of the state and administrative power to define, regulate, and assign value to women's lives through policies created predominantly by White men, with women and persons of color tending to be placed in subordinate positions (Bell & Chase, 1993; Marshall, 1993a).

In *The Feminist Case against Bureaucracy,* Ferguson (1984) asserts that the very organizational structure of a bureaucracy fosters unequal power relationships, treats workers like children, and reinforces isolation by separating workers from each other. Bureaucratically structured institutions such as schools are hierarchically structured so that workers are forced to comply and accept subordinated positions, not unlike patriarchal assertions of the second-class treatment of women and people of color.

Forceful and provocative feminist critiques demonstrate how arrangements of political structures, legal systems, and hierarchies and curricula in schools exclude the realities of women's existence and the legitimacy of women's needs (e.g., MacKinnon, 1982). Values and concerns traditionally associated with women are marginalized in the political arena and considered private concerns. The organization of schools can be especially oppressive and limiting for women and minorities who already deal with sexist and racist policies and cultures. The very structure of schools supports the silencing of these issues (Fine, 1991). The pushed-aside issues of girls' seeming need to be valued as sex objects, anorexia, teen pregnancy, sexual harassment, avoidance of "mannish" subjects and careers, and women's aversion to male-dominated educational administration cultures, then, become political issues, not private problems. This awareness has led some to a deeper understanding of the need to reorganize and restructure the dehumanizing aspects of schools embedded in these structures. Recognition provides a way to assess policy that goes beyond concerns for efficiency or standardization.

Feminist insights highlight the intertwining of power and sexuality, the construction of female identity and perceived social roles such as childrearing and caregiving, and implications of these for school policies and practices. Policy problems such as teen pregnancy can be seen as a desire for some women to fulfill their socially constructed feminine roles in society. Feminist insights about the complex nature of gender identity formation have also led to concerns about masculinity as a social and cultural construct (Connell, 1996; Reed, 1998). Although it took terrible suicide statistics and school murders, such as at Columbine High School, to get policy makers and leaders to acknowledge it, schools play a role in the social construction of masculinity. Researchers are finding that boys must operate under the oppressive assumption that they cannot display emotion or feeling. These repressed feelings, reinforced by schools, elevate rational and objective interactions by placing a high value on control and discipline. Boys' resistance to this emotional suppression can lead to violent emotional acts (Kenway & Fitzclarence, 1997; Shaw, 1995). Because male and female stereotypes are relational, researchers have increasingly found that gender equity cannot be achieved without attention to understanding how femininities and masculinities evolve and are coconstructed (Blackmore, Kenway, Willis, & Rennie, 1993). While oppressive masculinity "is an expression of the privilege men collectively have over women" (Connell, 1996, p. 209), it can also marginalize boys who exhibit feminine traits, such as feminized masculinities. The suppression of these alternative masculinities supports a dehumanizing system; thus, according to Kenway and Fitzclarence, "To ignore the emotional world of schooling and of students and teachers is to contribute to the repressions which recycle and legitimate violence" (1997, p. 128). In policy research, formation, and implementation, this awareness points to the need to include and acknowledge the emotional needs of those affected by policy.

Critical Race Theory

Feminists of color have made great inroads into understanding the gendered nature of racism, yet until recently relatively little work was undertaken on understanding racism as a theoretical construct. *Critical race theory* is a relatively new perspective developed by legal scholars (Matsuda, Lawrence, Delgado, & Williams-Crenshaw, 1993) and educational scholars (Banks, 1995; Ladson-Billings & Tate, 1995; Lipman, 1998; Lopez, 2003; Ogbu, 1994; Omni & Winant, 1993; Scheurich & Young, 1997; Zou & Trueba, 1998) that examines how racism is embedded into normative assumptions about policy, schooling, and research. These scholars view Whiteness (an elite, heterosexual, White male worldview) as an oppressive force in a society that marginalizes women, ethnic groups, homosexuals, the poor, and anyone not fitting the normative assumptions.[5] These theorists argue that research needs to subvert and expose how assumptions that place a value on Whiteness create racist interpretations of policy problems.

For example, Lipman (1998) studied two racially diverse junior high schools in the same district in order to understand the impact that racism had on school restructuring policy. Lipman (1998) found that because neither school came to terms with racist assumptions about students, the restructuring efforts ultimately failed. Her work points to the need for policy to take into account (1) how social context, such as racism, poverty, and historical attitudes towards desegregation, mediates policy; (2) how teachers' views of students can be shaped by ideologies around race; and (3) the need for marginalized groups to be included in decision-making processes.[6]

Heterosexism

Heterosexism is an emerging area of research that challenges the social constructions that give rise to the view of homosexuality as aberrant and the assumption that only two genders exist (Seidman, 1995). The terms *gender* and *sex* have been traditionally conflated and reinforce assumptions that there are only two official gender/sex distinctions: man and woman, male and female. In reality, however, there are actually multiple genders. The term *queer,* however, is gaining prominence to denote individuals who are bisexual, homosexual, transgendered, transsexual, and intersexed. Queer theory seeks to "highlight the ways such oppositions as knowledge/ignorance, voice/silence, and visibility/invisibility structure gay and lesbian lives and produce an unknowability of gay and lesbian identity and experience" (Talburt, 1999, p. 529).

The cultural proclivity toward acknowledging only two genders is widespread and deeply ingrained culturally. For example, when a baby is born with ambiguous genitalia—in that the child is not clearly male or female biologically—standard medical practice has dictated that the parents must select a male or female gender for their child. Once a gender is selected, the baby undergoes surgery to remove the nonselected sexual organs (Beh & Diamond, 2000). Issues around queer theory, such as transgendered experiences, have been almost completely ignored by policy researchers (Lugg, 2003). Although there is an emerging policy and politics literature related to racism and sexism, discrimination based on sexual orientation or sex identification remains relatively unexplored.

Fraynd and Capper (2003) provide one of the few studies that examine the precarious position of gay school administrators. In their study they examine the experiences of four gay administrators, two of whom are closeted (are not openly gay) and two of whom are openly gay. Their study investigates how cultural norms serve to frame homosexuality as a form of deviance. For example, state or district policies that do not acknowledge the possibility of same-sex marriages deny benefits to gay couples because they do not fit cultural assumptions that marriage is possible only between a man and a woman. Recognizing and critiquing heterosexist assumptions in education politics can support re-framed policy proposals that recognize sexuality and that scrutinize hostile school environments.

Cultural Production Theory and Cultural Capital

Cultural production theory acknowledges and builds on class inequities (emphasized in Marxian social reproduction theory; e.g., Althusser, 1971), but it focuses on how cultural knowledge (such as education, dress, taste, disposition, and language usage) is seen as "cultural capital"—a form of economic currency (Levinson & Holland, 1996; Lamont & Lareau, 1988). Cultural production theory builds on the work of Bourdieu and Passeron (1977) and views "culture as a continual process of creating meaning in social and material contexts, replacing a conceptualization of culture as a static, unchanging body of knowledge 'transmitted' between generations" (Levinson & Holland, 1996, p. 13). Cultural production theory offers a critique of the deterministic, structural analyses of oppressive power in educational institutions, which can generate a sense of hopelessness. While social reproduction theory assumed that if you were born in poverty, you most likely would remain in poverty, cultural production theory suggests that material wealth can be linked to education and knowledge about how to act and portray yourself in cultural settings. Thus, just because a child is poor does not mean he is doomed to live always in poverty. The notion of individual human agency—the idea that individuals produce culture as much as they are shaped by it—is seen as an important facet in understanding discrimination and oppression. Poverty and other forms of discrimination (such a racism and sexism) are not things that doom individuals or groups; rather, awareness of these oppressions can be used as a basis for resistance and action in the form of human agency. This approach offers hope for how individuals born into poverty have the potential to produce different cultural outcomes.

This recent theory lays the groundwork for people to sense that they have the means to escape from, or at least negotiate their own identities in, oppressive institutional and cultural systems. In contrast, reproduction theories view educational institutions as sites at which social inequities are reproduced. Although such theories are useful for identifying powerful oppressive forces, they leave us with a depressed passivity, a feeling that we have been ignorant cogs in this reproduction scheme. But cultural production theory bestows a sense of agency, a sense that, even as we identify structural oppressions, we can find ways to work the systems as individuals creating our own senses of self and as groups collaborating for more socially just systems. These perspectives shift away from determinist analyses by developing research approaches designed to allow us to understand how power and knowledge are produced in specific cultural contexts.

Thus, these powerful theoretical perspectives enable and support critique and the re-framing of politics. Even the simple process of labeling an educational issue can be oppressive, but new approaches to analysis of politics and policy can be used to support culturally negotiated, re-visioned, and re-framed issues. In recent years, for example, the label "at risk" has focused attention on certain students but also has become a catch-all category, allowing application of deficit notions to a broad variety of people (Margonis, 1992). Such categorization casts aside the values and goals of equity and social justice. It can funnel seemingly neutral problem definitions toward goals of transforming workers into middle-class citizens with good values and character but away from underlying economic and institutional injustices. Definitions such as these provide the grounding for policies and programs with, Margonis says, the "ideological strength [of] a deficit conception with egalitarian pretensions" (Margonis, p. 346). This is illustrated in policy deliberations over issues such as teenage pregnancy, single-parent homes, and minority achievement. Further, Fine (1991) has shown how student poverty coupled with dispassionate dropout policies that do not attend to students needs and concerns make many students want to leave school. Such identification and labeling of the issues is depressing and one wonders, "How have I participated in these injustices?" or "How can we get out of these traps that reproduce inequities?" But, students' choices about courses, behavior, and persistence in school, once framed as "the dropout problem"—with ensuing antidropout policies—can be re-framed in light of cultural production theory and research that focuses on the lived realities of girls and boys (e.g., Connell, 1996; McRobbie, 1975; Willis, 1977).

Understanding how policies marginalize differences such as gender, race, and class holds promise for exposing submerged issues in education (Levinson & Holland, 1996). The dynamics of race, class, sexuality, and gender privileges in postindustrial societies would give a reality twist to analyses of dropouts. Such twists will redefine questions about how children form their identities and make meaning for their lives. Theory grounded in experience holds promise for exposing submerged issues in education; for pointing to the need for policy research, politics, and policy making that is not disconnected from the realities of the daily lives of the individuals who inhabit schools; and for envisioning alternative frameworks to engage perspectives from the margin.

Strategic Democratic Possibilities

Education politics cannot be re-framed without new ways of thinking about democracy. Increasing numbers of democratic theorists share common beliefs in the ideals of community and democracy, and view the pluralistic and participatory ideals of democracy as worthy goals for policy and politics (Fraser, 1997; Mouffe, 1992; Mouffe & LeClau, 1985; Phillips, 1993; Young, 1990). To that end, it is useful to mention two dominant values in society that have shaped the meaning of democracy: egalitarian beliefs and meritocratic beliefs. The *egalitarian* strand stresses equity and equality and the role of government as ensuring that all individuals in society are valued equally, regardless of differences. The *meritocratic* strand stresses equality of opportunity but suggests that society is unequal for a reason:

Some individuals are not successful because they do not work hard enough or do not have the necessary ability. This meritocratic view can be detrimental to true democracy because it tends to exclude as worthy of participation those who are unsuccessful for whatever reason. It also does not take into account how forms of discrimination such as sexism, racism, poverty, and homophobia can have an impact on one's ability to participate in a democracy.

Utilizing an alternative, philosophically based theoretical framework to evaluate policy, then, can support creation of re-framed policies. Kahne (1994), for example, draws on the work of John Dewey to re-frame the analysis of politics and policy, focusing on how well the political arrangements and policies foster democracy for all involved. Kahne shifts the focus of analysis from individual student achievement to group, class, school, and community achievement. Traditional outcomes-based analyses often lose sight of the relationship between educational policy and the political processes of change within and around schools. Instead, Kahne advocates examining schools to see if they function as democratic communities. He offers an alternative framework for structuring policy debates so that additional substantive issues about democracy and schooling are not obscured. The following Lived Realities examines how theory can be used to re-frame the study of policy and politics such that it supports democratic ideals.

Lived Realities: Examining the Prospects of Democratic School Reform

In deciding on a research topic, Gerstl-Pepin (1998) was intrigued by the A+ Schools Program in North Carolina, an arts-based school reform program created by a grassroots policy formulation and implementation process. Yet the current frames for policy analysis available to her seemed inappropriate for capturing the grassroots nature of the reform. Traditional analyses could help her document the program's change process, but they did not provide a way to examine whether or not the program might represent a more participatory approach to school reform. Gerstl-Pepin decided to create her own framework to examine the extent to which the program might represent a democratic approach to school reform. She developed a theoretical framework building on Habermas' (1994) concept of the public sphere, a metaphorical space in a democracy in which citizens get together to discuss how to govern the country. The closest example of this is the media, which serve as the main arena in which citizens are informed about key policy issues. Specifically, Gerstl-Pepin's analysis provided a way to highlight how the program operated democratically, in that it created a space outside of the school bureaucracy, a counterpublic, for teachers, administrators, parents, and other staff to come together to discuss how to improve schools. It created an alternative policy arena, separate from the hegemonic center. In this alternative arena, the "often-forgotten players" could develop a sense of identity and agency and construct alternative policy narratives. This allowed Gerstl-Pepin to see how school bureaucracies resist change, because teachers are often isolated from each other and collaboration is not structured into the school day. Gerstl-Pepin wondered why other politics and policy analysis approaches had not attempted to examine this aspect of reform, as it seemed so central to school improvement.

In the preceding vignette, Gerstl-Pepin (1998) re-framed her analysis of a school reform movement to examine whether a grassroots reform movement might be able to promote a more egalitarian conception of democracy. This type of re-framing of politics places value on democracy and provides an example for how the framing and the implementation of policies can be assessed to determine whether they support or hinder egalitarian democracy.

While democratic analyses of policy such as Gerstl-Pepin's (1998) and Kahne's (1994) offer hope, they also present challenges. Meritocratic conceptions of democracy can serve dominant cultural interests at the expense of marginalized groups (Scheurich, 1998) and reinforce oppressive power relationships if all groups in society do not have equal representation in decision making. If oppression can be exposed and differences among people (race, gender, ethnicity, sexual orientation, etc.) accepted and valued in educational policy making, then there is hope that democracy might also move in a more radical direction (Mouffe, 1992; Mouffe & LeClau, 1985).

For example, Fraser (1994) suggests that the possibility for change occurs in democracy when counterpublics come together to critique existing inequalities. *Counterpublics* provide a way of conceptualizing groups that come together to critique harmful hegemonic assumptions. Central to this conception is the idea that democratic decision-making processes often do not provide space for critical discussion about areas of silence or inequity. Instead these discussion and moves for action occur in alternative spaces, such as interest group organizations, churches, or street corners. The Civil Rights Movement is one such counterpublic. Discussion about racism or segregation did not occur openly in Congress, legislatures, or the media until civil rights protestors brought these issues into the public consciousness. Groups came together in churches, on street corners, and in communities to discuss racial inequity. These dialogues served as the basis for civil rights demonstrations and political action (Fraser, 1994).

Democratic theories offer a way of seeing the fluidity of democracy and the need for critiques of democratic ideals that elevate meritocracy above equity. They provide a way to analyze the conduct of politics and the exercise of power and assess them against the ideals of democracy to determine whether they promote a more engaged and equitable society.

Social Capital Theory

As shown in Chapter 1, human capital assumptions are frequently used to justify public education with the rationale that an investment in schools is an investment in creating the skilled, workforce-ready people needed for the nation's economic development. In contrast, social capital theory studies the formation of movements that energize groups, communities, and networks to achieve some common good (Woolcock, 1998). Social movements can encompass and mobilize the common values, passions, and needs of those who want different policies, whether as grassroots organizing from the margin (e.g., for peace, for civil rights, for migrant farm workers' welfare, etc.) or as politically connected groups with resources for negotiating with the hegemonic center (e.g., League of Women Voters, ACLU) (Oberschall, 1993).

Social capital theory and research on social movements hold promise for changing the dynamics of politics, power arrangements, and policy through educator activism. Some educators retain a zeal for participating in societal change (Casey, 1993). But many learn professionalism, which involves the dispassionate and careful management of student progress. In order to be considered "professionals," educators may be socialized to deny their activist motivation to improve society through the education process. Generally, educators learn to work through the hierarchical system and must work through their superiors if they want their needs and problems represented to the political system. Social capital theory, by framing analyses of education politics and policy, can be used to highlight educator activists who take strong passionate stands, mobilize for action, and defy professional norms. This approach to examining policy can underscore how true leaders can create their own networks (Marshall, Taylor, & Gaskell, 1999) and join causes, taking strong, values-based stands (Casey, 1993). Challenges from heretofore disenfranchised, marginalized groups are in the purview of a real education politics, a politics that goes beyond and outside the hegemonic center.

Politics from Margin to Center

Traditionally, research on education politics and policy has focused on the center—the legislatures and boards and central offices that have the formal, legitimized power and authority for making policy (as we have seen in Chapters 1 and 2). Although it is important to understand the dynamics at the center, what about the views of groups who challenge dominant beliefs about policy? By focusing only on the center of policy making, the analyst of politics and policy can overlook important lessons from the *agency* of individuals actively engaged in resisting inequities that might be embedded in policy. Such an analyst might be led to believe that those at the hegemonic center are the real and only political agents, and that those at the center have the right to determine what educational realities, voices, issues, and needs are to be heard and addressed.

We are putting forth an alternative model for understanding educational politics and policy—a picture of possibility that draws from the previously discussed theories and that values the politics of challengers (see Figure 3.2). The *Politics from Margin to Center* model encompasses those who are often unrepresented, such as students and teachers, those not fitting within majority norms. This conceptual framework encompasses the theories of resistance and challenge—postmodern, feminist, and critical theories that support the possibility of emancipatory social action and individual agency.

Theorists note that those who decide the agenda in the public sphere arrange the "hegemonic mode of domination" (Fraser, 1989). Most of us were socialized to accept unquestioningly that values are allocated in hegemonic centers like legislatures, but alternative definitions of educational problems are expressed by disenfranchised groups and activist organizations (evident, for example, in home schooling and the women's movement). Opposition and resistance exist outside the centers of policy making—in the stories about why kids drop out, why women are too disgusted to become school administrators, why girls become pregnant, why educators fake their compliance with policy directives, and why parents are so cynical about pseudoparticipation structures. Alternative discourses exist about what really motivates teachers, what really goes on with kids, what alternative models women's leadership would offer. The lived reality of families, students, and educators is out there and often *not* represented by educational policy actors.

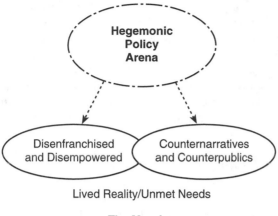

The Margins

FIGURE 3.2 *Politics from Margin to Center*
We suggest there is a pressing need to expose how the hegemonic policy arena can ignore the unmet needs and lived realities of marginalized groups. Those who feel disempowered or disenfranchised can create alternative publics and construct counternarratives with an alternative sense of priorities that can refocus the concerns of the center.

Chapter 1 introduced notions of language and symbols as political tools that powerfully convey ideologies. Theories that recognize that education politics and policy are about ideology conveyed through *talk* (rather than rational decision making) can be used as tools for constructing and negotiating politics. By focusing on the politics of discourse, using discourse analysis as a powerful analytic tool, we can display the language that mobilizes some policy logics and discredits others (Marshall, 1997b; Taylor, 1997). People use speech as a power tool. Gaining access to the public discourse is essential for this power. To expose this type of power, one can focus on the dynamics of power at the margin of political movements in education. This provides a way of showing how policy talk can be reconstituted, resisted, and strategically used in policy debates.

For example, through analysis of discourse, we can see how hegemonic notions about what constitutes "good leadership" (e.g., hierarchical authority) are conveyed into certification policies that emphasize individual achievement. The presentation of counternarratives (e.g., the valuing of caring, community-based models), as evidenced in the experience of successful, caring principals, provides a way of capturing marginalized voices. The dynamics of policy discourse between the margins and the center provides a way of re-visioning this political struggle in a way that validates the marginals as important political actors.

But, *naming* the *Politics from Margin to Center* and drawing the model helps. Marginal groups can use it as a tool when they are working with those in the center (e.g., legislators, editors, school boards, power elites, and funding agencies) who frequently cannot or will not see the margins. Viewing protests at school board meetings as the workings of counterpublics points to the ways that challengers' talk can permeate the boundary around that hegemonic center. Viewing conversations in the teachers' lounge as constructing a counternarrative—such as, "Accountability is turning our schools into factories"—can help educators deal with the stress of harmful policies. This new viewing, or re-visioning, can lay the groundwork for educators to engage as policy advocates, negotiating their own identities, articulating realities and needs in their own narratives, and engaging with other challengers in re-visioning democratic, socially just bases for school politics and policy.

Proactive Re-visioning and Re-framing

Theory provides a way of conceptualizing how we see the world, and methodology provides a way to connect theory to a defined process for conducting analyses of politics and policy research. What if politics and policies were approached using critical theories that are openly interested in bringing about social change and postmodern understandings that subjectivities and values are never sanitized out of analyses? These approaches differ significantly from the theories driving analysis in the first two chapters of this text. Adopting such perspectives means being openly political—acknowledging a values base and exposing societal inequities. Theory-driven analyses can encompass politics from the margins and provide a vision to frame what could be. This approach is driven by a proactive desire for a social justice that is compassionate and caring and incorporates passion and feeling. The aim is to expose the interlocking nature of oppressive relationships by challenging politics-as-usual, by re-framing hegemonic policy questions, and by providing practical examples of how policy can be framed to improve decision making.

Political negotiations over power, resources, and values occur in microinteractions and informal talk as much as they do in formal policy arenas. Openly political policy advocates place this battle at the center of analysis. Their purpose is to engage with others who know the everyday realities of children and educators and to expose political practices, policies, and structures that suppress issues.

Further, researchers and leaders with critical theory agendas would acknowledge that politics often takes place beyond traditional policy arenas. The definitions of school leadership, the microinteractions of students' identity negotiations, the juggling of different strategies and coalitions, all require different approaches to policy analysis (Marshall, 1997a). Proactive re-visioning seeks to improve the human condition and is found in emancipatory social science, policy, and leadership models. To reach the new visions, leaders and analysts must assist in developing radical alternatives, and actively seek to reconstruct our understanding of policy problems (Bobrow & Dryzek, 1987; Scheurich, 1994; Schram, 1995). These leaders share no illusions that research and re-visioning alone will somehow be able to save or liberate the downtrodden; rather, their focus is to provide alternative visions of what is and what could be. From this perspective, the practitioner-leader and researcher is proactive and engages the policy world, incorporating its values, yet producing policy recommendations that are strategically designed to problematize normative assumptions.

Promising Approaches to Analysis of Politics and Policy

In the past few years, an increasing number of methodological approaches have integrated theoretical perspectives that critique social and cultural inequalities that permeate schools and political processes (Carlson, 1993; Forester, 1993; Laible, 1997; Marshall, 1997a; Marshall & Anderson, 1995; Mawhinney, 1997; Pillow, 1997; Scheurich, 1994; Schram, 1995; Stromquist, 1995; Taylor, 1997). In the past three decades, several shifts in theory and research paradigms have influenced educational and policy research. These perspectives question the foundations of epistemology, or "how we know what we know" (Crotty, 1998, p. 8). Epistemological interrogation suggests that knowledge, including research, can be socially constructed and deeply subjective. This perspective rejects the epistemological assumptions that research is objective and free of bias. These openly political approaches are concerned with uncovering the fallacies in current policy assumptions and utilizing the theoretical approaches listed in the previous section (Scheurich & Young, 1998). In particular, the politics of language and symbols, critical policy analysis, and feminist critical policy analysis are three promising policy methodologies. An overview of these perspectives is offered in Table 3.3.

The Politics of Language and Symbols

Political negotiations over power, resources, and values can be embedded in language and political symbols. Policy studies that focus on language and symbolism focus on the "dimensions in which we act communicatively: those of making and testing claims about

TABLE 3.3 *Promising Policy Methodologies*

Policy Methodology	Purpose
The Politics of Language and Symbols	Problematizes language and symbols in order to show how political negotiations over power, resources, and values can be embedded in policy and politics. These types of policy studies vary greatly but share an interest in how the language and symbolism used in policy and politics are connected to historically situated social and material relations, identities, and ideologies.
Critical Policy Analysis	Examines educational policy and politics in order to understand the nature of relationships in social systems, with the purpose of eliminating those that maintain privilege and oppression. This approach embraces critical theory, focusing on social critique in an effort to transform society.
Feminist Critical Policy Analysis	Ensures that women's needs, concerns, and values are included in examinations of policy and politics. This perspective argues that these concerns need to be at the center of policy deliberations. It illustrates how mainstream hegemonic policy deliberations usually privilege male norms.

states of affairs in the world, about appropriate and legitimate social relationships, about personal and social identities, and about ways of framing issues at hand" (Forester, 1993, p. 12; see also Placier, 1996, and Taylor, 1997). For example, a derogatory label such as "children at risk" implies that students are deficient. The issue can be re-framed by articulating the possibility that students are instead "at promise" and unfairly disadvantaged from negative stereotyping (Swadener & Lubeck, 1995).

Further, *policy sociology* and *policy archeology* approaches examine how policy problems and solutions are socially constructed (Foucault, 1981; Scheurich, 1994; Ball, 1990b). Both of these approaches can be used to identify whether, how, and by whom the problem is framed and can identify the social processes through which some solutions are deemed viable and others not. The values bases, the beneficiaries, and the losers of educational policy directives can be unearthed through policy archeology, revealing the historically constituted, value-laden questions and problems. Such archeology disproves any assertions that policy analysis is value-free.

Further, Edelman's notion (1988) of *political spectacle* provides a way of conceptualizing language as a form of dramaturgy, a symbolic act in which "actors evoke symbols of rationality even when reason does not govern the act itself" (Smith, Heinecke, & Noble, 1999, p. 188). Symbols of rationality, such as census data, test scores, and public opinion polls, are used by political actors as a way to convince the public that a given policy is legitimate.

Examining language and symbols critically provides a way to determine how power operates in the words and symbols used to frame and define policy issues. It points to the power embedded in seemingly benign policy discourses. These frameworks provide a way of exposing how power can be hidden in policy language and symbols and provides insights into how these languages and symbols might be re-framed and re-visioned in support of social justice.

Critical Policy Analysis

Some people study education policy and politics in order to understand the nature of relationships in social systems, with the purpose of eliminating those relationships that maintain privilege and oppression (Ryan, 2001). This *critical policy analysis* approach embraces critical theory, focusing on social critique in an effort to transform society. These analysts are part of what Weiler calls "a long battle between those who would restrict access to knowledge and power to elites and those who seek a more equal and participatory society" (1993, pp. 210–211). Critical theorists and analysts of policy and politics expose policies and power arrangements that restrict access; their work often demonstrates how privilege is maintained and how the disempowered and silenced are kept that way, raising "serious questions about the role of schools in the social and cultural reproduction of social classes, gender roles, and racial and ethnic prejudice" (Anderson, 1989, p. 251).

Critical policy analysis, then, is a search for improvement of the human condition, knowing that to get there, analysts must assist in more radical alternatives, seeking a "reconstruction of political institutions and public life" (Bobrow & Dryzek, 1987, p. 181). One approach is to focus attention on communicative acts that create and maintain social relations. These imply a focus in policy analysis on "the dimensions in which we act communicatively: those of making and testing claims about states of affairs in the world, about appropriate and legitimate social relationships, about personal and social identities, and about ways of framing issues at hand" (Forester, 1993, p. 12). Policy analysts would have to pay attention to the policy deliberations "including such processes as how decision premises are covertly built into decision structures are the ways in which non-decisions can pre-shape political agendas" (Fischer, 1989, p. 950). Forester (1993) provides several examples of critical policy analysis by examining social policy issues such as toxic waste, Environmental Protection Agency budget reductions, and local health services. He concluded,

> This political and communicative rendering of the problem does not dismiss issues of interest but rather gives them a multidimensional cast—so that we can examine how . . . forces obliterate or dominate popular voice, so that we can examine particularly ways that citizens are (or are not) able to speak and act politically, to question facts, rules, or stereotypical identities. (1993, p. 130)

Policy analysis, then, must consider whether a policy will empower and democratize, whether it will dispense goods to the have-nots as much as it considers whether a policy is efficient.

This approach acknowledges that political agendas and negotiations over power, resources, and values occur during microinteractions and talk as much as they do in formal policy arenas. Such a critical focus can be very depressing, making one feel like giving up in face of such powerful oppressive forces. However, within this sort of inquiry, we can find great examples of human agency, in which individuals and social groups "culturally produce" alternative ways of being, alternative spaces, and power bases. Although economic and political systems create institutions that reproduce elite privilege, humans can negotiate their own ways of being, resisting, and re-creating what will be.

Feminist Critical Policy Analysis

To put women's and girls' needs and values at the center of policy deliberations is to be openly political, values based, and challenging to hegemony. *Feminist critical policy analysis* illustrates how the values bases of mainstream, hegemonic policy deliberations usually are openly political for the benefit of men. Noddings does this when she says, "Instead of asking why women lag behind men in mathematics, we might ask the following: Why do men lag behind women in elementary school teaching, nursing, full-time parenting, and like activities?" (1992, p. 66). By putting women at the center, with women's ways, needs, values, and choices as important, this analysis re-centers policy debates. If the maintenance of caring relationships is the central topic in the design of curricula, then developmental studies and family would be more than add-ons, electives, soft, and only for girls. Noddings continues: "With family life at the center of the curriculum, we could teach history, literature, and science more meaningfully than we do now" (p. 67). Education for citizenship would include neighborliness, helpfulness—things mothers inculcate in their children. Using feminine perspectives consciously as the standard for our educational assessments would promote social consciousness, an inclusion of peace studies, and serve as a useful critique of popular culture and gender relations that glamorize violence.

Lived Realities: Promoting Development via Girls' Education

After many days of preparation and practicing, Reba Conover (a pseudonym) had calmed her nerves and honed her presentation so that she was ready for her Senate testimony. Still, the challenge was to promote the doubling of the millions of dollars to the U.S. Agency for International Development (USAID), focusing on education and on girls in developing countries by getting the president to ensure that education assistance in the Foreign Assistance Act promotes gender equity. Her theme was "The Virtuous Circle of Girls Education." She quoted the former prime minister of India as saying, "Educate a boy, and you educate a person. Educate a girl, and you educate a whole family." The bill proposed a Gender Equity Index to measure outcomes such as enrollments, retention, and achievement data to get baseline data and then to measure progress over time. To provide convincing arguments, she emphasized that the bill, besides teaching girls to read and write, increased wages, productivity, and labor force participation; it increased agricultural productivity; it improved health and nutrition; and it enhanced environmental practices. With increased education, women would have better prenatal care and their children higher survival rates. Women would marry later and have fewer children, but with better health and nutrition. She summarized barriers to girls' education as long distances to schools with unsafe paths and roads; high costs (for uniforms or supplies), leaving families to invest in their boys, not in their girls; the predominance of male teachers; and traditional values that emphasize girls' housekeeping and childcare roles. She quoted the former chief economist for the World Bank, Larry Summers, who liked to talk about how educating girls gives "a higher rate of return than any other investment available in the developing world."

Reba, no fool, knew to promote with the logic that had the highest likelihood of breaking down the senators' resistance: Talking of high returns, as if the bill were the stock market, or a reduction in the birth rate, as if pregnancy for women of color were a disease to be eradicated, would lead to passage. But she hated doing so! Why couldn't it be enough to argue that foreign aid should eliminate barriers to girls going to school? Why did she have to keep quiet about the real issues with which the girls and women were struggling? What was wrong with this political arrangement that made her talk only within *their* parameters? Weren't there ways to re-frame these issues?

Feminist critical policy analysis connects feminist theories and policy questions as a way to re-frame policy.

What are the related issues that surface when gender is the policy issue? Some examples are the debate over how much the state should intervene in family and private affairs, and whether government should be satisfied with addressing (but not redressing) an equity issue.

Women-centered research and women-centered politics present a challenge to the male norms that have framed most research and political arrangements (Harding, 1987). Feminist theories re-frame all issues to focus on women. *Liberal feminist theory* frames research on the barriers to women's opportunity (e.g., sex role stereotyping and male norms about the workplace) and seeks to eliminate barriers to opportunity by enacting laws against them. Another strand is *difference feminisms,* which identify women's ways of thinking, moralizing, setting priorities, developing relationships and community, and cycling of lives. The message of difference feminism is that women are different, so our institutions and values must be changed to incorporate women's ways. *Power and politics feminisms* recognize that all meaning and valuing is politically constructed. The message of this strand is that we must focus on the power dynamics and the political processes through which male dominance is perpetuated. *Feminist critical policy analysis* examines the formal and informal processes of power and policy that affect women's advancement and full development. Feminist analysis assumes that where policy apparatus is male dominated, creating and maintaining systems that benefit men, women's issues, by definition, come to the policy system as a challenge, to be resisted. Traditional policy analysis assumptions and methods will not suffice to bring about change. Feminist theories of the state and alternative methodological approaches are needed in order to frame policies in ways that avoid male-centered assumptions.

Feminist approaches have a particular goal of identifying ways to make our policy system more democratic and equitable, with a valuing of women's needs, values, and perspectives. Whatever theory and methodologies guide policy analyses, political realities may determine how they are presented in the real world, as the Lived Realities on the previous page illustrates.

Conover's story shows the potential for strategies, politically attuned agendas that have the potential for improving education worldwide. As is true for any policy directions, to become authoritative and to have resources and enforcement, policy proposals must pass muster through the frameworks that fit the processes in the policy arenas and through the values of key actors; otherwise, they risk being treated as "hostile."

Frequently educators, analysts, and even privileged insiders in hegemonic arenas of politics pine for strategies, abilities, and support for presenting what they really know to be true and important, in the hope that these intentions could lead toward new visions, new ways of tackling issues. In the next section, and throughout the book, are examples of the beginnings of such re-framing and re-visioning, coupled with research and policy advocacy approaches to activism that can serve as inspiration in that quest.

Examples of Policy Re-framing: Accountability Policies

High-stakes testing, minimum standards, and holding teachers and school sites responsible for student test scores are the dominant policy instruments aimed at achieving school improvement. In the current policy context, no policy maker can be *against* accountability. But as educators and students live with the effects of accountability policies, problems are repressed and needs are left unmet. If political actors dealt with the realities of educators and children, if the dominant paradigm were shifted, what would policies encompass? With re-framing that embraces the desires of educators, the ideals of democracy and community, and policies purposefully embracing the needs of disenfranchised, often-silenced, and marginal groups, what would quality policies look like? Table 3.4 provides a quick view of the ways that theories and methodologies can assist in this re-framing.

The theories introduced in this chapter provide a way to re-frame questions, uncover interlocking systems of domination, re-value democratic practices, and elicit healthy rebellions. Qualitative approaches, in particular, flow from these theories and can comple-

TABLE 3.4 *Re-framing Educator Quality Policy*

Quality Issue	Dominant Policy	Missing Issues	Re-framed Policy Possibilities
Educators' Work Supports and Measures of Success	Administrators' competencies assessed by (a) test scores and (b) ability to quell unrest	Creates low morale, as administrators must focus on hierarchical control, domination of subordinates, and standardization	Judging administrator and teacher competency by ability to create pedagogical, structural, and curricular strategies to build community and address oppressions
	Increase requirements for teacher training and competency testing measured via standardized testing	Creates low morale, as teachers are demoralized by standardization and pressures to teach to the test	Valuing teachers for their contributions and providing support for their increased professionalism and competency
	Create merit systems so teachers are rewarded for excelling over their peers.	System of extrinsic rewards do not motivate teachers intrinsically and fosters competition rather than collaboration.	Focusing on building community and fostering collaboration within schools to ensure school success. Rewarding educators for making schooling democratic and socially just.
	Lowered requirements for lateral-entry non-teachers	Many teachers leave the profession due to dissatisfaction with working conditions.	Policies enhancing teachers' joy about engaging with students
	Merit pay will push teachers to succeed.	Teaching as a profession is not valued or respected as integral to the success of a democracy.	Placing a high social value on the work that teachers do every day. Creating supports and incentives based on teachers' narratives.
	Prescribed curriculum	Teachers are not seen as professionals who deserve the freedom and support to be curriculum developers.	Increase support for professional development approaches that support the teacher as a curriculum developer.
	Published student performance tied to educators' career survival	Creates tremendous pressure on teachers to view students as test scores rather than unique human beings with particular needs. Pushes special need and marginalized students out of school.	Focusing on student mastery of material and providing extra resources for students needing emotional and intellectual support

TABLE 3.4 Continued

Quality Issue	Dominant Policy	Missing Issues	Re-framed Policy Possibilities
Bottom Line	Higher test scores are used as *the* measure of school and educator quality. Educators and students with divergent goals do not belong.	Punitive, de-skilling of the workplace violates educators' sense of craft, separates them from each other. Students' individual needs and modes of learning must bc funneled into standardized, narrow curriculum.	Focusing on a community of collaborating and proud educators able to articulate and create nurturing teaching and learning environments and inspire excellence

ment openly political/activist researchers, because they can be used to study individuals, groups, and organizations traditionally excluded from the policy process. Quantitative research, more accepted in policy arenas, can strategically disrupt hegemonic policy discourses, but because it focuses on numerical data, it is not always useful for uncovering hidden meanings, experiences, and lived realities. (Recall our discussion of traditional policy research in Chapter 2.)

Quantitative approaches are particularly powerful and useful for identifying larger, more sweepingly oppressive structures such as the connection between socioeconomics and test scores. For example, the work of Berliner and Biddle (1997) examines how easily quantitative data can be misinterpreted and misrepresented. Specifically, they examine how data are often used to support public "myths" that assume that the American educational system is failing, when in fact there is much evidence that suggests that education has actually improved substantially for affluent schools and students. Berliner and Biddle (1997) suggest that a careful look at the available quantitative data suggests that school failure is tightly connected to societal and cultural inequities.

> Widespread poverty, inadequate job prospects, and lack of social services all contribute to loss of dignity in many families in the country and, therefore, to the loss of hope among children. This is especially so for the most vulnerable of our citizens, those who must endure the additional burdens of prejudice. Given these facts, "school improvement" often really requires improvement in the overall quality of life of the members of the community. Unfortunately many federal and state policymakers seem disinterested in this message. They ignore it at our collective peril. (p. 288)

Thus, this information is treated as "hostile data" or ignored by policy makers unwilling or incapable of dealing with larger social and cultural issues. Further, cost–benefit analysis conducted by Masse and Barnett (2002) indicates that investing in early childhood education affects the long-term chances of children living in poverty. These researchers suggest that investment in early childhood education is cost effective, because it will lead to a reduction in additional funds needed for elementary, middle, and secondary intervention; social services; and the criminal justice system. Strategic quantitative studies such as these that claim "objectivity" is much needed in order to raise these neglected issues. Additionally, though, there is an urgent need for policy research that captures the voices, experiences, and lives of individuals marginalized in policy discussions, and that connects them to elite policy-making arenas.

Many emerging research methods are centered on naming issues, exposing areas of silence, theorizing structures of inequities, focusing on ethics and the purpose and process of education, and discerning the problems inherent in the very structure, language, and assumptions that undergird research on politics and policy (Bloom, 1998; Lather, 1991; Gitlin, 1994).

Openly political and empowering theories (e.g., feminism, critical race, hetrosexism, cultural production, and democratic theory) and methodologies (e.g., the politics of language and symbols, critical policy analysis, and feminist critical policy analysis) are available for re-framing policy possibilities. The current policy directives affecting educators and students involve strict controls over competency in tightly constructed schemes of curriculum delivery and standardized testing. Analyses that focus on language and symbols could be used to reveal how these value bases and policy logics assume that competition and punitive measures will transform struggling schools. For example, narratives of teachers' career frustrations could highlight the incongruity of policies that discourage teacher creativity and sense of professionalism at a time when there is a growing crisis in terms of recruiting and retaining teachers. Policy re-framing requires policies that inspire new teachers and support career teachers by connecting to their narratives and needs.

Policy research would highlight educators' initial idealistic and ethical aspirations to make a difference and show how high-stakes accountability policies can cause emotional stress that gets in the way of that desire (Hargreaves, 1990; Sederberg & Clark, 1990; Czubaj, 1996; McNeil, 1987). It would reveal teachers' rebellions against the dispassionate and careful management of student progress. Moreover, it would be a positive framing around that rebellion, viewing it as an activist motivation to improve society through the education process. Policy formulation that acknowledged that teachers feel violated by workplace controls that tightly align teacher delivery of constrained curriculum (Wirth, 1990) and discredit the craft and emotional labor of teaching (Freedman, 1990) would incorporate lived realities.

What if the policy directives addressing teacher and student performance were re-framed and re-centered to capture teachers' and students' realities, and to incorporate what we learn from emerging theories and methodologies? The theories and methodologies outlined in this chapter, inserted into policy analysis, could elicit repressed policy issues, force these counternarratives into political debate, and re-frame policy about standardized curricula; about recruiting, retaining, and motivating educators; about chronic inequities; about dropouts; about school violence; and so on. Table 3.4 provides one example. It contrasts the dominant assumptions behind current teacher/student performance quality policies with such re-framed possibilities.

Summary

This chapter examined how policy generated from research that exposes the lived realities of the most disenfranchised—students—would re-frame schools in important ways. Rather than subscribe to norms that focus almost exclusively on test score outcomes, a policy researcher interested in re-framing could first recognize that students want a safe and nurturing place for exploring their identities. For example, feminist critical policy research provides a way to expose such issues as how policies can place an emphasis on academic achievement based on White middle-class cultural norms. Uncovering this hegemony helps to explain why policies often propel a segment of students to success and leave others behind. The bottom line of many accountability policies is that test scores are an effective measure of school quality. Missing from most of the dominant policy logics is an awareness of the critical need to create schools that are collaborative and nurturing communities and that are attentive to the needs of students, parents, and educators.

The remaining chapters of the book explore the traditional perspectives for framing politics and policy that seek to understand the centers of policy making. Additionally, alternative ways of framing policy that highlight the experiences of individuals and groups negotiating them on a daily basis are also examined. The intent of this book to provide an array of lenses for looking at policy, from microinteractions to the national and global levels of analysis, and to show how these levels are all interconnected. Finally, we also provide examples of the possible ways these approaches can be used to effect change.

Exercises for Critically Analyzing Policy

1. How are the theoretical and methodological approaches presented in this chapter different from the approaches outlined in Chapters 1 and 2?

2. Whose voices and needs are missing in the accountability rhetoric? Give specific examples.

3. Apply the re-framing perspectives presented in this chapter to a situation in which you might have found yourself recently. How does this re-framing allow you to see the issue differently?

4. If you were a principal in a school or a superintendent of a district, how would re-framing affect your work?

5. Choose a "hot" policy topic of importance nationally or in your state. Review print and electronic media stories for coverage of the topic, and go to relevant websites such as the state or national department of education to search for information. Analyze the policy using one of the traditional approaches outlined in Chapters 1 and 2. Then, use a theoretical perspective such as feminism or critical race theory to analyze the policy again and compare and con-

trast the two analyses. What were the unique contributions of each approach? What did each approach miss? Which did you like (dislike)? Why?

6. Identify an activist or special interest group in your state that is involved with educational issues (could be a small local PTA or community group or a group representing the often-silenced such as gay–lesbian alliances). Collect any documents the group has produced and informally interview a member of the group to learn about strategies they use for influencing educational issues. Create a list of strategies the group uses.

7. Select an educational "problem" that interests you. Then choose a methodology such as discourse analysis, narrative policy analysis, or feminist critical policy analysis to frame a possible research question. Look at the original sources that outline these approaches so that you can understand them more in depth. Then frame an analysis that highlights how the policy has misrepresented or ignored issues around social justice, such as sexism, racism, poverty, or homophobia.

Notes

1. A 1986–1987 survey showed that the education professorate, representing a variety of disciplines within teacher education, is approximately 65 percent male, while the population of teacher education students is 70 percent female (Ducharme & Agne, 1989). Most teacher education curricula treat feminist insights as too controversial, or as a set of issues that has already been managed (Hollingsworth, 1997).

2. For example, in recent years, the label "at risk" has focused attention but also has become a catch-all category allowing reemergence of deficit notions to a broad variety of people (Margonis, 1992). Such categorizing casts aside the values and goals of equity and social justice. Such categorizing funnels seemingly neutral problem definitions toward goals of transforming workers into middle-class citizens with good values and character, but away from underlying economic and institutional injustices. Such definitions provide the grounding for policies and programs with, Margonis says, the "ideological strength [of] a deficit conception with egalitarian pretensions" (1992, p. 346), as illustrated in policy deliberations of teenage pregnancy, single-parent homes, and minority achievement. The social construction, indeed the very definition of problems, occurs through the social processes of talk, interaction, and a filtering through values screens.

3. They found that a majority of educators perceived that the reform movements of the 1980s had not increased female or minority academic achievement, interest in math and science, entrance into educational administration, or retention in school. Even in reform eras, and even when abundant research points to inequities, educational leaders and policy makers find ways to make inequity a non-event.

4. The average after-tax income of the 20 percent of workers in the middle-income bracket was projected to grow by 8 percent between 1977 and 1999. The average income of the top 20 percent of households was projected to increase 43 percent in the same period according to an analysis of Congressional Budget Office data by the Center on Budget and Policy Priorities, a liberal think tank in Washington. . . . The analysis projects that the 2.7 million Americans with the largest incomes were expected to receive as much after-tax income as the 100 million Americans with the lowest incomes (Shapiro & Greenstein, 1999).

5. Feminist perspectives have to address how the mix of gender, race, and class affect patriarchy (Collins, 1990; hooks, 1984, 1989; Trinh, 1989). Women of color (Collins, 1990; hooks, 1984, 1989, 1996; Anzaldua, 1987; Villenas, 1996) and other theorists (McIntosh, 1988) have complicated the previous White, middle-class feminism. Many of these scholars reject the essentializing feminist perspectives that do not acknowledge the complex interaction between race, class, gender, sexual orientation, and other forms of "difference." Grounded in everyday reality, they can see that the sexual harassment of an African American girl from a blue-collar background may be ignored, compared with the same action perpetrated against a White girl whose father is a prominent local banker.

6. Another example could be the ahistorical and simplistic construction of the ideology of equal opportunity (Matsuda, Lawrence, Delgado, & Williams-Crenshaw, 1993) that is so prevalent in education policy but often constructed as if cultural and structural inequalities around racism could be wished away. The teachers, students, and parents working to get the students to those end-of-grade tests know that until you can show that every child has equal opportunity to all the things that help students do well in schools, it is unreasonable to hold children, teachers, schools, and districts accountable for standardized performance.

Part II

Multiple Arenas of Educational Politics

Our education system is like a three-dimensional puzzle. To put the puzzle together, one needs to view the puzzle from different angles, seeing one aspect of the puzzle at any given time. Because all of the pieces of the puzzle are interconnected in complex ways, we believe this approach can help make sense of the complexity by delving into only one piece of the puzzle at a time. In the next five chapters, we examine key facets of the puzzle, including micro (classrooms, schools, and hidden politics), district, state, federal, and international political arenas. The chapters in this section apply the methods for studying politics and policy presented in the first three chapters.

We all can identify with the presentation in Chapter 4 when it focuses on the interpersonal aspects of politics. At the micro level, we see how a nod or a scowl conveys a powerful yea or nay—whether it is in the classroom by a teacher encouraging some students' responses and denigrating others' or by a state board chairman giving "air time" to one superintendent's case and cutting off another's protest. In this arena, politics includes such personal power plays as how a senior staff member might maneuver to get first dibs on new textbooks and how three or four staff members might collude to say the same thing at a staff meeting in order to persuade the principal to take notice.

We expect to see democracy in action at the school district level. Chapter 5 explains the workings and the characters in district educational politics. In doing so, it shows why we are often disappointed in our quest for district exemplars of democratic access to policy arenas and in our expectation that district policies will ensure equal opportunity. Instead of those ideals we learned in eighth grade social studies, we see impediments to equality and democracy. We can then understand why districts' attempts, for example, to satisfy constituents that they are all being treated well and that the central office is truly responsive to their needs are persistent quandaries.

Similarly, the chapters on state and federal education politics provide a range of ways to understand and analyze what happens with elite policy players such as governors, Congress, appropriations committees, court decisions, regulatory agencies, and special interest groups. One must know that roadmap well enough to read the signposts; every educator, parent, and student is affected by state and federal education policy shifts. The ability to "read" the shifts, if not control them, provides one with some power. These chapters provide conceptual tools for that reading and for that power.

At first glance, studying the international politics of education seems like switching the U.S. roadmap for an unfamiliar global map. But Chapter 8 demonstrates that an isolationist stance cannot suffice. One learns useful alternative strategies from other countries' approaches to schooling. Also, the next time someone asks, "Why can't we just copy Japan's math programs?" or "Why don't the students in your school have the job skills they need?" your responses can be supported by comparisons with other countries' cultural values and socioeconomic conditions. Thus, educational leaders who will be policy advocates will learn, vicariously, how to ask questions about data and how to stick with and focus on what is important for schools during those times when political agendas threaten to wash over educational realities.

The chapters in Part II demonstrate in each arena the need for, and several ways to, re-frame politics.

4

Micropolitics

Uncovering "Hidden" Power

Guiding Questions _____

- What are micropolitical interactions?
- How can power be hidden or unnoticed in micropolitics?
- What are some of the lenses policy analysts use to study micropolitics?
- What do micropolitical analyses tell us about issues missing from policy discussions?
- For leaders and for researchers, what are some challenging and intriguing questions for re-visioning micropolitical analysis?

Examining politics at the micro level can conjure up images of smoke-filled rooms, secret deals, payoffs, ideologically driven decision making, and the hidden transgressions of the powerful. But it is not just about examining the seedier side of power. Micropolitical approaches can serve as a lens for examining the daily lives of the individuals most affected by education policy: people who work in and around schools. Micropolitics can be seen in seemingly mundane room assignments or in visibly thorny political tensions over a community tradition of a Christian prayer at the start of a high school football game.

The following four chapters in this book are dedicated to looking more at the very visible macro arenas of politics at district, state, federal, and international levels. Before tackling those governance arenas, this chapter explores the microinteractions of power at the site level where policy is played out in individual schools. This chapter also explores the utility of micropolitical analysis for uncovering subtle and covert power interactions in any arena of education politics.

Chapter 3 presented a model for reframing policy and politics that seeks to understand how certain groups are marginalized or work the system to gain power and support for their goals. This chapter builds on Chapter 3 by examining how micropolitics are entangled with issues of marginalization and oppression. This approach focuses on the interplay of power that is often hidden or unseen. The first section examines traditional approaches to micropolitics that explore how power is exercised via interpersonal organizational interactions at the school site (e.g., in classrooms, hallways, and offices). The following section explores emerging micropolitical perspectives that examine the personal side of power but are not restricted to school sites. This personal side of power can occur across different pieces of the policy puzzle, including state, federal, and international political arenas. These perspectives examine the political and policy implications of what happens in classrooms and seeks to connect them to broader political, social, and contextual processes occurring at the district, state, federal, and global arenas.

Defining Micropolitics

Everyone engages in micropolitics, even those who say they hate politics. Micropolitical analyses examine politics at the interpersonal level. Power in micropolitical arenas is often informal and understood, not elected, named, or appointed. Inequitable power relations relating to policy and politics are examined at an individual and/or local level. Micropolitical analyses examine political interaction in micro-arenas such as classrooms, corridors, offices, and lounges.

Micropolitics, first conceptualized by Iannaccone (1975), focuses on "the interaction and political ideologies of social systems of teachers, administrators and pupils within school buildings" (p. 43). This perspective conceives of the organizational context of schools as a discrete policy-making arena. Thus, micropolitical perspectives swing politics upside down. They invert the hierarchical paradigm by studying the nitty-gritty of politics at the school site, the political arena that is closest to educators' and children's experiences. Although the study of micropolitics has been defined in multiple ways, all variations share a common interest in examining "power, influence, and control among individuals and groups in a social context" (Willower, 1991, p. 442).

Micropolitical analyses can also move beyond solely focusing on politics within specific schools. Emerging perspectives broaden micropolitics to include how microinteractions of power relations relate to broader issues of social equity and justice. These can occur through direct conversations, through symbols, or in tacit language such as glances, smiles, sighs of disgust, and body movements. Building on the postmodern theoretical perspectives outlined in Chapter 3, these approaches focus attention on how language and symbols can be used as power tools. These microinteractions occur not only in schoolyards and faculty meetings, but also in the U.S. Senate, state legislatures, state departments of education, and interest groups.

Each year hundreds of new policies are created by elite policy makers far removed from individual school sites. By connecting macro policies with micropolitical perspectives, we can better understand the complexity and sometimes misguided and even damaging effects of large-scale policies that are created without input from individual school contexts. The following Lived Realities provides an example of how public perceptions of "educational problems" can be disconnected from the micropolitical realities inside schools.

Lived Realities: James's Story: Whose Perspective Counts?

James never would have read *Investor's Business Daily* normally, but he saw an issue of the magazine at a friend's house. One of the feature articles on the cover caught his eye: "Is America Running Out of Teachers? Data Show Shortage Is Exaggerated" (April 3, 2000, p. A24). The article implied that teacher unions were crying wolf and that President Clinton's and Secretary Riley's pronouncements about predicted shortages were off-base. It quoted the president of the National Center for Educational Information saying the shortage was only in certain subjects like science and math and in hard-to-staff inner-city schools. It said the crisis talk was a way to get higher salaries for teachers and more money for Schools of Education.

James's own experience as an African American high school teacher painted a different picture. James knew that minority teachers made up only about 5 percent of the teaching force and that minority students were expected to comprise up to 40 percent of students in the next decade. He had entered the profession so he could be a role model, and James believed minority students needed more role models to counteract the negative stereotypes they saw on TV. Now, however, he was contemplating leaving the profession. With the new state accountability program and federal pressure coming from No Child Left Behind, he was feeling increasingly disillusioned. He had selected his school because it served the poorest students in the district, but now, due to test score pressure, his school was being forced to adopt a comprehensive reform model that required proscriptive mandated lesson plans. The passion that led him to teaching was waning in the face of the imposed didactic teaching methods. More testing was not what his students needed; what they needed was hope and someone to care about them.

James felt that the new emphasis on testing made him feel more like a drill sergeant rather than a professional whose job was to foster a love of learning. He had to deal with daily bureaucratic imposition in the form of state- and federally mandated rules and regulations that seemed disconnected from his students' struggles. The structure of the school day meant that he had little opportunity to collaborate with his colleagues. He often felt isolated and alone in his classroom. Why did business reporting seem to devalue his work, and why was all the focus on salary? Why did the media seem to represent teachers in such a negative light? Sure, he'd like better pay, but he also wanted better working conditions and to be respected for the job he did. He also wanted more minority teachers.

In this story, teacher shortage discussions are relegated to debates over salary, while other issues, such as the dearth of minority teachers, teacher professionalism, and the dehumanizing aspects of school bureaucracies, are largely ignored. The policy disconnect between James's experience and national and state policy debates over teacher shortages shows how micropolitical realities can often get lost in policy discussions. In this case, James's reality is shaped by societal racism perpetuated in the media, dehumanizing bureaucratic structures, and embedded cultural assumptions that value test scores over developing a nurturing community. James's passionate desire to serve as a role model to counter racist assumptions and to help kids and their communities is a story that is missing from policy discourses. Oftentimes this type of disconnect remains hidden in policy studies, due to a lack of critical questioning around how policies can be embedded with racism, perpetuate the dehumanizing aspects of bureaucracy, and privilege individual achievement over community or democratic goals.

What makes micropolitical inquiry distinct is that hidden interplays of power and control serve as the starting point for these analyses. This chapter examines two distinct micropolitical orientations to examining politics and policy: (1) traditional approaches to micropolitics, which focus on a specific organizational *site* such as a classroom, school, policy-making board, or committee; and (2) two emerging perspectives, discourse analysis and sociocultural perspectives, which examine hidden interpersonal *interactions* involving power struggles that may cross policy arenas. The former refers to politics at the micro site level, such as approaches that examine power struggles over resources and curriculum as they play out in individual classrooms and schools. The latter two, which are discussed in the second half of the chapter, examine the multiple ways "hidden power" is exercised among individuals inside or outside of schools and offers a way of connecting macro and micro policy arenas.

What these approaches share is an interest in uncovering how power is exercised in specific political contexts. Micropolitical perspectives emerged out of the recognition that political analyses tended to focus on the elite and the powerful. Scholars acknowledged a need to understand the politics embedded in individual schools. In the following sections, we examine both of these approaches individually, but an analysis could actually encompass both perspectives.

The Dynamics of Site Micropolitics

Site micropolitics examine power dynamics and interpersonal interactions within individual schools and district governance structures (Bacharach & Mundell, 1993; Hoyle, 1999). This focus delimits policy analysis to a specific organizational context. This focus also brings additional attention on how school contexts and external policies interact. Noblit, Berry, and Dempsey (1991), for example, compared how teachers in two schools responded differently to district pressure for policies designed to increase teacher professionalism. Their study examines how school culture and context can affect the way in which policies can be interpreted differently in individual schools.

Micropolitical analyses generally examine schools as discrete political organizations. Because schools are viewed as organizations, these analyses utilize organizational theory, or perspectives, that conceptualize the structure, function, and features of organizations. Organizational approaches ask such questions as, "How are interactions structured?", "Who makes governance decisions?", "How are conflicts resolved?", "How is policy translated into practice?", and "How do power differentials affect interpersonal relationships?" What makes micropolitical approaches distinct is that issues of power and control are central to understanding the organizational life of a school. Organizational theory provides lenses to conceptualize schools as bureaucratic organizations. Implicit in many of these approaches is the assumption that bureaucracy imposes power structures that dominate school organizations. This lens comes from the work of Max Weber (1947), who first conceived of bureaucratic organizations as institutions where rule and regulations are designed to limit individual decision making and support hierarchical relations, increasing efficiency and standardized productivity. Subsequent political analyses (e.g., Ferguson, 1984) highlight power structures and elaborates on how bureaucracies channeled power through hierarchical lines of communication, opportunity structures, structured isolation, and inflexibility.

Micropolitical studies that look organizationally seek to show how interpersonal relationships are structured in terms of rules, norms, lines of communication, and decision-making structures. School organizations are replete with power structures that serve to control work and determine policy (Ball, 1987). Thus, a broader definition of organizations encompasses "the varied perceptions by individuals of what they can, should, or must do in dealing with others within the circumstances in which they find themselves" (Ball, 1987, p. 3).

Looking micropolitically, one can see that the unfortunate dysfunctions of bureaucracy are evident in the structure of the school day, in which many teachers work in isolation from one another with very little time for building relationships, co-teaching, planning, collaboration, nurturing individual students, professional community building, or participation in decision making.

Devolution and the Micropolitics of Inverted Bureaucracy

Decades of practice, reflection, and research have shown that educators and citizens are more likely to care about and help school improvement if they feel that it has been constructed to fit their specific local needs. Such an approach would be more democratic and community oriented (Mertz & Furman, 1997). Site-based management is the key policy strategy that policy makers utilize to address bureaucratic inflexibility. As a policy strategy it devolves some decision-making power to school sites, often with citizens' participation in site councils for setting site priorities. Such devolution may be mandated from the state or be a local option, with varying names and specifications, but when it happens it can bring huge shifts in district roles (Malen, Ogawa, & Krantz, 1990).

If site administrators make site-specific decisions and site councils set priorities for goals and budget, then what purpose does the district administration serve? Which leaders, district or site, have the responsibility to ensure that federal, state, and court mandates are adhered to? Is it not inefficient for each site to be creating its own personnel and staff development processes? Is it fair to hold sites accountable for results when, in fact, they have little discretion and flexibility, and power over agendas and budget really reside elsewhere? How can you expect administrators who are trained to manage by "running a tight ship" to now let go of hierarchical control, especially when they have no new training or incentives or alterations in their professional culture enabling them to think and act differently?

Research on devolution reveals gaps between the theory and reality:

1. The site councils tend to be parents who defer to professionals and traditionally support the status quo (Malen & Ogawa, 1988; Mertz & Furman, 1997).

2. Site-based management results in instability in relationships between school boards and principals, as each has different definitions and norms regarding roles (Opfer & Denmark, 2002).

3. Site-based management can create confusion over who is in charge and leave principals with responsibilities for personnel and special education, for which they are underprepared (Guerra et al., 1992; McLaughlin, Henderson, & Rhim, 1997; Marshall & Patterson, 2002).

When site-based efforts aim at reform, they are not a guarantee of improved learning opportunities for children. As Shields and Knapp (1997) note,

> The schools with the most promising reform efforts are those that set attainable reform goals with long time lines for accomplishing them; focus explicitly on particular aspects of the curriculum and instructional practice while refraining from making school governance the main preoccupation of the reform effort; and encourage collaborative engagement of staff members with one another and use professional development resources to further this end. (p. 294)

In other words, if the change to site-based is used to concentrate and collaborate on specific instructional goals, one might expect improved learning. But if the change is side-tracked by lots of attention to the politics—who wins and who's in charge of site governance—learning opportunities will probably be untouched.

The Utility of Site Micropolitical Analyses.   So, what does happen politically with the shift to site-based management? In case studies of sites, Noblit, Berry, and Dempsey (1991) found that the power shift can be used to advance preexisting political coalitions' agendas because it creates a temporary power vacuum. Further, by looking at the micropolitics of one district, Marshall and Patterson (2002) discovered how federal and local policies can be at odds with each other. Specifically, they examined how the development of new site-based management governance structures left many special educators, special education students, and their parents without clear guidelines about who was in charge of ensuring that the students were adequately served. The new organizational structure had the effect of denying many special education students and their advocates an outlet for expressing concern that they were not being served adequately under federal guidelines. So while the researchers examined individual school sites, they also sought to understand how struggles over power were played out among conflicting policies from federal and local policy arenas.

In New Jersey, thirty "Abbott districts" (populated primarily by poor, Black, and Hispanic students and under state Supreme Court scrutiny to provide a thorough and efficient education for its students) engaged in a site-based management reform strategy (Walker, 2002). Research, conducted by Walker (2002), explored political questions about devolution, asking whether it enables grassroots efforts to function in collaboration with school-based leadership, "to replace the dominance enjoyed by educational bureaucratic elites in local school governance matters" (Walker, 2002, p. 3). However, 43 percent of the site teams had at least half of their membership drawn from the teaching staff, and most teams lacked student representation. Parents and community groups accounted for only about 29 percent of the membership, limiting opportunity for the input from parents and community groups. Training, capacity, and knowledge in areas of responsibility affect participation. In the Abbott districts, however, state centralization was another complicating governance shift. New Jersey's School Review and Improvement (SRI) teams' oversight of all reform contradicted the assumption that site-based management freed sites from onerous rules and regulations. So the state giveth and the state taketh away power, flexibility, and autonomy. Further, issues of principals' role in successful devolution and issues of competing power and authority in areas of curriculum and school operations unmask major policy contradictions. Walker asserts that state elites and other interest groups may push for decentralization in order to protect their self-interests rather than well-intentioned democratic ideals. Then educators, parents, and community groups are responsible for implementing poor, contradictory practices, keeping them busy with new layers of work, which then fail, thus reinforcing "calls by economic elites for market-based solutions to the problem of urban education" (Walker, 2002, p. 20).

Micropolitical studies that focus on site micropolitics can highlight how power can limit and structure change in individual schools. They are limited, though, in highlighting how the individuals and groups working in and around schools exercise their own power.

Re-framing Micropolitical Perspectives

Micropolitical perspectives have tended to examine the implications of power and politics in organizational structures and arrangements in sites (Ball, 1987; Mawhinney, 1999). Although these perspectives are useful for understanding the dynamics of power relations at the site level, they tend to overemphasize cultural reproduction through structures of domination or hegemony. This underemphasizes individual and collective agency within those structures. In this section, we explore alternative micropolitical perspectives that can be used to re-frame micropolitics by highlighting human agency. As structures, the bureaucracies discussed in the preceding section are often imbued with assumptions that can discriminate against anyone who deviates from certain norms by virtue of their gender, sexual orientation, race, cultural capital, socioeconomic background, and/or religion. In *The Color of Bureaucracy,* Larson and Ovando (2000) suggest that educational bureaucracies serve to structure social, racial, and political problems. These perspectives indicate that the organizational structure of schools can serve to reinforce discrimination and oppression through seemingly rational and benign policies and structures.

For example, Scheurich and Imber (1991) examined one school district's community participation in defining the issues for its school reform agenda, especially focusing on school boundaries, busing, and closing or consolidating schools. The authors demonstrate that the district, embracing a cultural pluralist model, made seemingly well intentioned efforts at getting all segments of the community on committees. However, decisions were still made without Black participation and favored affluent Whites. The study concluded that "the recommendations of constituency committees can be ignored if they do not coincide with administrative or power-elite desires, thus the community is not participating, it is being manipulated" (Scheurich & Imber, 1991, p. 317). This lays bare the ways in which a district can assert participatory decision making and then "blame the victim"; when disenfranchisement is subtle and marginalized, groups (in this case, the African American community) just drop out.

Further, minorities and poverty-stricken students are often blamed for their own failure because they fail to accept the norms and expectations of an educational system that reflects wider societal norms. Girls are blamed for getting pregnant even as school policies and national politics ignore their needs. Studies that place micropolitics with larger social and political contexts go beyond the school walls to examine how outside struggles over power can affect individual schools. Studies on the cultural production of success in classrooms, for example, have examined the way that African American, Latino/a, and Native American students often feel pressure to "act White" in order to fit in and succeed in school (Fordham, 1993; Fordham & Ogbu, 1986). For many of these students, succeeding in school symbolizes a rejection of their home culture in favor of dominant cultural assumptions. Failure becomes a way for students to rebel against oppressive structures that require assimilation in order for them to succeed. But micropolitical approaches highlight the human agency of individual human actors. Thus, students, teachers, or leaders are no longer viewed as mindless actors trapped in inequitable educational structures. Instead they are viewed as agents who use micropolitical moves to resist oppressive structures by refusing to assimilate into dominant cultural norms.

As mentioned in Chapter 3, these studies of cultural production seek to highlight human agency and connect structural understandings of inequities with individual experience. Two promising areas of emerging micropolitical inquiry that seek to identify agency and support social justice are discourse analysis and sociocultural policy analysis. Discourse at the micropolitical level can be used to reify and redefine power relationships. Discourse analysis can be used show the arrangements of power relationships. Therefore such analyses can be used to reframe microinteractions and policies. For example, Fine (1991) re-framed the politics of dropouts by examining how the issue of dropouts is framed as a social problem. Her work suggests that socioeconomics are the central feature of why students "drop out," yet much public understanding of the issue blames students for being unwilling or incapable of staying in school.

Sociocultural analyses seek to connect the politics of the site-level context with larger social and cultural structures. Sociocultural analyses that focus on the practice of policy "give voice." They examine policy as a process embedded in historical, comparative, and localized contexts. The work of Murtadha-Watts (2001) provides one example of how micropolitical analyses can be used to highlight human agency. In this case, Murtadha-Watts (2001) examined how two African American women leaders in the Indianapolis school district were able to work the district political system to support a multicultural curriculum that valued the experiences of minority students. Both discourse analysis and sociocultural analysis are useful for asking questions raised by the theories and methodologies presented in Chapter 3. Each of these approaches policy by examining how individuals are affected by hierarchically driven policy by studying those individuals that bare the brunt of policy. They place school politics within a wider social and cultural context while also honing in on microinteractions such as language and symbols. Thus, both of these perspectives suggest that micropolitics at the site are not site-confined but intertwined with larger societal power and political arrangements.

Agency and Structure: The Personal Side of Power

Micropolitical analyses offer a way to examine the personal side of power by highlighting individual and collective human agency and how it plays out with particular social and cultural structures. Evidence of the power of human agency abounds in the success stories of political social movements that have struggled against policies that disadvantaged certain groups. This struggle for equity comes down to how individual identities are viewed in comparison with prevailing norms:

> Somewhere on the edge of consciousness, there is what I call the *mythical norm.* . . . In America, this norm is usually defined as *white, thin, male, young, heterosexual, Christian, and financially secure.* It is with this mythical norm that the trappings of power reside within this society.[1] (Lorde, 2001, p. 316)

On an interpersonal level, individual and collective identities form the basis for understanding how micropolitical power is exercised. In specific social and cultural contexts, how individual identities are shaped in relation to mythical norms can determine whether individuals feel discriminated against or disadvantaged. Thus, it is critical to acknowledge how individual and collective identities can shape and be shaped by micropolitics.

Discourse and sociocultural analyses promote both social and cultural critique. These center and focus awareness that power operates in micropolitics in ways that serve to privilege certain identities over others. Thus, discrimination is the exercise of power reinforcing privilege. Forms of discrimination, such as racism, classism, hetrosexism, sexism, and abelism, can be manifest in a multitude of ways within schools: individually, institutionally, structurally, and culturally (Pincus, 2000).

A single individual can discriminate against another. If, for example, a student utters a racial slur against another student, it is the individual and not the institution that is discriminating. Institutional and structural forms of discrimination are a bit more complicated to explicate. Institutional discrimination refers to policies created in an organization that are intended to have a harmful effect on minority race/ethnic/gender groups. An example of this is the "separate but equal" policy that served to justify the need for segregated schools. Many district leaders were well aware that the resources given to schools for African Americans were inequitable, despite attestations to the contrary.

Structural forms of discrimination are a bit more difficult to uncover. These forms of discrimination are often not intentionally discriminatory but are just as effective. For example, in many states and districts schools are financed equitably with money given to schools based on the enrollment of students. Although this policy seems fair, it does not take into account how some school districts are populated with wealthier parents who can pour additional resources into their children and their schools. It also does not take into account how some schools considered "better" for socioeconomic reasons may also be the same schools where the teachers are more experienced, are more educated, and thus receive higher salaries. Thus, complex understandings of the politics of identity serve as a backdrop for discourse and sociocultural analyses and can help render these often invisible relations visible.

The notion of identity politics emerged out of the Civil Rights Movement and the Women's Movement. These perspectives build on social capital theory and cultural production theory articulated in Chapter 3 in that they examine how individual and collective identities are shaped. Thus, identity politics uncover powerful forces that shape discrimination and inequity. Identity politics refers to members of oppressed groups who "organize to change their situation, as well as their feelings of self and place in the social structure" (Ryan, 2001, p. I).

Identity politics strategies can create further marginalization as groups focus on how they are different. They can often prevent groups from working together, even though they might share similar goals across characteristics such as gender, race, ethnicity, or sexual orientation. Identity politics, when tightly oriented around visible differences can limit the possibility of building alliances and coalitions across differences (Gitlin, 1995). Still, identity politics approaches have successfully highlighted how cultural assumptions embedded in educational curricula and structures have marginalized certain groups.

Identity politics serves as a way to unite marginalized groups around specific issues of oppression and, in the process, is one way to forge advocacy coalitions as mentioned in Chapter 1. Specifically, three prominent identity politics issues have had a significant impact on public education: the women's movement, which pushed for Title IX and equality for girls in schools; the Civil Rights Movement, which led to *Brown v. The Board of Education;* and Native American activism, which fought to reclaim Native American linguistic and cultural heritage and administration of tribal schools.

Reclaiming Indigenous Culture and Identity.   Native Americans and other indigenous groups (such as Native Alaskans and Hawaiians) have rallied together to force the federal government to relinquish control of the administration and curriculum of tribal schools. These groups seek to highlight the historical genocidal treatment of Native Americans and how schooling has sought to destroy their cultural heritage (Pewewardy, 1998).

In the nineteenth century, the federal government perpetuated an assimilationist policy toward Native American children, under the dominant assumptions that Native American cultural values and languages were inferior. The government took children away from their families and sent them to boarding schools, decimating many Native American cultural traditions and languages. Students were not allowed to speak in their native languages and had to renounce their cultural heritage, which was believed to be emblematic of their savagery. Not until the 1960s and 1970s did the federal government pass laws (the Indian Education Act of 1972, the Self-Determination and Education Assistance Act of 1975, and Title XI of the Education Amendments Act of 1978) that supported Indian self-determination (Pewewardy, 1998). Simplistic analyses of curriculum and school structures often ignore powerful messages about values and culture, but micropolitical analyses can show how these "areas of silence and non-events" (Anderson, 1990) can actually devalue a student's cultural heritage.

Strategies, such as reclaiming cultural heritage and identity within formal school structures, require attention to micropolitical features such as the curriculum. For example, the history books that for decades ignored the history of Native American mistreatment can be replaced by those that include information about Native American cultural heritage as well information about past inequities and oppression. Native Americans have benefited from participating in advocacy coalitions designed to promote their heritage and culture in schools (Pewewardy, 1994, 1998).

Critical Pedagogy and Resistance.   Indigenous groups and other minority groups, such as Latino/a, Chicano/a, and African Americans, pressure for critical pedagogy, the purpose of which is to support human agency—the sense that individuals can find the power within themselves and resist oppression (Zou & Trueba, 1998). Critical pedagogy evolved out of the work of Paulo Freire (1993), who suggested that for oppressed groups to overcome oppressive structures, they "must first critically recognize its causes, so that through transformative action they can create a new situation, one which makes possible the pursuit of a fuller humanity" (Freire, 1993, p. 29). Thus, Freire's work suggests that for social change to occur, members of oppressed groups need to understand their oppression so that they can be their own advocates for social change. Micropolitical analyses are effective at advancing this type of understanding when they highlight both how oppression plays out in schools and communities and how groups and individuals seek to change their situations.

Picking up on Freire's (1993) work, Ladson-Billings (1994) suggests that awareness of the politics of identity needs to be woven together with critical pedagogy in order to transform the education of minority children in schools. Her assertion is based on her work with effective teachers of African American children. Ladson-Billings found that effective teachers utilized culturally relevant pedagogy and placed a value on African American culture and thus the students' cultural heritage. Her work has been adopted to work with children from other oppressed groups, such as indigenous and immigrant children. For example, schools that serve Native American children have developed a "culturally responsive pedagogy" that celebrates Native American culture and language as a way to reach struggling children (Pewewardy, 1994). Thus, identity politics inspires ways for school teachers and staff to work together to build advocacy coalitions that focus on educational processes as a way to give voice to children.

The Utility of Analyses of Discourse and Sociocultural Forces.   Looking critically at policy language and examining specific words and practices can reveal oppressive and marginalizing forces at work. Recall, for example, the contrast between the passion inspiring James in the earlier vignette and the accountability policy realities he faces. At the micropolitical level, policy discourse that dehumanizes can be juxtaposed against the human and personal experiences of individuals who must respond to seemingly uncaring policies.

Similarly, sociocultural analysis critically analyzes policy language but does so in a slightly different way. A sociocultural analysis studies individuals within their particular context, such as a specific school or district. This approach situates our understanding of schools as embedded within a larger social and cultural context. This approach seeks to understand how individual cultural groups or communities respond to and are affected by policy. For example, Quiroz (2001) examined how one group of bilingual and middle school educators worked together to address the situated needs of their students within a school context constrained by inflexible district, state, and national accountability requirements. Recognizing the inequities faced by many English language learners, the teachers Quiroz

(2001) studied worked to help their students develop their identities as members of specific ethnic groups while simultaneously reconciling the need for students also to develop their identities as problem solvers and science learners. While the push for science standards focuses on content exclusively, the teachers Quiroz (2001) studied recognized that the content would not be achieved without attention to the students' individual needs and ethnic identities. Thus, Quiroz (2001) highlights how the lived realities of students and teachers can be at odds with policies that ignore individual student needs.

The Politics of Language, Symbols, and Discourse.   Words are not neutral and can be used to shape issues in such a way that garners support or opposition. A focus on discourse can show how policy language can reinforce inequities and create political conflict via how language is used to define educational "problems" (e.g., labeling such as "at risk," which suggests that these students are deficient in some way) and can limit the possibility for social justice. Language is a potential instrument of control. Gronn (1983) showed how words can be used to cloak power. A focus on discourse can show how issues may be presented as "facts," implying that there is no subjectivity in the interpretation. This can lend legitimacy to an issue, just as implying that a perspective is personal and thus subjective can imply that the issue is trivial.

Micropolitcal analyses that utilize discourse analysis can uncover power relations within language and interpersonal interactions. Corson (1995), for example, studied the micropolitics of discourse interactions of a governing board of a high school in New Zealand. In his study, he examined how discursive interactions shifted depending on how issues were presented and whether members of the Board personally supported the issue. Corson (1995) found that when issues have stakeholders who serve on the Board, the discursive interactions are more supportive. In the excerpt in Figure 4.1, Corson (1995) examines how discourse can be distorted and prejudicial. Figure 4.1 provides an overview of the discursive interactions of the Board as they discuss the proposal of a fundamentalist Christian sect wishing to use the school grounds for meetings on weekends.

The Board discussion in Figure 4.1 is structured in such a way that support of the sect's proposal is not possible. This is particularly apparent under point 16, when the secretary discusses her deflection of the groups' attempt to present their case before the board. By belittling the groups' rights, she effectively closes down the possibility that there might be a compromise decision that would allow the group to use the facilities. In particular, Corson (1995) found that issues can be distorted and left unsupported when "the interests of those with some stake in the matter under discussion are not represented among the participants in the discourse" (p. 99). This finding has potential implications for democratic governance. Without support of the Board, discursive interaction can distort and prejudice underrepresented groups' needs and intentions.

Sociocultural Analyses.   Sociocultural analyses merge sociological theory with qualitative research methods and conceptualize policy as a complex social practice (Levinson & Sutton, 2001). This approach developed out of cultural production theory, which was discussed in Chapter 3. It suggests that diverse groups come together in social and institutional

1. The Secretary of the Board steps out of her official role of objectivity to use an ambiguity in the text of the sect's letter to play for a laugh at their expense (232). She signals that she is not disinterested in this matter. She solicits comments on the ambiguity by putting a raised intonation on her words kitchen and hall (232 & 234) and by deliberately pausing in her reading (234).
2. On cue, several participants deliver laughter and ironic comments (235).
3. The Principal reinforces these with an audible aside (236).
4. The Chair adds a frivolous interjection (242).
5. Several participants reinforce the Chair's expression of mild contempt (243).
6. Pam adds an ironic exclamation (246) perhaps renderable as "I am impressed."
7. The Secretary inserts an extremely hostile aside into her reading of the letter, adding the absent caretakers's view to her own in a new layer of opposition (249–251).
8. With the groundwork for the ideology laid, the Principal introduces it and solicits corroboration with a raised intonation (256).
9. The Secretary responds, providing the first in a choir of enthusiastic statements creating and supporting the ideology (257).
10. Overlapping or continuous contributions reinforce the distortion until it becomes a forecast of school chaos, complete with alarm bells ringing (258–264).
11. With her chuckle, Shastra (Elected Teacher Representative) signals that she for once is aware of the cynical game that the Board is playing, but contributes to it nonetheless (265).
12. The Secretary interrupts Shastra, highlighting the number of alarms (267) and getting the response from the Board that she expects (268–269).
13. The Principal brings the discussion back to the point, but gives the Secretary grounds for another interruption (272–273).
14. The Secretary interrupts with a very hostile choice of words (274–275).
15. The three administrators suggest some genuinely undesirable consequences of agreeing to the request (277–300). Again, they back one another in overlapping contributions (290–292).
16. The Secretary makes a ironic characterization of her own actions, "flobbing off" the sect when they had asked to plead their case in person (304–305). (Note that this act is very prejudicial to discursive fairness because it occurs soon after the only moment in the debate in which some form of compromise action is foreshadowed [287–289], and it preempts other members from suggesting that the sect be allowed to vary their request or to state their point of view more fully.)
17. By now the request is tacitly defeated and the Chair offers a humorous allusion to a problem that has affected other Boards . . . in the country, when they have been "captured" by sectional interests (306).
18. A motion to decline the request becomes a formality. Rangi [elected parent representative] moves it *sotto voce,* and Fred hurriedly seconds it (318–319).
19. The chair gives a mild display of intolerant impatience in hurrying through the motion (321–322).

Source: From D. Corson. *Discourse and Power in Educational Organizations,* pp. 97–98. Copyright 1995 by Hampton Press, Inc. Used with permission.

FIGURE 4.1 *Discourse Interaction Excerpt from Corson (1995, pp. 97–98)*

contexts. These studies share an interest in examining "policy as a practice of power" (Levinson & Sutton, 2001, p. 1) and in questioning how issues of power influence ways in which policies are interpreted and put into practice. Issues such as racism and sexual discrimination are wider social issues that can be played out in individual schools. The implementation and interpretation of federal and state policies can be produced and reproduced within individual classrooms.

This perspective implies that policies have no meaning in and of themselves; rather they can be interpreted only within a given historical moment and social context. Thus, local and state policies as interpreted by one school may be vastly different, depending on the social context in which the school is situated (Levinson & Sutton, 2001). In addition, schools are also no longer the sole focus. Other organizations or community structures are also seen as sites where education takes place. Exploring how some inner city youth were successful despite living in communities struggling with gangs, drugs, poverty, and crime, Heath and McLaughlin (1993) focused on effective youth community organizations that helped struggling youth develop positive youth identities. In identifying disconnects between policy maker assumptions about youth and the reality of youths' experiences, they were conducting sociocultural analysis. Some of their findings included how youth saw their ethnic identities as secondary (assigned to them by people from the outside); instead, what was important to them was "achieving a sense of belonging and knowing that they could *do* something and *be* someone in the eyes of others had to come first" (Heath & McLaughlin, 1993, p. 6). Additionally, they found that gendered assumptions often caused policy makers to target boys as needing policy intervention, assuming that girls did not need the same support. This misconception contrasted starkly with the reality of the girls they studied who were struggling with similar issues.

Ultimately, McLaughlin and Heath (1993) suggest that studying effective youth organizations allowed them to understand that for organizations (such as schools) to be effective with struggling youth living in poverty, they needed to "share a conception of youth as a resource to be developed rather than a problem to be managed" (p. 217). Sociocultural policy studies provide a way of situating policy within a particular local context while connecting it to wider social contexts and issues and connecting human agency to wider issues of social inequities.

Micropolitical Themes

As we've discussed in the previous sections, there are at least three discrete micropolitical lenses that can be used to examine hidden interplays of power: organizational analyses, discourse analyses of both language and symbols, and sociocultural analyses. Table 4.1 provides an overview of these three perspectives.

Several orienting themes that cross these perspectives provide lenses for understanding the dynamics of micropolitics (Blasé & Anderson, 1995; Hoyle, 1999; Marshall & Scribner, 1991; Mawhinney, 1999). These themes (adapted and modified from Marshall & Scribner, 1991) examine ideologies and values, boundaries and turf battles, the maintenance of bureaucratic myths, problem definition as a study of power, advocacy coalitions and interest groups, and street-level bureaucrats.

TABLE 4.1 *Lenses for Micropolitical Analyses*

Micropolitical Lenses	Purpose
Organizational Analyses (site focused)	Utilize organizational theory as a way of conceptualizing and assessing power dynamics in school sites. Generally these studies seek to understand the structure of an organization—how individuals communicate and make decisions and evince leadership. Implicit in many of these approaches is awareness that bureaucratic structures dominate school organizations (i.e., rules and regulations are designed to support hierarchical relations and reinforce isolation).
Language, Symbols, and Discourse Analyses (interaction focused)	Focus on how power relationships can be hidden in seemingly normative language. This approach particularly examines how discourse and discourse processes can be used to support oppressive claims about states of affairs in the world, about appropriate and legitimate social relationships, about personal and social identities, and about how issues should be framed.
Sociocultural Analyses (both site and interaction focused)	Examine policy within ethnographic research that places it within a sociological and cultural context. This approach utilizes qualitative inquiry as a method for capturing policy practice. The term *practice* is used to describe how individuals and groups engage in situated contexts that both foster and limit individual agency.

Ideologies and Values

Stakeholders in school sites are individuals or social groups with conflicting values and political ideologies (Iannaconne, 1975). Interactions between students, parents, teachers, staff, and administrators create constant unresolved conflicts. Biases stemming from values or ideologies within an organization are often assumed, and thus taken for granted and left unstated. Yet many conflicts within an organizational context often result from the clash among goals and values (as outlined in Chapter 1, the conflicts among equity, choice, efficiency, and quality values). For example, parents' valuing of choice for their children and principals' valuing of efficiency in programming will often come into conflict in sites. Most organizational interactions tend to dismiss, evade, and avoid these conflicts in order to preserve the integrity of the organization. However, sometimes these conflicts serve as a way to mobilize bias to support a particular issue. For example, teachers and administrators might desire authority (based on their expertise) in regard to discipline or curricular issues, while parents and students might demand alternative choices and question educator authority over education. Later chapters examine how these value and ideological conflicts play out in micropolitical interactions at the state and federal levels.

Boundaries and Turf Battles

Turf battles may develop between groups who feel that their rights and responsibilities are being limited or infringed on by other groups (Hanson, 1979). They erupt over who's in charge, what areas and issues are controlled by whom, and even over who manages a storage closet or a group of students. Teachers and administrators may battle over schedules or teaching methods, while administrators and teachers may battle with students over appropriate behavior and dress codes. These battles also may develop in response to imposed rules and regulations by organizations and authorities outside of schools, such as mandated testing policies, which teachers may perceive an infringing on their authority to determine the educational needs of their students. But as we discuss in later chapters, these battles can also occur in micropolitical interactions at school board meetings, in state legislatures, and between the president and Congress.

Maintenance of Bureaucratic Myths

Individuals within schools or those making policy may subscribe to and assert bureaucratic myths. They may insist and accept that tasks and decisions need to be standardized and rule-driven. In doing so, they deny that political maneuvering also may be at work. Additionally, bureaucratic myths that things are functioning smoothly are fiercely maintained. Conflicts and mistakes are kept secret, confined within a particular school or segment of a school. Unspoken rules suggest that these conflicts need to remain private and away from public scrutiny.

Stakeholders within a school buy into a belief that these bureaucratic processes and rules are necessary to ensure order in a school. Control over students and teachers, which requires passive acquiescence to rules and authority, then come to be seen as required to ensure compliance and effective management. Teachers who have quiet students and orderly classrooms come to be seen as complying with norms. Teachers who promote active questioning and collaborative learning may be seen as out of control and ineffective. Raising questions and mentioning mistakes and stupidities can be seen as disloyalty to your site. Interpersonal conflict is seen as something that needs to controlled and managed (Opatow, 1991). Order and discipline are seen as normative rather than as a method of exerting power and control over students and teachers.

Problem Definition as a Study of Power

Language, symbols, and interactions can be used to convey messages about problem definition, defining what is "real" within a given organizational context. The individuals with power in a school site can define what key problems are and whether they need attention. This can serve to create a narrow definition of what constitutes legitimate issues for discussion. Individuals without power may find their issues dismissed as illogical, irrational, and unimportant (Marshall & Scribner, 1991). Problems that are not deemed legitimate are ignored. They become non-events, areas of silence. For example, schools and districts without sexual harassment policies ignore the possibility of harassment and leave little room for discussion of these issues (Laible, 1997). Thus, how schools and districts define problems can influence whether societal inequities such as racism or homophobia negatively affect student learning and opportunities for success (see, e.g., Larson, 1997, and MacGillivray, 2000).

Advocacy Coalitions and Interest Groups

As mentioned in Chapter 1, coalitions can form around a particular issue or topic. These groups use their agency to challenge policies. They may work outside of formal structures and accepted political arenas. For example, conservative groups have developed highly successful local campaigns to advocate for particular components of curriculum, such as ethical teaching in the form of programs on values clarification, or have removed other components, such as specific literature that they deem immoral or science curriculums that examine evolution (Baez & Opfer, 2000; Lugg, 1998). These groups can launch quiet campaigns to elicit support for their issues, which can involve into going door to door, writing letters, or calling up superintendents, principals, or school board members in order to rally support for or against policies. For example, African American community groups have rallied against local actions and policies deemed racist by protesting and using the media to bring previously pushed-under-the-rug "silent" issues into the open (Larson, 1997).

Strategies and political action can come from groups outside traditional policy-making arenas, which can either support or work against certain policies. Studies that explore the micropolitics of coalition building highlight human agency and seek to understand how policy change occurs.

Street-Level Bureaucrats

As mentioned in Chapter 2, the notion of street-level bureaucrats highlights how individuals can subvert and resist policies they deem do not fit with the needs of their local context (Weatherly & Lipsky, 1977). Individuals at the site level bear responsibility for interpreting policy and may or may not choose to implement a policy in the way that it was originally intended. Many policies may not fit the needs of the individuals or the community the policies serve. For example, some educators in California, working in schools in which the majority of students do not speak English, resisted the English-only mandates of Proposition 227 (Torrez, 2001). This perspective highlights how individuals resist, recreate, or ignore policies when they don't fit the needs of the students they serve.

Each of these themes represents aspects of micropolitical analyses that examine interpersonal interactions. They can be used to understand the complexity of local politics as they relate to larger policy issues. In the next section, we examine three emerging research perspectives—discourse analysis, critical ethnography, and narrative inquiry—that can be used to highlight human agency.

Uncovering Agency in Micropolitics

Understanding inequities and inequitable power relationships can leave one with an overwhelming feeling of depression. Given that there are a multitude of communities, schools, and children who face racism or poverty, who have lost hope, how does one maintain a sense of possibility? As mentioned in Chapter 3, approaching politics and conducting research to highlight human agency provides a way to uncover the subtle and no-so-subtle ways that individuals and groups resist inequities (Scott, 1990). In this section, we examine how discourse analysis, critical ethnography, and narrative inquiry can capture the subtleties of human interactions and provide a way of uncovering areas of "silence," as well as highlight alternative perspectives and experiences. Beyond research, school leaders and policy analysts can modify these approaches to seek new visions for framing their work with teachers, parents, and the various communities and for uncovering and undoing structures and programs that perpetuate oppression and dysfunctional power plays.

For school leaders wanting to empower and unleash agency, the traditional educational administration textbooks on public relations, personnel management, and organization theory will not suffice. Micropolitical lenses offer approaches to analyzing patterns and practices in and around their schools that get them closer to lived realities. For leaders and researchers who want to engage in micropolitical inquiry, naturalistic methods are needed that are more flexible and exploratory. While statistical approaches are effective at quantifying and determining causality (x causes y) or the effectiveness of programs or approaches (in terms of increased test scores), they are limited in uncovering how power may be hidden (recall the hidden power dynamics in the talk displayed in Figure 4.1).

Statistical measures can be used to identify problems once the problems have done their damage. They provide numerical data such as poor test scores, the outcomes produced by problems, or teacher credentials and other such inputs that may be problematic. These types of analyses, however, involve highly structured research designs that need to build on existing data. When previous study designs were structured on traditional social norms, new studies repeated and reified those limitations. They offered no possibility of exploring hidden or tacit issues. The powerful and often subtle micropolitics that undermine marginalized voices, the discourses that maintain areas of silence, and the identity politics and resistance strategies have to be uncovered with frameworks and themes from micropolitics. One must explore, searching for stories and researching with methodologies allowing for emergent data, because little may be known about a given topic. Many different qualitative methods can better expose submerged policy issues. Due to space limitations, we will only explore three methods in particular: discourse analysis, ethnography, and narrative inquiry. Each of these naturalistic methodologies provides researchers with a way to ground theory in the day-to-day experiences of individuals who are marginalized in most policy discourses. Further, these methodologies can be employed by educational leaders and policy analysts who are searching for insights about connecting these day-to-day experiences into more appropriate policies and practices.

Qualitative approaches are particularly promising because they can be used to study individuals, groups, and organizations that are traditionally excluded from the policy process. Much of the emerging research methods in this field are centered on naming issues, exposing areas of silence, theorizing structures of inequities, focusing on ethics and the purpose and process of education, and problematizing the very structure, language, and assumptions that undergird policy research (Bloom, 1998; Gitlin, 1994; Lather, 1991).

Discourse Analyses

As discussed in Chapter 3, political negotiations over power, resources, and values occur in microinteractions and talk as much as they do in formal policy arenas. Policy discourse analysis focuses on the "dimensions in which we act communicatively: those of making and testing claims about states of affairs in the world, about appropriate and legitimate social relationships, about personal and social identities, and about ways of framing issues at hand" (Forester, 1993, p. 12; see also Placier, 1996, and Taylor, 1997). Policy analysis would pay attention to the deliberations "including such processes as how decision premises are covertly built into decision structures or the ways in which non-decisions can pre-shape political agendas" (Fisher, 1989, p. 950). For example, a derogatory label such as the "children at risk" implies that students are deficient. The issue can be re-framed by articulating the possibility that students are instead "at promise" and unfairly disadvantaged from negative stereotyping (Swadener & Lubeck, 1995). This perspective can sensitize leaders and researchers to the importance of thinking about how power is conveyed in language through policy discourse and the way issues are framed. It provides a way of comparing dominant definitions of policy problems against local realities.

Critical Ethnography

Traditional ethnography focuses on describing cultural meaning systems within particular groups. The field of critical ethnography, in contrast, attempts to describe and understand culturally created social inequities in hopes of bringing about positive change (Anderson, 1989; Carspecken, 1996; Quantz, 1992). There is also a growing interest in postcritical ethnography (Noblit, 1999), incorporating insights from postmodern perspectives and questioning the oppressive and exclusionary nature of the research process and the researchers complicit role in that process. A postcritical ethnographic approach interrogates and problematizes the very process of conducting research itself. Research in this vein delicately attempts to balance the tension between using grand theories to understand overarching forms of social injustice and the lived realities of marginal groups. These perspectives are also useful for educational leaders and policy analysts in grappling with challenges to move beyond traditional educational administration control and management perspectives.

This approach to examining policy draws on anthropological and sociological perspectives, and feminist and critical theory. These approaches utilize qualitative methodology to place policy analysis within a political and cultural context. Studies that utilize this approach share a common interest in examining "policy as a practice of power . . . and . . . interrogate the meaning of policy in practice" (Levinson & Sutton, 2001, p. 1).

Drawing on critical race theory, numerous studies in this perspective problematized "White," objective epistemological assumptions that promote emotional distance between the researcher and the individuals they study. Chicana/o scholars, in particular, have been developing alternative epistemologies grounded in social justice concerns. Responding to a lack of Chicana/o voices in educational policy and research, they actively reshape assumptions and support the political action of marginalized communities. Critical Chicana/o researchers use the process of research not only to transform the academy, but also to support "the empowerment of Chicana/o communities" (Pizarro, 1998, p. 57). Thus, for leaders, politics is not just about placating disgruntled activists, and for scholars, research is not just about writing articles and getting published. The challenge of politics is also about making connections with and supporting communities engaged in political struggle.

In analyzing policy, educational leaders and analysts of policy need to "shift out of habitual formations; from convergent thinking, analytical reasoning that tends to use rationality to move toward a single goal (a Western mode), to divergent thinking, characterized by movement away from set patterns and goals and toward a more whole perspective, one that includes rather than excludes" (Anzaldua, 1987, p. 79). Thus, this perspective highlights the importance of not taking issues at face value. Embedded with within a cultural context, micropolitics must be examined critically in order to understand how inequities are embedded in politics and policy.

Narrative Inquiry

Additional approaches base their methodologies on capturing the stories, or narratives, of particular individuals, groups, or movements. Narrative methods have arisen mostly out of feminist concerns that place subjectivity at the center of the research process (Bloom, 1998; Lather, 1991). These approaches capture the fluid and changing stories and lives of marginalized individuals and groups whose experiences would otherwise remain tangential. Narrative methodology provides a way to critically examine whether overarching theories are meaningful to multiple lived realities. Despite this ability, "[narrative] . . . ways of knowing have been devalued in Western science, precisely because of their serendipitous ability to integrate the seemingly paradoxical" (Brody, Witherell, Donald, & Lundblad, 1991, p. 263). This approach offers a way to uncover the intricacies of meaning systems on a collective level. By capturing individual and collective stories, researchers can expose the emotional and personal results of societal injustice, and tell the stories of those creating change, thus giving testament to the power of individual human agency. Narrative policy research can use stories, scenarios, and tales when they know that "the issue's empirical, bureaucratic, legal, and political merits are unknown, not agreed upon or both" (Roe, 1989, p. 251). These narrative stories have the potential to create alternative visions of policy problems, and that transcend "boundaries to shape the formation of culturally appropriate social and educational policy" (González, 1998, p. 99). This perspective provides a way of uncovering areas of silence and giving voice to those whose perspectives have been marginalized.

The methodologies and theories discussed in this section offer promises for decentering and re-framing policies to incorporate educators' realities and the needs of people often relegated to the margins.

Emerging Micropolitical Challenges: The Politics of Denial and Areas of Silence

How can political actors and leaders persistently avoid seeing, hearing, and addressing race, gender, and class inequities; conversely, when they do pay attention? Why and how does this happen, and with what effect(s)? Although these are not new questions, micropolitical themes offer ways to demonstrate the power of interactions, language, and sociocultural forces to keep patterns of privilege in place.

Denying Class

Plentiful documentation on the harmful effects of tracking, racial segregation, and class inequities has been available for politicians and school leaders to use to mount the rhetoric and mobilize strategies for change, yet the problems persist, and the response is simply more documentation. Parents believe that higher-income schools are superior and want social class desegregation to better prepare their children for wider social interaction in adult life (Brantlinger, 1985, 1993). Social class standing influences adolescent behavior and the dynamics in classrooms, shown in stratified classroom arrangements in students' sense of belonging in school, in the ways student trouble making occurs and is interpreted, and, of course, in student persistence and achievement. After countless analyses of class differentiation (Oakes, 1985), Labarree (1997) posits that the way we make education a consumer commodity reinforces social stratification and creates a futile race to attain merit and credentials. Americans and educators believe the myth of meritocracy—that if you work hard and try hard, in school and in work, you will rise in social and economic status. They cling to this belief despite the profusion of data indicating that success in schools is directly linked to the socioeconomic background of the parents. Micropolitical realities and stories provide a way of understanding the persistence of hidden assumptions and inequitable power relations.

Sexuality and Violence as Areas of Silence

Sexuality is an area that is so ideologically charged that it often remains an area of silence. President Clinton's "don't ask don't tell" policy, for example, ignored homosexuality in the military, rather than dealt with discrimination head-on. A very limited amount of research specifically connects this topic with politics and policy. Homosexuality has both religious and scientific implications. Conservative religious groups and members of the scientific community have long supported cultural assumptions that heterosexuality is the norm and all other orientations are "deviant." One of the few educational policy researchers that dared to examine this taboo topic, Lugg (2003) explored the legal aspects of discrimination based on sexual preference, or being transgendered, a transsexual, or intersexed. The following Lived Realities examines the life of Jamie Nabozny, a real person who experienced emotional and physical violence as a result of educational policies that rendered his sexuality invisible.

Jamie Nabozny's story provides an example of the politics of denial (Marshall, 1993b). It shows how schools (and the teachers and administrators who carry out policy)

Lived Realities: Jamie Nabozny

By the age of 13, Jamie Nabozny knew he was gay. His fellow students decided that his sexual orientation was problematic. He experienced verbal and physical violence for four years beginning in the seventh grade. Jamie was often called "faggot" or "fag." The physical violence against him included beatings and a mock rape in which twenty student onlookers laughed and did nothing (Broz, 1998; Lugg, 2003; Robson, 2001). All of the attacks were perpetrated by male students on school grounds and property. The violence escalated in the tenth grade, when Jamie was so savagely beaten that he required extensive surgery (Broz, 1998; Lugg, 2003).

In the face of the physical and verbal assaults, Jamie repeatedly appealed for help from his teachers and school administrators. One of his tenth grade teachers called Jamie a "fag." He was told by his middle school principal that if he was "going to be so openly gay, that he had to expect this kind of stuff to happen" (Broz, 1998, p. 753). Jamie received little help or support from his middle school principal, assistant high school principal, or high school principal. The strain and violence Jamie endured ultimately led to two suicide attempts. He eventually

(continued)

Lived Realities   Continued

dropped out of school after being told by administrators that he should leave (Broz, 1998; Bryant, 1999; Lugg, 2003).

Ultimately, Jaime sued the Ashland, Wisconsin, school district in U.S. federal court for gender/sex and sexual orientation discrimination as well as for violation of his due process rights. The court rejected his claim that his due process rights were violated, but the court did rule that he had been discriminated against based on his sexual orientation. Nabozny was later awarded $900,000 in damages (Broz, 1998; Jones, 2000; Lugg, 2000).

can reinforce negative cultural assumptions about sexual orientation. There was no specific written policy at any of the schools or at the district that supported Jamie's harassment. Rather, the inaction of his administrators was a policy by default that supported the violence against Jamie. By not intervening and in some cases blaming Jaime for the violence, his administrators reinforced cultural stereotypes and supported his harassment.

This story highlights how discrimination based on sexual orientation is an area of silence that can be reinforced by micropolitical inaction and denial. It also highlights the need for school administrators and teachers that are sensitive to issues of sexuality and sexual orientation. Jamie's only recourse against discrimination was to sue his school district. He had to experience significant physical and mental violence and ultimately bring a legal suit against his school district before the pain he suffered was acknowledged. Sexuality and sexual orientation continue to be issues that remain shrouded in silence and inattention. The voices of students (and teachers) ignored by policy remains an area in need of further attention. Additionally, analyses that uncover the experiences of those who have experienced this type of discrimination and violence are needed to render this issue visible.

Media Misrepresentations

The media can be a powerful player in micropolitics. Media reports have the power to "name" issues and they also have the power to "silence" them. The media is a central player in how citizens learn about political issues. How does the general public think about schooling issues, about how well schools are performing? Print media and television news reports frame issues for local consumption. After the shootings at Columbine, for example, even schools and districts with well-managed discipline policies and safety records were called on to put safety on the decision-making agendas as media highlighted fears in communities throughout the country. School performance data, identified with specific school sites and districts, are headlines now in newspapers, and the public then bases its educational concerns on the performance data.

Public attention is drawn to, and frames education by, critical events like the Columbine shootings, but also to ongoing regularized performance (such as reports on school teams, honor rolls, or test results). Newspaper articles on charter schools, home schooling, immigrant families' children, and debates (e.g., on year-round schools, resegregation, and neighborhood schools) powerfully frame public perceptions.

Not only do public opinion polls gauge perceptions of issues in schools, they also are used by school leaders and politicians to buttress claims and to present a rationale for policy directions. The annual *Phi Delta Kappan* publication of the Gallup poll of public opinion on schooling gets lots of attention in education policy circles. Pollsters continue to notice that people give schools a much lower grade when speaking of schools generally, but grade their own children's schools higher. Examining how Nashville's two daily newspapers portrayed schools, Pride (1995) found highly favorable coverage. But a shift occurred after 1987, as stories began to focus more on "the system" rather than on parts, and the rhetoric of reform took "the system" to task. He notes that, at this time, nationally, the dominant narratives defining problems in education shifted from equity to efficiency, and demonstrates this shift in Nashville's media. Public assessments became more negative, voters turned down proposed tax increases, and, eventually, a new superintendent and mayor (imports from northern states) introduced reforms that included decentralization, privatization, parental choice, and an end to busing for desegregation. Discourse analysis can be used to uncover how the selective use of language can be used to frame political debates.

The media is a discursive arena that serves as the primary avenue through which most citizens receive information about policy issues and thus can support participatory democracy and encourage citizenship (Gerstl-Pepin, 1998, 2002, 2003). Yet often media do not: Only certain perspectives are deemed legitimate for coverage, and due to space limitations, not all perspectives are always presented. Critically examining media coverage (or a lack of coverage) of policy issues offers insights into policy-maker strategies and possible public or special interest group resistance. Noting which issues are ignored or are framed in limited ways can also provide a way of exploring which issues are ignored or "silenced."

In the following Lived Realities, Wendell High School (a pseudonym), located in the southeastern Appalachian mountains, drew national attention and was ultimately forced to make certain policy decisions based on a particular social construction of linguistic racism. At issue was the school's female sports mascot, the "squaw." Educational policies at the site and district levels are often conducted with relative equanimity until "hot topic" issues enter the media spotlight. As Native American tribes have been reclaiming their cultural identities and languages, the misuse of Native American cultural images and discourses by researchers (Foley, 1996) and the public (Basso, 1979) have been an increasing concern to Native Americans nationally.

Lived Realities: Uncovering Racism: Native American Mascots and the Media

The meaning of *squaw* became an issue for Wendell High School when a member of a Native American political action group attended a girls' high school basketball tournament and was disturbed to learn it was the name of Wendell's mascot. The tournament-goer informed the tribal leader of a local reservation, who in turn wrote to the school and district, explaining Native American concerns that the use of the term was racist. Local and national Native American groups asserted that the term had multiple derogatory meanings varying across tribal languages. For example, one group contended that the term was used by early settlers to demean Native American women as "whores," while another tribe asserted that the term was used to describe female genitalia.

Eventually, at the suggestion of members of a local Native American special interest group, the parent of a Native American student lodged a complaint with the Department of Jus-

(continued)

Lived Realities   *Continued*

tice (DOJ), arguing that use of the term created a hostile environment. (The school is over 80 percent White, and Native Americans comprise less than 2 percent of the student body.) The DOJ commenced legal action under the Civil Rights Act, and threatened to cut off $2 million in funds to the district.

Students and members from the community who had attended the school resisted getting rid of the name because they saw it as part of their local cultural identity. The administrators and teachers at Wendell and the school board sought to find a way to settle the issue that would appease both sides. Despite these attempts by the district and the school to resolve the issue, the school board decided to remove the name, citing the potential lawsuit from the DOJ as the deciding factor.

This story (drawn from Gerstl-Pepin, 2003) illustrates how cultural misconceptions and assumptions get in the way of recognizing the complex nature of how policy problems are defined. While *squaw* was a Native American word that had been co-opted by the colonizers, much of the problem with this issue was not only that it was degrading to Native Americans, but also that it was derogatory to women. The media and groups that rallied around the issue tended to focus exclusively on the Native American issue, while the sexist nature of the language was rendered invisible. The media increasingly provides limited and simplistic overviews of highly complex problems (Trend, 1994). There is no space for debate or open dialogue about issues. In this case, the media provided little opportunity for open dialogue. Additionally, the gendered nature of the debate was subsumed by a concern with racism.

The legal rhetoric defined the "problem" as a racial issue exclusively that could be resolved by only removing the mascot. The problem's framing did not leave much room for alternative perspectives, such as the need to address community misunderstandings about racism. As the school internally struggled to discuss the issue and arrive at an amicable solution, the assertion of the justice system led to a legally based decision to remove the mascot. The media represented dominant cultural beliefs that racism is a cosmetic issue. Ultimately, the removal of the mascot did not address the underlying racist and sexist categorizations that led to its original selection. Rather it allowed them to remain intact.

Gender, Sexuality, Character, Multiculturalism, and the Private Sphere

All sorts of issues are deemed to be private, sensitive, and unsuitable for public debate. Yet many of these issues have tremendous ramifications in school districts. For example, many women educators find it difficult to attain top administrative positions. In the administrative career track, race and gender issues are areas of silence, seldom addressed as district problems. Wondering how administrators learn to keep quiet about exclusion and discrimination in their administrative careers, Marshall (1993b) noticed that women and minorities talked about their careers as if there were no problems with discrimination. Within the same discussion, they told of situations in which a White man got a job the women were more qualified for, or in which they were placed in positions primarily to deal with racial tensions and not other organizational issues, or when men left them out of the loop in the professional culture. But insights from feminist and critical race theory highlight such politics of silence and denial. Chase (1995) found that women superintendents suppressed and modified their ways of talking about discrimination they had experienced. Sensitized research methods that asked difficult questions in order to captured women's narratives and struggles with sexism were devised by Skrla, Reyes, and Scheurich (2000). As scholars, they were "interested in piercing the silence at both the individual and professional level that surrounds women in the superintendency" (p. 45). To uncover silences, they went beyond merely documenting the chronic underrepresentation of women and minorities in leadership. Instead, their research provided a forum for discussion of "silenced issues," while at the same time highlighting the agency of the women interviewed.

Sex and sexuality, too, are taboo. Individuals who go to district schools have sexual identities, but these are treated as belonging to the private sphere, to be managed in private relationships. School boards and central offices do not get involved in discussions of the ways that cultural identities and gender constructions are intertwined. Thus, the district resists any policy consideration of matters like adolescent pregnancy and school-age parents. It resists the activists who want school programs to assist girls whose anorexia, whose boyfriends, whose socialization for passivity and the like will prevent them getting the full benefits of schooling, seeing these as personal and private family affairs. District policy makers treat gay/lesbian/bisexual issues, too, as not on the agenda and resist the requests of activists to provide psychologically and physically safe school environments. Still, within the discouraging accounts in which marginal issues and marginal groups' needs are shoved aside, there are glimmers, theories, and methodologies for constructing politics and policy more inclusively. Such purposeful delving into the thoughts and meaning making of the people involved in schooling can bring important policy insights.

Micropolitical perspectives uncover hidden power plays in how policy is constructed, implemented, and resisted, and in how it can be re-defined. Specifically, they provide a way of understanding how power relations structure local site interactions, how identities and constructed and reconstructed, how discursive interactions structure inequity, and how interpersonal interactions are shaped by cultural practices, language, and symbols. They focus on the everyday realities, street-level interactions, and often-silenced voices. Such insights provide a way of understanding persistent inequities, but they also show that a different politics is possible, one that re-frames and re-visions policy questions and methodologies.

Summary

In this chapter we examined the subtle interplay of power at all levels of policy making. Although micropolitical analyses have traditionally examined the specific micro sites, reconceptualizing such analyses as microinteractions allows us to see that micropolitics occurs across policy-making arenas. As we recall from Chapter 2, backward mapping, what goes on at specific policy-making sites, can be connected to politics at the macro level. One sees the need to uncover micropolitics, which are often in subtle nuances of words and hidden interplays of power. The lived experiences of teachers, students, minorities, those with limited economic means, individuals whose sexuality differs from the stereotypical norm, and any others marginalized by policies can be captured by naturalistic research approaches. Micropolitical analyses show us that we need to use multiple research methodologies to re-frame and examine the multifaceted interplays of hidden power that occur across political arenas. Human agency in the form of social action and resistance occurs in all arenas of policy making, including districts, states, the nation, and the world. The next four chapters weave together traditional perspectives and policy re-framing that highlight this human agency and political action.

Exercises for Critically Analyzing Micropolitics

1. Follow a current or past contentious issue reported in the national media (e.g., a mascot issue or a zero-tolerance policy). Are there any hidden issues related to race, religion, class, gender, or sexuality? How are issues framed? Use each micropolitical perspective—site organization, discourse analysis, and sociocultural analysis—to frame the problem. What does each perspective add to your understanding of the issue? Are there any limitations to the perspectives?

2. Track a recent piece of legislation (e.g., related to accountability or finance equity) that will have an impact on your school, community, or district via media coverage, public documents, and websites. Brainstorm with other members of the class about how this legislation will affect the sociocultural context of your school or district. Is the policy biased (structurally or culturally)? Whose voices are left out?

3. Critically examine the discipline or sexual harassment policy for your district or school. Does it seem equitable? What is the intent of the policy? Is it clear? Was it difficult to access? What kinds of resources and support are available for individuals who may have a claim? Does this policy address students and staff? Women and men? How about issues of sexual orientation? Are there any provisions for heterosexist or racist harassment?

4. For each of the micropolitical themes, recall one or two stories from your school life experiences that are illustrations of the theme and relate them to classmates. In your discussion, describe your role in the scenario, then try to identify the quiet conflicts, the power dynamics, the stakeholders and their resources, who or what "won," who or what was lost. Then brainstorm to imagine how the arena or the situation could be set up differently.

5. Examine the "political aspects" of your local school's or district's website. Is it targeted at enticing middle-class parents (e.g., it's a public relations piece that highlights the excellent aspects of schools and focuses on test scores), or does it seek to build community and function more as a community resource (highlighting community building events and resources for parents)? What images does it use (pictures highlighting diversity or examples of innovative curricula)? Is this information available to persons who do not have Internet access? Whose voices are missing? What issues are silenced? Are there any changes that could be made to make the site more inclusive?

6. Conduct a discourse analysis of media coverage of a recent piece of legislation that has had an impact on your school, district, or community. What language was used to define the problem? How was the "solution" to the problem defined? Which individuals or groups are quoted and who is considered to be an "expert" on the issue? Did any groups champion the issue? Were there any counterpublic or counternarratives that interpreted the policy differently?

Note

1. While Lorde does not include abelism or English speaking in the definition of the mythical norm, in education being able and speaking English would need to be added to the mythical norm (and there may be others that have yet to be uncovered).

5

Democracy and Community in District Politics

Guiding Questions

- Who are the key actors who make district policy?
- Through what processes do they interact? Who has power?
- What are the multiple lenses for analyzing district politics?
- Does democracy happen in districts?
- What discretion and power do districts actually have?
- What are the challenges and controversies playing out in districts?
- How do marginal groups and often-silenced voices get heard, expand, and subvert policy debates in districts?

The U.S. Constitution does not provide powers or obligations for schooling. Schooling, therefore, becomes a state prerogative, mentioned in state constitutions. State legislatures generally retain authority but defer to localities to generate local funds and to work out details of implementing policies and delivering services. School district governance brings citizens closer to democratic participation and immediate connection with issues of public policy than any other level of governance. We send children to those schools, have friends that do, have done so in the past, or plan to in the future. Unlike state and federal levels, we may personally know a district employee. We may listen to their opinions about how the school and district are operated or we may read about these issues in our local newspaper. District education politics is the closest we get to a representative democracy. We engage district politics with our emotions, our pocketbooks, our citizen involvement, our attention, and our curiosity. Unlike other levels of governance, the public expects community input and democratic responsiveness. This chapter examines how the promise of districts as inclusive communities utilizing democratic representative governance has yet to be realized.

It also shows why district leaders seem so attuned to managerial concerns and seek to avoid public controversy. Finally, it raises questions about whether districts really have much power over their own destinies anymore, given their vulnerability to federal, state, and judicial directives. This chapter walks you through the characters, policy processes, and political issues in school districts. We begin the chapter with a vignette meant to pique your curiosity and desire for concepts and research that help explain district politics. In the following Lived Realities, Bible as History, notice the superintendent's and board members' vulnerability as they get caught in values conflicts, and the ambiguities they face, as they seek to define the role of the central office staff and the superintendent while dealing with the highly charged issue of religion in schools.

Lived Realities: Bible as History

Voting 3 to 2, the Lee County, Florida, school board adopted a two-semester Bible-as-history curriculum in 1997, with national groups providing curricular guidance. The resurrection of Jesus would be presented as history. A Christian Coalition member on the school board argued, "The Bible is an integral part of the origins of our country" (Lugg, 2001, p. 3). Before the vote, the superintendent and the district lawyer warned the board of trouble, but the board fired the superintendent and the lawyer resigned! Conservative board members had help from groups ranging from those who wanted fewer school taxes to those who wanted to sell their fundamentalist curriculum materials. Nationally, Bible colleges, fundamentalist think tanks, and websites keep the Christian Coalition movement alive and well funded. Differences in philosophy and strategy among groups can be ironed out when coalitions are being formed. So symbols centering on morality, faith, and family can appeal to the ideologies of people who are not part of a Coalition group. The American Civil Liberties (ACLU) and People for the American Way (PFAW) helped community activists block implementation of the curriculum and campaigned to defeat the conservative majority on the board.

Bible battles are not new in education politics. Fundamentalist groups move beyond Bible studies to shape debates about school choice, vouchers and charters, home schooling, outcome-based education, phonics, sex education, evolution, prayer, and gay/straight student alliances. But the Lee County case illustrates how, in recent years, groups can use national mass media, marketing, and political clout to buttress local interest groups. Imagine superintendents trying to manage district politics when the full force of national organizations can be pulled in to influence the outcome of a curricular debate in their county. This vignette demonstrates the complexity of the values conflicts and the role ambiguities district leaders deal with as they define their roles. The characters that occupy positions on boards and in central offices have to stay on their toes to keep up with shifting demands. They make decisions that shape education while having to address the oft-conflicting and shifting community values and professional truths about what is right and good for education. District politics include many easily observable examples of power enacted through *symbolic politics* (please review the definitions and illustrations of these terms in Chapter 1). Because political players at the district level are central to understanding the subtleties of local politics, in the next section we examine the complexity and political nature of their varied roles.

The Characters on Boards and in the Central Office

Board members and central office employees play a critical role in shaping district education politics. Examining this arena presents many questions: (1) Do board members represent a particular neighborhood or the whole district? (2) Why do so few women and minority leaders attain the highest levels of district leadership? (3) How can districts be innovative? (4) Are district powers-that-be really representing their constituents? In the following section, we delve into some of these questions as we explore the unique dynamics of district politics and policy.

School Board Members

At a school board meeting, an observer may pick up on tensions, power plays, and rituals related to agenda items. Agenda items range from seemingly mundane topics (e.g., a school bus route) to items that elicit debates over the fundamental purpose of schooling (e.g., a debate over expansion of school-to-work programs). Boards sometimes deal with deep political governance and philosophical issues. For example, when a board has to decide how to respond to a federal government directive, members may debate whether such federal control is proper, and whether the directive is appropriate for the cultural values and needs of that community. Some board members rely on experts like the superintendent or the district's lawyer for recommendations, while others seem to amass their own information about issues.

Actions of boards sometimes raise questions of propriety. For example, hidden and private interactions among board members violate sunshine laws. These laws prevent members of a board from making decisions in private before a meeting, so that their public votes are often mere formalities. Newspaper reporters sniff out many such violations, but some may be hidden within the closed-door sessions in which personnel issues are decided. Some agenda items have hidden agendas. For example, when a board member asks why one elementary school's budget for paper supplies is so high, that might be the precursor to agenda-building for ousting a principal or for tightening district monitoring.

Unlike elections at the state and federal levels, school board elections are relatively nonpartisan, with little overt political party attention. In larger districts, running for school board is sometimes a stepping-stone to wider, more partisan political aspirations, while in smaller districts, it may be more reflective of community traditions. Often, though, people serve in order to lead the district toward the philosophy, the values, and the kinds of programs they prefer; to give to the community; and to have some power over what happens while their own children are in school. Some boards pay members a small stipend and expenses, but not enough to motivate members to serve.

Many states, and the state and national school board associations, provide training for new board members. Still, the requirements for running in an election are usually as minimal as being an adult, being a registered voter, and living in the district. So anyone could meet the requirements to be elected and, for example, push *back to basics* or seek to limit expenditures. Sometimes, people run and win as single-issue candidates, bringing attention to a particular need during their campaign and, if elected, during their tenure. Examples of such an issue might be a need for more bilingual teachers and better after-school programs.

In some jurisdictions, the powers of boards are limited by the demands and fiscal control of county commissioners, who determine budgets. All are limited by the public's willingness to pay more taxes or vote for bond referenda for new facilities. Of course, state and federal mandates, the need to avoid lawsuits, and the advice from district lawyers and superintendents constrain board members' actions as well.

Although touted as close to direct democracy, school boards do not reflect the diversity of school students and families. As with other arenas of governance in America, school boards are predominantly White, male, and middle class or wealthy. Women comprise more than 70 percent of the educators, more than 50 percent of the parents directly involved in children's schooling, and more than 50 percent of the citizens. But overall, 61 percent of school board members are male. Surveys show that 85 percent of members are White, 7.8 percent are African Americans, and 3.8 percent are Hispanic (*American School Board Journal,* 2001). A majority of members (67 percent) have incomes between $50,000 and $150,000. Looking at urban boards in 1915, Nearing found that business and professional groups predominated, with doctors, dentists, and lawyers comprising over two-thirds of the membership (Nearing, 1917, as cited in Bowles & Gintis, 1976). The reality is that often members of lower-income families who are struggling to make a living, and lack leisure time and flexibility, seldom run for school board membership. Yet these families are among those most in need of representation.

Further, at-large elections, which select 56.7 percent of school board members in the United States, make running difficult, because time, visibility, and money resources for campaigning must cover a whole district. Ward or district voting alleviates this barrier. This voting enables minority candidates to have the possibility of garnering votes from largely minority districts or wards. Many larger districts use ward voting and have higher percentages of minority members. Boards are strange bodies that clearly do not reflect, demographically, the people most involved in schooling.

The public schools are becoming more diverse. A panoply of minority students goes to U.S. schools. They include recent immigrants from war-torn countries such as Somalia and Bosnia, Muslims from various countries, and those who attend highly segregated schools (especially African Americans and Hispanics). In 1999, Hispanic students made up 16 percent of the student body; Asian and Pacific Islanders, 6 percent; and African Americans, 16 percent. While these minority students constitute almost 40 percent of the student body, school boards have only about 15 percent minority representation. Thus, minorities and members of disadvantaged groups are underrepresented by school board officials, and the ideals of representative democracy are undermined.

Central Office Staff and Their Political Orientations

Although some on the education career ladder remain building principals, some administrators take central office staff positions such as Director of Curriculum, Personnel Director, Director of Buildings and Facilities, Director of Gifted and Special Education, and Coordinator of Technology. The political lessons that they learn in the central office are well known by insiders but seldom studied by scholars. Nevertheless, the central office has powers in developing curriculum, writing and administering grant funds, and interpreting policy.

Central office power is exercised quietly. In the midst of time spent on meetings and phone calls and interruptions, central office managers spend a great deal of time on paperwork and talking with other managers (Hannaway, 1989). Talk yields both factual and value-laden, interpretive information about specific tasks or problems, and also the big picture. They place importance on tasks from federal and state directives and less importance on tasks that come from lower-level staff and school sites. Thus, student issues, curriculum problems, and parent/community concerns rate low attention (Hannaway, 1989).[1]

An overarching obsession of central office staff is the need to be in control—of personnel, allocation of resources, and the preparation and transmittal (and withholding) of information, according to McGivney and Haught (1972). Some of the tactics used by central office staff are known as "stacking the deck" and "lining up the ducks," terms used, for example, to control hiring and to modify reform proposals. More recent studies have focused on the role of central office staff in aiding or blunting reform, showing that

- "defensive behaviors [were] used by district members to sustain inert district cultures" (Rusch, 1998, p. 18); and
- the central office tends to hold onto power and to recentralize even while policies promote site-based management (Berne, 1995).

When districts *do* respond positively to reform initiatives, what makes that happen? Firestone's 1989 examination of districts' *will and capacity* to reform led him to focus on dominant coalitions (1989b). (These could consist of some combination of central office, city agency, principals, superintendent, board, and community group.) The will of coalitions to see and act on a specific policy was related to how useful the policy was to the coalition's larger agenda. Reforms were facilitated by the coalition's willingness and ability to mobilize the personnel, to forge the linkages, to find the technical specialists, to provide and sell the vision, to obtain the resources, to provide encouragement, to adapt standard operating procedures, and to monitor the reform. Reforms were facilitated when the central office fills the buffering function of handling disturbances that come from outside and inside, and by *consiglieres,* middle-level change agents, who have special interest, expertise, or roles in managing the reform closely.

Clearly, anyone with thoughts about new policy directions or effecting change in a school district must take into account the role and power of the central office. The central office is often the focus of anger and frustration for citizens, parents, teachers, principals, and interest groups. It is also the focus of attention for *condensation symbols* about red tape, bureaucracy, and waste.

Superintendents

Typically, superintendents move up the education career hierarchy by starting in the classroom. Often, during their ascension, they earn legitimacy with masters' degrees, state credentials or licenses for administration, and even doctorates in education. Through such formal education and through the informal socialization and sponsorship in the professional culture, these aspiring superintendents learn the need for networks and political savvy (Ortiz & Ortiz, 1992). As they perform administrative tasks they learn not only skills, but also attitudes that help them fit within the administrator culture (Ortiz, 1982). They learn early on to project a calm façade, even in disturbing circumstances, to keep disputes private, to limit their risk taking, and to display behaviors and values congruent with their administrative team (Marshall & Mitchell, 1991). As they ascend, they acquire political and expert capital that they will use on their paths to becoming superintendents.[2]

Evolution of the Superintendency.   A survey of education history highlights how the role of superintendent as manager developed, and also highlights the gender and race politics in careers. Historically, the county superintendents managed funds coming from the state, visited schools, monitored statistics, and trained teachers in methods and curricular content. They were attuned to teachers, curriculum, and children. District and especially urban superintendent positions emerged as work expanded to the point at which local elected and volunteer boards needed full-time administrators to manage daily operations of larger districts.[3] Teachers and administrators belonged to the same professional association, the National Education Association.[4] This changed, with professionalization of administration, reforms aimed at keeping politics and education separate, the tendency to see administration through military or through industrial supervisor lenses, and values and power conflicts among educators. In the 1920s election struggles within the NEA, gender and power issues were played out.[5] Led by Ella Flagg Young, women administrators, teachers, and reformers promoted platforms for instructional leadership on schools as centers of democracy and social reform. They lost to other platforms that focused on a powerful managerial and hierarchical view of administration. Thenceforth, teaching and administration became separate professions, with White men dominating power and policy positions and defining administration as an executive, male job[6] (Blount, 1998; Ortiz & Marshall, 1988; Tyack & Hansot, 1982). Teachers, the instructional function, and, for the most part, women were relegated to nonleadership roles close to children. Over the decades, in communities where boards expected superintendents to be business executives and also to be peers with others in the community power structure, these assumptions about school leadership were culturally embedded. Thus, the professionalization of school leadership cleansed and sanitized subtle political processes, which had the effect of excluding women, people of color, and people with alternative ways of framing issues. In recent years, scholars have researched these issues, but the cultural assumptions about school leadership remain intact (see exercise 3 at the end of this chapter).

By 2000, political pressures for reforming the definitions and requirements for school leaders had emerged in many states at the national level. The Interstate School Leader Licensure Consortium (ISLLC) (1996) proposed standards to guide state licensure and university graduate training for principals and superintendents. The ISLLC called for more attention to leaders' roles in instructional leadership and in inviting and supporting diverse community participation.[7] It remains to be seen, however, whether or how these school boards will view such orientations as powerful and capable leadership and recruit and support these new district leaders. Whether brought in as outsiders, usually to disrupt and forge new power relations and "clean house," or as loyal and deserving insiders who will work for slower and more subtle change; whether viewed as managers, CEOs, instructional leaders, community facilitators, or butt kickers, superintendents are always attuned politically as they make difficult decisions in the midst of value conflicts.

Interconnected Governance in Urban, Suburban, and Rural Districts

Town and city councils and county commissions affect school policies most when they determine tax rates, school sites, district boundaries, and other similar issues. From time to time, mayors, especially in large cities, take active roles in school management and policy.

Often in city politics, we hear of scandals when city and school politics intermix. For example, in describing how the mayor of New Orleans in 1912 intruded in the choice of a school superintendent, an editor railed against "the politics of coercion and cajolery, of hounding and trickery, with the instruments of the saloon and the brothel, the gambling house and the racetrack" (Ginsberg, 1990, p.109). Reforms of the Progressive Era throughout the country led to experiments with elected superintendents and with separating school board elections to be held at times different from other elections.

Conversely, in the same era but in Chicago, Mayor William H. Thompson led a charge for curriculum on American's multiethnic heroes of the American Revolution saying, "Never rest until the histories in use in the Chicago public schools are purged of their pro-British propaganda" (Zimmerman, 2002, p. 9). Such interest and intervention by civic government actors, whether in urban, suburban, or rural districts, can seem idiosyncratic or not part of their assigned role. A politician may see great financial and power advantage in using school budgets, or other individuals may choose to use their political office bully pulpit to take stands on education policy. This can happen in any size district, from New York City to the tiniest district in Montana.

Similarly, education politics cannot be separate from the politics and concerns of other agencies and offices of government. Any student problem (e.g., the star football player stopped for driving under the influence) or curricular debate (e.g., the details of parental consent for their child to attend sex education classes) may affect budgets and lead to debates over jurisdictions.

Ways to Look at District Politics and Policy

In this next section we examine the ways to conceptualize district politics and policy, focusing on schools boards' activities and their members, on superintendents' concerns, and on citizens' influence and perceptions of districts' policies. What do districts deal with? Board dilemmas mentioned in *The American School Boards Journal* archives presented the following challenges to board members, asking what they should do if

- a board member home schooled her children?
- the public overran their board meetings?

- their board traditionally prayed before meetings?
- several parents asked the board to change a teachers' grading scale?
- the superintendent recommended the use of drug-sniffing dogs?

These dilemmas are the surface effusions of the deep issues lurking in school districts.

Local Boards: Ho-Hum Rituals and Hot Contests

In one district, school board routines may include quiet rituals like polite introductions, prayer invocations, and the trotting out of children to receive awards; but in a ten-mile distant district, decades-old conflicts may erupt in loud altercations, in spite of Robert's Rules of Order and other procedures designed to control community input.

State policies determine many school board structures (e.g., number of members and length of term; whether members will be appointed or elected; or requirements for candidates). State policy makers, over the years, have altered the policies, trying to perfect boards according to some new idea and/or trying to set up boards that are more likely to pursue education the way the policy makers prefer. For example, North Carolina state policy designated boards ranging in size from three to twelve members over the decades. At one point in 1897, North Carolina boards were supposed to be selected by the legislature. At another point, county commissioners were to select board members to be "three men of their country, of good business qualification, and known to be in favor of public education" (Watts, 1989, p. 149). In the 1868 Constitutional Convention, boards were to establish free public schools "to provide separate and distinct schools for the black children of the state, from those provided for white children." However, "ample, sufficient and complete facilities must be available." While the 1954 Supreme Court decision in *Brown vs. the Board of Education* changed the former provision, state legislatures and courts have had the power to structure and restructure boards repeatedly over the years.

Many questions remain regarding how school boards are structured. When state policy makers change laws about local boards (e.g., increase the number of board members or allocate money for their training), what is it they are trying to affect in districts? Is it better to have appointed or elected members? Researchers cannot agree on which is more responsive. Some find appointed members to be more liberal on race issues and less likely to bend under public pressure (Crain, 1968). Others find elected members more responsive to constituents. Yet others found elected members more responsive to individuals, but less so to group pressures (Jennings & Zeigler, 1970). A survey of both elected and appointed Virginia board chairs and superintendents ascertained that elected boards were confronted with greater numbers of interest group demands and greater controversy (Feuerstein & Opfer, 1998). The top seven issues were school funding, capital improvement, population growth, technology needs, student achievement, testing and assessment, and diversity of student population.

Boards may be arenas for trivia and inaction, spending a great deal of time on regular routines and obligations. This may slow or blunt reform initiatives, as boards translate state and federal policies to fit with local preferences and values. But sometimes they are responsive to reform initiatives, especially when they see the usefulness, and when the initiatives also come with money and resources (Nowakowski & First, 1989).

Communities, District Conflicts, and Superintendent–Board Relations

Superintendents cannot stay removed and unaware of local constituencies and group demands in the subpopulations of school communities. Within the alliances, conflicts, and political interests, superintendents are often seen in the role of defending order and the status quo, "while communities push for educational innovations and accountability policies" (Bjork & Lindle, 2001, p. 79).

Research on how superintendents adapt their leadership to the power of school board and community characteristics holds important lessons. In an update of research from 1971, Bjork and Lindle (2001) used a typology of community power structures and assumptions about how those would affect school boards and superintendents (see Table 5.1).

In the 1971 research by McCarty and Ramsey, *pluralistic* was the most common type of community, followed by *inert*. In an *elite* dominating community (whether it is dominance by tradition or economic, ethnic, or racial groupings), the superintendent merely does the bidding of the board and constructs programs that reflect their values. *Factional* communities, with factional boards, require the superintendent to deal strategically with open conflicts of values and needs. In *pluralistic* communities and their school boards, superintendents must provide expert advice, as the board, representing multiple interests, must deal with issues without exacerbating differences among groups. Many a superintendent might wish for an *inert* community power structure in which the superintendent's expertise and decisions are respected as long as the status quo is maintained.

Analyzing a recent American Association of School Administrators (AASA) survey of superintendents, Bjork and Lindle (2001) found that pluralistic was still the most common type of district but the next most common was factional. Very few superintendent respondents viewed their communities or boards as dominated or inert. Also, superintendents with factional boards were not as likely to adopt political strategist role descriptions, as would be predicted by the model. Instead, almost half described themselves as a professional advisor—giving technical, expert, perhaps research-based judgments—and almost half said they were decision makers, with 89 percent saying their boards accepted their recommendations 90 to 100 percent of the time.

TABLE 5.1 *Community School Board Typology of McCarty and Ramsey (1971)*

Community Power Structure	School Board Characteristics	Role of Superintendent
Elite	Dominated	Functionary
Factional	Factional	Political strategist
Pluralistic	Status congruent	Professional advisor
Inert	Sanctioning	Decision maker

Source: From L. Bjork and J. C. Lindle. Superintendents and Interest Groups. *Educational Policy,* vol. 15, no. 1, pp. 7691, copyright 2001 by Sage Publications. Reprinted by Permission of Sage Publications.

Citizen Dissatisfaction and Influences

Very few citizens actually get involved in school board elections: There is low visibility, little competition for school board seats, and low voter participation. In municipal elections and bond referenda, city employees can have great influence when they organize to influence election outcomes. Sometimes citizens do, however, use their voting power to demand change.

Dissatisfaction theory has been used to frame research on school board elections. This theory calls attention to the ways that shifts in community values, economics, and demographics can be used to predict district outcomes: Superintendents working with boards and not changing as their communities change will contribute to board members' election defeats, leading to superintendent turnover (Iannaccone & Lutz, 1970, 1995). Where there has been significant influx of new citizens, new businesses, new values, or electoral conflict, with the citizenry demanding new priorities, board members can be voted out. Ultimately, this leads to board conflicts and strains board–superintendent relations, resulting in demands for a new superintendent.

How does dissatisfaction theory frame issues in different kinds of districts? One study hypothesized that people in *high-status districts* would have management resources like skills in conflict management, communication, and negotiation (Boyd, 1974). The study revealed that the political culture—that is, the norms, attitudes, and values concerning the proper conduct of politics—was as important as management resources. According to Boyd, "In white-collar districts politics in its broadest sense was shunned as unseemly" (1974, p. 3). Superintendents could use symbols and language about what's best for the community, marshal management resources, and capitalize on those norms. They could become educational statespersons and experience low conflict, unless they were naïve or not resourceful about working with community relations. Boyd says, "In blue collar districts competing interests and points of view tended to be an accepted fact of life and the competitive aspects of educational decision making . . . provided an enjoyable diversion" (p. 3). When board members identified with subgroups in the community, voting was more on the basis of ethnic or religious affiliation, and board members were often expected to take care of the needs of their particular constituents and even their relatives. Superintendents' expertise and decision making was not highly respected. Given these highly charged citizen issues, superintendents need to be political strategists, *acting* apolitically, as if the educational goals were all-important, while being politically strategic with interest groups.

Although in the early 1900s Ellwood Cubberly (1929) spoke of the superintendent as a highly regarded pillar of the community, a father figure, this may be mythical. Today the superintendent is often under attack and at the center of community conflicts. The tenure of urban superintendents is typically 4.6 years, according to *Education Week* (Borja, 2002). Superintendents' legitimacy, authority, and power in part come from the training and experience of their career paths and their master's and often doctoral degrees in education. But some business leaders, school boards, and other politicians increasingly act as if other sorts of managerial expertise (especially their own) should override that authority of expertise. Some states are deleting the traditional requirements that a person must have been an educator to attain licensure to be a superintendent.

Vulnerability to board, community, media, and even staff displeasure, and thus to being dismissed, is a reality for superintendents (Lutz, 1996). Superintendents may be no more vulnerable than other professional managers, but administrators generally do not have the tenure protections that teachers have. Politically and personally, whether the turnover is voluntary or involuntary, superintendents manage by negotiating contracts that make the district continue some pay if they fire a superintendent before the contract expires. They laugh and say, "I keep my bags packed," inflicting instability on their families, and/or they negotiate concrete performance goals to demonstrate how they did do the job. Apparently superintendents give satisfaction, because according to the survey by Glass and colleagues (2000), 80 percent of annual performance evaluations of superintendents by school boards were in the excellent or good category. Still, their frequent dismissals show that giving satisfaction and doing a good job do not suffice in this political position.

How are vulnerability and authority issues different for the rare superintendents who are female and/or a minority? The 2000 AASA survey (Glass et al., 2000) suggests that superintendents who were women or of color were more likely than White male superintendents to characterize their boards as dominated by elites. These superintendents also predicted that their boards would be less likely to accept their recommendations and decisions (Glass et al., 2000). Gender and race power dynamics, and historical preferences for their leadership on boards, in the community, and in the education professions, apparently provide White males with automatic legitimacy.

The following Lived Realities serves to highlight superintendents and boards in the cross-hairs, balancing use of their respective expert and electoral legitimacy with their staying attuned to interest groups demands.

Lived Realities: Converting Closets into Classrooms?

"This is not an optimal learning space," the principal said, with cynical understatement. In her elementary school, some English instruction and special education classes were held in classrooms made from converted storage closets, due to overcrowding. Springdale's officials must come up with a winning strategy to manage a set of dilemmas that are now being spotlighted by a local newspaper's series on overcrowding. The superintendent said the district needs twenty new schools and the $487 million costs cannot be trimmed without hurting the schools' quality. Add to that the costs of renovations for existing schools, and the building costs rise to $867 million, which county commissioners must approve. Voters must approve a bond referendum, which will result in a property tax rise. While many of these needs come from rising enrollment, some come from new federal requirements for separate classrooms for special English instruction, mostly for Hispanic children. Further muddying of the waters is the appearance that the district has ignored citizen and think-tank recommendations for more year-round schools, smaller class size, schools with fewer amenities. Constructing smaller middle and high schools, with no auditoria or auxiliary gyms, would cut costs. School board members, county commissioners, and the central office are fully aware that the 1999 previous bond issue for $650 million was voted down, yet they are also aware that parents will be ready, willing, and able to form lobbies protesting schools with few amenities. Board members are caught in the cross-hairs of conflicting interests and demands.

Interest Groups

Traditionally, educators have seen interest groups as selfish or threats to stability, although they see associations like PTAs as supportive and positive. Organizations trying to influence local education policy center their attention on, for example, low taxes, favorable salaries and working conditions, or protection of their favorite programs. PTAs generally are viewed as working for better support for schooling, and church and civil rights groups are viewed as promoting their ideological vision of the good society.

Early in the 1900s, the Progressive movement aimed to separate dirty politics, graft, nepotism, and special interest influence from school governance as a way of separating education from seemingly evil political influences. However, they, themselves, were a sort of special interest, as organized elites with skills in bureaucracies, usually White, and often men with management or business orientations. Cibulka (2001a) states, "The apolitical label of education Progressivism disguised complex and shifting political coalitions in which school professionals . . . were active participants" (p. 17).

As volunteers, as PTA members, and even as members of site-based committees, parents usually are acting as school supporters at their own children's sites. Parents as individuals may be powerful in swaying a principal to get the football coach to give one kid an extra chance. Individual power is transformed into interest group power when people attend meetings and agree to work collectively, more typically trying to exercise influence at the district level. Table 5.2 provides information from research on the influence of interest groups in Virginia districts (Feuerstein & Opfer, 1998).

TABLE 5.2   *Groups Interested in Influencing Board Decisions*

Respondents/Groups	Percentage of Total Identifying Group
Education Association/Teachers Union	65
PTA/PTO	56
Religious Conservatives	15
Taxpayers Association	10
Other Government Bodies	10
Boosters Clubs	6
Minority Organizations	6
Civic Clubs	5
Business Interests	4
Retired Citizens Groups	3
Media	2
Political Parties	<1
Groups of Concerned Citizens	<1
Neighborhood Organizations	<1

Source: From A. D. Opfer and V. Denmark. Sorting Out a Sense of Place: School and School Board Relationships in the Midst of School-Based Decision Making. *Peabody Journal of Education,* vol. 76, no. 2, pp. 102–118, 2002. Used with permission from Lawrence Erlbaum Associates, Inc. and the authors.

Beginning in the 1960s, with increased federal intervention and state control over education, more interest group activity was aimed at the state and federal levels. Interest groups and lobbyists are most visible as state and federal phenomena. Still, they can show their clout in local districts. Single-issue interest groups can actually elect board candidates. Bureaucrats, professional groups, and categorically funded programs have their own interest groups with state and national connections. National politics impinge on and create conflicts in local arenas. The lone, local activist can call on a national network of information and clout to advance her cause, be it autism or playground safety or calculus in the curriculum. As a result, local superintendents' and school boards' control over agendas is weakened.

Most noticeable are the parents, community pressures, and interest groups that *are* able to gain access to education decision arenas. But many are disenfranchised, literally, as are migrant workers' families; more subtly shut out, perhaps, are those whose demands are not presented in the orderly manner demanded by school board decorum and central office bureaucratese and protocol. In the midst of rhetoric for parental involvement for student success, the system creates barriers. One study, in schools with large numbers of migrant families, showed how their workplace and lifestyle hardships and economic and social discrimination have kept migrant families beyond the margin (Lopez, Scribner, & Mahitivanichcha, 2001). The opportunity and meaning of political involvement and participation in school events is very different for these parents than that of the mythical soccer mom or Rotary Club dad. Schools often limit their parental participation practices to "formal activities ignoring culturally specific perspectives of minority populations," confusing and frustrating minority parents (Lopez et al., p. 257). Grounding parental education programs in experiential learning, hiring parent involvement coordinators and liaisons, building programs on the identified needs of migrant families, recruiting school staff who are intimately familiar with the migrant life, making home visits, keeping continuous interaction to identify shifting needs—all are effective strategies when they are district- and building-level priorities. District leaders can re-frame parental involvement and bridge race and class divides for more democratic and equitable schools.

Power and Access in Districts

Power dynamics are displayed in the discussion of interest groups, citizen participation, the superintendents' roles, and board relations. In the majority of U.S. districts, school board and school finance elections are designed to take place at times other than partisan political elections, to keep "dirty politics" away from school issues. It is assumed, too, that the political party system is bad for education. As a result, board votes and the power they wield are more controlled by professional or by class power. Leading families, professional associations, PTAs, and the like can sway elections. School districts are particularly vulnerable to special interest politics. Most of the time, so few people vote, well-knit organizations can get their candidates elected. Often there is no developing a range of alternatives, so votes are either *for* or *against* the system's proposals. Ultimately, politics is either politics of influence, trying to influence current management, or politics for changing the management. Still, most board decisions are routinized.

Superintendents hold authority via their expertise, although they get much assistance from experts on curriculum, the district's attorneys, and the like. Superintendents socialize new board members into their roles and routines. In superintendent–board interactions, some board members can be seen as *passive acquiescent,* as they rely on administrative staff information and refer constituent needs to the superintendent. *Proactive supportive* members are actively involved and advocate superintendents' stances. *Restive vigilant* members personally visit teachers and the central office, ranging far and wide for information and overseeing constituent needs personally (Tallerico, 1989, p. 218). More controlling superintendents are inclined to channel selected information through study sessions and other informal means to board members. Less controlling superintendents tend to surface divergent expectations and negotiate agreements. Among other factors, superintendent–board dynamics and tensions are affected by sense of character, trust, sense of honesty, integrity, and forthrightness. Boards operate from a model emphasizing political self-interest more than a community and public good model, so they are more likely to respond to parents and community by getting involved in school management (Greene, 1992).

Much goes on behind the scenes, where pre-decisional social processes occur (Cobb & Elder, 1983). Boards' cultivation of information sources; participation in subcommittees; their "seed-planting of ideas and directions, bargaining, persuading, compromising, coalition-building, peacekeeping, scrutinizing, cheerleading, monitoring, challenging, and fact-finding" shape what happens in the decision arena (Tallerico, 1989, p. 224). Superintendents' ability to anticipate community and boards' *zones of tolerance,* their gate-keeping information, and their sense of timing affect *decision arena* activity. Ability and acceptance in the decision arenas, for board members and for superintendents, may come from casual socializing over golf as much as from analysis of policy alternatives or from courses on organizational dynamics.

With this terminology providing information and frameworks about boards, superintendents, communities, interest groups, and so on, we can notice much more when observing district politics, which will raise important questions.

District Politics, Business, Unions, and Outside Interests

While educators and parents are thinking about curriculum, testing, or the extracurricular events, a great deal of district political activity centers, instead, on nonpedagogical issues like labor negotiations and business contracts. In states and districts with strong unions, the policies and political dynamics of negotiating contracts are enacted between school boards and union leaders (representing teachers and noncertificated personnel). The power of teacher employees greatly increased as collective bargaining laws designated the unions as bargaining agents and required boards to negotiate labor contracts. That power is increased when unions determine that boards are not negotiating in good faith, and then threaten to strike. Unions' success in gaining rights for educators has been essential for maintaining some degree of status and protection, and quality of work life. Unions have been the agents for maintaining a stance of teachers as professionals, worthy of participation in establishing the policies that govern their roles. At the same time, unions get the blame for driving up the costs of schooling, for shielding mediocre educators, and for resisting innovative policy proposals that might jeopardize their constituents. Unions' power declined in the 1990s.

School board members get advice and even training, if they wish, on managing the impasses, fact finding, strikes, contingency plans, frictions, the legalities, and the communications involved in collective bargaining. To amass power and leverage, they learn to strengthen management rights clauses, strengthen teacher evaluation clauses, replace seniority-based salary schedules with performance-based pay scales, and eliminate class size limitation clauses (Munk, 1998.) While boards have the major responsibility in negotiations, the superintendent and central office provide most of the information boards need, weighing the implications of a salary schedule proposal for seasoned teachers' retirement decisions, managing communications, and being attuned to likely unions' reactions (Prosise & Himes, 2002). Bargaining may be a three- to eighteen-month process. Critics of collective bargaining point to the expense, the application of the factory model to schools, and the increased conflicts in board agendas. Still, a union is the traditional power tool used by workers to make demands for improved working conditions and pay, and is therefore politically useful for teachers.

Many people and groups have interest in connecting with schools. One outside interest is local universities, whose schools of education and social work wish to conduct research and collaborative arrangements with districts. One example is school–university partnerships, linking two different institutions, each with its own power system. Analyzing the ideological and political complexity of such linkages, focusing on the interests and resources of participants, highlights possible conflicts (Firestone & Fisler, 2002). Identifying the micropolitics of partnerships, with divergences of interest, multiple sources of power, and the potential for constant conflict helps to predict, and thus to deal with, the coalitions and conflicts that develop.

Boards, with advice from the central office, allocate large amounts of money, whether it is for new gym bleachers, architectural firms, or business contracts (e.g., with janitorial services, special transportation and security services, or food delivery). Because of the large sums of public money involved, there is potential for graft, corruption, and even organized crime. The advertising dollars spent at conventions and in publications aimed at boards and central office administrators give a hint of the importance of such business activity.

Business and the Curriculum

We can immediately see the connections between computers and curricular and pedagogical issues, but what do soft drinks have to do with classrooms? District policy makers must, in the midst of controversies heated up by a rise in the obesity rate and Type I and Type II diabetes, and by school parents, health professionals, and physical education teachers, make decisions about whether to accept lucrative contracts for installing soft drink machines. But these contracts would ease budget woes, perhaps even allow for hiring more physical education teachers or nutrition classes.

Similarly, curriculum packages, software, and hardware are marketed with strategies attuned to dominant discourses for achievement, accountability, and standardized delivery that will make teachers more productive. Computerized pedagogy infusion has economic and bully-pulpit support from the national policy level, as when President Clinton's 1996 *Technology Literacy Challenge Grants* subsidized districts' alliances with computer technology businesses. District policy makers accept this policy logic often without recognizing a trend to private-sector management, outsourcing, and, what Cuban (2001) calls "the wholesale embrace of market competition" (p. 11). Critics, like Cuban (2001) and Labarree (1997), note that this efficiency-oriented emphasis on individual human capital contributions can mean abandonment of historical goals of schooling, such as democratic equality. Critics may notice, but district policy makers may not, especially when business and national policy lures are strong.

Citizens' Direct Participation: Levies, Referenda, and Initiatives

Designed as mechanisms for allowing citizens a direct voting response to a specific question, referenda and initiatives are familiar tools in education policy at the state and local levels. They are often used for getting citizen decisions on bond referenda or for tax increases for building schools. State laws vary on whether school boards, county commissioners, or others set the tax rates that generate local revenues for schools. In many instances, those laws allow localities to use referenda or bond issues, asking citizens, through direct democracy, to vote on new expenditures. Needless to say, those votes are determined by voters' values, not simply by an objective assessment of the need. Do the voters believe the district is run efficiently, without fluff? Do the voters feel their children are going to be served by these new costs? Do the voters have a direct vested interest (e.g., their own families), or are many of them sending their children to private schools? Are they older or childless and less convinced that more education funds make sense for them? Is this happening in the midst of a recession or rising unemployment, hurting the chance of passage (Coombs & Bell, 1985)? Boards, the media, central office staff, and interest groups can get very involved in these campaigns. An interesting case study of a southwestern district demonstrated how the consensus and networking among district, chamber of commerce, and informal social networks of the power structure created a campaign in favor of a bond referendum, mobilizing only those voters primarily favorable to the district and its needs (Conners, 1981). Washington, DC, schools, governed by Congress, held a referendum on tuition tax credits (Initiative 7) in 1981. Citizen initiation also can be used to bring about major policy change. Examples include California's referendum to eliminate bilingual education, and Florida's referendum to guarantee a fixed percentage of the state budget for education.

Sometimes people vote in nonpartisan elections on the basis of whether it directly benefits them. In other instances, people vote with a "public-regardingness" (Banfield & Wilson, 1963, p. 234) motivated by a concern for a general public good. People with greater economic resources are more likely to believe that their voting makes a difference. Historically, they have voted in more elections than those with fewer economic resources, even in nonpartisan, local elections like those on school issues (Verba & Nie, 1972).

Table 5.3 is a shorthand summary of approaches to understanding and framing observations of district politics and policy. These frameworks outline structures, roles, and enduring questions about districts. Recent developments and current challenges are outlined in the next section, leading to the biggest challenge: how to do politics differently.

TABLE 5.3 *Frameworks for Analyzing District Politics and Policy*

Lens	Focus
Actors and Positions	How roles, tasks, and orientations affect politics and policy
Structures and Tasks of Boards	How rules governing boards affect board makeup, activity, responsiveness
Relationships	Power, dominance, and interactions among key actors
Elections, Dissatisfaction	How dissatisfaction leads to incumbent defeat of board chairs and then hiring of a new superintendent
Superintendent Authority	The sources of power and the vulnerability of superintendents to political forces
Interest Groups	Who influences boards, how, and with what effect?
Participation, Access, Democracy	Who participates in district politics and how accessible and democratic are boards; how do the district dynamics affect participation?
Influences	How unions, business, media, courts, and referenda affect district policy and politics

Controversies and Challenges for Districts

The characters, tasks, and politics of districts have endured, although with some alterations, over decades, even centuries. Recurring controversies regarding governance, state control, efficacy, efficiency, equity, and basic questions about democracy, however, present challenges to districts. Some of the challenges are related to persistent tensions over control, when localities resist or resent power and intrusion from other levels of government. Other challenges are related to persistent tensions over the "essential relationships between popular education and the politics of oppression" (Anderson, 1988, p. 1), as localities have continued centuries-old traditions of inequitable access and outcomes.

Democracy?

The role that democracy plays in district politics remains. Before we can examine this, though, we must first ask, "What constitutes democracy?" Does it involve extensive participation (a *pluralist* definition)? Is it representative, with elected elites making policy until countervailing forces remove them from office (*democratic elite*)? Or is it a question of electing expert neutral representatives that act in the best interest of the electorate (*administrative state*)? Any of these are viable expectations for district politics. However, the realities presented about boards, central office, elections, and participation indicate districts tending to retain power within an administrative elite.

Restructuring, Power Shifts, State Monitoring, Intervention, and Takeovers

When people want to shift power relationships, they raise questions. Should school sites make decisions? Should city hall run the school system? Should voting wards be changed? A century ago, Philadelphia had 545 members on the ward and central school boards, "545 more than were needed to run an efficient system, thought the reformers of that time" (Tyack, 1992, p. 172). Decades ago, a survey of big city mayors showed that they expected to become involved in school issues (*American School Board Journal,* 1969). New York City and Chicago governance changes in recent decades include strategies for creating tighter school–neighborhood–parent relationships. Chicago's School Reform Act created a system of school-based decision making that moved authority and responsibility to the school site through local school councils. The councils would (1) create a school site plan for improvement, (2) control discretionary resources at the site, and (3) determine school staffing. It was as if policy makers were recognizing political realities and the findings of decades of policy nonimplementation (see Chapter 2). However, this meant that Chicago would have over 6,500 school board members (Tyack, 1992) without clear evidence that such reforms brought measurable achievement gains (Hess, 1999). The democratic local-ism thrust of the reform could not be decisively implemented, clearly effective, or politi-cally viable because it was radical re-structuring, and was also something that was variably implemented (Bryk et al., 1998). According to Katz and Fire (1997), "Within the city many different reform stories coexist" (p. 118), so assessing the political and policy efficacy of such governance changes is a postmodern challenge.

Devolution and decentralization reforms have affected suburban and rural districts, sometimes creating politics and power shifts, and sometimes not. The structure and sub-stance of site-based management (SBM) vary widely across states and school districts. The assumption is that the SBM will bring decision making close to the parents and teachers who know the site needs best. In their analysis of a small city's implementation of SBM, Malen and Ogawa (1988) demonstrated the tendency of powerful principals to keep their power, controlling the agendas and the selection of site advisory councils. Goertz and Stiefel (1998) also found that principals retain considerable power in deciding how money is spent. Further, dilemmas arise when sites have discretion and responsibility but are held accountable for results out of their control, and have inadequate discretion over budgets. Without close analysis of intradistrict equity of resources, SBM can become a trap. Con-sideration of vertical equity, wherein schools with high proportions of needy students should receive more resources, makes allocation of resources and analysis of results of site performance quite complicated (Goertz & Stiefel, 1998).

After the 1954 *Brown* decision on desegregation, with increased federal and state cat-egorical programs creating new specialists, sub-bureaucracies, and often-contradictory mandates, parent groups, activists, and teachers demanded community control and curric-ular choices. The politics of New York City schools' 1960s reorganization created "frag-mented centralization" so that "everybody and nobody were in charge of public schooling" (Tyack, 1992, p. 172). Segal's analysis of the pitfalls of this decentralization says, "Pro-gram vulnerabilities in the context of politicized, often poor, urban communities led to un-intended widespread and systematic corruption . . . a majority of the cities' 32 school boards carved their districts into fiefdoms where jobs were doled out to loyal campaign workers, lovers, and family or sold for cash" (Segal, 1997, p. 1). In 1997, a new law stripped the community school board of many of its hiring and budgetary powers, consolidating power in the chancellor and central bureaucracy.

Recounting the changes in governance in Baltimore and Washington, DC, in recent years, Cibulka (2001b) concluded, "Whatever the changes, someone is sure to be irritated. This is because governance systems reflect certain values, advance certain interests, and contribute to or subtract from the power and prestige of various elected officials, school employees and their unions, and other constituencies" (p. 28). When Mayor Barry acknowledged that DC's governmental structure was not working, Congress appointed a financial control board. It discovered a diversion of $50 million from required fire-code repairs, sagging morale, high per-pupil costs, declining enrollment, White flight, and more scandals. All of this led the financial control board to fire the superintendent and create a new board, wiping away traditional school board authority, and hiring a retired Army general as superintendent. Later shifts included alterations of voting districts, election of a new mayor, restoration of some of the district's and the school board's power and sovereignty, and new proposals for changing the size and method of selecting the board of education.

In Baltimore, state officials reversed mayoral authority in 1997, changing the system in place since 1898, in which the school board was appointed and controlled by the mayor. Cibulka (2001b) shows how mayors' problems could be traced to the 1970s and 1980s, which saw Mayor Schaefer's public dispute with the first Black superintendent, conflicts between community activities and the mostly White school board, and the mayor's strong stand against the teacher union strike. Still, the mayor's office, using the power to give and take away jobs and appointments (patronage), had kept people in power who prevented much-needed reforms.

In the early 1990s, a trendy policy among states was some version of state takeover, wherein state departments of education would run districts where state policy makers declared local management to have failed. Dramatic state takeovers, like that in 2001 of Philadelphia schools (Borja, 2002), assume that another entity, like a university, corporation, or a state department, can solve intractable problems of failing districts. Philadelphia did, indeed institute the biggest school privatization experiment in the country, and radical reprioritization of district finances, with outside managers taking over forty-five low-performing schools. Some takeovers put control in the hands of state bureaucrats, but some takeovers became opportunities to outsource public schooling.

Although these power shifts make national headlines in the big cities, they are no less dramatic when governance shifts are proposed in rural and suburban districts. States have the responsibility to provide for education, and although they delegate it to local districts, they retain ultimate control.[8] Local control is a tradition, emanating especially from northeastern townships but resonating throughout American culture. It is a concept that provides families with a sense that they and their community-elected boards have a direct voice in the books, the curricula, the bus schedules, the location of the next new school, and the amount of property taxes to be paid for schooling. But that tradition is greatly undermined by (1) the growth of federal education initiatives, (2) court decisions, and (3) increased state power over education.

Federal and court controls over local districts came with perceived needs to jump-start innovation and with states' and locals' failure to address equity issues. A persistent and pervasive problem, surfacing in lawsuits in many states over many decades, has been states' inequitable and inadequate school finance policies. State formulae for allocating state funds, and for allowing locals' property taxes to be the main source of dollars for local districts, create some budget stability, because property taxes are less vulnerable than income taxes to economic cycles. But property taxes have huge and problematic results, especially in urban and some rural districts. With declining tax bases, needy children, costly deferred maintenance of facilities, and few incentives to offer to attract and retain good teachers, these districts cannot possibly provide the educational opportunities that many suburban districts do. Federal compensatory dollars aimed at making up such differences have declined in recent years. A consortium of North Carolina districts sued the state for inequities in distribution of funding, asserting to a judge that the formulae did not account for their special-needs learning, the education policy decisions about central office efficiencies, preschool programming, and class size. New tensions over power and control are played out now when local districts, parents, and educators' resist or protest the federal No Child Left Behind directives.

Consolidation

A profusion of small districts existed in the mid 1900s. Then, in a push for efficiency reforms, small districts were consolidated into amalgams. In these districts, board members represented a much wider range of interests. They were people with divergent values and demographic profiles. Central offices needed to serve wide expanses of schools, geographically dispersed. Where once the district office was several rooms next to the K–12, comprehensive school that served one community, consolidated district offices had to provide services to schools that were geographically distant. At present, consolidations are proposed primarily for delivery of specialized needs. Districts consolidate their delivery of special education services. Districts consolidate (often under court order) their efforts to desegregate. As one could predict, consolidations are unpopular, create huge resistance, and rarely occur without huge brouhaha.

Parental Choices: Vouchers, Charters, Home Schooling, and Magnets

Districts have had the luxury of assuming that most families will have children, and that state law will enforce compulsory attendance laws. They have also assumed that state and local dollars will be funneled to them, as the dollars follow the children to the public school fund. But the long-cherished notion that local schools can best serve the local community has been eroded by national concern over student academic achievement. In the past, American valuing of the ideals of free access to public-funded schooling has been steady, with noted exceptions (such as "separate but equal" segregated schools and the viable faith-supported schools, especially urban Catholic systems). Dissatisfaction and desire for alternative curricula and structures lead parents, and the politicians who represent them, to demand flexibility and choices for their children. States allow home schooling, usually loosely monitored, for children's attainment of minimum curriculum but no state funding. Therefore, home schooling is usually available to more affluent families with the luxury of one stay-at-home parent. These options, along with private schooling, have sometimes been used to allow families to maintain racial segregation (Lugg, 1996). Magnet schools provide options, with public funding and within district management, not only to provide interesting specialized curricula (e.g., arts, international studies, and sciences), but also as a way of attracting both White and Black families to choose a magnet and thereby integrate schools. Both Republican and Democratic presidents have provided at least rhetorical support for charter schools, which are *not* always managed by districts but do receive public funds. Finally, vouchers, promoted more by Republican platforms and permitted in some circumstances by a recent Supreme Court ruling, allow families to receive public funds to help pay for their children to attend private schools, including private religious schools. Fighting against these policy moves, as teacher unions have done, makes education leaders appear defensive or at least anti-reform and even anti-family, anti-choice, and anti-American.

Research offers a few insights:

- Urban parents often choose to keep their children enrolled where they would have been assigned; more minority parents are exercising their right to move their children from an urban to a suburban magnet school (Goldring & Hausman, 1999).
- Existing power structures control charters; they use standardized assessment measures for accountability purposes (Office of Educational Research and Improvement, 2000). State scrutiny and pressure to compete for clientele inhibits experimenting (Gerwitz, Ball, & Bowe, 1995; Whitty, Power, & Halpin, 1998; Opfer, 2001b).

Scrutiny over charters, vouchers, magnets, and other forms of choice are tested under state provisions for thorough and efficient education. They are challenged to be cost effective, but the more overarching questions have to do with how they affect districts' possibilities for enhancing democracy, access, and equity.

Equal Access and Rights

Huge political controversies explode over questions about a school district respecting and expanding rights. Districts face volatile and sensitive challenges.

Diversity. Given the assumption that one goal for schooling is for socializing children for adult roles, and given the diversity of population, should school experiences encompass all cultural and personal expressions? Who, or what, has the power to decide? Often courts guide districts in such decisions. For example, the Boys Scouts of America have long used school facilities that now may be prohibited because the Scouts discriminate against and exclude gays. In many districts, violations of U.S. constitutional amendments go unnoticed because dominant community values support, for example, infusion of religion in schools. The Supreme Court's *Mergens* decision (*Board of Education of Westside Community Schools v. Mergens,* 1990) declared that if a school has allowed noncurricular opportunities or activities for any group, then all groups are allowed, be they Christian clubs or Gay–Straight Alliances, under the Equal Access Act. Ironically, the very groups wanting Christian clubs want to ban Gay–Straight Alliances from school premises, but *Mergens* supports equal access.

Expression of personal rights comes into conflict with dress codes (whether it is about a swastika-bearing sweatshirt or a burka), demands that girls have equal access to the good soccer fields, and decisions over districts' responsibilities regarding bullying and sexual harassment—all fall to district powers-that-be, but under the direction of laws and court precedents.

Resegregation, Equity and Achievement Gaps.   Districts' attempts to provide thorough and efficient education systems can be facilitated when neighboring districts coordinate and combine their service delivery. Metropolitan districts have been created to combine the minority populations of inner-city schools with Whiter suburban districts. Regional, county, and intermediate districts have been created so that localities can cooperate in meeting special needs, ranging from special education to advanced arts and sciences programs. Such consolidations can promote equity and efficiency. However, resistance to change and to redistributive policy is a political reality.

Toss into a big pot these unsolved, persistent challenges: schools' inability to fix the unequal outcomes for minority and poor children; school funding inequities; tracking; schools inadequacy in preparing girls to get equal pay when they move from school to the job market; concentrations of minority children in special education and as dropouts; and patterns whereby poorer children get less qualified teachers. Festering in that huge cauldron will be the most troublesome and interconnected challenges for school districts. Past policy that kept the cauldron on simmer sometimes and some places includes the separate and unequal segregated districts, busing (and its permutations, such as metropolitan plans), and magnet schools (Orfield, 1994). In fact, courts are allowing resegregation and there is a re-emergence of a substantial group of American schools "that are virtually all non-white which we call apartheid schools" (Frankenberg, Lee, & Orfield, 2003, p. 5). These authors note that urban schools have lost most of their White populations; many of the most rapidly resegregating school systems since the 1980s are suburban. Welner and Oakes (2000) describe the political tensions in a district that adopted a three-year plan to phase in de-tracked, heterogeneous classes. Upper-tracked parents made angry calls and formed "Parents for Excellence," with threats to put the children in private schools. Realtors and homeowners complained about property values. Proponents of de-tracking were drowned out, and school board members' "political expediency (and survival)" led to repeal of the policy (Welner & Oakes, 2000, p. 12). Tradition and entrenched interests and powers undermine political moves for equity.

Courts and Funding Equity

Inequities among, and also within, districts persist in spite of court cases emanating from the Fourteenth Amendment to the U.S. Constitution, guaranteeing that no person may be denied "the equal protection of the laws." Other court cases stem from the requirement in most state constitutions that states must provide "thorough and efficient" systems of education. Most state systems of distribution of school financial support have been challenged in court, with the courts using criteria of equality, efficiency, and adequacy, leading to analyses of equity of facilities. With demands and monitoring of high performance standards for students, the emphasis in the future may be more about spending what is needed for the school or the student, not solely on the district (King, Swanson, & Sweetland, 2003).

Funding Inadequacies and Restrictions

The logic of basing funding so much on property taxes is fatally flawed. The disappearance of manufacturing and the middle-class tax base of major cities, and increasing burdens of homelessness, children in poverty, and increasing costs for urban education, all escalate the urban tax burden (Ladd, 1998). Public sentiment against chronic hikes in property taxes in the 1970s and 1980s resulted in passage of Proposition 2½ in Massachusetts, and California's Proposition 13, which rolled back tax rates and restricted the rate of tax increases. Minnesota and some other states followed suit. Such limitations reduce the flexibility of local governments in decisions about spending and taxes. While working with increased funding limitations, districts face increased demands for meeting the special needs of children with disabilities and children from non-English-speaking families. Federal and state aid has not adequately supported its mandate to districts to meet these needs. These are chronic inadequacies, and they will not be fixed in the midst of economic recession, even if there were the political will and the valuing of public education required. The emerging policy logic supporting choice undermines that will.

The Overarching Challenge: Expanding Democracy and Community

Traditionally the dispassionate, disconnected scholar observes a school board or analyzes superintendent career patterns with little attention or useful insights regarding the persistent inequities in access and outcomes that are perpetuated through district dynamics. The unasked questions, areas of silence, and non-events remain at the margin. Re-visioning and re-framing can come from the challenging theories and alternative research methodologies suggested in Chapter 3, however. They focus on the margins and create strategies for purposefully identifying the subtle and overt exercises of power, which have the effect of repressing dissent, burying challenges, and pushing aside the unmet needs of some in favor of others. The topics discussed earlier in this chapter are in need of further exploration because existing and traditional district politics and policy research do not adequately address the following questions:

- Why do poor and minority families *still* have little to do with school decisions affecting their children, who still underachieve and drop out?
- Why don't women and minority educators protest their lack of access to the top jobs in district leadership?
- How can districts continue to function with all the federal, state, and court mandates that often promote equity but then have contradictory directives and are often under- or unfunded?
- How can educators believe that key policy makers intend to provide support for public schooling when they hear themselves blamed and held accountable for system in-

adequacies, or when they see policies that give funds to families who dislike public schools?

• When policy makers have clear evidence that something is not working, why don't they fix it?

• How can citizens believe assertions about schools as bastions of democracy, community, grassroots, and local control when they see so much contrary evidence?

Or, by re-framing, with a more constructive stance, we should ask these questions:

• What alternative arenas exist for developing counternarratives and empowering counterpublics in school districts?

• When educators and/or parents do initiate empowering change, how does that happen?

• When the usually disenfranchised succeed in getting district responses, how does that work?

• What are useful and effective strategies for getting dominant elites to look at and engage in searching for answers for often-ignored problems, either from the research, the testimonials, or the lives of people?

• What training, experience, and licensure requirements would enhance the likelihood that school district leaders would be capable and willing to take strong action for more democratic education policy?

Such questions are unsettling because the potential solutions cannot fit within existing ways of thinking, or because they are not top priorities for powerful question framers. They are issues from the margin, which some policy advocates and marginal groups will promote. Maintenance of political will to sustain equity policies is part of the challenge (e.g., for special needs, gender equity, federal loan programs to equalize access to higher education).

The remainder of this chapter demonstrates some ways to grapple with these tough issues at the district level, asking questions about democracy, using critical and feminist frameworks and methodologies that enhance our abilities to uncover the meaning-making of marginal voices, and advocating more democratic policy making and more expanded views of community.

Deconstructing and Critiquing Democratic Schooling

The preceding descriptions of the realities of districts stimulate critique of the limited democracy in districts.

Community Participation and Democracy

Lenses from critical theory raise questions about the depth of community participation in educational affairs. One inquiry into issues of race and class used the U.S. Census and the Council of Urban Boards' survey of school districts to examine districts with large percentages of African American students (Hess & Leal, 2001). Finding that citizens did have greater institutionalized access to the educational policy process, the authors speculated that this was White activism in response to the presence of a larger African American population. Latino student population increases, however, did not bring increased Latino opportunities for participation. Southern districts were the least likely to provide citizens with access to decision making. Also, districts with higher incomes, with lower student–teacher ratios, offered more access to decision making. The authors concluded that the poor, with little historically demonstrated solidarity or organizational effectiveness, have little political efficacy and voice, and that one must distinguish between opportunity to participate and deep participation and not be fooled by proxies like programs and statements providing opportunities. Analyses must look deeper than questions of attendance at board meetings or voter participation. Devoid of assessments of actual degree and meaning of participation, those proxies are merely politically correct symbols.

How does one examine whether policies for increased equity are meaningful or merely political symbols? Multicultural policy is an inadequate response to racial conflict, and community members know this. For example, after a racial incident in a Midwestern district, administrators focused on managing potential conflicts with the community and the board, and African American participants' reactions varied in relation to their social class, gender, and status as district insiders. This demonstrates the usefulness of multiple lenses for analyzing politically and racially charged events, as participants each have their own views of the situation (Placier, Hall, McKendall, & Cockrell, 2000). Using questions and perspectives from critical policy analysis elicits nuances beyond the hegemonic center of politics. As Anyon (1997) says, rather than blame students, parents, or school personnel for their actions, we need "to illuminate how economic and political decisions by others—over many decades" (p. xix)—have created a context full of inequities, exclusions, and inadequacies that require concerted social action by all, not just by educators and in schools, to change.

Hopeful Re-framing

Structures for participation and for legal equality that are insufficient to ensure that all participants are meaningfully included may, instead, be a mask for domination (Fraser, 1994). As discussed in Chapter 3, critical race, feminist, democratic perspectives highlight how seemingly rational policy processes and distributional justice are inadequate. Undoing social and institutional practices that have embedded patriarchal, racist, and elitist assumptions requires more than token policy statements. What seems like reasoned deliberation still reinforces the racial, socioeconomic, and gender power status quo, further disadvantaging traditionally disempowered groups. Democratic theorists argue that deliberation among equals in the public sphere is essential in legitimate democracies (Benhabib, 1996; Fishkin, 1997; Mansbridge, 1980). However, political equality, equality of resources, power, and knowledge for that democratic ideal would need to be assured. Democratic deliberation is enhanced by methods that equalize the political clout, resources, and knowledge of those from marginal groups.

Our critical lenses and cynical anger help reveal exclusions and evasions, but they can be depressing. To demonstrate examples of re-framed politics and to end this chapter on a more hopeful note, we provide instances in which district politics and policy moved toward deeper and wider democracy. Later, in Chapter 10, we offer action plans and constructive strategies for educators' political strategies.

(Un)Silenced Voices.   Searching the margins of district politics, one finds the great potential of people expressing counternarratives and alternative proposals for policy. One example comes from Boulder, Colorado, where Abu-Haidar (2001) tracked three Latinas' struggle to be heard in the antagonistic politics that were fueled by the proliferation of charter schools and other school choice options. One of the women, Mata, spoke of "the fear that the people in the community don't like the fact that schools are getting diverse. People are hiding behind school choice to avoid diversity. I'm going to make people [on this committee] uncomfortable" (Abu-Haidar, 2001, p. 10).

Emotions flared over the racism and elitism, but also over parents' rights to seek advantages for their kids. Top-down board decisions to close several schools led the board to bring in mediators, focus groups, study circles, and town meetings. Citizen advisory groups' *issue booklets* became part of wider deliberations that included teacher unions, the city council, the chamber of commerce, the student council, the League of Women Voters, a pro-voucher group, the Latino community, the Asian community, and several school improvement teams—thus representing both mainstream and traditionally marginalized groups. The Hmong representative, feeling as if she did not know how to participate, resigned. The Latinas, however, created their own subgroup, invited community allies, and used new discussions to formulate a written proposal for new choices, including bilingual and other ignored equity proposals.

The Latinas' actions were examples of the power of a counterpublic, a separate deliberative body apart from domination of the mainstream political arenas where they could formulate their vision, their counternarrative (Fraser, 1994). Thus, members of marginal groups, anticipating being silenced or given mere token audience, created their own agendas and their own arenas for debate. The social capital and power of group negotiation works better than operating as the sole voice, which may be seen as a token, symbolic representation. Further, expanding the range of ways and places for agenda creating provides a multiplicity of public arenas, allowing subordinated groups to strengthen their group positions and identities.

Expanding the Agenda Topics and the Meaning of Community.   Do we have a democratic and representative public sphere and a real community when policy arenas and committees are predominantly male and women's perspectives and needs are trivialized? Sexual harassment, rape, domestic violence, and even school bullying have been kept off public policy agendas or have been dealt with in ways that concentrate on individual behaviors and legal rights more than on the institutional arrangements that have allowed such injurious use of force and power (MacKinnon, 1989). Research (e.g., American Association of University Women, 1992; Stein, 1993), lawsuits, Anita Hill's 1991 Senate testimony against Supreme Court nominee Clarence Thomas, Title IX, and the Women's Movement have created language and policy for redress. For example, the phrases *school bullying* and *sexual harassment* have different policy-framing meanings than they did decades ago.

Laible (1997) examined a school district's responses to demands to develop a sexual harassment policy. Her analysis incorporated feminist critiques that women's issues are often seen as private-sphere, family, personal, emotional, and concerning relationships. She wondered how women's perspectives might alter the definitions of social problems. In her case study of a school board, she found members whose values derived from personal experience and advocacy (including assisting women and girls in filing complaints), as well as board members who would prefer to avoid the issue, saying that a drafted policy should be vague, without reference to "horrible facts that might make for bad law" (p. 209). Because the vague policy failed to recognize the fear and power preventing a victim from filing a complaint, several activists went directly to a female board member and asked whether her seven-year-old granddaughter would be helped by the drafted vague policy. Because the policy also failed to recognize the fear and power issues preventing a classified employee from complaining, the union president spoke with higher-ups. Policies had to address class/power/hierarchy dynamics if they were to make any difference, given the micropolitical forces at work in school settings.

Without the counter-hegemonic moves of people demanding that the policy drafts had to incorporate the wider definitions of the issues, the board would have produced a general, weak, and token policy, "reinforcing the status quo, normalcy, and (patriarchal) order" (p. 212), and affording no protection to the victims of sexual harassment. Laible (1997) showed how placing the voices of women and children in the center of policy discourse helps challengers devise forceful and imaginative political strategies to get deeper, more expansive, and effective policy when powers-that-be propose simplistic and token solutions.

The preceding examples show district politics re-visioning and re-framing in ways that enhance democracy and lay the groundwork for relational social justice. Knowing the barriers usually created by the dominants and the exclusivity of district politics, an educational leader, who views *politics from the margin* (see Chapter 3) as natural and healthy challenges and as ways to facilitate the strengths from diversity, can create structures that invite and support the democracy and the widened view of schooling that can come from the usually disempowered. By so doing, agendas are expanded and democracy is enhanced.

Summary

Roles and structures for districts have evolved over more than a century. The hope for democracy in district politics for education, with all voices heard, is not realized. Professionalization of roles of educators has reinforced managerial control, separation of managers from teachers, and educators from the community. The patterns of interactions between school boards and community power structures have reinforced patterns of privilege. Still, by critiquing district patterns, school leaders can re-frame district politics to build on the insights and potential social capital of unsilenced voices.

Exercises for Critically Analyzing Democracy and Community in District Politics

1. To learn to use publications critically and also strategically, go to your university library and search for references mentioned above—by McGivney and Haught, by Hannaway, and by Firestone. All make points about central office political activities and roles. Assemble them, and assemble definitions of the words *normative, empirical,* and *theoretical.* Which study matches with which definition? How do you know? What kinds of words do you find, and what characteristics are present in an article that is clearly normative? Clearly empirical? Clearly theoretical? What are the situations in which you would find normative most useful? Empirical? Theoretical? Why is it important to know which kind of journal article you are reading?

2. Collect your local newspaper for two to three months. Select all news, editorials, and letters to the editor on schooling topics and classify them into categories such as "Informational" (e.g., lunch menus), "Positive Public Relations" (e.g., awards), "Negative P.R." and "Controversies." Create a system for assessing the amount in each category and analyzing the tenor of the portrayal of the schools' management of the controversy. Present the findings to the school board and the local newspaper editor.

3. Gender and race politics in educational administration affect everyone, yet they are often treated as unmentionables. Read recent research publications on women in the superintendency (e.g., Alston, 1999; Blount, 1998; Brunner, Grogan, & Bjork, 2002; Brunner, 2003; Grogan, 1999, 2000; Jackson, 1999; and Skrla, Reyes, & Scheurich, 2000) and summarize the findings. Ask a classmate or friend who is a female administrator whether there are situations in which she knows it would not be a good idea to make a point about sexist or discriminatory practices she notices. Keeping details confidential, bring your findings to class for a discussion that culminates in proposed ways to restructure district practices to

be centered on supporting women's access to administrative positions. Then generate a class discussion focusing on how school leadership, values, policies, behaviors, and values might be different if women and persons of color had been, over the century of the profession's existence, proportionally represented in positions of power. Identify structures for recruitment, promotion, and retention of students and faculty who are women and of color and aspects of the curriculum that address gender, power, and leadership in your graduate program and state and national policies for administrator licensure that address these issues.

4. Make a list of six to eight observations of how politics and governance works in your district (e.g., central office staff provide all information, which is seldom questioned; the board chair has been the same person for eight years; there are tensions among board members, which seem to be related to race; and so on). Then compare those observations with the observations made by classmates in neighboring districts, and discuss the meanings and sources of these differences.

5. What is the most controversial issue dealt with in your district in the past three years? (e.g., dress codes, consolidation with neighboring districts, busing). What actors and groups took positions? What did they have to gain or lose? Who "won"? How did the controversy change the district? What policies and what political arrangements were changed by the events?

6. Generate a class list of the various ways business interests affect local school districts, directly and indirectly.

7. Conduct a class debate focusing on the arguments for and against non-educators becoming school superintendents.

8. Return to Chapters 1, 2, and 3, which provide traditional frameworks as well as challenging theories and methodologies for analyzing education politics. Make a list of the ones that

provide, in your view, the best insights for understanding several of the sections in this chapter. (For example, which lends useful insights for understanding central office politics, or mayors' involvement, or business and the curriculum?)

9. Peruse your state and local newspapers for the education reporting of journalists, the editorial commentary, and the political cartoons. They often focus on the wheelin' and dealin' and partisan politics as well as the foibles of key actors in state politics. Choose an issue or a policy (e.g., computer literacy curriculum requirements, testing for home schooling, requirements for school adminstrator licensure, expansion of charter schools, or whatever is "hot" in your state) and collect an array of such commentary to display to your class. Lead a discussion about how the various frameworks for analyzing policy help make sense of the actions, the behaviors, the discourse, and controversies.

Notes

1. Amazingly, Hannaway conducts and reports this research as if school management is the same as all management. In fact, the reader's only solid statement that the study is one of schools is in the Appendix!

2. Colloquially, there are three superintendent types: butt kicker, knight in shining armor, and consolidator. Scholars clean up the language and trace the history of the role (see especially Callahan, 1967; Tyack & Hansot, 1982; Iannaccone & Lutz, 1995; Blount, 1998). Analyses of career patterns have developed themes; one is the distinction between local and cosmopolitan, the latter to national networks and more likely to move from district to district and state to state. Another theme is the tension between task specialization and generalized leadership.

3. Teachers and administrators belonged to the same professional association, the National Education Association.

4. Cubberly (1929) is credited with the creation of the executive officer professional manager superintendents, arguing that they should have scientific expertise, developing curricula, and recruiting men to Stanford for professional training.

5. Conservative forces were playing on other fears; an NEA Journal in 1919 printed an editorial called "Why We Are Not Bolsheviks" (Lugg, personal communication, 2003).

6. For details of this gender/power struggle, see Ortiz and Marshall (1988) and Blount (1998). For details of the conceptualization of the superintendent-as-executive, see Callahan (1962).

7. But some business leaders, school board, and other politicians increasingly act as if other sorts of managerial expertise (especially their own) should override that authority of expertise. Some states are deleting the traditional requirements that a person must have been an educator to attain licensure and certification for the superintendency. The National School Board Association is open to the idea, arguing that superintendents are like corporate executives, in charge of huge budgets and personnel systems, so prior experience as leaders in business or the military makes sense. Our larger cities, especially like Los Angeles, Philadelphia, New York, and Seattle, have tried out the idea of hiring non-educators to run their huge operations. These have included a former governor, a former accountant, and a retired military leader, stimulating provocative questions about the tasks, skills, and aptitudes seemed to be the prerequisites for school leadership.

8. Hawaii is the exception, where the state department of education manages all schools.

6

State Policy Shifts and Cultural Idiosyncrasies

Guiding Questions _____

- What roles do individual states play in directing education?
- Who are the key players in state educational politics and policy making?
- What are the primary policy mechanisms through which state educational policy is formulated and implemented?
- What are some of the lenses that policy analysts and scholars use to study the state level?
- Whose experiences and concerns are often neglected by state policy?
- What are some ways to be political actors and influence state policy making?
- What are some of the policy issues in need of further research?

State level politics are fascinating. Newspaper articles on budget struggles, on proposals for statewide student testing policy, or on state funding of schools provide peeks at the actors and the controversies. Have you ever wondered why state policy makers seem to approach educating children and structuring schooling in such varied ways? Power struggles occur in state policy-making arenas that are linked to specific state politics, values, and cultural contexts. One group of state policy makers might remove reference to "evolution" in its science textbooks, while another state might leave it up to individual districts to decide. Some states have teacher unions that strike regularly, while other states have state constitutional provisions that make union strikes illegal. Each state has its own set of power struggles and definitions of the meaning and purpose of public education. These struggles are linked to state policy shifts and specific cultural meaning systems and idiosyncrasies. This chapter examines how various state educational roles have evolved over time and identifies key players in the policy formulation and implementation process; explores key issues and controversies facing states, particularly with a focus on politics (e.g., accountability); and examines some proactive ways of examining and re-framing state policy.

Shifts in the Role of State Education Policy

Because the Constitution does not explicitly give the federal government the right to govern education, by default state policy makers are primarily responsible for education policy. Although individual states have always wielded a certain degree of power over the education of children in their states, this role has continued to evolve over the years. The historical development of individual states varies depending on contextual factors, such as degrees of industrialization, natural resources, economic development, geography, agriculture, size, ethnic and racial diversity, immigrant influx, and/or a historical reliance on slave labor. Differences in these contextual factors created wide variability in how state political systems developed and how education policy is formulated and implemented. In particular, states have developed individualized policies and procedures pertaining to such issues as assessment of students, allocation of funds, development of state curricula, school reform initiatives, and licensure and preparation of educators.

In addition to how they differ, states have developed policy networks to share information and policy ideas across states. Two of the most prominent policy network organizations are the National Governors Association (NGA), a coalition of state governors, and the Council for Chief State School Officers (CCSSO), an organization of the key educational officers of each state. The political influences of these organizations have risen in recent years as federal policy makers have pushed for greater local control of schools. Such networks spread common ideas and discourses for policy logics, mechanisms, and political strategies.

Who's in Charge? Shifts in Control

In the 1980s, governors were clamoring to be seen as "education governors" as never before. With the media-enhanced crisis generated by *A Nation at Risk* (ANAR) in 1983, politicians, state department of education bureaucrats, and state school boards swung into action, generating legislative fixes. Concomitantly, beginning in the 1980s, the Reagan administration led the charge to devolve (take power from the central government and give it to states) and thus reinforce individual state's rights over education policy (Clark & Astuto, 1986). This devolution signaled the beginning of an important shift toward increasing individual state control and responsibility for education (Furman & Elmore, 1995). State policy makers' increasing awareness of global competition has also led to an increased interest in educational issues. This interest has been stimulated by powerful interest groups such as the Business Roundtable, a coalition of CEOs from major companies, that has advocated for accountability measures nationally (Reyes, Wagstaff, & Fusarelli, 1999). To that end, state governors have been interested in working together to develop national goals. In 1989, the nation's governors met (with the highly visible participation of Governor Bill Clinton of Arkansas) to lay the groundwork for educational reform legislation known as America 2000, which resulted in the passage of Goals 2000 at the federal level in 1994 (Sikes,

1995). Goals 2000 was a set of national curriculum guidelines that outlined what students needed to know to be prepared for the twenty-first century. Passage of this legislation signaled an interest on the part of state governors in having some national guidelines or a set of goals while maintaining the individual state's primary authority over education.

Focusing on Accountability

Originally, the shift in emphasis in favor of state responsibility led to a focus on increasing standards, such as increased curriculum requirements, in many states. Very quickly, this change led to the reasoning that increased standards had to be monitored and enforced, and thus came a policy logic focusing on accountability, starting sometimes with tests for teachers, sometimes with tests for graduation, and sometimes with tests for administrators. As of 2003, the District of Columbia (DOC) and all of the fifty states use tests to assess student learning. Additionally, the DOC and forty-seven states publish "report cards," data on schools concerning performance measures tied to test scores. To graduate from high school, students in nineteen states are required to pass a test. In five states, student promotion from grade to grade is tied to test scores. Additionally, the DOC and twenty-two states are legally authorized to take over, close, replace staff, or level other punitive measures on individual schools identified as failing. Florida and Texas are considering connecting teacher evaluation and salaries to the test score performance of their students (Education Week, 2003). Thus, state control, quality, and accountability converge in the dominant policy logics around which state politics swirl.

State Contexts and Idiosyncrasies

Individual states' roles in developing education policy relate to each state's unique political conditions. Education initiatives compete for funding with projects such as road repairs, state zoos, children's immunization and dental health plans, criminal justice, and prisons. Additionally, teacher unions can be a factor that affects state policy making. The American Federation of Teachers (AFT) and the National Education Association (NEA) are unions that operate within individual states and are organized through a national organization that connects states. Thus, each union can be a powerful state-level interest group as well as have an impact on national politics. The impact of these unions on a state level varies greatly, however, because several states have antibargaining laws that prevent union members from striking. Without the threat of a strike, districts and state policy makers may feel less obligated to respond to union concerns (Lieberman, 1997).

State policy makers often view education as a variable in economic development, based on the assumption that educated workers represent a form of "human capital." Indeed, a state's reputation for productivity in education can be used to entice big businesses to locate in a particular state. Although all states make some attempt to promote economic development, some states have been more effective than others. Some have strong economic bases in the form of industry, while others are relatively poor by comparison. As Chapter 5 notes, funding inequities create huge challenges for districts, and the state becomes the plaintiff in lawsuits over these disparities. Furthermore, the differences among states in their resources, economic health, and revenues have resulted in a wide variability in state monies available for expenditures on public schooling.

Special interest organizations such as conservative religious organizations or such business lobbies as the Business Roundtable (BRT) can also have an effect across states. Rarely are businesses or nonprofit organizations confined to a single state. Many large companies and special interest groups often have offices in several states. For example, to lure business to a state, companies often want assurances that the educational system in that state will provide qualified local employees and "quality of life" for employees relocating from other states. The BRT, which started in 1989, has been working closely with policy makers in all fifty states to advocate for increased accountability (McDaniel & Miskel, 2002). So while states can differ greatly in terms of resources and cultural contexts, they are also influenced by national movements toward greater accountability and national standards. Even global competition rears its head, affecting state coffers and expanding student populations as states compete to garner the bounty of multinational corporations and as workers move to certain states in search of accessible jobs.

In this chapter, we introduce you to the key state policy makers, key policy issues and processes, ways of analyzing state politics and policy, and the key challenges and controversies facing state policy making in the current political climate.

Key State Policy Makers and Arenas of Power

Just as there is great variability among states in terms of resources, geography, and values concerning the purposes of education, the states' individual political systems also vary. Although the key players in the political system differ in terms of who wields power on a particular issue, there are some way to make sense of this variability across states.

Hierarchies of Power

One way to make sense of these competing players is to recall the circles of influence and hierarchies of power, introduced in Chapter 1 and displayed in Figure 1.6. In their comparative study of state policy making, Marshall, Mitchell, and Wirt (1989) developed this model to show how individuals and groups assert power and influence in education policy making. They grouped the key players together according to which ones were perceived to be most influential in creating policy at the time. The insiders (members of the state legislature) are closest to policy making and are primarily responsible for passing legislation and allocating resources. The near circle includes the Chief State School Officer (CSSO), governor and executive staff, legislative staff, teacher organizations, and education interest groups. While those in this circle cannot directly pass legislation, they can influence the legislative process. The far circle (state board of education) has less of a direct influence on policy makers, but it is primarily responsible for translating legislation into policies for individual schools and districts. The last two groups—the "sometimes" players (school boards' associations and administrators' association) and the often forgotten players (courts, federal government, noneducator groups, lay groups, education researcher organizations, referenda, and producers of educational materials)—vary greatly in influence, depending on the issue.

These hierarchies of power and influence vary from state to state, and the power that each player in the model wields is dependent on the particular issue in question. Political coalitions among these groups can form around an issue, or a key player can emerge with enough political clout to force the issue through. Table 6.1, adapted from Marshall, Mitchell, and Wirt (1989), shows a sample organizational table, derived from a study of twelve states, of the key policy actors and their relative closeness to policy making, and provides specifics in terms of the mechanisms through which these key players can potentially influence state policy.

As Table 6.1 shows, state legislatures (including individual members and staff personnel), governors (including executive staff), and the CSSO tend to be the key players in formulating educational policy. Bureaucrats play a more formal role in terms of influencing policy. For example, the CSSO of a state may be either elected or appointed. The State

TABLE 6.1 *A Snapshot of Key Policy Actors at the State Level*

Influential Policy Actors	How They Influence	Clusters of Influence
Individual Legislators State Legislature	Draft, propose, and vote on legislation	Insiders
Chief State School Officer	Have authoritative responsibility for managing policy	Near circle
Legislative Staff	Advise legislators	Near circle
Governor and Executive Staff	Champion issues	Near circle
Teacher Organizations Education Interest Groups	Lobby for issues	Near circle
State Board of Education	Act as conduit for state policy	Far circle
School Boards' Associations Administrators' Association	Lobby for issues	Sometimes players
Courts	Determine constitutionality of legislation	Often forgotten players
Federal Government	Control the distribution of federal funds	Often forgotten players
Noneducator Groups Lay Groups	Lobby for issues	Often forgotten players
Education Researchers	Evaluate policy and suggest changes	Often forgotten players
Referenda	Can approve additional funding	Often forgotten players
Producers of Educational Materials and Tests	Determine curriculum content	Often forgotten players

Board of Education (SBE) is composed of bureaucrats who are primarily responsible for turning state legislation into policy guiding practice. Additional interest groups (such as teacher organizations, parent groups, and educational researchers) use more informal processes to influence policy.

Table 6.1 presents the hierarchy of power and influence of states studied in the 1980s; of course, this assessment is a snapshot of the hierarchies then, but we really need a motion picture, because the power relations are dynamic. These hierarchies may have shifted since the 1980s and will differ from state to state, but serve as a reminder to analysts that they do exist. One can identify the hierarchy and circles of influence as part of any analysis of state education politics and then use that information to feed information to the powerful play-ers. We can understand why a certain policy was approved when we identify the insiders and the near circle and see how the policy met with their political needs and their policy logics.

Although the insiders are primarily responsible for writing legislation, each of the players in the process can influence legislation and agenda items. A great deal of education politics emanates from their competition with each other to determine who will guide edu-cation policy. Any program needs key political supporters, or a champion, in order to make it through the state policy process. Thus, the dynamics of competition for power combine with the presentation of the logic, the need, and the utility of any proposal as potential champions assess the political and the educational benefits of a given program.

We can understand each of these key actors (and actor groups) by determining their relative power and influence and their closeness to the center of education politics. For each actor, we might also ask questions about the size and professional expertise of their staffs, whether (as for state boards) they are elected or appointed, and whether they are well paid. For legislators, it is useful to examine the degree to which they have backgrounds in edu-cation. For state departments of education, we might ask about the proportion of staff who are political appointees with no civil service status (and thus will be changed with political shifts) and those who are career bureaucrats. For interest groups, we can ask about the de-gree to which they collaborate (e.g., to increase state funding for schooling) as opposed to the degree to which they compete with each other, and which groups work together for which issues.

Given that state policy-making processes and outcomes are so varied, how do we begin to understand state policy? In the next section, examples of lenses are provided that can be used to understand how state policy is formulated and implemented and how state policy affects schools.

Ways to Analyze State Politics and Policy

With such variability across states, a variety of lenses is needed to make sense of differ-ences and similarities. As you recall in Chapter 2, we discussed the proclivity of the gen-eral public for comparing states based on certain outputs (such as test scores) or certain inputs (such as education funding). For example, Scholastic Aptitude Test (SAT) scores are often used when making state comparisons. States that regularly rank near the bottom in test scores are assumed to have failing educational systems, yet making these comparisons based solely on outputs overlooks additional factors that may be influencing test score outcomes. For example, the proportion of overall students taking the tests varies greatly from state to state from as little as 10 percent in some states to over 70 percent in others (Berliner & Biddle, 1997). Using output data such as SAT scores without placing them within a larger conceptual context is problematic.

What are some lenses or conceptual frameworks that have been useful when trying to understand how states formulate, implement, and monitor education policy? Understanding and analyzing state educational policy making has been a difficult challenge for researchers. Each state has its own constitutional charge for educating students. Policy analysts must understand each state's approach to allocating funds, formulating and implementing policy, assessing and monitoring student learning, and its unique set of resources (such as the strength of the economic base, size, diversity, geography, etc.). Because of variability in terms of state politics and policies, it is often difficult to compare an individual state's approach to state policies and systems with that of other states. Thus, most analyses of states have tended to focus on individual states, or comparisons among select states.

To make sense of state policy processes and outcomes, there are multiple conceptual lenses and models that can be used. In the following section, we examine some of the more prominent approaches.

Structural Policy Mechanisms

Each state has a set of organizational structures through which policy is formulated and transformed into practice. Examining policy mechanisms provides a way of analyzing formal state policy-making structures. Table 6.2, adapted from Marshall, Mitchell, and Wirt (1989), outlines seven primary mechanisms and their purposes. While each of the mechanisms can be used as policy conduits at the state level, some states have devolved control of these areas to individual districts. Additionally, states vary greatly in terms of which policy mechanisms they choose to emphasize. For example, a state like Kentucky has placed significant emphasis on equalizing funding on school finance, because it is under a court order to do so. In contrast, a state such as Georgia, which is more concerned with economic development and bringing new businesses to the state, has emphasized statewide testing and assessment in an effort to raise test scores. Without legal pressure to equalize funding, school finance is a lower priority issue in Georgia.

Sometimes policy mechanisms are combined. Nevertheless, analyses focused on identifying the policy mechanisms can be used to sort out policy confusion. For example, North Carolina, a leader in promoting accountability policies, has developed a set of diploma tracks (referred to as "pathways") that simultaneously cross several policy mechanisms. In the eighth grade, students must decide what they want to do upon graduation: (1) attend a four-year university or college, (2) attend a technical or community college, or (3) enter the workforce. Students with disabilities can elect a fourth track created to fit their needs. The requirements for each track are significantly different so that students who later decide to switch tracks would almost have to start over again, possibly adding a year or two to their studies. The program requires that schools organize themselves to accommodate students in the four different tracks, and it covers three policy mechanisms: school program

TABLE 6.2 *Key Policy Mechanisms*

Policy Mechanism	Purpose	Example
School Finance	Allocates human and fiscal resources to schools	Formulas for allocating funds to schools
School Personnel Training and Certification	Creates criteria for getting or keeping jobs within school systems	Licensure requirements
Testing and Assessment	Specifies the timing, content, and consequences of testing, including distribution of data	Accountability programs
School Program Definition	Defines program planning and accreditation related to the duration, content, and method of instruction	State-approved school reform models
School Organization and Governance	Determines who has authority and responsibility	Site-based management
Curriculum Materials	Provides development and/or selection of instructional materials	Statewide curriculum guidelines
School Buildings and Facilities	Controls the design, placement, and maintenance of school facilities	Regulations determining building design

definition, testing and assessment, and school organization and governance. Similar forms of tracking are being set up in other states as well; for example, Massachusetts instituted the MCAS, a graduation test that students must pass to obtain a high school diploma (Vogler, 2002).

Analysis of policy mechanisms provides a method for sorting through, and thus, in some instances, identifying which parts of a policy are working and which are not. By analyzing the policy mechanisms used (or proposed), we also can begin to identify the values being pursued and predict some fallacies and conflicts in state policies. In sorting out the political and policy strategies for addressing the needs of African American and Latino students who attend resource-poor schools, we can, for example, identify the need in such schools for teachers with good mathematics preparation, which would help the students complete the requirements that make them eligible to apply to a four-year college or university. Take, for example, a statement by an African American parent who was asked about the new requirements, saying of the North Carolina Pathways reform: "What does this mean for Black and brown children. . . . It's like they're categorizing these kids by eighth grade and telling some you're going to work at IBM, and you're going to work at McDonald's" (Jackson, 2002/2003, p. 6). State definitions of what constitutes a "pathway" in North Carolina and the requirements for receiving a diploma can have great implications for students' ability to gain access to higher education. By analyzing this situation with a lens such as policy mechanisms, we can more effectively identify a particular policy proposal and how it is tied to a mechanism (e.g., educator training and certification). At the same time, we can begin to tie the policy proposals to potential constituent demands (the mother in the preceding example), to policy advocacy coalitions, and to potential policy champions who would shepherd the proposal forward on the political agenda.

Another example that provides insight concerns the many states that have started to move toward tighter restrictions on graduation requirements; this is accomplished through legislation that exerts tighter control over the policy mechanism—school program definition. By tying the awarding of a high school diploma to a particular test score or a set of prescribed courses, the state can control a student's ability to earn a diploma. By pulling apart this intertwining of program definition and student testing mechanisms, we can see how it supports tracking. Tracking describes how schools sort students into particular ability groups, such as the college track and the non-college track (Oakes & Lipton, 1999). This type of sorting mechanism determines which are destined for higher education and which are destined for blue-collar or unskilled positions. Although many policy makers are touting this as a new phenomenon, this form of curricular tracking—grouping students according to their "intellectual abilities"—has been around for decades. In 1959, James Conant suggested that the role of the comprehensive high school was to group students according to their goals and abilities (Rury, 2002). So, this old approach to reform has been revived as policy logic, even though none can assert that it has a legacy of success. Subtle changes in areas such as graduation requirements, licensure for teachers and administrators, and testing program can have a powerful affect on educators and on students' daily lives.

Understanding the Policy Process: The Arena Model

Understanding policy making as an arena—a specific site where power is enacted in order to initiate, formulate, and implement public policy (Mazzoni, 1991)—is particularly useful at the state level. This perspective asserts that policy-making arenas are *not* value-neutral in how power and access are allocated. As mentioned in Chapter 1, four potential arenas exist. The subsystem predominates in states as an arena, often hidden from public view, where a small group of elite policy makers (e.g., legislative committee members, bureaucrats, and insiders) engage in pragmatic political decision making. Most state policy for education is formulated in this way—in incremental changes to the existing policies. However, when major changes are to be proposed, policy makers must make visible, ideological appeals in the macro arena.

Major changes, such as authorizing state-funded charter schools or requiring all teachers to have state certification in speaking Spanish, involve ideological policy shifts or radical structural changes. In these cases, policy makers need an arena large enough to make speeches that manipulate symbols and shift values. The macro arena encompasses new actors and media outside the subsystem, widening the audience. The commission arena operates when an elite policy maker, such as a governor, establishes a commission, in which groups that traditionally do not directly make policy, such as parent groups and other educator organizations, are given a formal role in policy making. The leadership arena, then, encompasses the interaction between elite policy makers and the interest groups that may influence their decision making and support for a particular policy or program.

In the arena model, shift occurs when outside pressure pushes the macro and micro arenas to produce a policy change that may support innovative approaches to education or represent little deviation from a previous policy. The arena model highlights the importance of media coverage in drawing the public's attention to issues, specifically how the media covers the macro arena while giving little attention to the micro, commission, or leadership arenas, where the majority of decisions concerning policy take place.

We can identify the subsystem at work in any state capital by simply observing where those individuals concerned with education policy cluster. In the 1980s in Pennsylvania, for example, education lobbyists and legislative staff could be seen clustered around the capitol office of Jim Gallagher, long-standing Chair of the House Education Committee. Those in the know recognized that Gallagher was the subsystem's epicenter, where all alterations in education policy ideas emerged.

Mazzoni (1991) used the arena model to examine Minnesota's 1985 legislative session and how the governor and additional members of the legislature built support for choice legislation. While the legislation for school choice in K–12 legislation ultimately failed to pass, an open enrollment program for higher education was successful. This success was attributed to the House majority leader, the "idea champion" for the legislation, who was able to successfully garner support for open enrollment. The model suggests that the reason the higher education piece of the bill was successful, while the K–12 component failed, was due to two reasons: (1) It had a successful "idea champion," and (2) it received relatively little media coverage, which meant that groups who might have opposed it did not know about it.

Even controversial programs can pass with the right support, as the following Lived Realities shows. For politically controversial topics, it can be advantageous for programs to maintain a low profile and to stay out of the media spotlight.

Lived Realities: Under the Radar

The allocation of funds for programs can determine whether a program survives or fails. No funds, no program.

One program—the A+ Schools Program, an arts-based reform program in North Carolina—silently built up support through a quiet lobbying effort in the legislature and the governor's office. Then-governor Jim Hunt was considered an education governor. Arts reform was often a highly political issue, because many policy makers saw the arts as "frills" and not a necessary basic of education. The reform was developed out of an art institute that was funded by an endowment administered by one of the most powerful families in the state. The head of the foundation, William Friday (a former head of the North Carolina's university system), wielded a great deal of political clout in the legislature and with the governor. At every opportunity, he lobbied legislators and the governor for support of the program by extolling the program's potential at raising the achievement level of minority and lower income students. His supportive efforts helped persuade the speaker of the House to support the program.

(continued)

Lived Realities   Continued

Additionally, one of the governor's chief advisors was a former art teacher who had been asked to advise the program and to help decide whether the program was feasible in the state. In 1994, with the clout of the governor's advisor, the head of the foundation, and the speaker of the House, the program was funded (at a reduced rate) at a time when no other new programs were being funded in the state. The coordinator of the program suggested that the program was funded because it had "slipped under the radar" of the media and groups who might have opposed it. The program was not written in as legislation per se; instead it was written as a renewable budget item. Discussions about the program were confined to negotiations in the Senate and House budget committees and in the subcommittees on education. Legislators outside of these inner circles would have no knowledge of the program.

With a "new" legislature that had been voted into office on promises of slashing taxes and spending, funding for a new art program seemed almost impossible. What also made this so unusual was that an arts program was being funded at a time when "basics" (e.g., writing, reading, and math) were being emphasized and a high-stakes accountability program was under development. Having key political players as advocates and supporters of the program and slipping "under the radar" meant that no organized opposition from the public or other legislators formed against the program, so the program was funded when many other programs were eliminated.

As the preceding vignette reveals, media reporting and public interest are not needed in order for a program to receive funding and support. What is important is that the proposed program or policy be supported by key players in the state policy-making process, in this case a subsystem (which is true for the other levels of education politics as well).

Comparing Outcomes: Rational Choice and Institutionalism

As mentioned in Chapter 1, political scientists who study education policy have tended to examine policy via a lens of rational choice theory (e.g., Chubb & Moe, 1990; Schneider & Ingram, 1997). Central to this approach is the assumption that humans are rational decision makers. Building on this assumption, these approaches examine outcomes (predominantly measured via standardized student achievement scores). These studies strive for objectivity in their research and seek to understand why, given all the options, certain decisions are made and what those decisions imply for certain policies.

Chubb and Moe (1990), in a prominent institutional analysis of education, utilized a highly sophisticated statistical model to examine the role that organizational control plays in limiting student achievement. They assert that education as an institution has remained stagnant because it has been increasingly bureaucratized by progressive politicians and special interest groups who "gained increasing public authority and used it to support and impose a bureaucratic system" (p. 46). Chubb and Moe's (1990) solution to this over-bureaucratization is for schools to become individualized, choice-based, free-market organizations operating with a certain degree of autonomy (free of bureaucratic entanglements) to compete with each other over resources (e.g., funding, teachers, and students).

Descriptive Cross-State Comparisons

Descriptive cross-state comparisons identify certain input, outcome, or process indicators in individual states as a way of comparing state policy. These studies have generally fallen into two categories: (1) studies that examine outcome measures exclusive of state contexts and (2) studies that examine how contextual factors, such as a state's political culture, can affect state policy.

Outcomes-Focused State Comparisons.   As mentioned in Chapter 2, studies organized around outcome measures tend to focus more on quantitative comparisons of standardized outcomes, such as test scores or funding differentials (see, e.g., Grissmer et al., 2000; Wong, 1999). For example, Wong examined how states varied in terms of the amount of aid they provided to schools and how this reflected state policy shifts in finance reform.

Structural Comparisons.   In their study of governance in twelve states, Campbell and Mazzoni (1976) examined how contextual features of states related to differences in state education politics. An mentioned in Chapter 2, these types of structural approaches are useful for building a conceptual model of policies and politics. In comparing differences among education power dynamics in school governance models in twelve states, Campbell and Mazzoni (1976) explored whether the method of selecting the state superintendent and the state board affected the power dynamics of effectiveness of school policies. Fifty-eight percent of state board members said that legislators became involved in school issues in which the state board had the authority to make the decision. Elected state superintendents had higher power rankings; where superintendents were appointed, boards without the power to select the superintendent had lower power than others; and state superintendents' backgrounds were in teaching, principalships, superintendencies, and higher education—they were all men and two of the twelve were African American. The framework guiding this research is presented in Figure 1.4 in Chapter 1.

From a different angle, two decades later, Lusi (1997) examined two state departments of education (Kentucky and Vermont) that were given the responsibility of carrying out major educational reform. Lusi's study entailed an analysis of organization, management, and personnel, as well as the political and state context challenges and the particular content and goals of the reform. She recommended that, to be more effective implementers of reform, departments need staff with more expertise in reform, need to know schools and districts, and need to make reforms locally appropriate. Many staffer functions are tied to specific federal categorical areas, so working with systemic reform is tough.

Some scholars study state contexts with a particular focus; for example, Hasazi et al. (1994) compared how four states implemented the "least restrictive environment" provision of Individuals with Disabilities Act (IDEA). They discovered that the degree to which a state supported the implementation of the policy had a direct impact on the degree to which the policy was implemented.

An emerging conceptual framework for making cross-state comparisons is structural network analysis. Using social network analysis, Song and Miskel (2003) compared reading policy networks in eight states. They found that the state reading policy networks were highly differentiated in terms of their influence on reading policy and suggested the need for more research into how special interest groups relate to policy making across states. As Song and Miskel noted (2003), there is a critical need to understand how interest groups "link to and interact with each other and how they connect to and intersect with policy elites, political parties, the mass media and the broad public" (p. 4).

Cultures and Assumptive Worlds

As mentioned in Chapter 1, Marshall, Mitchell, and Wirt (1989) found that states' political cultures affect the development of educational policy. In different states, with different political cultures, people have different views about what government and governmental agencies are supposed to do. Tacit, unwritten cultural rules function as a set of assumptions that guide policy makers as they determine what is acceptable and expected in terms of their role in the policy process. Policy makers are thus

> socialized within their subcultures to adopt shared understandings about what is right and proper in their policy environments. Their perceptions of the expected behaviors, rituals, and feasible policy options are a perceptual screen that guides their behavior. (Marshall & Mitchell, 1991, p. 397)

Political culture can shape these tacit rules and reflect the political values of the more powerful players in the political process.

Assumptive Worlds.   The "assumptive worlds" cultural framework is useful for examining why some states implement federal and national priorities in different ways and may have diverse and varied reform agendas. Understanding that a hidden set of values can permeate policy decisions and constrain alternatives that do not reflect dominant values provides a key to understanding how marginalized voices can easily get lost in the policy process. If the rules of the policy process are governed by the assumptions of elites, then disenfranchised groups who do not know the rules of the game will find it difficult, if not impossible, to have their voices heard. This suggests that to influence state policy making, attention must be given to understanding the "assumptive worlds" of the state policy-making process. Marshall, Mitchell, and Wirt (1989) identified four central questions to ask when trying to understand the assumptive worlds of particular state cultures:

1. Who has the right and responsibility to initiate policy?
2. What policy ideas are deemed acceptable?
3. What policy-mobilizing activities are deemed appropriate?
4. What are the special conditions of each state? (p. 37)

In case studies of the political dynamics of six states in the 1980s, the stories from insiders revealed much information. Insiders understood the particular limits on state superintendents' right to initiate policy. When an errant CSSO got out of line in Pennsylvania, powerful legislators put him in his place by stalling his initiatives. Similarly, when the state board challenged a legislator, he was reminded, "We created you and we can dissolve you" (Marshall, Mitchell, & Wirt, 1989, p. 40). Risky political behaviors included initiating policy ideas that defied traditions or defied dominant values, such as demanding equity programs when quality was the dominant value, or raising questions about a special program that advantaged the constituents of a powerful senator. Insiders learned, too, that they needed to "know their place" and cooperate with those in power, bet on a winner in political battles, and carefully use policy issues networks to legitimize policy proposals. They found that using experimentation and consultation with outside experts should be done only with accompanying sponsorship from powerful actors. Insiders' understanding of the rules of the assumptive worlds enabled them to maintain their position in or near the power centers. Challenging these rules meant taking a risk. If you win, you get more power, but if you lose, you will be sanctioned by exclusion from policy arenas. Staffers, bureaucrats, and lobbyists, as well as legislators and CSSOs, know, or quickly learn, these rules.

Such cultural understanding constrains the possibilities for innovative activist education proposals in state policy systems. For example, Sacken & Medina's (1990) study of the 1984 passage of bilingual education legislation examined whether the law could have been more far-reaching, given the traditionalistic political culture of the state. They showed how the proponents of bilingual education in Arizona worked the political scene with full knowledge of the constraints of a political culture and dominant values that would allow only token legislation and voluntary bilingual programs. Additionally, Gerstl-Pepin's (1998) examination of a reform process in North Carolina revealed that the program was successful because the leaders of the reform were well versed with the assumptive worlds of policy making in North Carolina. Specifically, these reformers knew how to create a network of powerful policy insiders (legislators, legislative staff members, lobbyists, staff members in the governor's office) to support their program. They contacted these individuals personally and educated them about the program, emphasizing the aspects that would appeal to each individual (e.g., arts integration, minority students, the correlation between the arts and test scores). As the reform developed, they nurtured these relationships through personal contact (phone calls or personal meetings), always keeping key players informed of program successes as they developed.

Cross-State Cultural Comparisons

Just as states vary depending on their physical and financial attributes, state cultures also vary. Cultural lenses provide an additional way of comparing states. As mentioned in Chapter 1, policy-making cultures tend to fall into three primary categories: traditionalist, moralistic, and individualistic. These political cultures are not defined by borders but by the *traditions* brought by populations migrating and settling in areas of the United States. Nevertheless, it is possible to identify the dominant assumptions of the political culture within any state border. These differing cultures represent varying views of the purposes of schools, which translate into differing approaches to education policy. Using this model for understanding state culture, Marshall, Mitchell, and Wirt (1989) were careful to point out that these categories are by no means exclusive or exhaustive. For example, Florida is both traditionalistic and individualistic, while Wyoming is both moralistic and individualistic (see Figure 1.7 in Chapter 1).

Moralistic, Traditional, and Individualistic Political Cultures.   In primarily moralistic state cultures such as Maine, Oregon, Wisconsin, and fourteen other states, people believe that government and governmental agencies function openly and work to promote the public good, that politicians promote the public interest, and that government should take action and initiate programs to improve society. The atmosphere of the New England town meeting carries over as government agencies and policymakers listen to open debates and hear the needs of citizens.

In contrast, Louisiana, Virginia, South Carolina, and thirteen other states have primarily traditionalist state cultures. In these states, people believe that certain elites always have managed public policy, and probably should. Their ties with other elites and their family names bestow on them governing privileges. They believe that government is there to maintain the status quo, and much activity centers on maintaining social, kinship, and personal relationships. Politicians pay attention to and decide to focus on issues (e.g., housing developments, pre-kindergarten child care) more because of some personal or social connections than because of some experts' reports.

Pennsylvania, Indiana, Connecticut, and fourteen other states have primarily individualistic state cultures. In these states, government is seen as a kind of marketplace, existing for economic purposes and running like a smooth, efficient business. Politics and policy operate as an exchange: "You scratch my back and I'll scratch yours" is the thinking. Issues, ideologies, and studies recommending certain policies or programs are not useful unless they serve utilitarian purposes in this exchange. People involved in politics are sometimes viewed as amoral and potentially corrupt, as if involved in a dirty business. The enterprising settlers in the mid-Atlantic colonies, such as in New Jersey and Maryland, developed the individualistic culture, and it spread as their descendants moved throughout the United States.

Political culture, therefore, can aid our understanding of the seemingly idiosyncratic state attitudes toward education policy. Such cultural approaches are particularly powerful when combined with the rules of the assumptive worlds, such as the notion that political action must acknowledge the special conditions of each state. This sheds light on differences among state political support for higher education, for example. In West Virginia's traditionalist culture, Marshall, Mitchell, and Wirt (1989) found mixed emotions about the importance of higher education for social mobility. As an example of West Virginia's assumptive world concerning mixed attitudes toward higher education, one insider reported a common attitude: "I went to first grade, then I went to second grade, and by golly by then I decided that going to higher education was not for me!" (Marshall, Mitchell, & Wirt, 1989, p. 49). On the other hand, such states as California and Wisconsin, which have moralistic cultures, support politicians' initiatives and value citizen access and improvement through higher education.

Each of these lenses provides a way to conceptualize state politics. Through them, we may look at the centers of power, at how formal policies are structured, and at how rational decision making and informal and tacit assumptions shape politics and policy.

TABLE 6.3 *Lenses for Examining State Education Policy and Politics*

Analytical Approach	Purpose
Structural Policy Mechanisms	This perspective examines the formal structures that guide state policy making, transforming policy into practice.
Arena Model	This perspective views policy making as an arena, a specific site where power is enacted in order to initiate, formulate, and implement public policy. This perspective acknowledges that policy-making arenas are *not* value-neutral in how power and access are allocated.
Rational Choice and Institutionalism	Central to this approach is the assumption that humans are rational decision makers. This approach focuses on outcomes (predominantly measured via standardized student achievement scores). These studies strive for objectivity in their research and seek to understand why, given all the options, certain decisions were made and what those decisions imply for certain policies.
Cross-State Descriptive Comparisons	This perspective identifies certain input, outcome, or process indicators in individual states as a way of comparing state policies. These studies have generally fallen into two categories: (1) studies that examine outcome measures exclusive of state contexts and (2) studies that examine how contextual factors, such as a state's political culture, can affect state policy.
Assumptive Worlds	This perspective suggests that that a hidden set of values permeates policy decisions and constrains alternatives that do not reflect dominant values. This lens suggests that dominant cultural assumptions help to explain how marginalized voices can easily get lost in the policy process.
Cross-State Cultural Comparisons	The "assumptive worlds" perspective provides an additional lens for comparing states. State policy-making cultures tend to fall into three primary categories: traditionalist, moralistic, and individualistic.

Controversies and Challenges for States

State politics and policies have shifted over time in relation to issues such as national concerns, shifts in federal policy, changes in economic conditions, value shifts from elections, changes in relative power of the two dominant political parties, and changing demographics. Certain issues are seemingly chronic, pressing, and unresolved by the current ways of "doing politics" in states.

Inequitable Funding and Resource Allocation

The inequitable funding of education is one of the most controversial issues that states face. While the federal government provides funds to targeted programs, such as those aimed at high poverty schools (ESEA, Title I) and special education (IDEA), individual states and districts are responsible for securing the bulk of the funds for education. Funding for education comes from a variety of sources: state taxes, local property taxes, federal and private grants, corporate and business sponsorship, revenues, local fundraising, and state funding formulas. Because states often provide over 50 percent of the funding, they bear the primary responsibility for public education (Wong, 1999).

Schools often receive a set amount of funding from the state based on an array of factors, such as number of pupils, experience of the staff, and sometimes even test scores. But these differential funding systems and the array of additional funds that can be given to schools have meant that there is a great disparity in resources between schools. One of the biggest causes of these disparities involves the tax base in which a school is located. While state funds may be "equally" distributed according to a state formula, individual schools receive differential funding from their districts because their tax bases vary greatly. (District funding is discussed in greater depth in Chapter 5.) Some districts have a wealthier tax base, and thus have more money available to spend on their schools (Burrup, Brimley, & Garfield, 1999).

At the heart of state controversies over funding is that inequitable funding often affects high-poverty schools the most. This is true particularly for inner-city schools that serve large numbers of children of color and for rural schools situated in high-poverty areas (Ryan, 1999).

The resource and funding disparities among schools has led to several court cases in such states as California, Texas, New Jersey, and New Hampshire because they have failed to address inequitable funding between districts. In New Jersey, the state supreme court ruled, in *Abbott v. Burke,* that the state needed to provide additional funding to resource-poor districts (Ryan, 1999). New Hampshire and California also went through similar legislative processes as the result of litigation, but their legislatures responded by requiring that property taxes used for education be capped, which made it difficult to raise additional funds to address disparities. States such as Kentucky, Vermont, Tennessee, Massachusetts, and Washington, in contrast, adopted legislation in response to litigation that sought to address funding disparities. In the case of Kentucky, the legislature dismantled their previous inequitable funding system in favor of a comprehensive program targeted at addressing differential funding among districts. In another example, Vermont responded to a state supreme court ruling in 1997 by passing Act 60 (later amended as Act 68), legislation that effectively created a statewide property tax aimed at redistributing additional funds from wealthier districts to districts that have smaller tax bases (Ryan, 1999). State court and legislative battles over funding continue to be waged. Although courts can rule that state funding allotments are unconstitutional, it is still up to state legislatures to decide how to address inequities. A state, such as Kentucky, can respond by revamping its system in favor of more equitable funding, or it can respond similarly to California and create legislation that actually increases disparities by limiting the use of property taxes.

English Language Learners

Conflicts over how to teach English language learners (ELLs) have become increasingly salient for many states. While the states that border Mexico (such as California and Arizona) have dealt with large numbers of language learners in schools, other nonborder states are beginning to face this issue as well. States such as Florida, Georgia, North Carolina, Massachusetts, and Maine are finding increasing numbers of ELL students in their classrooms.

Much controversy remains concerning how to educate these students. Some groups believe that these students need to be taught via English immersion (not being spoken to in their native languages), while other groups believe that students should be taught via bilingual education (spoken to in their native language and in English). The research does not fully support either approach: Some studies suggest that students who learn via English immersion tend to learn to speak English at a faster pace (Moses, 2000), but other research shows that students in an immersion setting can miss valuable content learning and are forced to reject their cultural heritage (Krashen, 1999). In a small school in which four or more languages are spoken, it might be difficult to find trained teachers who are fluent in each particular language. However, for a school with large populations of certain groups, such as Latinos/as, it is more feasible to find trained teachers who are bilingual.

While decisions about how to teach these children have been traditionally left to individual schools and districts, states are beginning to weigh in on this issue. California and Arizona in particular have passed legislation (Proposition 227 and Proposition 203, respectively) targeted at restricting students who are considered language-minority and limited in English proficiency (Mora, 2002). Antibilingual legislation is also being considered in Colorado, Massachusetts, New York, Oregon, and Utah that would effectively require that students not be taught in their native languages. Many of these policies carry punitive measures for individual teachers by opening them up to a possible legal suit if they ignore state law and teach children in their native languages.

Vouchers and School Choice

Another highly charged issue is school choice via vouchers, tax credits, and charter schools. This issue is deeply complex and is tied to cultural values such as "choice," which embodies a belief that parents have a right to have educational options for their children (discussed more fully in Chapter 1). On one hand, those who oppose school choice feel that it works against the notion of schooling for democracy. Without state-supported schools, in which individuals from different backgrounds come together, how will citizenship be promoted? On the other hand, religious groups advocate for choice because they are disenchanted with public schools for not placing a high enough value on individual responsibility and the teaching of ethics and morals (Herrington, 2000). Additionally, groups such as the Black Alliance for Educational Outcomes have promoted school choice as a way to serve low-income minority children who are currently not being served by inner-city public schools (Bracey, 2002). Still other groups see school choice as privileging certain parents who have the know-how and savvy to work the system to ensure that their children get into the best schools possible (André-Bechely, 2003).

Vouchers represent a more radical policy instrument (mentioned in Chapter 2), one that allows students to use public money to attend private schools. Essentially, vouchers favor educational privatization over education for the common good (Bracey, 2002). Vouchers take public money and use it to fund private schools. The voucher debate has centered around two main foci: (1) a concern that families should have the freedom to select an appropriate school for their children and (2) critical examinations of who benefits (or is penalized) from these types of policies (Moses, 2000). Critics of vouchers are concerned that they will privilege parents who can afford additional expenses and provide transportation. Additionally, due to concerns about separation of church and state, many policy makers are unsure about using public money to pay for religious education.

Charter schools, as a policy instrument, are less radical than vouchers. Essentially, charters are publicly funded but are independent from an individual district. They function more as a self-contained organizational structure. Charter schools have been popular because they are free of bureaucratic red tape and are seen as an alternative for low-income communities. There is some concern, however, that charter schools are not really free of state bureaucracy or racial segregation. Although some charter schools may be able to institute school uniforms or alternative curriculum foci, many are still assessed by the same standardized measures as public schools. Opfer (2001b), for example, suggests that charter schools in Georgia are restricted from having innovative curricula because they must follow the same accountability requirements as other public schools. Since they rely heavily on recruiting students, they must be mindful of test scores. The issue of school choice, whether in the form of vouchers, charters, or another choice option, cuts at core values embedded in democratic ideals, religious beliefs, and social inequities, such as poverty and racism (Bracey, 2002).

Testing and Assessment

For a number of years now, there has been an increasing interest in holding schools accountable for test scores. States are responding to this issue in a variety of ways, most commonly by developing testing systems to evaluate students. High-stakes testing programs attempt to hold schools accountable via test scores. As noted earlier in this chapter, all fifty states and the District of Columbia have some testing program in place, and twenty-two states can level punitive measures against schools that are deemed to be failing (Doherty & Skinner, 2003).

The passage of the No Child Left Behind Act (NCLBA) in January 2002 means that schools that receive Title I funds will risk losing federal funds if their test scores are not high enough. NCLBA also requires that states develop their own reading assessments if they want to qualify for additional federal funding. This increased pressure from the federal government has meant that even states who previously have avoided high-stakes accountability are now being forced to address this issue if they want to ensure a steady inflow of federal funds.

Massachusetts has experienced student protests over the controversial MCAS test. If students don't pass the test, they do not receive a high school diploma, which can limit their access to higher education and federal support for college. Business leaders in this state have come out in favor of the MCAS, yet many students question the role it plays in limiting the future prospects of those who do not pass. It has been suggested that the MCAS has improved teaching practices (Vogler, 2002), yet many questions remain as to its negative impact on students who do not pass the test. Numerous other states, such as Texas, North Carolina, and Georgia, have wrestled with the notion of ending social promotion and tying test score performance to whether a student can continue to the next grade or receive a diploma.

In Arizona, political support for a more authentic form of assessment—one aimed at promoting higher order thinking—was considered by state policy makers. Just before its implementation, the program was scrapped in favor of the preexisting high-stakes, standardized assessment already in use. Research was cited as the reason for the demise of the program; however, Smith, Heinecke, and Noble (1999) suggest that the decision was more about politics than whether the program was effective. It wasn't that the authentic assessment was not working; rather, key policy makers felt the state should use standardized assessments instead. Moves toward more authentic forms of assessment, such as essays and word problems, would require greater state expenditures. These tests are generally more costly because they are not multiple-choice, cannot be processed by a computer, and require trained graders.

Curriculum Battles

As mentioned in Chapters 4 and 5, the curriculum is often a point of political contention. With the push toward standards, states are now moving to a statewide curriculum that serves a guide for what teachers should be teaching in each grade level and course topic. With this new emphasis, states are more central players in writing standards (Placier, Walker, & Foster, 2002).

A curriculum comprises the knowledge that schools are to impart to students. According to Cornbleth and Waugh (1995), "Different values and interest are sustained or modified depending on which curriculum knowledge is . . . selected" (quoted in Placier, Walker, & Foster, 2002, p. 282). There are two key components of curriculum: (1) The "official curriculum" is content knowledge that leads to building student skills, such as the ability to read and write; and (2) a "hidden curriculum," which is often ignored—for example, the pledge of allegiance teaches nationalism and patriotism, and individualism is prized as students are primarily valued for their individual academic achievements (English, 1991). These hidden values teach students as well.

For example, for decades the experiences of women and minorities were absent from core curriculum materials. Multicultural movements suggested the need to expand the curriculum to include the perspectives of marginalized groups and value their contributions to history as well as their cultures (Placier et al., 2000). As mentioned in Chapter 4, these same movements also advocate for culturally relevant pedagogy that addresses the needs of minority children (Ladson-Billings, 1994).

Despite these equity concerns, much of what is driving state standards within high-stakes accountability contexts is increasing test scores. In the case of Missouri, state standards were written by a politicized committee. The resulting standards appear seemingly value-neutral and present a simplistic view of content and process (Placier, Walker, & Foster, 2002). The push for high-stakes accountability raises many questions about exactly *what* is being assessed and measured by standardized tests. With the passage of NCLBA, this question becomes even more pressing.

"Crises" over Educator Quality and Quantity

The political dynamics of educator recruitment, retention, assessment, and promotion are heating up. Many states have teacher shortages, particularly in the area of special education, English as a second language, and the mathematics and sciences. Complicating this shortage are funding constraints, the powers of teacher education programs and state credentialing boards, and pressures from teacher and administrators' associations. Identifying and supporting a viable policy proposal requires listening to the varied demands of all of these potentially powerful groups. Further, it is difficult to find, without major re-framing of extant policy logics, a mechanism that will recruit and retain teachers, especially for schools that serve students who traditionally do not test well, given an increasing focus on accountability. As illustrated in the vignette in Chapter 4, "James's Story," discussions about teacher shortages are often reduced to discussions about salary. Deeper discussions about teacher professionalism tend to remain hidden. The Lived Realities on the next page highlights some of the complexity that surrounds this issue. As this story shows, many teacher-quality policies often assume that teachers are currently not working hard enough. Although there are teachers that need professional development or should not be teaching, these policies often penalize good teachers who work with struggling children. Because test scores are tightly aligned to socioeconomics and race, and teachers are often blamed for any educational woes, questions are raised concerning the need to support teachers who feel their professionalism is under attack.

Re-visioning and Re-framing Expanding State Policy

We have looked at who the key players are in state politics and some of the key issues facing states. Now it is time to delve into an example of how policy research can be used to uncover issues that may be marginalized or excluded in mainstream policy discussions. In this section, we explore two examples of how state policies can be re-framed and re-visioned.

Exposing Marginalized Issues in Anti-Bilingual Education Legislation

Proposition 227 in California provides an opportunity to examine how policy research can be used to uncover and unearth critical policy issues. California is responsible for approximately 45 percent of the United States' immigrant students (Rumbaut & Cornelius, 1995). Proposition 227 has been seen as a direct threat to the 1974 U.S. Supreme Court decision, *Lau v. Nichols,* which supports the right of language-minority students to equal access to curricula and methods that can help them be successful. *Lau* is considered as important to proponents of bilingual education as *Brown v. Board of Education* is to proponents of civil rights.

Several policy researchers have begun to tackle this issue by taking a sociocultural approach to exposing hidden assumptions and inequities within policies that oppose bilingual education (Mora, 2002; Moses, 2000; Torrez, 2001). Moses (2000) and Mora (2002) critique the hidden values in state policies such as Proposition 227 and suggest that they represent a desire on the part of some policy makers and interest groups to maintain the privilege of English as the preferred language. By privileging English, both researchers suggest that an ELL student's heritage, home language, and culture are devalued.

Moses (2000, 2002), in particular, places the political and value-laden aspect of the policy issue at the center of her analysis. Utilizing a sociocultural approach that values cul-

Lived Realities: Am I Not Working Hard Enough?

Ms. Williams had been a kindergarten teacher at Sweetwater Elementary School in Georgia for the past twenty-five years. Her teaching assistant was one of her former students. One of the little girls in her class was the daughter of another teacher at the school, who also had been one of her former students. Ms. Williams had seen the school go from a homogeneous, thriving middle-class school serving children from the surrounding neighborhood to a high-poverty school serving primarily immigrant children whose first language was not English. Although many young upper middle class families lived in the surrounding neighborhood, most of their children went to private schools. Ms. Williams didn't mind the change; in fact, she welcomed the opportunity to serve children who needed extra nurturing. She was often given the most difficult children because she had a reputation for being effective with struggling children. She had seen many reforms and policies over the years. It seemed as though someone always had a great idea about how to "fix" education. As a master teacher, she would take aspects of the reform that seemed to work with students and integrate them with her own style, which involved using music and drama to help the students develop a love for reading and school.

What Ms. Williams sometimes found hard was that her class sizes often approached twenty-five students. She found it difficult because her room was relatively small, and with so many children whose parents did not speak English (or any single language), it was difficult to reach so many parents. She often used her own money to buy the children books because they had so few at home. Despite these hardships, she firmly believed in what she was doing, and she had nurtured so many children and seen them grow into successful adults; she was proud of her accomplishments. What was troubling her now was the new testing program being instituted by the state. If the school's test scores did not increase, then the entire school would have to adopt a very proscriptive school reform model. She found this troubling because she had always worked hard at her job and felt like a professional. She knew that the schools with the higher test scores also tended to have more White students and wealthier parents. She could have transferred to one of those other schools many times, but she elected not to because she felt she was needed at Sweetwater. She wanted to continue her legacy, but it was getting increasingly difficult. The new reform model would mean that she might not have the opportunity to use music in the same way. Some of her colleagues were talking about transferring to other schools. Why was it that policy makers always thought they knew how to fix education? Ms. Williams was not opposed to innovation or trying new things; she just wished the policy makers would acknowledge how hard she was working. She came in at 6 a.m. and often did not leave until after 4 p.m. It seemed that state policies always implied that she was a failure, that she was not working hard enough, yet the thousands of students she had nurtured over the years told her a different story. This new accountability program would make it hard for her. Many of her junior colleagues were talking about leaving the profession. Was she really not working hard enough?

ture and contextual issues, she suggests that policies that privilege English are oppressive because they support a "common culture" that is inherently racist and asssimilationist. This culture requires that "people of color change their identities in order to participate successfully in the dominant culture" (Moses, 2000, p. 339).

Additionally, Moses (2000) suggests that policy debates have ignored how bilingual education policy has fostered "heritage language students' self-determination" (p. 342). By allowing students to speak in their native languages, these programs give students greater power over decision making and their own learning. When students are placed in a situation in which they do not have the language to speak, raise questions, or understand the content of the lesson, they are effectively excluded from the dialogue, are "silenced," and thus lose any possibility of self-determination. Advocates for ELLs focus on the importance of valuing a student's native language and culture. Rather than viewing English as *the* only language, these perspectives suggest that valuing a student's native language is a way to value the student's native culture and, ultimately, the student.

Leadership for Social Justice

The increasing emphasis on standards has led many states to rethink they way in which they license and prepare educational leaders. The push for standards at the national level has also focused attention on leadership preparation and led to the creation of the Interstate School Leaders Licensure Consortium (ISLLC) standards for school leadership. The ISLLC standards are a set of national standards developed by the CCSSO as a guideline for leadership preparation programs.

At the same time, educational leadership scholars have felt increasingly concerned that social justice issues need to be central to educational leadership preparation (Marshall & McCarthy, 2002; Rapp, 2002). A group of leadership scholars committed to social justice formed an advocacy coalition (see Chapter 1 for a full description of the advocacy coalition framework) to make social justice an important focus of leadership preparation. This group convened regularly at professional meetings and stay connected via an e-mail listserve to discuss ways to conduct research aimed at highlighting the need for leaders who are sensitive to social justice. One outcome of the group was a collaborative research project designed to examine whether the translation of the ISLLC standards into state policy supported social justice. Scholars in seven states—Georgia, Indiana, New Jersey, New York, North Carolina, Ohio, and Texas—examined the connection between ISLLC, state licensure policies, and social justice (Marshall et al., 2001; Cambron-McCabe, 2004). The research project highlighted the need for policies that are intentional in their support for leadership preparation and for licensure that builds the capacity to support social justice (Marshall & Ward, in press). The re-framing of state policy around leadership preparation by these scholars led to an increased awareness that leaders need training in how to support social justice goals.

Hopeful Reconstructions

How can activist, re-visioned policies make it through the state political process? We end this chapter with a few heartening examples. Given that researchers have identified how an exclusive focus on English immersion can be detrimental to student self-worth and likelihood for success, what are some possibilities for addressing these issues? One group, the National Latino/a Education Research Agenda Project, based out of the *Centro de Estudios Puertorriquenos* at Hunter College, was formed to advocate for issues related to the long-term life prospects for Latino/a students and their communities (Pedraza, 2002).

This project brought together various constituencies within the Latino/a community to form a coalition aimed at identifying key issues and conducting research in support of Latino/a children. To that end, the project developed a national advisory board of practitioners, researchers, and community advocates to develop a research design to give "voice" to Latino/a perspectives on school reform. The group utilized a participatory action research design, which invited the participants in the research study to act as co-researchers. This methodological approach inverts the traditional approach to research, in which the researcher assumes the privileged position as the "authority" and "expert" on the research topic. The purpose of the research was to develop an empirical research base in order to document issues that have been ignored or minimized by policies and/or previous research. Such documentation is useful for educational leaders, as is the idea of inverting roles and thus shifting the power in collaborations.

Summary

This chapter examines the policy shifts, accountability pressures, and cultural cultural idiosyncrasies woven throughout state policies and politics. The national push for accountability, coupled with federal moves to devolve decision making to the state and local levels, has created a new emphasis on state responsibility for monitoring and supporting school reform. Increasing numbers of states are responding to this change by creating high-stakes accountability reform models that emphasize testing. NCLBA, which will be discussed further in Chapter 7, has reinforced this emphasis on holding schools accountable via standardized test scores. Yet, despite this shift toward accountability, states' assumptive worlds continue to frame policies differently in terms of how they monitor, assess, and fund schools. The focus on accountability has minimized a multitude of issues, such as funding inequities and poverty, English language learners and cultural imperialism, and school choice and democracy, that need to be addressed in order to support social justice.

Exercises for Critically Analyzing State Policy Shifts and Cultural Idiosyncrasies

1. Go to the Texas and North Carolina department of education websites and critically examine their accountability programs. How do they define *success?* How is learning measured? What happens if a school's scores are low? What do the programs have in common, and how are they different? In light of the issues discussed in this chapter, are there any issues that are not included in the information (e.g., issues related to differential resources or diversity)?

2. Use your research skills to find articles and information on Goals 2000. Examine all sides of the issue, including which groups opposed the legislation and who supported it. What was the crux of these arguments? Can you see any way that ideology might determine a state's set of curriculum standards? How could policy makers really think they could get their states to reach these goals?

3. Go to your state's department of education website and locate state codes related to current policies. Identify two to three laws that pertain to each of the policy mechanisms listed in Table 6.2.

4. Brainstorm research ideas aimed at exposing marginalized voices and groups in your state. Which groups or individuals are currently ignored or harmed by current policies? Which issues need attention?

5. Create a personal advocacy plan for influencing policy (accountability, teacher quality, site-based management, or one of personal interest) in your state. Which organizations could you join that are currently active in areas in which you are interested? Who are the key players (or advocates) that you could influence? What mechanisms could you use to influence policy (e.g., letters to politicians, affiliations with advocacy groups, or policy research that needs to be conducted)?

6. Look up your state's accountability policy (or a neighboring state's if your state has none). Then, go back to Chapter 2 and review the three overarching approaches to studying policy: structural, cultural, and policy studies and analysis. Use each of these lenses to examine the policy. What does each lens tell you about the policy? What do you want to know more about? Now, use either a sociocultural framework or discourse analysis to examine how one school is responding to the legislations. What are the "unintended consequences" of the policy? Are there any groups who are being harmed by the policy?

7. Reflect on your state's dominant political culture (traditional, moral, or individual), using the following political culture questions (adapted from Fowler, 2000, p. 99):

Traditional

- Is political participation viewed as a privilege for an elite few?

- Do most political leaders belong to an elite group?
- Are government bureaucracy and civil service systems viewed negatively?
- Are most political conflicts played out within a single dominant party?
- Is government's major role seen as maintaining the status quo?

Moral

- Is political participation valued?
- Are issues and principals important in political conflicts?
- Are government bureaucracy and civil service systems viewed positively?
- Do two parties exist with different ideological platforms, supplemented by occasional third-party activity?
- Is the government's major role seen as advancing the common good?

Individual

- Is politics viewed as a "dirty" marketplace best left to a few professionals?
- Do two political parties exist that are businesslike organizations, characterized by a high level of cohesiveness and competition?
- Are government bureaucracy and civil service systems viewed ambivalently—efficient but restrictive due to the system of mutual favors?
- Is government's major role seen as favoring economic development?

7

Federal Policy Communities, Interest Groups, and Standards

Guiding Questions _____

- How do federal politics and federal educational policy making have national impact?
- Who makes federal policy?
- Can federal policy be implemented effectively?
- What are the ways of analyzing federal politics and policy?
- How do individuals and groups influence federal education policy?

Have you ever wondered how the federal government influences educational policy? Have you ever wondered what politicians in Washington, DC, could possibly know about the real issues in classrooms and in families? Title I, free and reduced lunch programs, and the No Child Left Behind Act (NCLBA) are all federal policies that affect individual schools. You may be familiar with the titles, but how are these policies created in the first place? Who decides that schooling and lunches are related or that federal policy can require that school sites collect specific data. What are the politics affecting the legitimacy of such policies? This chapter focuses on understanding the shifting federal governmental role in educational policy making. Symbolic politics (see Chapter 1) can be powerful at this level. If a sitting president or powerful member of Congress chooses to champion an issue, he can use his position to focus national attention on the issue. He can also promote his policies via legislation in Congress.

Federal educational policy making is often dismissed by those who study education, because over the past two decades these funds have made up less than 10 percent of the total funds expended on education. But are those at federal level only minor players in understanding policy and politics in education? To address this question, we will examine how the federal role has changed, identify key players, determine key policy mechanisms, and explore how to influence the policy process.

The Evolving Federal Role in Education

Understanding the federal role in educational policy making requires understanding its evolving relationship with states' policy making. The original framers of the Constitution wanted to give states ultimate power over education, so that this power was not placed only in the hands of a few at the federal level. This decentralization of education policy laid the basis for an ongoing struggle between federal and state policy makers. While state constitutions require state decision makers to set their own education policy, federal policy makers debated over how large a role, as leaders and financiers, they should play in this process.

The emergent federal role in education dates back to the formation of our country. The framers of the Constitution were concerned with the development of an informed citizenry. The development of the Department of Education—the primary organization responsible for implementing federal education policy—dates back to 1867 (Vinovskis, 1999). The office was initially created as a research center and was housed first in the Bureau of the Interior and then in the Department of Health, Education and Welfare. It was not until 1979 that then-President Jimmy Carter, under pressure from the National Education Association (NEA), lobbied to elevate the head of the Department of Education (DOE) to Cabinet status. The legislation barely passed. Many groups and members of Congress were opposed to the DOE because they saw it as an attempt to usurp state and local decision-making power over education.

Republican reaction to President Carter's elevation of the DOE saw it as the creation of further bureaucracy and an infringement on state's rights. When Carter lost his bid for a second term, the Reagan administration sought to shift decision-making power away from the DOE. In an effort called *devolution,* and calling it "the new federalism," the Reagan presidency (1981–1988) sought to diminish the federal role in education, to give funds directly to states, and to minimize the DOE (Clark & Astuto, 1984). Republican resentment of the newly created DOE was so strong that in 1982 the Reagan administration proposed to take away the newly awarded Cabinet status of the secretary of education and eliminate the DOE. Although this attempt failed, the powers of the DOE were greatly diminished under the Reagan administration. Despite this diminishment of DOE power, the NEA had proved itself a powerful interest group in Washington.

While the Reagan administration sought to curtail the powers of the DOE, a report released during its tenure simultaneously served to support the need for a DOE. In 1983, the Commission on Excellence released *A Nation at Risk* (ANAR). This report criticized the public education system and made the case that the prosperity of the United States was in danger due to a failing education system. ANAR argued that a strong national educational system was needed to ensure a strong economy. ANAR served as an important touchstone in support of the DOE and led to the creation of the standards movement.

A national focus on standards originally came to fruition via the National Governors Association, which advocated for America 2000 and Goals 2000, national-level policies that emphasized the need for national standards. Presidents George H. W. Bush and

Lived Realities: The Creation of the Department of Education

Unlike many previous presidential candidates, Jimmy Carter's successful 1976 bid for the Democratic nomination relied heavily on developing grassroots support. His grassroots effort drew particularly on the National Education Association (NEA), which at the time was the largest union of elementary and secondary teachers and one of the largest unions in the United States. It signaled the first time the NEA had supported a presidential candidate and had become actively involved in a presidential election campaign. NEA members were trained in the specifics of political organizing. As reward for NEA support, Carter made a campaign promise to support the creation of a Department of Education (DOE) as a way to highlight the federal role in education and consolidate federal programs, which were spread between several different agencies.

Once Carter was in office, however, two of his chief advisors—Joseph A. Califano, Jr., the secretary of Health, Education and Welfare (HEW), and T. Bertram Lance, the director of the Office of Management and Budget (OMB)—were against the creation of the DOE. Califano and Lance both felt that an additional federal department and cabinet member would increase federal bureaucracy and limit the government's ability to coordinate programs for children. When over a year after he took office Carter decided to have the OMB study the feasibility of creating the DOE rather than moving ahead on the plan, the NEA responded with a letter campaign from its members. They made it clear they would withdraw their support if he did not create the DOE. Finally, in 1978, Carter made good on his promise and lobbied Congress to create a department of education. After much political infighting over which programs should fall under the umbrella of the DOE, the Senate and the House dropped their respective bills. In response, the NEA went after the support of individual representatives, and the president and his staff personally became very involved with the lobbying effort. Finally, in 1979, both the House and the Senate narrowly passed bills in support of the creation of the DOE.

Important educational programs successfully lobbied to not be included in the DOE. These programs included Head Start, which remained in HEW; Native American schools, which remained with the Bureau of Indian Affairs; a number of science education programs, which remained with the National Science Foundation; and the school lunch program, which remained with the U.S. Department of Agriculture. Those within these programs felt they were already appropriately situated. The Head Start program, for example, had been successful under HEW. Because Head Start is a family- and community-based program, its administrators were concerned that the DOE's focus would be school-based, and thus limit their ability to be effective. So, while President Carter and the NEA had successfully led a coalition to create the DOE, many education programs remained disbursed among other agencies.

William Clinton both championed the need for the federal government to lead the nation toward national standards. Clinton's successor, George W. Bush, continued the focus on national standards with NCLBA. A key facet of the NCLBA emphasized the use of standardized test scores as a way to hold high-poverty schools (designated under Title I) accountable for their performance. While each of the three presidents that succeeded Reagan focused on national standards, they also continued to emphasize the need for local control over schools. So although the federal role is seen as guiding the nation in school reform, it also acknowledges the importance of local decision making. Before discussing the federal role in greater detail, in the next section we examine the key players and arenas of power in which they operate.

At the Constitutional Convention centuries ago, the framers of the Constitution could not have envisioned the federal role, the federal powers, and the key actors involved today, nor could they have anticipated the need for facing national educational challenges. Given that local districts and states alone cannot or will not solve all schooling challenges, the following issues are open for highly politicized debate:

1. How far, and with what mechanisms, should the federal level go in creating funding equity?
2. What should the federal level do with national education challenges, such as the special needs of immigrant families?
3. Should the federal level coordinate policy, given that national economic development, family, health, housing, and defense policies can intertwine with, affect, and be affected by how well education systems are doing?

This list could go on. The Bill of Rights' equal protection clause has been used as the most accepted grounding for any federal role. Therefore, the least contested rationale in policy discourse for federal initiatives is grounded in arguments for equal access to schooling. However, other rationales (e.g., national strength, economic competition) hold, and even flourish, when crises open policy widows.

Key Players and Arenas of Power

To understand education policy making and implementation at the federal level, it is important to understand the key players that drive policy. Unlike state policy, federal policy is less likely to legislate on the specifics of how states or individual schools should educate their students, but it can still have an impact. The president of the United States and Congress are the major political players in federal education policy. The political clout of the federal level is enhanced when there is alignment between the party affiliation of the president and the majority party in the U.S. House and the Senate.

Beyond the president and Congress, there are a number of other players who influence federal policy. The secretary of education's primary role is to support the president's education policy platform. The Secretary also oversees the Department of Education, which is responsible for writing regulations that enact federal laws and distribute funds to individual schools and districts. (Specifics on the different kinds of federal funding are discussed in the next section.) Also, with the devolution of power to the states, the president and the secretary of education use the media to launch public relations campaigns to support their particular philosophies of education.

In presidential politics, campaigns are not won or lost on the platform statements on education. Still, there are real differences in education philosophies, as was evident during the 2000 election contest between Al Gore and George W. Bush. Gore favored universally available preschool, while Bush wanted to reform Head Start. Gore wanted to provide federal dollars for school construction, and Bush did not. Gore strongly opposed vouchers, but Bush would provide them to students in any persistently failing Title I schools. Campaign promises for education, along with ideas for housing, welfare and family support, economic development, the environment, and so on, are part of the domestic program that voters care about. Once a candidate is elected, however, the actual proposals he or she proposes can become mired in the political maneuvering of Congress. Despite these pitfalls, the rationales used for federal education policy proposals can still be uncovered in the language of platforms and speeches. Look, for example, at this excerpt, immediately following his words about jobs and the economy, from President Bill Clinton's 1994 State of the Union address: "We can . . . put our economic house in order, expand world trade, and target the jobs of the future . . . [if] we give our people the education, training, and skills they need to seize the opportunities of tomorrow. We must set tough, world class standards for all of our children. . . . Our Goals 2000 proposal will empower individual school districts to experiment with ideas like chartering their schools to be run by private corporations." One can see not only the proposal, but also the policy logic and the linking of education as human capital development with a valuing of business expertise! As another example, William Bennett utilized his position as secretary of education as a "bully pulpit," a public position from which he could use "moral suasion" to convince state governments and the American public to support the Reagan administration's platform on education policy (Clark & Astuto, 1986). To this end, Bennett developed his rhetorical strategy around the concept of the "three Cs." The three Cs emphasized the need to focus on curriculum content, parental choice, and the development of each student's character. His focus on content emphasized the need to concentrate on the basics of reading, writing, and mathematics, and on the "new basics" of science and computer skills. Bennett focused on parental choice to promote parental influence on the content of their children's education and to give parents choices for where their children attend school. His focus on character promoted school-based character education programs to teach students discipline and respect for others. Thus, instead of mandating that states take up these policy foci, Bennett used public relations (and some discretionary funds) to support these issues at the state and local levels. In these cases, the media served as an outlet for the political strategies of the key players and, in effect, became key players.

The key players in federal policy making are always shifting, depending on interest, their relative political power in Washington, the power of interest groups, and the available resources. Presidents play a key role in agenda setting; however, their power depends on a number of factors, including public opinion, the political context (health of the economy, international upheavals, personal scandals, and how strong their respective party is in the House and Senate). Individual members of Congress also serve as key policy makers by authoring individual bills on education. In 2002, for education initiatives, the "big four" were the chairmen and ranking Democrats on the Senate and House education committees (Schemo, 2002). The Individuals with Disabilities Act (IDEA) is one policy that was instigated by members of Congress. As with legislation instigated by a president, legislation initiated by congressional members requires support and depends on a number of key contextual and political factors.

Lobbyists and special interest groups influence the policy-making process in numerous ways. For example, they contribute money to campaigns, develop partisan research favoring specific policies, or threaten to withdraw support, which could translate into lost votes and contributions. At the national level, interest groups run the gamut from conservative groups, such as the Heritage Foundation, to liberal groups, such as NEA and AFT. The need for campaign contributions from major interest groups can greatly limit key actors' freedom to support education policies. For example, in considering school violence prevention, the NEA and the National Rifle Association might take very different stands, and both exercise power through their large constituency bases, the contributions they make, and their lobbying strengths. In these ways, we see the reality of how partisan politics affects the course of education policy.

Additionally, educational researchers (including think tanks) and the media can have an impact on policy. Often though, research and media organizations are used by policy makers to support a particular policy. While both of these often seek to be seen as unbiased or not endorsing political platforms, they both can be used to support political policies or pressure politicians to address issues. Table 7.1 provides an overview of the key players in federal policy making.

George W. Bush, for example, was seemingly successful at convincing Congress to support his No Child Left Behind Act. Yet despite Bush's interest in the legislation and a supportive Congress, appropriations for Title I, which funds the NCLBA, were cut. Thus, funding allocations provide help for only one-third of eligible children (NEA, 1999). The media's absence of critical attention to issues such as the lack of adequate resources for programs serves to support the NCLBA rather than subject the policy to a possible critique. Rod Paige's role as the secretary of Education has largely been to create public support for

TABLE 7.1   *Key Players in Federal Policy Making*

Player	Role	Example
President	Can set agenda for federal policy making	George W. Bush's development and support of the NCLBA.
Congress	Can set agenda for federal policy making	Passage of the NCLBA and reauthorization of IDEA and ESEA
Secretary of Education	Creates regulations and interprets legislation via the DOE	Rod Paige's promotion and support of the NCLBA
Supreme Court	Interprets the constitutionality of state and federal legislation and regulations	*Brown v. The Board of Education* (desegregation of schools)
Lobbyists and Special Interest Groups	Can lobby president and Congress to influence what gets on the policy-making agenda	NEA, AFT, Business Roundtable
Educational Researchers (University-based, Think Tanks, and Institutes)	Conduct research that provides justification for, assesses the merits of, or failures of legislation	RAND, the Heritage Foundation, Brookings Institute, DOE-funded research
Media	Serve as an outlet for information about policy issues	Newspapers, television, radio, the Internet, and magazines

the NCLBA via "moral suasion" in speeches, interviews, and public appearances (Paige, 2002). In regard to the NCLBA, the Business Roundtable has been an important interest group that lobbies in favor of greater accountability. Because the federal role in education is limited to its control over federal funding, its influences are tied to the money it allocates for particular programs. For, example, the NCLBA exerts a force over schools and districts by threatening to take funding away if schools' test scores remain low or if they are found in noncompliance with federal regulations.

Federal Policy Mechanisms

What is the federal role in education, and what are the mechanisms through which policy is created? Given that individual states have very different ways of funding education and differential resources, great disparities exist between the resources available to individual states. Although states have the constitutional right to govern education, the federal government can affect state policy via such political levers as agenda setting, legislation, judicial interpretations of the Supreme Court, and spending billions of dollars on various educational programs. Over the years the federal government has stepped in numerous times with funding for programs such as the Food Bill (free and reduced-price lunch program), the Elementary and Secondary Education Act (ESEA), and Title I, and with such policy directives as Title IX and IDEA. Federal funds and legislation have been largely targeted at students and schools that required additional funding beyond what they received locally and from the state. The free and reduced-price lunch program is aimed at providing food to children who otherwise might not eat.

Although many policies are created at the federal level, Congress is notorious for underfunding legislation, which effectively weakens the policy. For example, the FY2000 educational appropriations bill, H.R. 3064, included an initiative for class-size reduction. However, the program's funding was frozen at the 1999 level, and then an across-the-board cut of 1 percent was levied. Every school district would receive 1 percent fewer dollars, not enough to fully maintain the 29,000 new teachers hired. At the same time, the bill allowed communities to use the class-reduction money for any educational need, which means that communities with voucher programs like Milwaukee and Cleveland could use class-reduction dollars to fund vouchers (Levin, 2000). Just as a lack of funding can weaken a federal policy, a lack of specific regulations means that some funds can be used in a way not originally intended by policy makers.

Legislation and Funding Mechanisms

Federal funding generally falls within three different types that range in terms of the freedom the local level has in meeting their specific needs. General aid represents the greatest freedom for individual schools and districts, while categorical aid is the least restrictive. Block grants fall somewhere between the two in that the money is often not tightly regulated, but when applying for grants, schools must be specific regarding how they intend to use the money.

General Aid. These funds are broadly targeted to an issue such as school improvement. There are few federal guidelines that mandate how the money should be spent.

Block Grants. These funds fall between general aid and categorical aid. Although these funds are not tightly regulated, individual schools must specify how the money is to be used.

Categorical Aid. These funds are tightly restricted and must be used in accordance with federally specified guidelines.

Table 7.2 shows that the federal expenditures for elementary and secondary education are relatively small compared with state and local contributions, yet federal funding represents over $22 billion per year.

For the past twenty years, federal expenditures have hovered between 9 percent and 6 percent of the total expenditures on elementary and secondary education. Because the percentage is relatively small, the influence of the federal level is often dismissed, because it constitutes a small portion of overall funds. Any superintendent, principal, parent, student, or teacher, however, is aware of the way in which federal legislation such as IDEA and the free and reduced-price lunch program affect individual schools and districts. For example, IDEA not only brings money into schools and districts to support students with disabilities, but also provides legal protections, which can lead to legal action if schools are not seen as complying.

The regulations that accompany federal funding—created largely by congressional mandates or staff within the DOE—place restrictions on how funds can be utilized by individual schools and districts. Regulations that specify how funds are to be used can have an impact on how policy is implemented at local sites. For example, for a school to qualify for schoolwide Title I funds, the majority of a school's students must qualify and participate in the school's free and reduced-price lunch program. This schoolwide designation means that funds can be used to pay for additional staff or materials, which can be used for

TABLE 7.2 *Expenditures for Elementary and Secondary Education*

	Total	Federal Expenditures (percentage of total)	State Expenditures (percentage of total)	Local Expenditures (percentage of total)	Percentage of Gross Domestic Product
1980	96,881	9,504 (9.8)	45,349 (46.8)	42,029 (43.4)	4.0
1985	137,295	9,106 (6.6)	67,169 (48.9)	61,020 (44.4)	3.9
1990	208,548	12,701 (6.1)	98,239 (47.1)	97,608 (46.8)	4.3
1995	273,149	18,582 (6.8)	127,730 (46.8)	126,838 (46.4)	4.4
1999	347,378	24,522 (7.1)	169,298 (48.7)	153,558 (44.2)	—

Note: Data in millions of dollars.

Source: From Burrup, P. E., Brimley, V., Jr., & Garfield, R. R. (1999). *Financing Education in a Climate of Change,* 8th ed. Published by Allyn and Bacon, Boston, MA. Copyright © 2002 by Pearson Education. Reprinted by permission of the publisher.

all the children in the school, not just the ones who have signed up for the lunch program. But, a school that does *not* qualify for schoolwide Title I funds faces much tighter restrictions on how those Title I funds they do receive can be spent: Title I teachers may be hired with those funds, but they are not allowed to work with students who are not designated Title I. Also, any materials purchased with Title I funds may not be shared with any other teachers or students. This creates a bureaucratic layer in the school in which division between Title I students and teachers is reinforced.

Equity Values in Federal Legislation. As mentioned in the beginning of this chapter, the federal role in education is most easily justified by the need to enforce equal access and to address the weaknesses and inequities inherent in state education policy.

There is a tradition of federal education equity initiatives. Federal action attempting to redress perceived inequities in education dates back to the 1870s, when federal policy via the Bureau of Indian Affairs sought to use education programs to assimilate American Indians and Alaska Natives (AI/AN) into westernized culture. The intent behind these programs was to teach AI/AN children how to speak and write English and to act in accordance with American cultural norms. AI/AN children were seen as savages in need of taming via education. It has only been in the past thirty years that AI/AN tribes have been successful in their activism and have taken control of reservation schools and created programs that value AI/AN culture (Lipka, 2002).

Despite this federal interest in educating AI/ANs, the federal government primarily allowed individual state governments to handle domestic issues. This *laissez faire* approach—avoiding governmental intrusion or regulation of business—changed dramatically after the Great Depression (Patterson, 1996). For example, out of concern for widespread poverty, the School Lunch Act was created in 1946 and was housed in the Department of Agriculture, where it resides today.

In the 1960s, under the leadership of Lyndon B. Johnson, Congress passed the Great Society programs aimed at waging war on poverty. Many observers and policy makers at the time linked education to curing poverty, and these views drove passage in 1965 of the Elementary and Secondary Education Act (ESEA). The centerpiece of ESEA was Title I, which provided additional resources to schools and districts to support the education of low-income students. Additionally, Title IX of ESEA sought to redress the inequities perpetrated against AI/ANs by providing additional funding to districts that educated AI/AN students. Project Head Start also was funded in 1965 in response to research that suggested that children living in poverty are less academically prepared when they enter school (Vinovskis, 1999). Head Start focused on providing early childhood education and fostering parental involvement in that education. (As noted in Chapter 2, Head Start was terminated briefly but was reinstated after a more complete and favorable evaluation and, perhaps more importantly, after large numbers of activist constituents demanded continuation of its services.) Table 7.3 highlights key federal equity policies.

Although federal funding is a relatively small portion of the money expended on education, it has provided additional resources and services to students living in poverty and to children with disabilities. It has, concomitantly, provided legitimacy and rationales at state, district, local, and micro levels for parents, activists, and educators who face resistance when they need special provisions for students with unequal access to the benefits of schooling.

TABLE 7.3   *Key Federal Equity Policies*

Policy	Intended Purpose
Free and Reduced-Price Lunch Program	To provide nutritious meals to children who might not otherwise eat
Project Head Start (1965)	To provide early childhood education for children living in poverty
Individuals with Disabilities Education Act (IDEA) (1975)	To support and protect students identified as having a disability
Title I of the Elementary and Secondary Education Act (ESEA) (1960)	To equalize educational opportunities for lower income children
Title IX of ESEA	To promote gender equity in schools

Quality Values and Development Goals in Federal Legislation.   Federal initiatives for assuring education quality have a history as well. Federal allocation of acreage for schools in frontier lands and for land grant colleges demonstrates some shared concern at the federal level for developing human capital throughout the nation. The provisions in federal funding to support curricular experimentation in math and sciences in the 1960s and the Pell grants for college students are similar investments for quality.

A major event that deepened federal interest in quality goals for education was the 1957 Russian launch of *Sputnik,* the first successful space satellite. With the Cold War at its height, the launch of *Sputnik* created public concern that the American education system was technologically inferior to Russia's and a risk to national defense. As a result, Congress passed the National Defense Education Act of 1958 to provide additional funding to schools and states in support of science, mathematics, and foreign language instruction (Rippa, 1992).

A later significant shift in federal policy toward quality goals was the creation and passage in 1994 of Goals 2000: the Educate America Act. This program emerged out of meetings with the National Governor's Association, which agreed that there needed to be a set of national standards for elementary and secondary schools (Fritzberg, 2001). Researchers, education interest groups, and expert panels debated contentiously over the issues of what standards, what topics, how to measure progress, and, of course, who would control it all. Ultimately, Democrats and Republicans could not agree on how to interpret the standards for the states, did not fully fund the program, and subsequently eliminated it in 2000. Goals 2000 took its place in a long line of underfunded federal education initiatives that demanded change without the resources necessary to accomplish such change.

The new president and majority party in 2001 passed a new policy: George W. Bush's No Child Left Behind Act (NCLBA) represents a further step toward national standards. The program is aimed at schools identified as Title I and requires that students be tested annually in grades three to eight. If a school's test scores do not meet the standards, it risks punitive measures, such as reduced funding. The NCLBA is a good example of a dominant discourse and a mobilization of a mindset and logic pervading state and national policies. Thus, accountability as a dominant way of framing education policy in states can also drive federal policy. Table 7.4 highlights the key developmental and quality policies.

Although the NCLBA is listed as a policy aimed at improving quality, it also attempts to encompass equity, excellence, and choice goals. The policy is a component of Title I of ESEA and is targeted at high-poverty schools. The NCLBA clearly has an "equity" component in that it is targeted at failing children in high-poverty schools. But it also emphasizes efficiency and choice. Efficient, cost-effective, aggregate standardized test scores are the designated measure for determining which schools are failing. Additionally, parents of children whose schools continue to fail will have the "choice" of sending their children to a neighboring nonfailing school. Policies such as the NCLBA pursuing multiple values and using multiple mechanisms and instruments often create what a Washington policy analyst called "the mother of all unintended consequences." Despite the inclusion of additional value frames, the policy is predominantly focused on quality values, as evidenced in its concentration on standardized test scores as the measure of success.

Supreme Court Decisions

The states have the right to create and implement education policy, but state policies must operate within the context of constitutional law. Because Supreme Court Justices are presidential appointees, the political composition of the court (i.e., which political party made the nomination) is central to its decision making. The power of the court rests in the hands of seven judges, so one or two retirements from the court during a given presidency may have a big impact on whether a court decision might represent more conservative, liberal, or centrist leanings.

One of the most significant Supreme Court decisions in the past century was *Brown v. The Board of Education* (1954). This landmark case ruled that the "separate but equal" policy of racially segregating students in schools was unconstitutional. Specifically, the court found *de jure* segregation, meaning the segregation that was not the result of choice on the part of students and parents but enforced by school district policies, to be unconstitutional. Because almost 40 percent of students were attending schools considered to be segregated *de jure* at the time, this policy had a great impact an state educational systems (Ravitch, 1983).

TABLE 7.4 *Key Developmental and Quality Federal Policies*

Policy	Intended Purpose
National Defense Act	To assist states in funding science, mathematics, and foreign language instruction
Goals 2000: Educate America Act (1994)	To assist states in developing common performance standards and assessment tools
No Child Left Behind Act	To promote literacy and testing standards for lower income children

Although the Supreme Court does not directly make policy, its decisions can invalidate federal, state, or local policies. The *Brown* decision forced many school districts to develop desegregation policies or face litigation. While the political pressure came from the federal level, the costs involved in integrating individual schools and districts had to be provided by the state and local levels. Legal scholars refer to the decision as an example of an act of judicial activism, a reinterpretation of constitutional law in order to promote social change (Kalodner, 1990). Once the decision was made, the court's role evolved into a regulatory function in the sense that litigation could be brought against individual districts that were still segregating students to separate schools.

In the past few years, the Court's original ruling in *Brown* has undergone another reinterpretation, with respect to what actually constitutes *de jure* segregation. Many school districts across the country have seen schools resegregating by race and socioeconomics (Orfield, 1994). At the same time in the past decade, federal courts have started to interpret this segregation as constitutional, because they see it as the result of geographic segregation and not intentional on the part of school districts. Reinterpretation has left the determination of whether segregated schools are constitutional up to the interpretation of state courts (Green, 1999).

As mentioned in Chapter 6, twenty years after *Brown,* in 1974, the court also ruled on another landmark case, *Lau v. Nichols.* In the *Lau* case, the court decided that language-minority students had the right to equal access to curricula and teaching methods that can help them succeed. In both the *Lau* and *Brown* cases, the court addressed the issue of the rights of minorities to receive equal access to education. The Court also has handed down decisions on the importance of providing special education services for special needs children and has stepped in when state funding methods have unfairly disadvantaged low-income districts. There are myriad of other issues the court can decide to take up at any time, from school prayer to curriculum content. As a political player, the Supreme Court can make a significant impact on education policy. All it needs is the right case and the willingness of all seven justices to agree to hear it.

Executive and Congressional Appointments and Staffs

As the chief executive, the president, with the advice and consent of the Senate, selects and appoints people to key positions that affect education. Cabinet members are often appointed primarily for their ability and willingness to work closely with and advise the president, along with running an agency and symbolizing national interest (e.g., in education, health, etc.). Overly independent and controversial Cabinet appointees often do not get or keep their positions. Jocelyn Elders, surgeon general in the Clinton administration, famously spoke out in favor of sex education and birth control availability for adolescents and was forced to resign. William Bennett held tremendous power as secretary of education by articulating a philosophy and policies that harmonized with administration values and goals. Even something as seemingly straightforward as the appointment and duties of the commissioner of education statistics can get caught up in political tensions (as will be illustrated in Chapter 8). Power in these appointments is not only symbolic. Political appointees manage huge bureaucracies that disseminate money, determine which aspects of congressional policy will actually get emphasized in policy regulations, and interpret legislative intent.

For Cabinet posts and a wide range of agency positions, appointments often are token rewards for loyal party workers who demonstrated their worth and their agreement with the values and goals of the party during electioneering. Political stances toward education can be initiated by using the mechanism of appointments. President Bush enacted his stance on accountability by creating (through legislation) a new agency. Strategically named the Institute of Education Sciences (IES), he appointed researchers who would support his stance and sought to eliminate from the national education research database (ERIC) any research findings that did not fit with the policy goals of his administration. Stone's (1997) instruments for structuring implementation (mentioned in Chapter 2), specifically the strategy of promoting certain *facts,* provide a way of seeing Bush's strategy as a method for ensuring support for the implementation of the NCLBA. Key political appointees, rhetoric supporting the effectiveness of accountability, and the removal of contradictory research data worked together to buttress the implementation of the NCLBA.

In Congress, committee chairs and membership powerfully shape the destiny of education policy possibilities. Political parties' caucuses promote senators and representatives to education committees based on their seniority, interest, and status. The party with the majority, in each chamber, has the right to appoint the chair and members. These powerful committees define policies, judge their legitimacy, and hold hearings that are about policy alternatives, about constituencies' needs, and, sometimes even about research, evaluation, and policy analyses that could inform decisions.

Staff members in Congress and the executive branch are appointed because of their loyalty and their expertise. They often have the most expertise on issues and feed that information, as well as useful rhetoric, to their bosses. They also assist in dealing with lobbyists, with constituent demands, and with public relations. At the same time, campaign staffers are working, as are policy makers, with an eye to mobilizing support and raising money for the next election. In her shadowing of Senator Culver of Iowa, Drew (1979) noted countless instances in which scanning a staffer's summary was Culver's only preparation for his next action, in which brief contact with a constituent or a lobbyist shaped the senator's questions, and in which a brief visit to a boys' detention center was the basis for major policy planning.

In his sociocultural approach, Weatherford (1981) identifies how one becomes a "Congressional Big Man . . . in a national milieu of volatile ideological stances, voters, and tactics, there is still a need for a certain underlying constancy in tactics if the politician is to succeed" (p. 78). He may change his stand, but he may not change the clan mentality of his own personal political organization. Weatherford (1981) asserts that congressional control over their bureaucratic agencies is a crucial political skill. He gleans insights from comparisons with Watusi warriors, pointing out that the Watusi's elaborate displays are not what gives them power so much as their ability to control tribes with oratorical skills and ritual, using battle only as the last resort. Placing former staffers in prominent lobbying jobs is a strategy Big Men use to control lobbies. Rituals, taboos, courtesy calls, the power of the dance, the hidden authority, and the power of the undramatic media expert, policy analyst, or lawyer are realities observed in "tribes on the Hill." In more recent years, the power of seniority was illustrated when a congressional insider commented, "Thurmond is like royalty, and he can get what he wants around here." The insider was referring to Strom Thurmond, who at the time was using his position as a long-term senator from South Carolina to get his inexperienced nephew appointed to a high position.

Research as a Strategic Tool

Members of Congress (or their staff), the president, the secretary of education, and lobbyists and special interest groups can use research to support or oppose legislation. Though strategically placed research also can be used in state and local arenas, most of the research available to date has focused on how research has been used to influence federal policy. Looking at Congressional Committees in particular, Weiss (1989) provides a framework (Table 7.5) for looking at how legislators can use research to frame policy issues.

Research and information can be deployed on behalf of specific values or presuppositions to support or reject policy options. For example, data on literacy rates and test scores on math and science have been used to argue that America's educational system is in crisis and to suggest a need for a national focus on school reform (Berliner & Biddle, 1997). *A Nation at Risk* (ANAR), Goals 2000, and the NCLBA are all examples of federal initiatives that use data to argue for a greater federal role in education.

Research data also can be used to support the platform of a particular politician. For example, Gerstl-Pepin (2002) found that in the 2000 presidential election, George W. Bush used research produced by the Rand Corporation (Grissmer et al., 2000) to support his credibility as an education president. Specifically, Bush used the fact that the report suggested that the accountability program he instituted as the governor of Texas might have caused an increase in test scores. The research became evidence that he had credible and success-

TABLE 7.5   *Legislative Uses of Analytical Information*

Function That Information Serves	Use to Which It Is Put

Support for preexisting position
  Certifies that the position is right
	Political ammunition
	  Reinforces advocates' confidence in their stand
	  Strengthens coalition
	  Persuades undecided members
	  Weakens opponents' case and support

Warning
  Signals that a problem is (or is not) severe
	Reordering the agenda
	  Moves the problem up (or down) on the policy agenda

Guidance
  Indicates better alternatives
	Design of activities
	  Leads to legislative provisions, amendments, further questions

Enlightenment
  Offers new constructs, new ways of thinking about issue
	Modification in thinking
	  Reconceptualizes issues
	  Raises level of discussion

Source: From Carol H. Weiss. Congressional committees as users of analysis. *Journal of Policy Analysis and Management,* vol. 8, no. 3, p. 425. Copyright 1989 by the Association for Public Policy Analysis and Management. Used by permission.

ful experience leading education reform, even though later reports (ignored by the Bush campaign) called those conclusions into question.

As recounted in Chapter 2, policy analyses, evaluations, and policy studies are used and abused. Countless similar stories can be told of political agendas driving research. But federal support of education research and development is miniscule. DOE, in 2000, had authority over just $210 million for research and development, while the Department of Agriculture had almost $2 billion, NASA had almost $10 billion, and Health and Human Services together with the National Institutes of Health had over $8 billion (American Educational Research Association, 2000a).

Media

The role of the media in federal educational policy has generally focused on the role the media plays (1) in representing issues (its degree of autonomy and its strategic use by politicians) and (2) in electoral politics.

Federal-level policy makers often operate as "doctors of spin," seeking to use the media to present their issues and concerns in the best possible light (Spring, 1998). The media are set up as political players in their own right and wield a tremendous amount of power in terms of how they choose to represent issues to the public. The media then can be viewed as a vehicle for politicians to advocate for issues via such strategies as moral suasion, used by such political players as George W. Bush and Rod Paige in championing the NCLBA. It also can be seen, however, as a political entity of its own, one that wields tremendous power in determining which issues are covered and how issues are presented. For example, an insider in the George H. W. Bush administration suggested that the media's penchant for political sound bites resulted in the Bush administration emphasizing "family" in the 1988 election (Spring, 1998). Peace was also a value that Bush had emphasized in a speech, but the media chose to highlight "family," which ended up being the focus of the 1988 Bush campaign.

Additionally, the role of the media in education issues and electoral politics is a relatively unexplored topic (Opfer, 2002). Media coverage can focus attention on a particular issue at the expense of other issues, but does it affect whether or not a candidate is elected? At the federal level, September 11, 2001, led to an increased focus on "homeland security." Though education is often seen as an important issue at the federal level, foreign policy and the state of the economy tend to be perceived as even more critical (Gerstl-Pepin, 2002). Clearly, the media are key players at the federal level; however, much more research is needed to understand how the media do or do not influence educational policy.

Multiple mechanisms can be used to influence or create policy. In the next section, we examine how to make sense of the multiple arenas and mechanisms through which federal policy is influenced, developed, and implemented.

Conceptual Lenses for Studying Federal Policy

An array of lenses can be used to study policy and policy making at the federal level (Chapters 1 and 2 provide numerous examples). In this chapter, we focus on three of the more prominent approaches used at the federal level: values focused, evaluation/outcome focused, and process focused. The values focus seeks to understand the ideological nature of policy making and how policies represent certain value stances. This approach dates back many decades to the work of Easton (1965a), who argued that policy represented the "authoritative allocation of values." The implementation approach examines the outcomes of a given program or policy. These approaches can be either summative, aimed at judging whether a program is effective or not, or informative, aimed at understanding the process of implementation, such as the unintended consequences of a given policy. The process focus approach, such as the concept of "policy windows," seeks to understand how policy streams converge at a particular time, creating an opening for action, to become part of the political agenda, and then are ultimately transformed into legislation or policy.

The Values Approach

As mentioned in Chapter 1, the values approach focuses on identifying which values are represented by a given policy. These studies focus on understanding how educational politics and the resulting policies represent a certain set of beliefs about what should be the purpose of education. This approach was discussed at length in Chapter 6 as a way that is useful for understanding state policy. These approaches help to analyze the dominant values and to identify how and where values shift over time. In the earlier discussion of funding and legislation mechanisms, this approach helped identify the shift in values toward policies that focus on quality.

Education leaders and policy analysts use this values approach to help them understand politics as a battle over values. Policies reflect particular stances, such as equity, excellence, choice, and efficiency, the four core values that are often in conflict in political debates (Stout, Tallerico, & Scribner, 1995). When looking at federal policies, this approach tends to focus on value conflicts between the Democratic and Republican parties and the interest groups they represent, or it addresses the deeply held values within our culture. Using this approach, one can identify how presidential administrations or members of Congress reflect certain values stances or how their stances and their policy proposals reflect deeper societal fissures.

Recently, values approaches have expanded beyond the four core values and become more nuanced. Labaree's (1997) work identified three key goals concerning education as a public good and how these goals conflict and compete with one another. The first goal is *democratic equality,* which implies that the purpose of education is to prepare students to participate in democratic politics on an equal basis. The second goal is *social efficiency,* which emphasizes that the goal of schooling is to prepare students for the economic world of work. The third goal is *social mobility,* which views education as a "private good designed to prepare individuals for successful social competition for more desirable market roles" (Labaree, 1997, p. 42). The first goal is to prepare students to be political actors in pursuit of equity, but the remaining two goals seek to prepare students for market competition. Essentially, these goals conflict because they are at odds with each other. *Competition,* by definition, means that some will succeed while others fail, which is at odds with the desire for democratic equality. As Labaree suggests, the idea that schools should be making workers more than making republicans has undermined the ability of schools to act as a mechanism for promoting equality of access and equality of treatment. The notion of educational equality is at best irrelevant to the expansion of GNP. . . . (p. 49)

The federal government's shift to block grants is one example of the move toward fostering competition among schools as a means to improve schools. The limitation of this approach is that it does not ensure that all students will receive the resources they need. Schools must compete with each other over limited resources just as students must also compete with each other for merit.

Education as a means for individuals getting what they need for themselves and their families has become a dominant goal with significant political clout. According to Labaree (1997), "Public education has increasingly come to be perceived as a private good that is harnessed to the pursuit of personal advantage" (p. 43). This shift in focus, Labaree suggests, has had profoundly negative consequences by not emphasizing the need for schools to pursue education as a common good. Labaree's concerns are echoed by Boyd (1991), who identified a startling political turn in the 1980s away from policy aimed at ameliorating social justice issues toward policy aimed at fostering competition. Additionally, Kahne (1994), mentioned in Chapter 3, makes this emphasis on competition problematic and suggests that policies should be assessed for the degree to which they develop citizens and community relationships. Rather than buy into a competitive value system, he suggests that schools could value democratic participation as much as they value test scores.

Clark and Astuto (1986) provide a detailed examination of how the values of excellence and choice were represented in the federal educational policies of the Reagan administration. They argued that excellence was represented in policies that fostered institutional competition, such as awards to principals and teachers, merit pay, and career ladders for teachers. Choice, they argued, was represented in policies that emphasized tuition tax credits and vouchers.

Federal policies often support certain values. "Equity" values, for example, are seen as guiding policies such as IDEA and Title I, which are both aimed at providing extra resources for students who may be disadvantaged due to poverty or disability. Goals 2000, in contrast, which focused on national standards, could be seen as a policy that represented the value of excellence. These approaches focus on how certain policies privilege certain values over others and can aid our understanding of why some policies are selected over others.

The NCLBA represents an interesting case in that it clearly represents the conflicting values of excellence and equity. Excellence is valued, because the law expects that Title I schools that serve high numbers of children in poverty must increase their students' test scores. Equity is also valued because the policy provides additional resources for high-poverty schools. Yet because equity is considered to be achieved when aggregate scores reach minimum standards of literacy, there is no provision to ensure that students will gain knowledge about their own political agency. Increased test scores are thus equated with democratic equality. Additionally, because the NCLBA was underfunded by Congress, it does not reach all of the schools in need of additional resources.

Implementation Studies

As noted in Chapter 2, key questions about implementation are "How should policies be implemented?" and "What results or outcomes result from implementation (or a lack thereof)?" When applied to federal policy, using this implementation approach means focusing on questions such as "Is the program effective?" "Are the layers of the education system responding and complying or resisting?" and "Is this program meeting its goals?" Since the 1970s, implementation research underwent three primary stages (Odden, 1991b). In the first stage, studies focused on macro-implementation issues, such as whether federal policies were implemented at the local level. The 1968 Vocational Education Act and ESEA were some of the policies studied. In the second stage, implementation studies such as the Rand Change Agent Study (McLaughlin, 1990) sought to understand what happened to federal monies and federal policy intentions in the 1960s. McLaughlin found that federal policies were implemented at the local level but rarely in accordance with the original intention of the policy. The study examined four federally funded programs: the Right-to-Read program, the 1968 Vocational Education Act, and Title III and Title VII of ESEA. The results of her study highlighted effective projects and noted that these projects were the result of localized mutual adaptations rather than uniform implementation of federal policies or procedures (McLaughlin, 1990). These findings highlighted the need for local flexibility and the need for schools to adopt programs to fit their specific needs. The five-year (1973–1978) study was funded by the U.S. Office of Education.

Studies like the Change Agent Study raised awareness that federal programs were implemented but not necessarily effective. The question for much of the implementation studies that followed focused on how to assure not only implementation but also that the program was effectively achieving its goals. These studies vary in their approach (Odden, 1991b). For example, McDonnell and Elmore (1991) argue that policy implementation depends on instruments such as incentives, mandates, regulations, and funds. Thus, education leaders and policy analysts can focus on the mechanisms through which policies are implemented. McLaughlin (1990) takes a different approach and, based on her earlier findings with the Change Agent Study, suggests that analysis should focus on micro-interactions at the local level, because these sites are "critical" for implementation to occur. Despite this awareness, education systems' lowerarchies and street-level bureaucrats have the power to resist and even re-create policy intentions (detailed in Chapter 2), and despite the critical component of micro-interactions and micropolitics (discussed in Chapter 4), federal programs have tended to leave it up to state governments or local districts to determine if changes have been implemented. This often means simply filling out forms that indicate minimal compliance. It also means, especially for policies that disrupt assumptions and practices and challenge the powers-that-be, that compliance will be cynically opportunistic and the backlash will build up. In this way, "paperwork" becomes a negative condensation symbol, collecting the array of emotions toward government intrusion, mandates from above, states' rights, lack of respect for teachers' hard work, and so on.

The NCLBA represents a significant change in the governance policy mechanism. Instead of direct federal imposition and scrutiny, the governance mechanism shifts the implementation, control, and monitoring to state responsibility. However, the NCLBA directs states to use standardized test scores as the primary method of assessing the implementation effectiveness of policy. So federal policy tells states what to do, tells them how to do it, gives them the responsibility to implement, and allows them few options regarding policy instruments and mechanisms for monitoring and enforcing. Thus, for states whose policy makers might want to focus on classroom practice, federal policies emphasize test score outcome measures, leaving little leeway for state and local alternative approaches.

Studying Current Implementation Policies. In recent years, federal policies have shifted away from categorical programs that target specific groups to ones that are more interested in promoting whole school reform. Multiple policies now affect schools and districts, so implementation studies need to look at whether the array of programs is having a positive or negative effect. Title I funding and NCLBA, IDEA, the free and reduced-price lunch, school improvement grants, standards, and standardized testing are all aspects of federal policy foci that can have an impact on a given school. For example, Peterson, Rabe, and Wong (1986) traced the evolution of Title I of ESEA and how the policy shifted its relationship with the local level. They demonstrate the difficulty of understanding federal policy implementation without understanding the evolving relationship among federal, state, and local governments in the implementation of a given program. With the shift to state testing and assessment programs, individual states have chosen to multiply the forms of assessment.

Process Analyses

As mentioned in Chapter 1, an array of conceptual approaches can be used to analyze the policy formulation process (e.g., assumptive worlds, policy communities, policy issue networks, and policy streams). These conceptual lenses share an interest in identifying who the major players are in terms of making and influencing policy. What are the key policy issues? Who makes policy? Who decides which issues are important? Why are some issues raised and others not? How do issues get on the public agenda? One of the most prominent approaches to understanding federal education policy making is the concept of "policy windows." One good example of this approach examines the confluence of forces that create a window of opportunity for policy shifts. Kingdon (2003) identifies three key policy streams: problem recognition, policy proposals, and politics.

To understand these processes in education, it is important to think of them as part of a policy community focused on bringing about a policy change. The policy community includes bureaucrats, Capitol Hill staffers, academics, interest groups, media representatives, and researchers. The policy community can be influenced by shifting public opinion, elections, changes in administration, and shifts in partisan or ideological groupings in Congress (Kingdon, 2003).

The concept of a policy window is useful for understanding the increasing national push for standards and the influence business interests have had on education. Business leaders have formed national coalitions, such as the Business Roundtable, intent on promoting standards in education and holding schools and teachers responsible for student performance (Borman, Castenell, & Gallagher, 1993). These special interest groups have influenced individual states such as Texas and North Carolina, which have instituted high-stakes accountability programs. At the national level, a policy window opened with the bipartisan support of Goals 2000. Support for the NCLBA signals a continuing interest nationally in promoting standards and high-stakes testing as a way to improve education.

In the following Lived Realities, a little-known senator from the state of Vermont changed the balance of power in the Senate by changing parties in response to party resistance to increasing special education funding. Despite this dramatic shift in power brought about by his principled stand, special education did not fit the push for higher standards.

Lived Realities: Sometimes One Vote Can Make a Difference

When George W. Bush took office in 2001, it looked as though the Republicans would be able to dominate policy making at the federal level. For the first time since the Eisenhower administration, Republicans were in control of the House and the Senate. It looked good for the Republican plan to cut taxes and keep the budget at its previous levels. But for then-Republican senator James M. Jeffords of Vermont, tax cuts were not high on the priority list. Jeffords, a long-time supporter of the Individuals with Disabilities Act (IDEA), was not going to support the Republican budget without assurances that additional funding would be allocated to IDEA. Jeffords, chair of the Senate Education Committee, felt that the biggest failure of federal government in regard to IDEA was its inability to pay its fair share of the funds required to provide for disabled children. The cost of educating a child with a disability is roughly twice the cost of educating a student without a disability. Jeffords felt the federal government had a responsibility to IDEA, which dated back to 1975. When IDEA was created, federal policy makers intended to shoulder about 40 percent of the cost of educating a disabled child. Jeffords believed that the federal government had never shouldered more than 15 percent of the cost. He was concerned that small communities, which are numerous in his home state of Vermont, would disproportionately shoulder the responsibility of educating a child with a disability. Educating just a few children with a disability could devastate a small district's education budget and result in higher property taxes and public resentment against special education. Jeffords wanted the Republican leadership to fund IDEA to the intended 40 percent commitment and shift the program from a discretionary program (a less stable position) to a mandatory spending program (which would assure funding). The Republican party line, however, did not see the increase in spending for IDEA as necessary. According to Jeffords (2001), "Only in Washington, D.C., I suspect, is spending for educating disabled students across the nation considered a pork barrel project" (p. 75). Ultimately, Jeffords did not side with the Republican leadership, and instead supported a bipartisan plan that allocated more funds for education. Republican backlash was strong and Jeffords decided to leave the party and become an Independent. His actions tipped the balance of power in the Senate toward the Democrats, significantly curtailing Republican power (Jeffords, 2001).

The Jeffords vignette shows how difficult it can be to influence federal policy when a policy window is not open to support an issue. Unlike the reauthorization of the NCLBA, which promotes the establishment of a national testing program (Lewis, 2002), fully funding IDEA lacks the same support at the federal level. Standards and national testing in the current policy window are seen as important to the economic prosperity of the nation, whereas IDEA was perceived as important but not critically in need of additional federal support.

Policy Communities, Assumptive Worlds, and Realities of Partisan Politics. For members of Congress and for the president, the constraints of regulations and traditions, the constitutional balance of powers among the executive, judicial, and legislative branches, and the realities of electoral politics greatly affect the stances they adopt in education politics. Strange things happen because of dictates from centuries ago, such as the phenomenon of the Electoral College structure and the Supreme Court ruling on the Florida vote in the 2000 presidential election, leading to Bush being appointed as president, although he did not win the popular majority vote. Strange behaviors happen, such as the rituals of congressional politeness (as when you know two Representatives totally disagree and will fight to the end, but you hear, "I have utmost regard for my esteemed colleague from North Dakota, but I must adamantly protest the veracity of his statement about vouchers."). Political analysts, staff, pollsters, campaign managers, and "policy wonks" (people with special expertise or a habit of constantly examining political intricacies) provide a running commentary on what the electoral effects would be for a politician to take a stand on an issue. The specter of a third-party candidate or two appearing and ready to take up causes that get too little voice in the two-party competition is always a possibility, or at least a worry, for siphoning off votes.

The competition for power between Republicans and Democrats is a reality affecting all federal actors and all education policy. Policy communities in Washington, DC, norms, and shared understandings about rituals and hierarchies are the context within which education politics are conducted. When Senator John Culver worked for passage of a strong Endangered Species Act, and spoke out about how Senator John Stennis' amendment would "eviscerate" the bill, he then "worked the floor," talking with others to get a sense of what the vote would be. During the vote, Senator Robert Byrd put his hand on Culver's shoulder and said, "I'll vote with you but there's something I want to talk with you about." But Culver, seeing that he was twenty votes short, replied, "Not right now but I'll talk to you when I need you" (Drew, 1979, p. 159). Countless similar stories of bargaining, trading votes, voting strictly along party lines, and constantly campaigning for the next election show that these behaviors are accepted in this policy community.

The intricate calculations of power plays; maneuvering around constitutional, legislative, and agency rules; working party politics; and calculating the timing of initiatives requires skills that would be envied by world-class chess players. Party balances of power and control and timing of the momentum of a policy proposal greatly affect results. For example, Congress adjourned in 2001 without a House subcommittee agreement on the bill to reauthorize the Office of Education Research and Improvement (OERI). The president had expended most of his education efforts getting confirmation of his secretary of education and passage of the NCLBA. When a new OERI bill was marked up, voted out of the House, and referred to the Senate, Senator Jeffords had left the Republican party, giving the Democrats control and putting Senator Edward Kennedy in as chair of the Senate Education Committee (American Educational Research Association, 2002a). By the time various groups pay attention and reach compromises, it might be too late for getting House and Senate votes and a presidential signature. Still, the chess players find devices for passing noncontroversial bills.

Challenges to Dominant Politics and Policy

That array of approaches for looking at policy and politics discussed in the previous section tends to focus on elites, the key policy makers. As with the other levels of policy discussed in Chapters 4 to 6, approaches that focus on elites exclusively often miss the voices and experiences of individuals and groups that are excluded from these power arenas. These approaches also are less intentionally critical of existing power structures and inequities. This issue is particularly heightened at the federal level, where policy making is often geographically far removed from the everyday lives of the individuals most affected by the policies. The voices of welfare parents, children with disabilities, children living in poverty, and children of color who deal with racism are often not included in policy deliberations at the federal level.

Traditional approaches, such as Kingdon's (2003), do not always bring marginal voices to the process of analyzing and understanding policy. At the federal level, two approaches in particular—interest group analysis and discourse analysis—provide alternative ways of framing federal issues. Both of these approaches tend to highlight marginalized and excluded groups and provide examples of the ways in which individuals influence federal policy processes. These approaches, along with the more traditional lenses mentioned previously, are highlighted in Table 7.6.

Interest Group Analysis

To be effective in analyzing and influencing politics, one must identify the goals and strategies of relevant interest groups, as a number of studies do (Lugg, 2001; Opfer, 2001a). Studying interest group inquiry is an outgrowth of the literature on values and on understanding hierarchies of power and assumptive worlds in policy communities. But an emerg-

TABLE 7.6 *Lenses for Examining Federal Education Policy and Politics*

Analytical Approach	Purpose
Values focused	Examines the extent to which policies represent certain values (Labaree, 1997)
Implementation focused	Focuses on outcomes by examining the effectiveness or intent of a program (McLaughlin, 1990)
Process focused	Examines the process by which policy decisions are made (Kingdon, 2003)
Interest group analysis	Shares a common interest in exposing how inequitable political decisions can be when certain interests and values dominate (Opfer, 2001a)
Discourse analysis	Examines how hegemonic policy language can privilege certain knowledges, which can in turn reinforce social inequities (Gerstl-Pepin, 2002)

ing group of studies focuses on the politics of interest groups. These studies share a common interest in exposing how inequitable political decisions can be when certain interests and values dominate. The significance of these studies is in how they highlight the inequitable distribution of power within the federal system. These studies, embedding power distributions into their analysis, offer a sharp contrast to the more descriptive studies listed previously.

These studies usefully highlight the power of non-education groups. Given the inequities in the political system, what is needed are additional studies that examine policy advocates and interest groups aimed at addressing such issues as poverty, racism, homophobia, and sexism.

Troubling the Language of Policy Discourse

Discourse analysis (as mentioned in Chapters 3 and 4) arose out of Foucault's (1981) notion that language is not value-neutral but a form of symbolic power. Policy studies incorporating discourse analysis examine how policy language can represent certain values and how these values can reinforce social inequities.

For example, Gerstl-Pepin (2002) analysis of media coverage of the 2000 presidential elections suggests that the media elevate the candidates' issues and agendas while minimizing alternative voices and issues from marginalized groups. She utilizes the concept of the public sphere (Fraser, 1994; Habermas, 1994) as a way to conceptualize how the media play an important role in supporting democracy. She suggests that the media serve as an arena of discourse where citizens learn about political issues, but also adds that this arena is hegemonic in the sense that issues of the elite are privileged. Gerstl-Pepin (2002) found that in privileging candidates' concerns, only nominal attention was given to negative or contradictory views of Gore's and Bush's support of high-stakes accountability and standards, and thus the potential for democracy was limited. For example, in the 2000 presidential election, the concerns of Bush and Gore dominated press coverage, while minimal air time was given to the third-party candidacy of Ralph Nader. Instead of covering his views on issues—he was referred to in the press as "the termi-Nader"—the media instead portrayed him as the candidate who might take votes away from Gore's bid for the White House (Gerstl-Pepin, 2002). By minimizing Nader as a viable candidate, his views on education were ignored.

Influencing Federal Policy

You may ask yourself, "How can I play politics and influence federal policy?" There are multiple ways. You can write detailed letters or e-mails directly to the president, White House staff, members of Congress, or congressional staff; join a union or group that has its own lobbyist (making sure she understands your concerns); and/or conduct research aimed at improving practice, highlighting the negative or positive consequences of federal policies. Of primary concern is garnering enough support to ensure that your issue is on the agenda. Typically, agenda setting involves three stages: diagnosis, softening, and activating. The diagnosis phase involves assessing the policy context to identify opportunities and constraints. The next phase, softening, involves making the context receptive to a particular policy initiative. The softening phase is the most delicate. It involves naming and framing the issue, negotiating and bargaining, assembling sponsors and supporters, promoting media coverage, getting key endorsements, building coalitions, and building momentum. Once the policy context has been softened, the next phase is activating change. This phase involves getting a decision maker or legislator to put an issue on the agenda (for a fuller discussion of these specific strategies, see Jansson, 2003).

Lived Realities: Lobbying to View Art as a Basic

When Goals 2000 was being drafted in Congress, arts organizations were following its progression with interest. They became aware that the arts were not being included in the legislation, and thus not deemed as critical to a child's education (diagnosed the oversight). Arts organizations formed a coalition in 1995—the Goals 2000 Arts Education Partnership—to advocate for the inclusion of the arts, and created a set of national standards for arts education (softened the context). This sparked an intensive lobbying effort on the part of arts organizations for an amendment to Goals 2000 that added the arts as an important component to education in the next century (activated change) (Sikes, 1995). The coalition utilized all phases of agenda setting—diagnosing, softening, and then activating—to get the arts included in Goals 2000.

Realizing the need for arts advocacy at the federal level, the Partnership has continued to grow and has evolved into the Arts Education Partnership (AEP), which is administrated by the National Assembly of State Arts Agencies and the Council of Chief State School Officers. This national coalition of arts, education, business, philanthropic, and government organizations seeks to promote the importance of the arts for learning and school reform via advocacy and research.

The example of the AEP demonstrates how vital advocacy and coalitions are at the national level. The arts are often viewed as a frill and not integral to public educations; without organizations such as AEP, the arts might not have a strong advocate in Washington, DC. Anyone is invited to join the AEP and can attend meetings or support their work. If there are educational issues that you feel particularly strongly about, then it is essential that you connect to organizations that strategically seek to influence federal policy. There are many organizations (unions, professional associations, etc.) that have lobbying efforts in Washington.

The key first step in influencing federal policy is to connect to national organizations and special interest groups that are involved in and knowledgeable about federal policy issues. The teacher unions (AFT and NEA) make it a point to stay current on educational issues, but other organizations also may prove useful, depending on your interests. National organizations for principals and superintendent organizations, such as the National Association for Secondary School Principals (NASSP), have started to take a more proactive stance with regard to education issues. Many of these organizations have their own lobbyists who advocate for their members. Joining and making your concerns known to the leader of the organization is one way of getting involved. Because the federal policy-making process is relatively closed to outsiders, joining an organization with connections and a proven track record of advocacy is an effective way to be more involved.

For example, NASSP has a website that tracks current education issues being considered by Congress. If you log on to the website, you can find out the names, mailing addresses, and e-mail addresses of your representatives, senators, and local media outlets. The website even provides sample letters that you can personalize or edit to suit your concerns and viewpoints. Figure 7.1 is a sample letter from the NASSP website.

Staying informed on key issues is also important to prepare for potential impacts in your own community, school, or district. Personal letter writing, such as the example provided by the NASSP, is another way to be more involved. While the letter provides an example for how to individually lobby Congress, it also points to some shortcomings of this type of approach. Generally, a personal and individualized letter is more likely to garner a

---

Dear X:

As a secondary school principal and member of the National Association of Secondary School Principals, I urge you to support S. 1248, the Individuals with Disabilities Education Improvement Act, and vote in favor of funding IDEA at its intended levels.

I believe this law is a real improvement over the current IDEA and it will do a great deal to help my school and others better serve students with special needs. In addition, I understand that an amendment will be offered by Senators Hagel and Harkin to mandate full funding of IDEA over an eight year period.

Providing the necessary resources to fulfill the obligations of IDEA is essential for all students to achieve. Currently, the federal government is providing only approximately 19% of funding instead of the 40% promised by federal law. As a result, the burden has fallen on states and localities to supplement these deficits with funds allotted for other worthy education programs. The current federal commitment to IDEA is insufficient and ominous considering that many state education budgets have been reduced significantly. It is unfair to expect states and localities to continue to make up these differences in funding levels considering that IDEA is a mandatory federal law. In addition, and more importantly, it is unrealistic to expect academic improvement for all students without the resources necessary to implement federal mandates.

Please work toward providing educators with the necessary tools and resources to properly implement and fulfill the promise of IDEA. Thank you for taking the time to consider this important issue.

Sincerely,

Your Name Here

FIGURE 7.1 *Letter for Influencing Federal Policy*

Source: Letter for Influencing Federal Policy. Retrieved on April 2, 2004 from http://www.capwiz.com/nassp/issues/alert/?alterid=5435486&type=CO. Copyright 2004 National Association of Secondary School Principals. www.principals.org. Reprinted with permission.

response. Additionally, this letter is missing four key components that could be used to sway the reader: The letter does not (1) provide evidence of timeliness (e.g., is the issue currently being considered by Congress?), (2) reference a particular bill or policy, (3) explain the experience or expertise of the writer concerning education, or (4) connect the writer to a particular constituency (e.g., union organization, professional organization, etc.).

Although individual letters do make an impact, politicians tend to be more responsive to large organizations that claim to represent large numbers of voters. So it is important to be affiliated, in policy advocacy coalitions, with organizations that carry clout in Washington. However, it is also critical to make your organization aware of your own concerns and interests. They must represent their constituents, so make sure they are representing your concerns.

Summary

In this chapter we have examined how the federal government has become an increasing presence in educational policy. Policy communities such as Congress, presidential administrations, and special interest groups (e.g., business lobbies) have collided to push for an increasing emphasis on national standards. Yet understanding federal policy depends on understanding the impact it makes in states, districts, micropolitics, and schools. Making these connections is critical to understanding the interplay between these pieces of policy puzzles. As we have shown in this chapter, there is an array of policy lenses available to help you make sense of how federal policy affects education nationally and locally, and we suggested strategies for becoming more knowledgeable and proactive toward federal policy making. In the next two chapters, we focus on the interconnections between policy-making arenas and how to use leadership, politics, and policy making to advocate for and support social justice.

Exercises for Critically Analyzing Federal Policy Communities, Interest Groups, and Standards

1. Read through *Education Week* from the past month (or go back further if Congress is not in session) and identify an education policy issue that is being considered by Congress. Then go to the Thomas website (http://thomas.loc.gov/) and track a specific component of the proposed legislation (e.g., focus on one particular aspect), discussions and debates, and committee reports concerning the topic. Write a position paper about the topic and send it to the key members of Congress engaged in discussion around the issue. (Also write to your own representative and senator).

2. Go to the Department of Education website and track current policy issues. Ask yourself the following questions:

- What grants are being offered?
- What research projects are being funded and reported?
- Does the Department of Education website represent certain values about education? (excellence? equity? choice? efficiency?)
- Does it support current presidential or congressional initiatives?

After examining these questions, what research is needed on federal policy that is not addressed by current funding priorities?

3. Conduct a literature review and identify three journal articles that examine some aspect of federal policy. What approaches do they use? Are the views critical of social inequities? Are

the articles useful for influencing practice or policy? If so, why; if not, why not? Do the articles identify issues in need of further study?

4. Go to the National Center for Education Statistics (NCES) website (listed at the end of this chapter) and look at how much funding your state receives from the federal government. If these funds suddenly disappeared, what kind of consequences would they have for education in your state or community?

5. Conduct a media analysis of a recent piece of federal legislation. (The LEXIS-NEXIS database is an excellent source for recent newspaper articles and television and radio broadcasts.) Identify the key players in the policy process. Who were the champions? Who were the detractors? Pay particular attention to which individuals or groups perspectives were not included or were possibly misrepresented.

6. Get together with your classmates and brainstorm ideas for research aimed at including marginalized voices in the federal policy-making process. These groups could be teachers, parents, building administrators, district administrators, students, or community groups.

7. Building on exercise 6, now think of a research project that could be used to advocate for a change in federal policies that would be inclusive of these groups.

8. Policies such as the NCLBA, pursuing multiple values and using multiple mechanisms and instruments, often create what a Washington policy "wonk" would call "the mother of all unintended consequences." Examine the NCLBA legislation and identify the values pursued, and the mechanisms and instruments for implementation, and predict the likely unintended consequences.

9. Review the abstract terms presented in Chapters 1 and 2 (e.g., coalitions, issue networks, values shifts, policy mechanisms, mandates and capacity-building policy instruments, and redistributive policy) and make connections to the content of this chapter. For example, what are some value shifts that have

occurred in state politics and policy making? What issue networks have been influential?

10. Obtain a copy of the State of the Union address via the internet (http://whitehouse.gov/) and identify the strategies used in this bully pulpit to shape educational policy. What policy logics are presented for education proposals and how are symbols used to persuade the public?

11. A list of emerging controversial issues was presented earlier in the chapter. Add five issues to the list and explain why you think these are being or will be debated at the federal level.

12. Using the policy window framework and your knowledge of education politics, list two or three events or crises that might open windows for policies that value equity? Now create three events or crises that might open a window for policies that value excellence.

13. Journalists, editorial commentary, and political cartoons often focus on the wheelin' and dealin' and partisan politics as well as the foibles of key actors in federal politics. Choose an issue or a policy (e.g., safe sex, school lunch subsidies, charter schools, or whatever is "hot" in Washington) and collect an array of such commentary to display to your class. Lead a discussion about how the various frameworks for analyzing policy help make sense of the actions, the behaviors, the discourse, and controversies.

14. You are a constituent. For that reason, your representatives in Congress might actually respond (or get a staffer to respond) to a curious and knowlegeable request from you for an interview. Find, through websites, what congressional committees your representatives are on and what issues are current. Write a one-page letter, asking for their insider insights via e-mail, phone, or brief personal interview. Use some of your political framework terms (e.g., *values conflicts, policy mechanisms, policy logic, partisan politics*), because they might intrigue them.

8

Global Education Politics

Guiding Questions _____

- What is political about making international comparisons?
- In analyzing different countries' education policies, what factors should be compared?
- What methods are used for comparing countries' policies?
- In what arenas are global education politics discussed, and who are the key players?
- What political and policy strategy insights can be learned from global perspectives and comparative policy analysis?
- What do international comparisons reveal about goals for education?
- How do nations' policies converge?
- What are challenges and controversial issues in education globally?
- What is it like to study politics and policy in another country?
- What are theories and methods for raising new questions internationally?

Perhaps one thinks, "Why do we need to study education in other countries?" and "I suppose international should be addressed, but is it really significant for understanding issues in my own country?" Educational leaders cannot ignore the global and international aspects of education policy. Education leaders and politicians hold assumptions about how the U.S. education system compares with Japan's, with Finland's, or with South Africa's. Concerns with global economic competition make comparisons in other areas unavoidable. Yet without awareness of problematic aspects of international comparisons and a deeper understanding of how countries differ in relation to the values, resources, and goals they have for education, one tends to jump to erroneous conclusions.

The Politics of International Comparisons

International comparisons are used to generate political action for national policies. Beginning in 1967, the International Association for the Evaluation of Educational Achievement (IEA) administered math achievement tests to large samples of same-age secondary students in twelve countries. The comparisons led to shock on the part of U.S. policy makers that the data seemed to reveal that in some instances, the U.S. students' scores lagged behind those of comparable countries. This was used as evidence to declare a crisis: "International comparisons of student achievement, completed a decade ago, revealed that on 19 academic tests American students were never first or second and, in comparison with other industrialized nations, were last seven times," pronounced *A Nation at Risk* (1983, p. 8). Debates ensued, and continue until now, over the meaning and relevance of the measures and the validity of the comparisons. Politicians made use of the data to legitimize attacks on public schooling as well as serious questioning of current ways of doing things for schooling, families, immigration, the economy, and so on.

National Assessment of Educational Progress (NAEP), the SAT, and other scores get reported in rather skewed ways in the media and by political groups. Bracey (2002) asserts that positive reports often are buried and negative reports are hyped, as when columnist John Leo's sarcastic headline was "Hey, We're No. 19!" while, as Bracey says, the TIMSS Final-Year Study compares "apples to aardvarks" (p. 50) (referring to Trends in International Mathematics and Science Study [TIMSS]).

Berliner and Biddle (1995) detail the range of problems with international comparisons in general, not just in math and science. They show that the South Korean student is made to care about his performance, knowing that his score contributes to his nation's honor. They show that American students' opportunity to learn the higher-level mathematics being tested was not equal to Japanese students.' Reanalysis of the data by Westbury (1992) showed that when comparing American students who had actually *had* the algebra curricula, then their scores were similar to Japan's. Berliner and Biddle (1997) point out, too, that

> Americans tolerate enormous inequities in funding for schools that serve the rich and the poor . . . schools in slum neighborhoods must contend with dangerous and decaying buildings, gross overcrowding, violence, inadequate funding for even basic instruction. This problem is not faced in other Western countries, where equal basic support is normally provided to each student in all public schools. (p. 58)

So, when the National Center for Education Statistics disaggregate data, it could show that states like Iowa, North Dakota, and Minnesota did about the same as those in high-achieving foreign countries, whereas Louisiana and Mississippi, with high poverty and low per-pupil support, fared in student achievement about the same as struggling, underdeveloped countries.

As every educator knows, tests do not measure some very important goals being accomplished in classrooms across the United States. International comparisons have, understandably, focused on the curricular goals that countries have in common. They have often not measured educational goals related to democracy, creativity, and empowered citizenship. They do not ask questions about how students actually use the schooling in, for example, vocational accomplishments or lifelong learning. Nevertheless, educators', parents', and some politicians' understanding and valuing of such wider goals have been pushed aside in vigorous dominant discourse about "the education recession" (W. Bush) (Bracey, 2002, p. 45), and the clamor for students to be prepared for the twenty-first century workplace. Selected and simplistically analyzed evidence from international comparisons provides fodder for those who believe that government dollars for public schools is not a good investment in the United States. Bracey and others provide extensive evidence that certain groups in "the education industry" are in favor of vouchers for private schools and of charter schools, for example. One can assume that international assessments are political footballs tossed around in education policy debates in other arenas.[1] District politicians and state legislators, too, can make political hay with such assessments. In that political fray between the extremes of political groups wishing to show "we're number one" and those highly critical of "the education establishment," the useful insights from international comparisons are sometimes lost.

The Lived Realities on the next page demonstrates that thinking globally about education leads educators and researchers into minefields of contentious international competition. TIMSS provided useful information, readily available for policy insights. The lessons learned from this TIMMS vignette suggest that, in politicized environments, even with well-designed studies, even with expertise in explaining findings and anticipating how the findings will be used in political contexts, partisan pressures and nationalistic urges to be the best may take over. Even with careful management of research, international comparisons will be used and abused in partisan politics and for opening policy windows and developing policy logics.[2] Thus, one must be prepared with knowledge of the actors, arenas, and structures; the various ways of looking at international politics and policy; as well as the continuing global education challenges and controversies.

Actors, Arenas, and Structures for International Policy

Politicians like to use comparisons with other counties to generate rationales for policy proposals. International organizations, national governments, nongovernmental organizations (NGOs), and comparative education scholars expend much thought, energy, and resources identifying trends, progress, and methods for comparing systems for schooling in different countries. While there is no global Education Policy Congress, there are a variety of NGOs like UNICEF, UNESCO, the Asian Development Bank, the World Bank, United Nations Development Program (UNDP), the Rockefeller Fund, and the Carnegie and Ford Foundations that study international education. These organizations use resources, expertise, research, and recommendations to examine the status of education globally and to push toward certain goals (Morales-Gomez & Torres, 1992). UNESCO's mid-1900s' origins set goals for understandings of people and for promoting tolerance and peace while working toward universal literacy through universal primary education. The U.S. Peace Corps works on education where countries express a need, and U.S. (and other countries') foreign aid is targeted toward education needs in some instances.

Lived Realities: TIMSS Lessons

The panic was big enough to generate more than a thirty-second report on the *CBS Evening News*. Later, newspaper headlines conveyed alarming messages, and the ensuing articles told American families and educators that school performance was an embarrassment for the strongest and supposedly most technologically and economically advanced country.

"Anytime you're part of an election, they're gonna look for the data and try to put their spin on it," said Pascal Forgione, recalling his years as the Clinton-appointed commissioner, heading the National Commission of Education Statistics. In a phone interview in 2002, he proudly explained how "probably the greatest education statistics agency in the world" carefully designed the TIMSS. Rather than relying only on outcome data, researchers compared videotapes of classroom instruction and interviews of teachers in select countries. As a result, they found, for example, that U.S. math teachers were covering twice as many math curriculum objectives as Japan, where the school year is 220 days. Rather than simply dispensing the data, they developed a TIMSS Tool Kit so that math specialists and school board members could be guided in understanding how to think about implications of the findings as they redesigned curricula and teacher training. Although the researchers sought to collect comparable and representative data, they knew to simply drop out the country where they were told which schools to observe, and they knew that they were really assessing only the Hebrew students when they were collecting data in Israel in the midst of an intifada.

International comparisons, carefully constructed, can be used to guide policy. They can also be used to manipulate public opinion. Forgione recalled, also, how "these people love to use you," as TIMSS was used by "some of the people who don't like public education, to say, 'the longer you're in U.S. schools, the worse you do.'" He laughed about how, when the findings that the United States was second only to Korea in fourth grade were released: "So who wanted to be with me reporting that? Clinton, in the Rose Garden! But when we reported that only Cyprus and South Africa were below us in twelfth grade, I reported that alone, in a hotel. Often, they'd as soon have me report the data alone in a closet!" He described how Gore "had to invent it! When we had our reading result, he got up and reported on only the 96 and 98 results where we had made growth, but if you go back to '92, that growth is wiped out. When I got up and revisited all the data . . . the vice president didn't like being criticized." He learned, too, that his own credibility for reliable, honest, and ethical reporting was essential because sometimes it comes down to "do you trust the commissioner?" At the same time, he maintained relations across partisan and political lines with political figures like Secretary of Education Richard Riley and former Secretary William Bennett, always emphasizing his goal of providing data in a timely and policy-relevant manner.

Thus, the politics of managing data reporting and interpreting cannot be ignored. Some statisticians, Forgione said, "would rather shoot the data up in a rocket and maybe it would come down somewhere and be used . . . but your values have to say we can do timeliness and usefulness. It about how you make data useful without being a prostitute."

According to Samoff (1999), "The grid of internationally active education organizations is dense" (p. 63). These researchers cooperate in order to measure achievement and identify troubling trends. Some forty thousand firms now qualify as transnational corporations and are emerging as major players for social and public services, like education

(Stromquist & Monkman, 2000), worrying analysts and activists about globalizing forces. Churches and religious groups have long been leaders in education programs. Troubling aspects emerge, however, through bitter memories of colonially imposed controls and from resentments of foreign values being imposed in the name of helping, foreign aid, and assisting underdeveloped nations and cultures. Foreign aid to developing countries, from the United States, Canada, and the United Nations World Bank, for example, creates dependence and shapes preferences for educational and social programs. For example, Senegal and Tanzania modified their education and training programs to reflect funding sources' priorities (Samoff, 1999). So there is no official arena for making global education policy (perhaps excepting the UN), but there are an array of actors trying to influence it.

Trends in Cross-National Comparison of Educational Policy

Educators and some politicians, from time to time, wish to concentrate exclusively on domestic concerns, but global interdependence makes isolationism impossible. By comparing how countries educate their citizenry, we can learn from their successes and failures to draw lessons across time and space. Rose (1993) states, "The experience of seeing a program in effect elsewhere demonstrates that it can be realized in at least one place" (p. 2).

Traditions from Comparative Public Policy

Comparative analysis of policies is used for guidance in designing better public policy to gain a deeper understanding of how governmental institutions and political processes operate as they deal with concrete problems. Increasing international interdependence demonstrates the importance of understanding what neighbors—near and far—are doing (Heidenhemier, Heclo, & Adams, 1990). As Becker (1986) says, "Since the end of the Second World War there has been a growing tendency to see educational policy as something that links nations together. . . . A permanent exchange of problems, expectations, and solutions are helpful to all nations" (p. 209).

Cross-national policy analysis requires perspectives that are sensitive to the complexity of differing national identities, economic and political structures, histories, cultures, and values. Heidenheimer, Heclo, and Adams (1990) identify six such perspectives:

1. *Socioeconomic theories:* Assuming that nations respond to general processes of economic growth and social modernization with basically similar policies
2. *A cultural values approach:* Emphasizing the deeply embedded cultural ideas arising from the distinctive historical experiences of nations
3. *A party government approach:* Assuming that partisan politics matter, so policies will vary with partisan shifts
4. *Political class struggle:* Assuming that the fundamental dynamic of policy development lies in the contest between business forces driven by capitalist accumulation, and workers and their representatives

5. *Neocorporatist framework:* Assuming that one should look to the broader system of interest organizations and representatives whose influence and bargaining create policies
6. *Institutional-political process:* Assuming the need to put the "state" at centerstage (whereas other perspectives treat policy as the result of outside pressures)

None of these is the "right" one, but each has embedded assumptions. The framework chosen, though, affects what is to be focused on and what will be emphasized, measured, and reported (and what will be left out).

If, instead of thinking about theory and frameworks, one assumes, with a medical diagnose-and-prescribe lens or with missionary passion, that the goal is to fix another country's schools, one may not worry about underlying theory and method. For example, thousands of pages of analyses of education in Africa in the 1990s, conducted by expatriate-led teams, found the needs to fix their systems, given the deterioration in quality, misallocated funds, inefficient management, recommending expanded private schooling, introducing double shifts and multigrade classrooms, and so on (Samoff, 1999). But developing countries are suspicious of ex-colonials' recommendations, remembering centuries of forced compliance with the laws and customs of European rulers. They may view recommendations to concentrate on basic education as patronizing and intended to undermine support for higher education, thus keeping developing countries behind and dependent on countries with greater research, intellectual, and technological advances. Always look for the assumptions, theories, and intentions that frame any analysis of countries' educational systems.

Without knowing which theoretical frameworks guide the analysis, one is easily led astray. Even seemingly atheoretical descriptions and unassuming approaches to analysis are suspect, if not irresponsible. Further, international comparison and recommendations for reform and improvement are often full of Eurocentric biases. To start, one must identify the various theories that do drive international analyses of schooling.

Approaches to Comparative Education Policy

What, then, are useful and responsible approaches for comparisons? Building on frameworks from previous chapters (especially Chapters 1, 2, and 3), recall how theories, frameworks, and lenses affect what one sees. Think about what theories and methods one would use to ask deep questions and to make comparisons across the globe.

One could focus on the structures of education institutions' mechanisms for improving the status of individuals and distribution of rights and opportunity within a society. In that tradition, and guided by a liberal paradigm, many studies track the progress and identify the facilitators and impediments to change. This descriptive approach emphasizes the structures of policy, often glossing over cultural impediments to change, and has been inadequate for explaining the persistence of poverty and inequality or for guiding educational change (Moralez-Gomez & Torres, 1992).

A range of approaches recognize processes and cultural underpinnings of politics and policy in analyses of international education policy. Critical theory, in contrast to the liberal and structural approaches, has focused on political, social, and educational processes by which inequalities in a country are reproduced by the education system. These Marxist analyses highlight the ways capitalist practices have created international labor, market, banking, military, and even cultural forces that reinforce business oligopolies and spread into the ways in which business interests dominate education policies. While powerful for identifying persistent oppressive forces, these theoretical framings have little power for prescribing change. They help indict systems and blame people, including educators, who reproduce inequities. They offer few remedies for working within current systems of governance. Still, seeking imaginaries and alternative ideas, such as "revolutionary citizenship" (McLaren & Farahmandpur, 2001), can stimulate new thinking about educators as activists, as workers at the task of supporting schooling that empowers children and challenges status quos.

Further, a significantly different model emanates from human capital theory, leading to questions about how the intertwining of policies and processes in educational systems contributes to the preparation of children to enter into and contribute to strengthening a countries' productivity. Human capital theory concentrates, then, on human resources. This model dominates much of the work of private foundations, the UN, and much foreign aid, which focus on developing the capacity of individuals within targeted countries to improve their country's economy.

Social capital theory offers another frame that focuses on how social networks, relationships, and movements generate power for individuals and groups to alter society. So the questions and foci are widened, acknowledging that people with common values and motivations can challenge dominant values and practices. Social capital and social movement theory encompasses relationships, networks, and also the power of nongovernmental agencies. Thus, one can see how education policies and political choices are shaped by forces and values beyond those in government offices. This theoretical framework is most conducive to research and policy action that embrace the politics from the margins and the possibilities of effective educator/scholar policy advocacy.

Such theories help guide analyses. Still, the theories have not solved the problems faced by marginalized groups and in countries whose totalitarian or authoritarian regimes do not promote education for empowerment or equity. (Nor have they solved inequities in the United States.) Theories are still needed that can (1) expand and raise the quality and support for education while, at the same time, integrating marginal groups into the system of education—that is, increase quality and equity at the same time; (2) expand the definitions of "useful knowledge"; (3) expand the range of groups involved in education decision making; and (4) recognize the extreme diversity of context wherein teaching and learning take place (Moralez-Gomez & Torres, 1992). Comparative analysts, then, are still searching for theories that encompass the full extent of the diversity and contexts of schooling. Still, their search for such theories, building on an international array of education systems, is important for understanding U.S. challenges regarding diversity of contexts, useful knowledge, and raising support for quality education and equity.

Relevant Questions for International Comparisons

If the secretary-general of the UN, concerned about ways to improve the world through education, decided to get baseline data about how countries are doing and what needs fixing, he would commission studies. What would be the research questions, and what would be compared? How would one compare countries' accomplishments and challenges?

Various kinds of input–output analyses are the most visible and frequent methods for comparing countries' education systems. It is relatively easy to measure a resource that is put into schools, such as number of teachers teaching in their field, or numbers of students on free or reduced-price lunch. Similarly, one can quantify outputs of an education system, such as percentage of students who graduate, apply for postsecondary education, drop out after the eighth grade, and participate in extracurricular activities. But any educator or citizen can see immediately that important inputs and outputs are not measurable and that such an approach pushes aside important cultural and economic differences. It matters whether a nation's economic health promises jobs for graduates when one is assessing that nation's graduation rate. Youths may sense that the diploma will make no difference, given their lack of vocational opportunities. When comparing the percentages of women who finish postsecondary education, it matters whether countries place value on women's education. Even if policies provide governmental resources to support women, analyses miss part of the story if university study is seen culturally as a barrier to marriage. Interpretations are flawed when forceful but nonmeasurable cultural values are left out of analyses. Finding appropriate ways to compare education systems is a huge challenge!

After reviewing technical and political issues, Nuttall (1994) concluded that, in comparing countries' education attainments, the measurements should be

- policy-relevant;
- policy-friendly (timely, comprehensible, and few in number);
- derived from a framework (defensible in research terms and including alterable variables, and thus oriented toward action);
- technically sound (valid and reliable); and
- feasible to measure at reasonable cost.

A cultural critique of the meaningful recommendations of any measures (what goal indicators are relevant culturally) would include the following: (1) what indicators that connect to the country are explicit policy goals; (2) what the country measures and monitors and what that monitoring says about progress in attaining explicit goals (and gaps); (3) insiders' critique of the monitoring/evaluation; and (4) insiders' explanations of gaps. Even with the most careful attention to validity and comparable data collection, international comparisons are highly politicized. Still, for future international comparisons, one can work for designs that ask appropriate questions. Also, one can exercise appropriate cautions when seeking and borrowing policy strategies from other countries. In spite of the tendency to politicize international comparisons, efforts such as TIMSS and others have great potential for lending insights for curriculum design, for equity and diversity questions. They can help in the search for answers to recurrent questions about the effects of length of school day and school year, about inclusion of civic and character education in the curriculum, and about the effects of immigration and new populations on personnel, curriculum, and testing, and so on.

Identifying New Policy Strategies

What studies usefully illuminate education politics in other countries? When education policy scholars compare countries, they often tend to conduct case studies of countries with similarities in the direction and evolution of governance and organizational reforms. Here are a few random examples:

* Derqui (2001) compares school autonomy reform in Brazil and Uraguay, addressing the specific political motivations for the reform.
* Lee (2001) found policy variation and convergences in school reform initiatives in Japan, Korea, England, and the United States. Whereas the United States and England focused on raising standards and tightening curriculum and assessment, Japan and Korea moved in the opposite direction, deregulating schools and diversifying curriculum and assessment.
* Leithwood (2001) classified leadership practices from a study of four countries instituting accountability policies.
* Enslin and Pendlebury (2000) demonstrated that principles of nonrepression and nondiscrimination have to be actively promoted in curriculum to meaningfully override the South African legacies of oppression.

Additionally, the following studies on current policy issues show how other countries are dealing with issues that are policy trends in the United States:

* Benveniste (2000) examined national reports to see how assessment policies in Uruguay reflect the country's commitment to equal opportunities for students.
* The Educational Testing Service (2002) provides useful comparisons in *The Twin Challenges of Mediocrity and Inequality: Literacy in the U.S. from an International Perspective.*
* Rajput and Walia (2001) focused on reforms in teacher education in India in an evolution from a reverence for the master teacher to a more westernized process, in the context of widespread illiteracy and high unemployment.
* In "I Love Teaching but . . . ." Scott, Stone, and Dinham (2001) identified international patterns of teacher discontent among 3,000 teachers and school administrators in Australia, New Zealand, England, and the United States.

This is a tiny sample of the international research that has been conducted. Searching for descriptions and analyses of alternatives can be fruitful. Ignorance of international insights from trends, philosophies, alternative goals, and neat policy strategies make educators less than they can be as intellectual and as policy advocates. Still, the policy strategies that fit dominant policy logics elsewhere, or that meet needs in other cultural and political systems, are not automatically transferable. Lessons can be learned, but simplistic exportation will not work.

Identifying Differing Goals and Values for Education

Is education for vocational and workforce development or for empowerment and full citizenship? Chapter 1 introduced the notion of analyzing education politics through a framework of political socialization, calling attention to the assumed goals served by public education. In 1816 Thomas Jefferson said, "Enlighten the people and tyranny and oppression of both body and mind will vanish like evil spirits at the dawn of day" (as cited in Mapp, 1991, p. 266). His assertion, embedded in assertions for American public education as a cornerstone of democracy, is challenged every day in policy and practice. For example, for many, schooling is good for training for the workforce, plain and simple.

Analysis of the politics and policies in other countries provides fascinating insights about conflicts and choices regarding the purposes of schooling. For example, Prost (2000) traced the debates over the *baccalauréate* professional diploma in France, evoking controversies about raising educational expectations of high school students for a more highly qualified workforce. The vocational versus college preparatory "tracking" that marks the French system of education became a hotly political debate.

From comparative and historical analysis, one can see how schooling has been used to politically socialize citizens and future citizens, such as young children and immigrants. This socialization can harness and homogenize populations, even when policy rhetoric focuses on development and freedom. Questions about how education has been used to maintain white colonial power through history to the present pervades Spring's (1998) analysis of education policy. He argues that an ethos of "white love" energized the British and U.S. policies to bring the English language and customs to help colonial subjects improve and fit Western standards.

By studying debates about the purpose of schooling, in Tanzania or in Canada, for example, one can see more graphically how the goals and international debates are like and also *not* like those in the United States. Thus, comparative education policy studies provide perspectives that help us see one's own systems' assumptions. To do that, however, one must use approaches that incorporate the particular and subjective values and interpretations of insiders in Tanzania, the Ukraine, and Saskatchewan, Canada.

What a delight it is, in conducting such international comparisons, to encounter surprise discoveries in foreign education systems! One can see clearly just how embedded assumptions are about separation of church and state when comparing how schools and religion mix elsewhere. Case studies tracing the increased influence of religion on public schools in Alberta, Canada (Taylor, 2001), are useful for comparison of the phenomenon with the influence of religion on public schools in the United States. Analyzing the debates over public funding to religious schools in any country is useful for showing how discourse is used by competing groups to control the political arena.

Views about what is "right" for education and for the policies and structures for schooling create recurring conflicts, debates, and political struggles. In Tanzania as well as in the United States, people debate about these kinds of questions: What do people think schooling is for? What are the dominant goals and values that education systems should be guided by, and should promote? What structures work well for accomplishing educational goals?

Even within the most totalitarian state, one would still not find agreement on the purposes of schooling. However, the answers provided by whatever or whomever has the most power when decisions are made are the ones that will be promulgated as the right ones. Not all governments really attempt to provide schooling for all children. Often, schooling is available, but economic and cultural forces determine who attends or who is successful. For example, some cultures keep girls out of school so they can care for their siblings. Studying the debates, decisions, and reforms as foreign countries grapple with the questions about the purpose of education is tremendously instructive. When the U.S. educator reads about the policies and structures in Great Britain, Germany, and France, which designate whether a child of twelve or thirteen will be prepared for a trade or for college, she might first say, "How awfully presumptuous—we would never do that so early!" Then, thinking more, she might say, "But, are there ways we do that, subtly?" So, seeing the other systems' policy purposes and assumptions help us ask questions about our own.

International Sharing and Borrowing

One frequently asked question is, "Do countries borrow ideas for education policy from each other, and if so, how and why?" Another question is, "Do trends, reforms, or problems in education occur similarly in several countries?" These are policy-borrowing, networking, and policy convergence questions that tend to make us wonder how much education policy really *is* connected and global.

How Policies Converge

With the UN, the European Union, and other such forces working toward global treaties and sharing for development, and with the recognition that economies are interdependent, political scientists have been asking questions about "the tendency of societies to grow more alike, to develop similarities in structures, processes and performances" (Kerr, 1983, p. 3), especially in societies with a progressively more industrial infrastructure shaping policy choices. These are particularly interesting lines of inquiry, which help us look at Burger King in Paris and then wonder how French education, immigration, and labor policies compare with those in the United States, and how that affects the workforce flipping the burgers. Such questions get much more complicated when you think about the Burger King in Beijing, where communist and capitalist economic ideologies are mixed.

The tradition of comparative case studies of nations dealing with similar problems within similarly advanced industrial democracies dealing with the problems in similar ways is well established. Bennett's (1991) review mentions these kinds of convergence:

• In policy goals, or coming together with intent to solve common policy problems
• Of policy content, or similar statutes or rules

- On policy instruments, or tools to administer policy
- On policy outcomes or consequences
- On policy style (e.g., processes that were conflictual, consensual, incremental, pluralist, etc.)

Although fun and interesting, these studies should be viewed with caution, as "convergence should always be seen as a process of becoming rather than one of being alike" (Bennett, 1991, p. 219). Also, when you find broad correlations and then claim convergence of any public policy, this "in some ways resembles photographs taken from a high-flying aircraft: the main features stand out, but much detail is lost—and the lost detail may be important" (King, 1981, p. 316). Nevertheless, convergence takes place these ways:

- *Through emulation:* Looking abroad and sharing ideas, drawing lessons, and imitating ways of solving policy problems
- *Through elite networking and policy communities:* People in a profession share their transnational concerns and ideas for solutions (e.g., the idea of ombudsmen from Sweden)
- *Through harmonization:* Broadly shared motivation and regular interaction, leading to transnational agreements to coordinate policy solutions (e.g., environmental pollution)
- *Through penetration:* Where powerful external actors get involved in internal policy formulation (e.g., when multinational business practices force a country to adopt their ways of doing things or be left out) (Bennett, 1991).

Comparative policy analysis has to acknowledge that "not all polities have interchangeable parts of conveniently identical systems" (De Leon & Resnick-Terry, 1999, p. 11). Also, what works in Malaysia might not work in Massachusetts. But policy pinching has proliferated from national down to local levels, as urban planners look over European cities' public transportation, for example (De Leon & Resnick-Terry, 1999). Further, with issues like the environment and terrorism, methods for managing and policy making simply *have* to be international in scope, because borders are permeable and because acid rain does not respect a national boundary. At the very least, a nation's policies must be made with recognition of the impact of related policies in neighboring countries. For example, the freedoms of speech and access to higher education in Singapore may have inspired the brave but tragic protests for similar freedoms that occurred in the Tiananmen Square protests in the People's Republic of China in 1989.

Continuing Challenges and Controversies

There is no authoritative legitimized policy arena for debating and attempting to solve global education challenges, yet many challenges and controversies in other countries have global implications.

Equity, Marginal Groups, and Social Movements

Looking abroad, one learns that schooling is often part of societal hopes for "betterment," and education politics can be the epicenter of politics from the margin. Groups seeking democratization, rights, and economic improvements enter the fringes of school politics to ensure that schools provide the needed access to policies and structures. While this is true in the United States, it can be seen graphically in studies of countries with more contentious and varied politics. Sadly, too, international analyses of politics from the margins reveal a common theme: Policies constructed to increase the access and voices of the less privileged often flounder as they encounter conflicting policies or lackluster support for implementation. Poverty, class division, and unequal access to the education and other social supports persist in every country.

Still, as other countries struggle to address the needs of marginal groups, the struggles, successes, roadblocks, and failures are instructive. Important policy and politics questions can be asked: What political strategies enable marginal groups to get their needs met? What approaches to policy formulation have some success in getting regimes to take access and equity and inclusion goals seriously enough to make policy and allocate budgets that benefit marginalized groups? And what policy implementation strategies increase the likelihood that such policies will make systemic change? Once again, examples serve to stimulate continuing interest and quests:

- Dura-Bellat (2000) outlines the social inequalities inherent in the French education system.
- Thrupp (2001), comparing England and New Zealand, suggests how social class might influence the direction of national policy.
- Moving on to Australia, Meadmore (2001) analyzes how a nineteenth-century law calling for a "free, compulsory and secular" education saw redefinition in the 1990s.
- The shift in Argentina in recent years to a dual public/private system of education is the focus of Naradowski and Andrada's (2001) research, showing that the shift gave those with greater economic means the ability to flee public schools.
- Does civic education encourage democracy and tolerance? Pedahzur (2001) shows that, in Israel, it has failed to encourage more democratic values.
- According to Shimizu (2001), current Japanese educational reforms reduce curriculum content and lower academic standards.

These studies provide insights for several potentially transferable policy strategies (Wong and Balestino, 2001). Clearly, from glancing at the contents of studies from around the world, many countries are enmeshed in troublesome and chronic challenges for meeting the needs of marginal groups.

In Pursuit of Equity in Education: Using International Indicators to Compare Equity Policies (Hutmacher, Cochrane, & Bottani, 2001) is an excellent compilation of baseline data with a focus on equity and marginalized groups. It can help raise more complex questions about poverty's effects on urban and rural education, gendered opportunities, enrollments, adult literacy, and more. Figures 8.1 and 8.2 show examples of the kinds of available information.

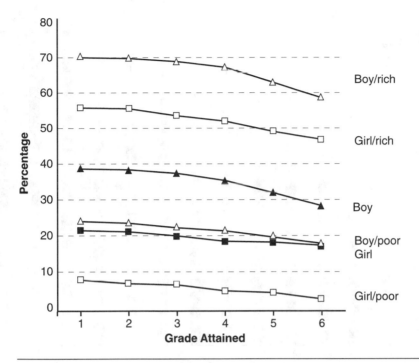

FIGURE 8.1 *Educational Attainment by Grade, Gender, and Wealth (percentage of 15- to 19-year-olds), Niger, 1997*

Source: From W. Hutmacher, D. Cochrane, and N. Bottani. *In Pursuit of Equity in Education: Using International Indicators to Compare Equity Policies.* Copyright 2001 by Kluwer Academic Publishers, Boston. With kind permission of Kluwer Academic Publishers and the authors.

As mentioned in Chapter 2, baseline data and input–output analyses, as in Figures 8.1 and 8.2, generally create as many questions as they answer. When one sees outcomes, it leads to questions about a country's values, economic and political situation, and cultural assumptions that led to these outcomes. Therefore, the search expands for comparative analyses that provide outcome data as well as cultural and political context. For example, Fulcher's (1989) multinational study of disability policies gives the reader a sense of the reasons for the variations among countries' treatment of children with disabilities.

The Evils and Benefits of Globalization and Internationalism

Internationalism connotes moves toward cooperation and sharing of knowledge and advances, as when Russia and the United States share a space station or international conferences of physicians and scientists convene to confront the spread of HIV/AIDS. How countries' policies are affected, and should be affected by global pressures, however, is an emerging important question.

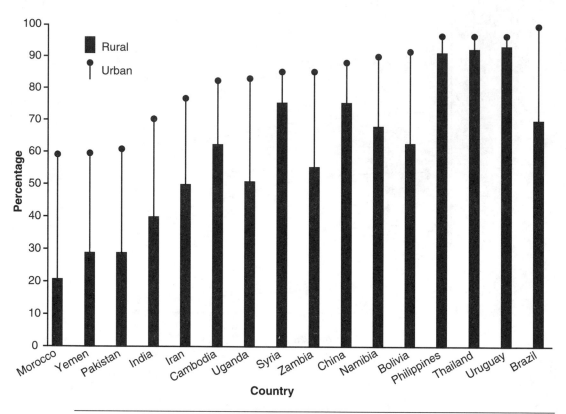

FIGURE 8.2   *Adult Literacy Rates by Location in Selected Countries, Early 1990s*

Source: From W. Hutmacher, D. Cochrane, and N. Bottani. *In Pursuit of Equity in Education: Using International Indicators to Compare Equity Policies.* Copyright 2001 by Kluwer Academic Publishers, Boston. With kind permission of Kluwer Academic Publishers and the authors.

Global Forces.   The term *globalization* connotes the changes in the economy, labor force, technologies, communication, cultural patterns, and political alliances affecting nations, especially centering on the interdependence of economics and trade among countries. Some 40,000 firms now qualify as transnational corporations and are emerging as major players in social and public services, like education (Stromquist & Monkman, 2000). Global forces can erode national cultural identities but can also provide an emancipatory "transnational imaginary" (Gough, 1999, p. 67). The limited cultural assumptions that shape identities can be flung aside, at least in fantasy, when, for example, the Afghan child sees girls' opportunities across the globe. Borders are permeable and fluid, as students seek entrance to higher education outside their native countries and as workers migrate for jobs.

Cultural and educational effects associated with globalization include an increase in cultural homogeneity and the erosion of native language and cultures. With globalization comes increased migration, with accompanying fragmentation of family and community connections and, through convergence (discussed previously), the global discourse of education reform centered on making schools efficient in preparing children for the workforce in the competitive market economy and making universities responsive to market needs.

Dilemmas and questions arise. For example, should indigenous groups in Latin America try use schooling to affirm their ethnic identities, or will they more effectively fend off exploitation by getting the language and vocational skills for jobs in new economic systems? Should university faculties worry that their traditional independence is undermined by grants from transnational corporations and by tenure reviews that place high value on work that responds to global market forces, such as technical applied research more than basic research? When Gerber Foods funds major studies of children's nutrition around the world, should scholars refuse to go along, worrying that the corporation makes them lackeys to economic forces that attune advertising so that mothers globally eschew breastfeeding?

Questions from Theory. Theoretical frameworks for pondering globalization include liberal, descriptive, and structural, which focus on the development of human capital and on education's relationship to economic development, and the more critical perspectives, with each raising important points worthy of investigation. For example, liberal, free-market thinking about globalization is optimistic, with a view that the reduction of barriers to trade will increase efficiency, international access to world resources, and the benefits of technological and scientific advances. The argument follows that this will allow people to cross boundaries to seek better political and economic conditions and will increase growth of international pressures for "good," such as peace, democracy, civil and human rights, and ecological preservation.

Arguments for economic rationalism, for planning and policy using logics about market forces, have been applied to school policy. Such logics brought devolution to site-based management, with tightened accountability for results and with parental/consumer choice, increasing competition and market-based governance of schools, especially in Great Britain and Australia (Henry et al., 1999). From this perspective, schools then need corporate partners, often leading to industry-oriented curricula and abandonment of generalist courses. School managers, competing for student dollars, cannot afford the risk of admitting students whose backgrounds will require great expenditures of resources and may result in lower performance scores. Structural inequalities are thus created and multiplied by competitive education (Henry et al., 1999). In reviewing the "rightist policies" of market competition, Apple (2000) argues that the increasingly individual and privatized decision making ruins any chance of collective education action. He believes collective action is necessary in order to improve educational opportunities for all, regardless of class, race, and gender. Yet "middle class parents have become quite skilled in exploiting market mechanisms . . . [bringing] their social, economic, and cultural capital to bear upon them" (p. 8).

Critical theory analyses highlight the history of colonial imperialism and the current evils of globalism in undermining labor power and the corporatization of schooling as business needs prevail in education policy goals discussions. For example, McLaren and Farahmandphur (2001) suggest that the World Bank's recommendation to developing countries that their curricula be tied tightly to performance standards and outcome measures creates international imperatives that emphasize controls to align teacher work toward such goals.

A critical feminist slant, applied to international questions, refocuses attention on social policy and educational structures, asking whether, for example,

1. countries have policies and structures in educational systems to help girls and women have more choice beyond the areas traditionally viewed as the private sphere (marriage and family, childbearing and childrearing);
2. policies and programs undermine and invalidate patriarchy in institutions (e.g., courts, social and welfare agencies, professional and craft associations) and empower girls and women to recognize and fight against oppressive practices, violence against women, discriminatory labor practices; and
3. education can prevent women from being caught in perilous and oppressive employment, especially in sweat shops, prostitution, and so on.

At first glance, globalization forces make women and children more vulnerable. NGOs struggle to combat the trade in children for pornography and prostitution, which is more globalized than ever. No global pressures stopped the Taliban from taking schooling, employment, and access to health care away from women in Afghanistan for years. At second glance, international movements working for women's rights range from those of the UN to the Ford Foundation to trade unions to *Ms. Magazine.*[3] Nongovernmental policy advocacy coalitions provide the social capital and attention to address these issues. Thus, thinking about issues from an international perspective can remind us of areas in which education and wider social issues intersect but are often ignored. How often do school administrators and education policy officials ponder the ways in which students are affected by issues like women's access to health care or children's vulnerability to sexual exploitation? Thus, feminist analysis of global issues serves to remind us of important but often forgotten issues.[4]

As this section has shown, the issues raised and the conclusions or actions recommended for globalism depend on the theory being used to frame the analysis.

Engaging with Globalism.   Rather than interrogating questions of good and evil, some analysts focus on how to work in increasingly globalized education politics and policy contexts. In their discussion about the future of democracy and social justice in education, Henry and co-workers (1999) suggest, "We cannot afford simply to retreat to traditional social welfarism or indeed to the emerging forms of backlash national chauvinism" (p. 85). They suggest that the answer is to engage with global forces in order to mitigate the worst potential consequences. They recommend that one must first recognize that market forces are not reified entities with lives and persona. Instead, social relations, aspects of culture, including policy preferences in nation states, can modify the social effects of markets. Social movements by consumers, owners, and workers have the capacity to affect national, and thus supranational, structures.

Protests at the World Trade Organization, resolutions by international trade unions, and environmental activism renew democratic politics. The Internet provides new tools for such movements. The battering taken by the working class poor, women, and minority individuals in competitive markets provides renewed motivation for social movement activism. Educators need to recognize that these international issues *are* their issues.

Global Framing of Policy Discourse.   An increasingly global political discourse dominates education policy framing. The dominant discourse has become one of economic rationalism. In many countries, politicians, educators, and citizens who raise questions or present alternative policy discourses (e.g., proposing non-economic goals for schooling) challenge the assumptive worlds, risk losing power, are not heard, or, if heard, are subject to a "discourse of derision" (Ball, 1990b, p. 18). Economic rationalism is a dominant discourse affecting education policy in many countries, with forceful arguments that (1) goals and functions of schooling must contribute directly to economic productivity (e.g., children must learn the skills needed for economic development) and (2) schools must be structured to maximize cost effectiveness.

This policy logic, in the context of the economic competition of globalization, affects education in the following ways, according to Carnoy (2002):

1. Governments, as they need to reduce expenditures for public services and encourage competitiveness, seek nongovernmental supports for education.
2. More emphasis on postsecondary education with increased valuing of knowledge-based skills as countries compete to attract transnational corporate capital
3. Emphasis on testing for the efficient production of measurable outcomes, especially in science and math, as education is being compared internationally

Decentralization has been seen as a way to reduce central expenditures and bureaucracy and increase efficiency through competition. The promotion of school choice is a response to consumer demand, especially as families see their children needing to be competitive globally, with credentials for widened labor markets (Green, 1999).

Global markets create the need for global skills and even languages. One example of the push for advanced competence in math and reading in the U.S. curriculum is that they are "prerequisites for global participation and critical sources of social and technical power for individuals and nations . . . (and) education policy and standards of practice become too important to be left to educators . . . far too technically complex to be left to well-meaning but unscientific practitioners" (Mitchell & Boyd, 2001, pp. 72–73). Another example is the training in business schools that includes preparation to handle business meetings within Japanese or Argentinean cultural contexts. High-tech firms, whose needs are not met by U.S. schools' technical training, recruit skilled computer programmers from India and Israel. At the same time that these global currents increase demand for higher skills, they also can create greater inequality in access to high-quality education and greater income gaps.

Is globalization overwhelming and evil? Nations have "lost some of their capacity to make national-policy independently" (Dale, 1999, p. 2). Yet is it that powerful? Noting effects on curriculum, Gough (1999) saw global themes as an explicit focus in curricular areas like development education. The UN and UNESCO developed teacher education modules and curricula on the global environment, peace, and industrialization in developing countries. He credits transnational social movements for these global themes; however, he doubts that they reflect a "transnational imaginary" (p. 76) that has transformed curricula or that school children and future politicians are truly learning to think globally enough to recognize that their countries' rubbish or logging policies must be attuned to the globe's policies.

Thus, this section has demonstrated that educators, in looking internationally, find wider perspectives on some of the same puzzles and challenges faced nationally and locally, such as the need to deal with local conditions and values to achieve equity, to recognize the needs of marginalized groups, and to work with the demands of social movements. But looking internationally helps educators become more astute in seeing how dominant values frame countries' policies and how theories frame analyses of countries' education systems. It also helps educators see the need to take a position as world citizens on global issues and on dominant policy logics such as economic rationalism.

Politics from the Margin: An International Example

As mentioned throughout this book, the voices and needs of less powerful groups are often missing from mainstream policy and policy analysis. This is true in analyses of international education policy and politics. As detailed in Chapter 3, approaches exist, from theory and from emerging methodologies, for exploring such politics from the margin. This section describes a social movement, in which individuals' and groups' sense of agency created alternative ways of being, alternative spaces, counternarratives, and power bases within counterpublics. While economic and political systems create institutions that pay attention to the needs of dominants and reproduce elite privilege, people still negotiate their own ways of being, resisting, and re-creating in those alternative spaces. This becomes the social capital that re-frames politics.

This section traces the evolution of Australian gender policy coming from the margins. It is an example of critical policy analysis, a search for improvement of the human condition through finding alternatives that can reconstruct political institutions and public life. It is an example of a kind of policy analysis in which the researcher seeks to understand policy making that can empower and democratize. It shows how evaluations, studies, and analyses can raise fundamental questions or help open conversations with the powerful and get the oppressed to see that they have been oppressed (Friere, 1985), as discussed in Chapter 3. The study uses feminist analysis, assuming that where policy apparatus is male dominated, women's issues, by definition, come to the policy system as a challenge, to be resisted. Thus, traditional policy analysis assumptions and methods do not suffice.[5,6]

Studying Australian Gender Equity Policy

What can be learned from Australia's national and state policy formulations for Gender Equity Policy (GEP)? Marshall was curious, on hearing from Australian scholars that their national policies were strong, even providing good jobs for feminists working in bureaucracies (femocrats) to implement and monitor the policies and programs. There, scholars even received government funds to study gender issues, curriculum writers' gender equity materials were supported and disseminated by government agencies, and the Victorian Ministry of Education ran special programs to promote women into administration. This contrasted much with her experience and analysis of gender equity policy in the United States (e.g., Marshall, 1997b, 2000a, 2002). Researching this could be a great way to do truly different education research, getting other politics scholars and policy makers to see how blind they've been to ignore gender politics (and the idea of traveling to Australia was rather appealing, too). With the help of Australian scholars, Marshall used documents and face-to-face interviews with the "femocrats," activists, and policy makers who were deeply involved in the formulation and implementation of Australia's policies.

An Analysis of the Structures for Gender Policy Formulation

At first, wondering how gender got on the agenda, Marshall used descriptive, mainstream approaches like Kingdon's theory of policy windows (1984; previously discussed in Chapters 1 and 7), emphasizing questions about the cultural values and politics that might support openness to gender policy. She also used, as her framework for interview questions, the taxonomy of seven policy mechanisms (discussed in Chapters 1 and 7) to get respondents to think about which mechanisms were most effective.

The first analysis, emphasizing the structure of education policy, identified the policy mechanisms viewed as powerful for effecting gender equity (Marshall, 2000a). Two policy mechanisms, Curriculum Materials Development and Program Definition, were seen as the most used and powerful policy mechanisms to effect policy. Nonsexist curricula, program development for learning and teaching that incorporated girls more, inclusive curriculum practices, designating ways to incorporate materials for elimination of sexual harassment and antiviolence, targeted innovations in frameworks with equal opportunity for girls, incorporating the contributions of women into Australian history—these were seen as strong and successful GEP initiatives.

Personnel Training and Certification was the next most powerful mechanism. In their training, certification, selection, promotion, and staff development, GEP was actively promoted. Interviewers had training to avoid and prevent sexism, and the Advanced Skills Awards included equal opportunity policies. The state of Victoria had a mentoring program and assertiveness and skills training to support women interested in becoming principals.

Through the Finance policy mechanism, the federal government targeted funding for gender research, for "catalyst teachers," for TV ads to get girls into math, and for policy analyses to monitor how gender was addressed. "In every grouping (for example, for kids in poverty, for disabilities), there would be a gender analysis to see that access didn't impact girls more than boys" (p. 374) and government subsidies of $300 bonuses to schools for every girl doing 300-level math. In addition, government agencies reported *A Women's Budget,* demonstrating how that agency had addressed the needs of women citizens overall. The policy mechanism, Testing and Assessment, was not as much of an obsession in Australia as it was in the United States, according to one informant. However, testing regimes were monitored to see that there were no negative effects on girls.

This analysis used policy mechanisms and a theoretical model that was values-neutral, as if gender policy were just like any other policy. But respondents said things like, "These questions are good but the real story is about the communicating . . . vision and leadership, the symbolic acts, the political model" (p. 378), and the most vibrant political activity was encompassed in informants' stories about the politics from the margin. The framework "Politics from the Margin," presented in Chapter 3, had not been developed yet, but it would have greatly assisted in finding a better way to make sense of the data.

A Politics from the Margin, Feminist, and Discourse Analysis

So why not listen to the data and try another approach to analysis? Indeed, the data begged for feminist critical policy analysis (Marshall, 2000b). The data were replete with insights that required recognition that gender policy was a challenge, from the margins of politics, to make the hegemonic center incorporate their needs and values. It required approaches from feminist theory. Further, it required recognition that when politics and policy are centered around ideological shifts, the focus needs to be on symbols (not structures), and so discourse analysis was a powerful methodological and theoretical approach for analysis.

Traditional policy frameworks were useful: Policy windows honed in on questions of why Parliament paid attention to feminists' demands; analysis of values shifts focused on questions about how equity values gained prominence (recall Chapter 1). But feminist critical policy analysis (recall Chapter 3) raised new questions:

- Any policy focus on gender, race, and class inequities redistributes goods and benefits; such policies take away from the ensconced and institutionalized privileges. Resistance and backlash will be fierce.
- When one focuses on gender, different feminist philosophies have different policy implications. Power and Politics feminisms recognize that women are placed at the margin of policy arenas, always viewed as challengers and upstarts. Liberal feminisms assume that governments can and would correct sexist practices, eliminating barriers to equal opportunity. Women's Way feminisms focus on women's special values and life choices, seeking understanding of how they should be revalued. Increasingly, feminist philosophies demonstrate how race, sexuality, and class biases are intertwined in gender regimes, recognizing the error of essentializing women by putting all women in one category, as if equity for women could be doled out simplistically. Thus, analysis of GEP needs to identify these feminist philosophical debates.
- When one recognizes the need to understand the power of words and symbols as they are mobilized in power plays in policy formulation, the focus is on ideological politics (Ball, 1990b). But women and women's needs have not been "out there" in public policy discourse (Blackmore, 1989; Eisenstein, 1993; Marshall, 1997a; Pateman & Gross, 1987). So, one must look beyond the mainstream policy debates and look toward the margin. It is important to identify the counternarratives (oppositional stories) and counterpublics (oppositional arenas of discourse) of members of subordinated groups that formulate oppositional "interpretations of their identities, interests, and needs" (Fraser, 1994, p. 117).

Thus, with feminist critical policy analysis and discourse analysis lenses, one must ask what were the counternarratives and the counterpublics. What happened to move GEP demands from the margins to the center?

As one activist said, "Making people talk about gender . . . with different groups in key positions forcing that dialogue will get people aware and making decisions they wouldn't otherwise have made" (p. 129). (All data in this section are from Marshall 2000b).

With these new frameworks for analysis, the same data reveal powerful lessons for doing outsider-in politics. This analysis shows how

- activists used national cultural values for giving everyone a "fair go" could be capitalized upon, when connected to girls' disadvantage in access to the benefits of school and employment;
- Australians' need to be caught up with international progress could be used to connect the international women's movement, justifying GEP;
- electoral politics, with government polling on domestic violence, were already creating a dialogue on gender;
- women from unions, parent groups, bureaucracies, and in schools had built networks, which were greatly facilitated by government-funded national conferences;
- the preexisting Association of Women Educators (AWE) were lying in wait for the GEP cause; and
- employment issues about free childcare, abortion, equal pay, and women in the administration were clearly equal opportunity demands.

With these as counterpublics, ready to assert counternarratives about what education systems ought to be doing, a strong politicking from the margin could be mounted. Joan Kirner, a mother wanting to get beyond cake sales, joined in the articulation of the challenge from the margin. She eventually became premier and then minister of labor in the state of Victoria in Australia. She said, "I'm a very strong unionist, feminist" (p. 131) and was angry that pregnant women teachers were forced to retire; she said, "My campaigning career dovetailed really into gender equity" from parent activism with reading feminist writers, into fundraising and demanding resources for education, leading to a slogan of "no fundraising without representation. . . . We argued for a *real* say. . . . My feminism grew out of saying, 'As a mum, I want to have a say. . . . Its no good just baking cakes.'" The Women's Electoral Lobby was there for her to connect to at the time. Similarly, others saw the numbers of men who were making decisions about women's lives and "how male educators dealt with power and hung onto it" (p. 132) and became activated. The feminist analysis and the discourse analysis continues, identifying the following:

- The networks and coalitions emerging among femocrats, outsider activists, and unionists who collaborated with AWE and the Women's Electoral Lobby to gain passage of key national legislation
- Activists' strategies for amassing people, using symbols, pamphlets, discussion papers, and scenario writing, using the media, and, in unions, establishing goals for having women in leadership match the percentage of women in membership
- Constructing common counternarratives by agreeing, on the surface at least, about when and where to promote certain issues and philosophies and guarding their images and strategically positioning GEP on the education-to-work idea

- Anticipating resistance and backlash but aligning with the "fair go" ethic and focusing on men's daughters; learning to "stage-manage" and use humor to jolly people along
- Using and publicizing research to legitimize the debate and to maintain the GEP focus when policy attention waned
- Expanding to connect to issues beyond education, recognizing GEP connections with sexuality, identity, violence, ethnicity, and emotional and family issues
- Living with and working together despite the tensions between femocrats and outsider activists, in spite of being sometimes isolated and marginalized
- Using new priority areas (curricular emphases on excellence, school climate, key learning areas) to infuse gender equity within them

One femocrat summed up enforcement of GEP, saying, "We made it happen by the three Fs: fear, funds and fairness, in that order" (p. 131). But, as values shifted, GEP was seen as finished, accomplished, and the clamor was "What about the boys?" and social justice was called "educational claptrap" by one key education official, GEP activists devised strategies for maintenance and managing the backlash. They modified their feminisms to show how feminism could benefit boys and to tie into the ongoing governmental concern about violence, thus "lock[ing] onto whatever argument you can" (p. 146).

Thus, the analysis of GEP using discourse analysis was very powerful in identifying political strategies used by this outsiders' movement to challenge hegemony. Compared with the analysis of the structure and policy mechanisms (discussed above), discourse analysis captures the life of GEP and displays the earthy and useful dynamics far better. Further, the strategies used by femocrats parallel those displayed in the Chapter 3 vignette, in which Reba Conover knew to present to the Senate her agenda for girls' education in words and values attuned to those of the dominants.

Finally, for those of you who might be still wondering how this could be useful, Marshall used this research as the basis for an article telling U.S. educators what can be learned about political strategies from the margin generally and about strategies for building and maintaining momentum for getting male-dominated policy makers and educational leaders to take education gender equity policy seriously (see Marshall, 2002).

Summary

Threaded through this chapter are reminders of reasons for the politicization of global educational comparisons; of the actions, theories, and methods for international education policy; of the ways to discover new strategies by borrowing insights from other countries. The chapter presents the challenge to identify ways in which politics and policies converge internationally and to ponder the effects of globalization. As global citizens, too, we see the chronic challenge to adequately support systems that will provide equality of educational opportunity, especially as regimes around the globe often pay, at best, lip service to reforms that redistribute opportunity and resources. Finally, this chapter provides an example of international policy research that tries out two different frameworks. Readers, now, can never again ignore international education policy news, never again travel without wondering about the status of families and education access in foreign countries, and we hope you will be inspired to conduct research on international education politics.

Exercises for Critically Examining Global Education Politics

1. In the year 2230, could there be a global curriculum and unified international educational system? Or is this suggestion preposterous? Construct a classroom debate. One side should argue why there will and should be, and another will argue why there will not and should not be.

2. Brainstorm an idea for an international research study. What is most interesting, why, and how would you start your analysis? Would you ask these questions?

    a. How does democracy affect education practice?

    b. How does increased centralization affect education policy?

    c. How does religion affect education policy?

    d. How do cultural assumptions about women affect education policy?

    e. How does the military get involved in education policy?

    What other questions would you ask and why?

3. Suppose you are a member of the UN Committee that directs studies and establishes guidelines in the attempt to get countries to equalize the access and effects or outcomes of schooling. With Figures 8.1 and 8.2 in front of you, and with your knowledge from previous chapters, what kinds of further studies and different ways of measuring equity would you propose, and how could you and your committee begin to put pressure on countries to make their education systems more equitable?

4. Often people want to focus just on education policy issues pertaining to their own country. Using the points made in this chapter and your own reasons, tell why the following groups need information regarding education policies in foreign countries:

    a. Members of Congress

    b. Local and state school board members

    c. Parents and other citizens

    d. UN and World Bank research directors

    e. Teachers and administrators

    f. Big business

    g. The military

5. Find several examples of international policy studies around a specific issue (e.g., women's literacy, vocational education, the arts) and try to identify the assumptions being employed. Because you know that researchers and policy analysts have theories framing their work that focus their questions about the politics and policies for deciding about pedagogy, about teacher training, the organizational structure of schooling, the curriculum and materials used, and so on, find evidence of those theories. Sometimes scholars, sponsoring organizations, and authors lay these out explicitly, but sometimes not.

6. Widen your understanding of how other countries organize education. Read one of the many books that describe and analyze the educational systems of different countries. Some are descriptive, rather like education-focused *National Geographic*, without the beautiful pictures. Here are some examples: (1) Mazurek, Winzer, and Majorek (2000) provide a well-organized overview of a range of countries, from Papua New Guinea, to Brazil, to Greece, and Israel. (2) Mungazi (1993) examines how a country's education systems reflect national character. (3) If you are interested in how children fare around the world, *Statistical Handbook on the World's Children* (Kaul, 2002) provides useful information. It shows how nutrition, violence and war, education, child labor, infant and maternal mortality rates, and the like, convey messages about countries'

ability and will to care for their children. (4) *In Pursuit of Equity in Education: Using International Indicators to Compare Equity Policies* by Hutmacher, Cochrane, and Bottani (2001) provides information on literacy levels in developing countries, countries with high percentages of poor children who never enroll in school, the ways disparities between rich and poor and girls and boys affect enrollment and progression through primary education, and resources for disabled or disadvantaged students.

Notes

1. In 2003, the deputy secretary of education asserted that we couldn't make good use of international comparative studies. Others from the Bush administration asserted no interest in additional studies like TIMSS (Research Policy Notes, 2003).

2. Here are some resources for further analyses of TIMSS:

    Koretz, D., McCaffrey, D., & Sullivan, T. (2001, September 14). Local flexibility within an accountability system. *Educational Policy Analysis Archives, 9*(44). From http://olam.ed.asu.edu/epaa/v9n44.html.

    O'Leary, M., Kellaghan, T., Madaus, G. F., & Beaton, A. E. (2000, August 21). Consistency of findings across international surveys of mathematics and science achievement: A comparison of IAEP2 and TIMSS. *Educational Policy Analysis Archives, 8*(43). From http://olam.ed.asu.edu/epaa/v8n43.html. This study investigates discrepancies between countries' scores on two international science assessments and offers hypotheses to account for the differences.

3. *Ms. Magazine* expends a large percentage of pages focusing on conditions of women internationally, but we doubt that many policy makers are subscribers.

4. Examples of feminist critical policy analysis exist (Marshall & Anderson, 1995). Examples of cross-national feminist critical policy analysis exist as well. Arnot and Weiler (1993) collected studies of feminist analysis of education policy in settings ranging from Maori women to women academics in Britain and Black American women teachers. Arnot, reviewing these, concludes that, while the analyses reflect differences in national circumstances, they share these theory-building challenges: They challenge the "master narratives" of Western thought and they are played out in the midst of "the realignment of politics following the success of neo-conservative forces in the 1980s" (p. 210) and the "rapid growth of world wide corporate capitalist economic system" (p. 210).

5. See other examples, such as Kelly, G. P., & Elliot, C. M. (1982). *Women's Education in the Third World: Comparative Perspectives* (Albany, NY: State University of New York Press) and many others for useful scholarly insights, and see *Ms. Magazine* for journalist and activist commentary on current issues.

6. Look at the full analysis for detail (Marshall, 2000b).

Part **III**

Making Connections for Policy Action

Having a range of insights about theories, concepts, models, and research provides one with plentiful ways to navigate education politics. A healthy suspicion of the politics of knowledge and identifying how such politics sway us to premature closure can help re-frame education problems. Now we are ready to plunge into re-visioning.

First, recognize that we are plunging into complexities where no political or policy move stands alone. All levels are interconnected, and further, education issues are often tightly interconnected with other social and economic issues. Chapter 9 maps some of these complexities and also makes the point that policy issues and allies are constantly shifting, so taking action and making moves in this environment is not so much following a roadmap but more, really, like constantly recreating the map. Groups who were once opposed to your goals suddenly become the strange bedfellow allies in your coalition. Or, where once you used phrases and stories about equal opportunity and that worked so well to rally people to action, after values shifted, those phrases just don't work any more.

With knowledge of these complexities and a determination to revision education politics, Chapter 10 shows how educational leaders can be policy advocates. They can use the practical knowledge of arenas of power, their sense that education politics needs re-visioning to include the voices and needs of the marginalized, and the promising emerging theories and methodologies for studying and doing politics differently. By knowing enough about power and enough about critique, you cannot be seduced by quick-fix promises. By knowing enough about collaboration and coalition and by recognizing the viability, credibility, and potential strength of education policy generated from participants' needs, you can generate education policies that fit with rhetoric and lived realties. By seeing examples of policy advocates who successfully maneuver political dynamics, you can keep your jobs and pay your mortgages even while taking bold stands. There are no Don Quixote nor Joan of Arc models of bungling or self-sacrifice here! In this section, we acknowledge the incongruities and interconnections you will encounter doing education politics but challenge you to dare be the creators of the new and evolving roadmaps of policy advocacy for education.

9

Intertwined Policies, Pendulum Shifts, and Interconnections

Guiding Questions _____

- How do national, state, and local governments and organizations interrelate, complicate, and affect politics and policy?

- How do agencies dealing with children and families compete, conflict, and cooperate with education agencies?

- What coalitions develop for policies affecting children's education?

- How do national movements and trends develop, shift, and affect state, district, and site politics?

- How do outside actors (e.g., business interests, courts) influence all levels of education policy?

- In the complex interrelationships and politics among agencies and levels of governance, what happens to education policies?

Realities and Interconnections

As I enter the room there is a strong smell of urine. The windows are closed, and there is a board over the glass pane in the door . . .

The children notice my arrival and look at me expectantly; I greet them and turn to the teacher, commenting on the broken pane of glass in the door. She comes over from her desk and says, "Jonathan put his hand through the window yesterday—his father passed him on the street and wouldn't say hello. Jonathan used to live with him, but since he started living with his mother, the father ignores him."

"These kids have hard lives, don't they," I say. At that, she begins a litany of the troubles of the children in her class: Derrick's father died of AIDS and another is sick. One girl's father stole her money for drugs. On Monday a boy had been brought to school by his mother, who said that the boy had been raped by a male cousin on Thursday, but that "he was over it now." The teacher was trying to get the boy some counseling. Two boys were caught shaving chalk and "snorting" the dust, and "they aren't getting any counseling either." One boy had a puffy eye because his mother got drunk after she got laid off and beat up the kids while they were sleeping; last night he had hit her back while she was sleeping.[1] (Anyon, 1997, p. xiii)

Anyon's interchange with a teacher in a second grade classroom at Marcy Elementary School (a pseudonym) highlights some of the stark realities facing children who live in challenging situations. The children in Anyon's study inhabit a community struggling with ghettoization and stigmatization. Many of the children she encountered had needs that went beyond what a school alone can provide. Many came from broken homes, lived on welfare, suffered abuse, engaged in violence, lacked proper medical care, and had little hope for the future. Teachers and school administrators interface with a range of community and governmental services in order to attend to student's needs. These complex issues are not exclusive to Marcy Elementary. Startling statistics reveal that 67 percent (or over two-thirds) of sexual assault victims are children under the age of twelve. Even more astounding are figures that suggest that almost a fourth of sexual assault offenders are juveniles who perpetrate 40 percent of offenses against victims under the age of six (Snyder, 2000). With such realities, children's experiences beyond the school walls matter. To truly transform schools via policy, Anyon (1997) suggests that the struggling communities in which many challenged schools are embedded need attention; "long-lasting, substantial educational improvement will not occur in the schools in our impoverished cities without the restoration of *hope* in the hearts of all involved—students, families, teachers, and administrators" (p. xvi). Think of the complexities to be encountered in politics and policies for grappling with such immense, wide-ranging, and deep-seated problems and for revisioning for such hope!

The previous five chapters examined specific components of the *policy web,* the multitude of interconnected and sometimes conflicting policies and policies that ensnare schools like Marcy, which struggles with an array of local contextual issues and community issues. Each of the chapters has shown that understanding this policy web requires an understanding of traditional models that focus on the power centers of policy making and politics, as well as approaches that seek to uncover and validate excluded voices such those of the students in Anyon's study. Now, in this chapter, we delve into the interconnections between levels of policy making and how this policy web of connections encompasses organizations and groups outside of education. Given the complexity of the "web" of connections, this chapter suggests that policy change requires policy actors and policy makers to be *strategic* about advocating for change. Every policy decision can elicit unintended consequences that may affect other levels. Additionally, to create policy change, attention must be given to each facet of the policy web and the multiple contexts in which they operate.

The Policy Web of Leadership

Think about a day in the life of a principal. A typical day might start with the need to co-ordinate with the Public Works Department over a snow day, or the Sanitation Department over a broken sewer line. It might be followed by a dispute between a divorced couple concerning who is responsible for picking up a child from school. It might involve strategizing with the central office or parents to prepare for an upcoming bond issue. At the same time, the principal knows she must also deal with personnel issues emanating from her efforts last year to forcibly retire two teachers (one who is jaded, tired, and ineffective and another who has emotional outbursts at students and refuses to seek counseling). She has to prepare for the looming court cases. She also has to recruit two new teachers to take the teachers' places, knowing that the neighboring district is offering low home mortgage rates and other recruitment benefits. After school hours, she rushes to the superintendent's strategy session on developing a campaign to convince voters to pass a bond issue for a much-needed facilities upgrade *and* she heads to another meeting on the district's standardized implementation of the antiviolence policies (where some principals are fudging their site statistics to avoid being labeled as a bad school). By 7 P.M. she is gobbling fast food while trying to look attentive in her graduate organizational theory class. Finally, she dozes off, wondering how scholarly work is going to help her cope with tomorrow's long to-do list. The class discussion wanders, and she cannot see how the professor can be lecturing students about working with the whole child and the whole family. Does the professor have any idea how hard it is just to get together the social worker, the parent, the truant officer, and three teachers, never mind to get them past their distrust of each other to generate strategies to help just *one* kid who is floundering?

Meanwhile, as her superintendent creates a strategy for the campaign for the bond issue, she knows the realities about competition for funds. Schools, libraries, departments of welfare, and public health agencies are all trying to tap into the same pots of public (and some private) funds to provide the array of services they know will help the children and families they serve. They compete, ironically, although they share many common goals and clientele.

Think about the superintendent looking over the agendas for the next several board meetings, jumping past the mundane ceremonial awards and information items to concentrate on trying to plan for managing when the superintendent and board will be debating the political aspects of myriad health-related, financial, ethical, legal, and cultural issues.

Channel One and Pepsi are both offering contracts that will create revenue streams, but some parents object to the advertising content and nutritional compromises. Should the Boy Scouts use schools for meetings? Some of the members of the board want to meet the budget by eliminating the band, the debate team, and the drama club. Also, several board members are pushing the governor and the chamber of commerce as they try to entice some big company to locate in that county and bring in tax dollars. Because of this, the superintendent is being pressured to put a very positive spin on some rather negative statistics about the schools. She has also gotten wind that the gay and lesbian group, GLSTN, and People for the Ethical Treatment of Animals (PETA) will be lobbying for local curriculum alterations to infuse their message in the health and social studies curriculum, and they may stage some dramatic, attention-getting media event that could upset the board meeting. Additionally, the new federal and state guidelines related to accountability and testing will have an impact on the several elementary schools in the district with high numbers of African Americans, which could stir up the local community activist group that advocate for children of color.

Reading about the complexities of such lived realities, one can see the following:

- No education policy issue is solely about the classroom, as it extends to societal goals and dilemmas.
- No dilemma in education ever gets dealt with completely, as one pressing demand overlaps with another.
- Education policies are usually carried out via interconnecting and often competing demands from international, federal, state, local, and micro levels.
- Political and policy demands force decisions and action that create further dilemmas, paradoxes, and peculiarities.

The reality of the policy web of leadership is that the educational context in which leaders work is complicated by an array of policies created in a multitude of policy-making arenas that are entangled with local, national, and global politics. Understanding this reality is an important facet of understanding how policies and politics might be re-visioned and re-framed.

Re-visioning and Re-framing the Web of Intertwined Policies

Is it not interesting that models and theories for analyzing the politics of education, especially those in Chapter 1, center on the arenas of power, the hegemonic center, which is a far distance from any first grader? We call Figure 9.1 Centering a Child in Multiple Contexts (developed by Adler, 1994). It begins with a very different premise, one that places the child at the center of the policy web and examines the complex societal assumptions and policy norms, powerful structures and systems, and people who can shape a child's life. Such a model is useful (and more likely the theory most in use for framing the daily decisions of educators, parents, and social workers). This model could be an excellent stimulus for re-visioning children's needs and and serve as a starting point for re-framing policy to address those needs.

This model provides a way to invert traditional arenas of policy inquiry by presenting a more holistic view of how multiple policy arenas can focus on the needs of one child. The model starts with the needs and experiences of a single student and moves outward in order to understand the complex array of policies and practices that have an impact on that student's needs and realities. The student is enmeshed within a particular family and home situation, educational needs, economic situation, and psychological and physical health conditions, which are embedded in broader structures, such as the specific issues facing the community in which the child lives, and the tangled "web" of district, state, and federal policies based on assumptions that might be racially, culturally, and/or economically in-

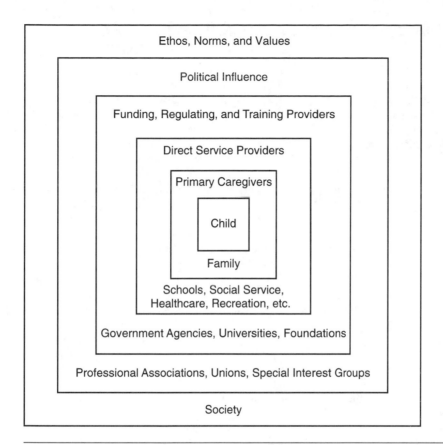

FIGURE 9.1 *Centering a Child within Multiple Contexts*

Source: From L. Adler and S. Gardner, eds. *The Politics of Linking Schools and Social Services.* Copyright 1994 by Taylor & Francis Publisher. Used by permission.

equitable. The Lived Realities on page 240 provides an example of how the model might be used to examine the politics of linking schools and social services through the hypothetical experiences of Ryan Franklin.

Harriet's struggle to figure out a way to serve Ryan's needs illustrates how educating children often involves a complex web of government services, special interest groups, the criminal justice system, business interests, medical services, community contexts, policies, and politics. Giving up on someone like Ryan does not mean that the policy problem will go away. Ryan's chances for incarceration and unemployment rise sharply if he does not complete school. Placing Ryan's needs at the center puts a face on one reality of the dropout "problem," which shows how intertwined it is with the economic realities of impoverished communities. Members of these communities face limited housing and job opportunities, business leaders' desires for skilled labor, juvenile justice concerns about truancy and delinquency, and federal and state policies emphasizing standardization over individual student needs and realities. As Ryan's story illustrates, education policies and politics are

Lived Realities: Re-visioning Policy Problems through Ryan's Eyes

The rules said, on no uncertain terms, that Ryan Franklin had to be suspended from school for a month after the coach found him smoking pot in the locker room. He had already had run-ins with the courts (for truancy), and, although his high school couldn't see the records, it was rumored that he had to report to juvenile justice supervisors because of his involvement with drug dealers. Academically, Ryan is deemed a failure by state and federal accountability measures that show him as performing below grade level. Diagnosed with a behavioral disorder, his Individual Education Plan (IEP) team (the organization of which is specified by the federal law IDEA), which includes a psychologist, special education teacher, and his regular classroom teacher, have been working hard to help develop life skills and modify his behavior.

Principal Harriet Stone is torn. Cheap labor in Third World countries has driven most clothing manufacturers overseas. Unable to compete with the low wages paid outside of the United States, the local clothing manufacturing plant to shut down, costing Ryan's father his job. Ryan's father left town shortly thereafter, leaving his mother to raise their three kids. Harriet knows that Ryan's mother works two low-paying service jobs to make ends meet. If sent home, Ryan will be unsupervised, loose in town, just looking for trouble. He may hang around nearby, looking for his friends after school. At the very least, he will miss schoolwork and probably therefore fail his classes, even though he has a chance of making passing grades and graduating. More dire threats loom from his obvious connection with older men who offer him a place to hang out and money to run errands related to their drug-dealing business. Harriett has phoned Mrs. Franklin on numerous previous occasions and knows she is afraid of her supervisor at work: "He's always saying, 'I can't rely on women like you. People like you can't control your home lives so I can't count on you to be concentrating on your work.'" Her fears were exacerbated by the threat that she and her three children could be thrown out of their public housing because of the "one strike and you're out rule" to prevent drug dealing there.

Principal Stone has a tremendous investment in these issues, not just for Ryan's sake, but also because she researched the issues and tried, unsuccessfully, two years in a row to win the special federal funding for an alternative in-school suspension for just such circumstances. She even campaigned for two county commissioners and a judge whose campaign promises included special funding for an alternative school. Such campaigning raised awareness that students like Ryan needed options, but the funding still wasn't there. Further, she knows that, without training, supports, and incentives to change his ways, Ryan is a threat to other students, both in school and in the community. Harriet knows that, even if she gets through and convinces the Department of Human Services and Social Welfare or Juvenile Justice to supervise Ryan, they have no daycare responsibility or facilities.

Sitting in her office at 8 o'clock in the evening, Harriet was determined to identify the ways Ryan's situation could be addressed. She started diagramming the complexity and interconnections of Ryan's situation. On a notepad, she drew Ryan at the center. Her depiction included Mrs. Franklin's limited work opportunities, the family's lack of housing options, his IEP team, and the realities of district, state, and federal politics and budget choices shaped by business interests. On a fresh sheet of paper, Harriet drew Ryan again, but this time she surrounded him with an (imagined) alternative school, tutoring and an after-school program, housing and family support systems, job training for his mom, and community counseling services.

inextricably bundled together with an array of wider social policy issues. In this case, Ryan needs support services that don't exist within the school.

Anyon's suggestion that the struggling communities in which schools are situated need help, coupled with the bureaucratic limitations of the principalship and the need for connected services for Ryan, points to the multifaceted challenges any leader or policy maker faces that seeks to improve schools. The lives of children, their families, community members, the individuals who work in schools, and various politicians are all interconnected in policy webs that cross different policy-making arenas from school board meetings to congressional hearings. Policies and political strategies are needed that are sensitive to these realities. In the next section, we explore the specifics of the array of policies and politics that affect children's lives.

The Politics of Policy Making for Children

The public programs and policies meant to meet the needs of children and families come from fragmented public services and fractured governance structures—multiple programs and agencies. The following lists some embarrassing results of federal and state policies in the United States. Many of these policies are constructed as if most families had stay-at-home moms to carry out a wide range of social, health, recreational, cultural, and educational services. But according to the Forum on Child and Family Statistics (2002),

- in 2001 19 percent of children in the United States had at least one foreign-born parent;
- the birth rate for adolescents was twenty-seven births per 1,000 girls aged 15 to 17 in 2000;
- 23 percent of eighth grade students had used illicit drugs in the previous thirty days in 2001;
- 16% of youth ages twelve to seventeen experienced serious crime victimizations;
- while the percentage of youth aged sixteen to nineteen neither working nor in school declined to 9 percent in 2001, the percentages for Black and Hispanic youth are 14 percent and 13 percent, respectively;
- 25 percent of Hispanic children, 13 percent of Black children, and 7 percent of White children were not covered by health insurance in 2000; and
- 69 percent of children lived with two parents in 2000.

The dominant values and key actors driving education politics have placed the needs of families and children at the margin. The structures of politics, too, weaken political momentum. Currently, no Department of Children and Families exists (although Congress and legislatures certainly hear from advocates). Coordination among agencies would allow children's advocacy groups to push for holistic, umbrella policies and budgets that touch on realities faced by families and children and the agencies, including schools, who try to support them. If educators and advocacy groups had access to the reins of power and budgets to create the supports children need to do well in schools, we would have very different politics. But conflicts of values and priorities would continue, as some would focus on health, some might demand marriage-first clauses for family assistance, some would demand phonics as the answer to early schooling difficulties, some would concentrate on housing, some on providing breakfast, and some on preventing unwanted pregnancy. Sources for these varied priorities include, among many others, people's professional training and organizational needs. The person with the degree in school psychology sees things differently than the social worker, who sees things differently than the Immigration and Naturalization Service (INS) officer and the lobbyist from the American Association of Retired Persons (AARP). Even in cases involving groups that ostensibly have common interests in helping children in, say, an expanded free milk program, interest group politics are brought to the fore, as groups compete to get credit, control, precedence, and turf (see Koppich, 1994, for a more in-depth discussion). To serve children and families, programs are needed that expand policy boundaries, necessitating the crafting of comprehensive and coordinated public policy.

Pendulum Swings of Webs of Control, Values, and Priorities

Looking historically, one can identify shifts in political views about government responsibility and goals for intervening for families and children. The Roosevelt New Deal era created a social services paradigm shift by creating an alphabet soup of federal agencies that focused on relief and support for families while jump-starting the economy. In the 1960s President Kennedy and then-President Johnson's Great Society created optimism and faith in government's ability to fix poverty, create jobs for the unemployed, provide health care, develop programs for impoverished children and youth, feed the hungry with food stamps, offer public assistance for housing, and, notably, federal aid to stimulate innovation and equity through federally funded incentives to schools (Title I of ESEA). According to Koppich (1994), "These new federal initiatives were woven into the fabric of large-scale social reform. In effect, the government created and sanctioned expansion of what constituted human services and the redefinitions of who was eligible to receive them" (p. 54). Funds targeted to specific populations were to be dispersed through state government agencies. Federal funds came with federal rules that required states and local communities to meet certain conditions to qualify for categorical funds (money distributed based on certain criteria, such as family income). Interest groups developed to keep those programs going as they built constituencies. This targeting helped create constituencies for programs that then learned to compete with each other. Title I of ESEA and bilingual education programs developed constituencies with lobbies and trained professionals who could, themselves, become political factors. The *Lau v. Nichols* 1974 Supreme Court decision (making school districts responsible for assisting limited- and non-English-speaking students) and the ability of groups to get states to fund bilingual and English as a Second Language (ESL) programs can be seen as an outcome of this type of constituency creation. Conversely, current attempts by conservative groups to mandate English-only programs (as mentioned in Chapter 6) in California and Massachusetts can also be seen as another outcome of constituency creation.

To proponents of broad-scale policy change, the 1970s, especially under President Nixon, seemed to be a period of backsliding and losses. Federal support for the *Lau* decision was "more symbolic than vast" (Koppich, 1994, p. 55). However, the previously created constituencies, with their professionals at work, kept many budgets and funds like Title I, now Chapter I, intact. Also, this was the era when Public Law (PL) 94-142, the Education for All Handicapped Children Act of 1975, was passed. The law represented a major federal policy shift, with clear equity goals and specificity regarding methods for monitoring and redress, requiring (not just encouraging or allowing) schools to create free and appropriate educational services for physically and mentally handicapped children.

President Carter's administration continued the programs of the 1960s and saw "a growing public perception that poverty, the foundation of many categorical entitlements, was fading as an urgent social issue" (Koppich, 1994, p. 56). Ronald Reagan's election, as mentioned in Chapter 7, can be seen as a "turning point" election, signifying a nationwide realignment of values. In Reagan's (and later the elder Bush's) education policies, new policies and new terminologies emerged. "The new federalism" meant deregulation and diminution of federal roles for education. First, the "new federalism" sought to get rid of federal involvement in education, disbursing federal money in block grants and leaving it up to state governments and political forces to set priorities. Many interest groups were successful in convincing Congress to keep the categorical protections. They argued that block grants were really just ways to cut the Great Society domestic program funds and ideals. Some lobbies shifted their work to state capitals. Some priorities that were once protected by targeting of categorical funding were now left to flounder and try to convince state politicians to fund their goals and programs. With this shift in values, a "discourse of derision" began in earnest, using new words like *educationist,* laden with anti-educator and anti–education researcher rhetoric. Educators were mistrusted and assumed to promote public schooling in order to maintain (union-supported) vested interests and categorical funding. In response, the Reagan administration sought to cleanse them from the Department of Education

As mentioned in previous chapters, in 1983 *A Nation at Risk* evoked fear that public schools were failing, and governors conferred on new plans for states to take initiative for solutions. New assumptions emerged from new dominant discourses: Market forces would weed out the incompetent; competition for merit pay would inspire teachers; and competition among schools for the dollars of children's vouchers would motivate schools to improve. Performance standards would inspire excellence and character education would transform classrooms to be full of self-disciplined and drug-free children. The dominant values were quality and excellence, and many equity-oriented social programs atrophied (Boyd, 1991; Clark and Astuto, 1986). After withdrawing federal oversight, the secretary of education assumed a "bully pulpit" role to advise and exhort, while each state bore the responsibility to make it happen.

Most recently, the No Child Left Behind Act (NCLBA) of 2001, championed by George W. Bush, represents a major federal policy shift toward federal intrusion into education. Although the bill has an equity emphasis in that it targets low-income children, in reality the major force of the legislation is that mandating test scores serve as *the* indicator of student achievement. The NCLBA is also severely underfunded in comparison to the financial costs that schools, districts, and states will incur in trying to implement the policy. Students like Ryan, who are barely hanging on by a thread, don't just need to raise their test scores, they need a wide array of services designed to keep them emotionally and physically healthy, in school and away from criminal activities.

In this recounting of policies, many shifts occurred in the direction, goals, and respective roles of different governance levels. Consequently, shifts also occurred in the kinds of policy logics, mechanisms, and programs created to address the shifted focus. In each instance, the politics of the time, the competition for benefits, the power struggles among key actors and partisan groups, the lobbying of interest groups, the crisis definition du jour—all played a part in shaping policy choices.

Swings in Federal Effects on States.   States look to the federal government for initiatives affecting the entire citizenry. Thus, we rely on the national armed services and on the national Environmental Protection Agency, because defense and environmental needs clearly cross state lines. Although education and child welfare needs cross state lines, for the most part states still retain their independence in making such policy. Still, national policy and initiatives, mandates, and funding do directly and indirectly frame state policy. As recounted in Chapter 7, the federal Supreme Court has jurisdiction when citizens' civil rights are compromised, so state and local policies denying civil rights can be adjudicated at that national level.

An analysis of how one state's policies (California) played out in the national context is instructive in demonstrating how national rhetoric, policies, and values affected state priorities (Koppich, 1994). In the booming economy of the '60s and '70s, categorical programs were created and expanded in education, health, juvenile justice, and welfare. Then Proposition 12 tax reform, which amended the state constitution to limit local property tax increases, placed the burden of social programs on the state budget. State-level interest groups intensified their efforts.

In the 1980s, state advocacy groups "did their best individually to define themselves for policy makers and thus grab 'their' share of a shrinking fiscal pie" (Koppich, 1994, p. 56). But with the accompanying reduction in federal regulatory and fiscal influence, the state dominated in the programs most affecting families and children. As a result, too many children slipped through the social service cracks; the state adopted a *triage* approach, serving only the most immediately threatened or damaged children, and services were fragmented, with little or no collaboration. "By the end of the late 80s, California boasted 169 different children and youth-serving programs overseen by 37 separate entities located in seven different state-level departments" (Koppich, 1994, p. 57). Legions of lobbyists tried to affect this scattered complication of funding streams. In 1988, Californians voted for another constitutional amendment guaranteeing that 40 percent of the state budget must go to K–14 public schools before any other money was spent. This was meant to stabilize education dollars and protect education from interest group politics. This Proposition 98 was dubbed "the mother of all categoricals." But with declining state revenues and a swelling (increasingly non-English-speaking) school population, the funding was insufficient. Shifting federal policies that devolve power to states without creating organizational capacity can lead to an array of disconnected programs and fractured services. Without coordination, these detached policies and programs allow many children and families to fall through the cracks.

To summarize, the past forty years have witnessed (1) the pendulum swing of federal initiative from the strong Great Society interventions to the devolution and diminution of the 1980s, (2) the ways in which the use of categorical grants and targeting created constituencies and interest groups, (3) how federal policy directions affected a state directions, (4) a dramatic overall increase in activity of influential interest group politics, and (5) an increased federal emphasis on accountability. Educational policy has been increasingly affected by pendulum shifts in voter sentiment and economic conditions. These insights are important to keep in mind because they highlight how deeply federal and national shifts in values and politics can affect states, programs, and the needs of children. Given this context, they also highlight the need for flexible policies and programs that keep the needs of children and families at the fore, even within shifting political contexts.

Interconnections and Paradoxes

The lines of separation and convergence among international, federal, state, local, and site governance are not clean and clear. As such, they lead to policy webs of strange connections and paradoxical disconnects. Suppose, for example, that several advanced-placement English students request to read *Exploring the Koran*. The teacher's response to this request is a policy decision that potentially crosses all levels of policy making. It is political and related to values, cultural assumptions, and judgments about whose purview it is to govern and about the purposes of education. The teacher's response connects to legal issues such as free speech and student's rights, the political dynamics of school board decisions, teacher unions, the Christian Right, the American Civil Liberties Union, and state curriculum guidelines. What happens to children in classrooms is more a function of an array of contextual factors, such as site policies that allocate teacher responsibilities, the economic and social health of community in which the school is situated, and the specific needs of students and staff. The president and Congress seldom think about such minutiae, as the paradox of Figure 9.2 illustrates. Yet many educators, children, and families are faced with the realities created by these shifting policy webs and policies that do not fit their needs.

The Paradox of Policy Intent and Unintended Consequences

With the political maneuvers of several levels of governance acting in often uncoordinated ways, the policies produced create strange juxtapositions and paradoxical effects. Unintended consequences result. A few historical events serve to illustrate the paradox of good policy intentions and the political and structural realities of unintended consequences. In 1972, with a two-foot-high stack of federally required paperwork in front of him (the state plans for federal education aid for Minnesota and Kentucky), Caspar Weinberger showed Congress the ensnarling red tape and governmental paralysis wrought by federal regulations. As secretary of Health, Education, and Welfare (HEW), he urged Congress to allow flexibility for comprehensive educational planning, and fewer strings attached to funds to promote greater use of financial aide. Murphy (1973b) describes lessons learned when, subsequently, Congress provided Title V money to states via State Education Agencies (SEAs) without restrictions, so they could strengthen their abilities in managing the array of federal programs entrusted to them. Staffing of SEAs was weak, and reformers hoped their management could undergo a thorough overhaul. However, the funds were used to provide

FIGURE 9.2   *Square Peg in a Round Hole*

Source: Copyright 2003, Tribune Media Services, Inc. Reprinted with permission.

more of what they had already been doing. Murphy studied nine states, finding, for example, that Massachusetts' weak state agency did use Title V money to beef up its research and statistics departments and to regionalize its services. New York created some small projects, but most involved cosmetic changes rather than substantive structural or cultural change. In contrast, South Carolina's SEA used the money to significantly strengthen their ability to manage federal programs. Murphy (1973b) found that "Title V enabled the SEA to build the basic organizational infrastructure necessary to shift from a traditional passive role to a new planning orientation" (p. 369). Thus, the funds allowed the South Carolina SEA to increase its influence with the legislature by conducting research and developing plans and objectives.

For most states, though, the increased funds to SEAs had little effect, because appropriations were tardy, preventing preplanning and making it impossible to hire good staff in mid-year, and state legislatures refused the money to make SEA salaries competitive. Also, critical gaps in SEA services took precedence, so major rethinking and restructuring could not take place. SEA organizational and political situations blocked the intended reforms. These old stories hold lessons that policy makers seem to ignore in paradoxes of policy consequences: (1) Intended results cannot be expected immediately, as they were to be implemented in rational organizations free of bureaucracy, organizational histories, and politics; and (2) federal, state, and local political and organizational realities complicate fulfillment of policy goals. The following Lived Realities illustrates these points by offering insight into the connectedness of federal and state policies, and especially how federal policy makers often assume states have the organizational capacity to do programs and evaluations when they often do not.

Lived Realities: Congress's Grand Plans Meet the Realities of State Capacities

Imagine her surprise when, in her role as consultant/evaluator, Professor Darleen Opfer found herself teaching Senator Ted Kennedy about the capacity of states to implement and evaluate federal programs.

Georgia was one of thirty-six states that received $8 million a year for three years to focus on improving teacher quality. Following the congressional directive, state policy makers created a state consortium made up of the Board of Regents for the University System, the Professional Standards Board, Office of School Readiness, and the Georgia Department of Education. Professor Opfer was charged with designing a methodology to evaluate the Title II Teacher Quality Initiative.

She found that Georgia, and in fact all of the states, looked at what they had been doing and essentially doled out the money for doing more of the same (although they sometimes added on to what they had been doing), instead of doing a master plan. For example, they raised Graduate Record Exam (GRE) and Scholastic Aptitude Test (SAT) requirements for prospective teachers and raised required credit hours for degrees—but there was no new innovation or rethinking of quality issues. Instead, Opfer found that Georgia put the money into 106 existing programs via the "gunshot approach" (e.g., they just shot money into existing programs without evaluating their effectiveness).

In her last, third year, the evaluation report was sent to Congress and the Government Accounting Office (GAO). As a result, members from Congress visited the state to see "a model program." Dr. Opfer quipped, "It was a model just because we actually had information—only a few others had done evaluations." Senators Kennedy and Ted Miller spent a day going through the program, asking what works and what needed to be improved. They were intrigued with Opfer's list of evaluation don'ts and decided to use them in the reauthorization of the federal policy. Her evaluation recommendations:

- *Clear Evaluation Criteria:* Choose your evaluation criteria and your evaluation team *before* you grant funds.
- *Technical Capacity:* If you're going to ask states to do something like improve teacher training, ask first whether they have the technical capacity to figure out what teacher workforce issues are. Ask first whether they already have data on what teacher prep is like.
- *Define Terms:* For example, what is a teacher? Do you include teachers teaching out of field, just a body in the field, or do you only count certified teachers teaching in their field? Are there databases available to report on defined data?

Paradoxically, although well-intentioned federal policy and monies did get some states to cosmetically pay attention to the issue teacher quality, these changes did not lead states to actually improve teacher quality. Georgia could only report on how many people participated in the training for science and math—but couldn't say whether it was an increase, because they had no baseline data. This vignette illustrates how policies are often disconnected from the lived realities in implementation sites. The devolution of federal funds to states, while well-intentioned, does not ensure that states have the organizational capacity to utilize funds effectively. In this case, an evaluation of how the federal funds were used is critical to understanding whether funds were directed toward the intentions of the policy. But this issue it not limited to the interconnections between state and federal governance. At the local level, multiple policies can bear down on individual schools and districts sometimes with perplexing results.

The next Lived Realities illustrates the waste and foolishness resulting from districts implementing complicated policies with different and sometimes paradoxical goals. In this case, many layers and levels of interpretation collide at the expense of children with special needs.

Lived Realities: Confounded Policies: Who's in Charge: Site, District, State, or Federal?

Laureltown is a district known for attracting and empowering its teachers, its respect for citizen input, and relatively fine services for special education. So when the school board enacted its site-based management policy, these factors could be strengths. But policies are not implemented in vacuums, as Laureltown's ensuing dilemmas illustrate.

Policy implementation is chaotic when directives are ambiguous and conflicting. As required by federal law, Laureltown was implementing several federal policies simultaneously. It was implementing the Individuals with Disabilities Act (IDEA), which specified that students who have IDEA-eligible disabilities needed individualized education plans (IEPs) and required they be educated in the "least restrictive environment." Additionally, the district also was required to implement the Americans with Disabilities Act (ADA), which protects children and adults with disabilities from discrimination, and Section 504 of the Vocational Rehabilitation Act of 1973, which commands that schools provide "reasonable accommodation" for access to educational programs (with no federal funds for implementation). Laureltown had adopted the "inclusion" approach to IDEA, requiring that students be served in regular classrooms as the first and preferred option in a continuum of services. State policy directives assumed that those closest to the situations could best make their own policies, so Laureltown also decided to implement site-based management.

IDEA, ADA, and 504 required hierarchical top-down controls and federal audits, and gave lobbyists and parents the legal ammunition to make demands for children with disabilities. Site-based management, in contrast, allowed sites to create decision-making bodies that were sensitive to local governance issues. Individual school governance structures in Laureltown, however, were unprepared for the additional responsibilities that the federal policies required, such as the coordination of services, professional development, personnel recruitment, managing sophisticated lobbyists and parents, and generating creative solutions to curriculum and testing modifications. The central office focused on being "just an interpreter of rules," thus divesting itself of power, leaving principals feeling they were "waffling" on student placement decisions, and leaving sites to implement policies without consistency around the district and with concerns about inequities, children slipping through the cracks. With little guidance on how to implement and maintain federal policies, principals and teachers were left to make up solutions as problems occurred (see Marshall & Patterson, 2002, for a full rendering of the Laureltown case.)

The story of the Laureltown district illustrates how when legislators, regulators, and bureaucrats make policy, they often forget that schools are already responding to an array of different policies. Many of these policies are developed with a different set of goals and assumptions about the structure of schools. When implemented at the same time and place, they can cause ambiguity and conflicts.

Teacher quality and special education are just two examples of a multitude of educational issues that can get caught in a tangled web of conflicting policy goals and assumptions. In the following section, we examine the interrelated issues of bilingual education, English language learners, and immigrant populations.

The Paradox of Ignoring Race and Culture: The Immigrant Experience

Looking beyond the borders of the United States, one can begin to see how local schools often deal with issues of international consequence. Many immigrants come to the United States to seek economic opportunity that may not be afforded in their home countries, plus they may be frustrated by a lack of educational services provided for poor children. Some immigrants, such as those from Rwanda or China, may come here to flee political persecution. Many Americans forget that the United States was founded by immigrants, as Figure 9.3 illustrates. International relations and events can have a powerful effect on local schools, economically and culturally. Immigrants cause previously homogenous schools to

FIGURE 9.3   *Taking Back America*

Source: Copyright © Steve Kelley, by permission.

have to rethink cultural norms, such as celebrating Christmas or Easter. Yet, at the same time, immigrants often face blatant racism and unwelcoming communities that are unwilling to embrace a change in their own community identity (Suarez-Orozco, 1998; Villenas, 2001).

How educational organizations, policies, and politics deal with immigrant children, their language, and ethnic identity shows the multilevel complexity of this policy issue. Differing local contexts mean that local schools, districts, and states respond differently in how they serve English language learners (ELLs) and their families. Some communities welcome immigrants, acknowledge racism, and celebrate diversity, while others do not. For example, some communities, such as Burlington, Vermont, have been supportive of immigrants. The refugee resettlement program in Burlington has been a preferred site for Bantu refugees due to the small size of the community, the community's development of communitywide antiracism policies, lack of a Somali population (which might cause ethnic conflict), and the availability of Swahili translators (Burlington Free Press, 2003). Other communities, however, have not been as supportive of refugees. In these communities, localized racism can surface in many ways. For example, Goodkind and Foster-Fishman (2002) studied Hmong refugees in one medium-sized Midwestern community and found that they felt excluded from meaningful participation in their community due to language barriers and discrimination.

While educators are concerned with education in the classroom, immigrant families often need help that goes beyond the classroom. For example, immigrant families may subsist on a limited income and speak little English. The bureaucratic forms and paperwork required to enroll children in services in a district can be overwhelming. They may not know about the free and reduced lunch program or may have cultural concerns about receiving handouts. While many school districts provide services to translate documents into other languages, many schools and districts are unprepared. These children may need health care or afterschool care, which schools are unable to provide. ELLs and their families require services and supports that go beyond the school walls.

While the 1974 *Lau v. Nichols* Supreme Court decision established the right of language-minority students to equal access to curricula and methods, the reality is that services for these children vary greatly from state to state. Arizona, California, and Massachusetts (see Chapter 6) have instituted stringent policies aimed at preventing bilingual education by requiring that teachers not speak to children in their native languages. What this essentially does is privilege English language while paradoxically devaluing the cultural heritages, ethnic identities, and thus the experiences of immigrants. This paradox points to the need for policies that *embrace race and culture* by acknowledging racism and valuing the histories, cultures, languages, and experiences of students (Moses, 2002).

Interweaving of National and International Politics

Chapter 8 discussed comparing countries and international relations. International relations among countries range from cooperation and economic competition to domination, colonization, and various kinds of war. The United Nations World Bank, UNESCO, and foreign aid from the United States and other countries contribute to the ability of developing countries to expand their economies, education systems, and healthcare services. But this is all done in the context of interconnected systems of world trade, military alliances, and agreements aimed at calming territorial tensions. International debates involve cultural clashes over what democracy, health, and education improvement should look like in developing countries.

National partisan politics, national cultural clashes, and even the values of individual key actors can have a huge impact on policy choices. For example, 170 countries—not the United States, however—signed something as straightforward as the international treaty for the rights of women and girls, including their rights to access to schooling and health care. In 2003, Senate ratification of the Convention of the Elimination of all Forms of Discrimination against Women (CEDAW) was held up in the Senate Foreign Relations Committee. Senator Biden and human rights advocates assert that the treaty would be a tool for women fighting for equity in inheritance, education, and employment and against tragedies like sexual trafficking, rape, and murder, while alarmists worry that it will destroy the traditional family, devalue Mother's Day, and give women the right to choose whether or not to have a baby. A then-ailing Senator Jesse Helms had enough support, even from his hospital bed, to prevent ratification, keeping the United States in the company of Somali and the Sudan as nonsigners. Such an example demonstrates how something as simple as statements that girls should have access to school are caught up in complicated political rhetoric and are held up by their association with non-school issues related to patriarchal controls.

Further, interconnections occur among foreign countries' education policies and international political relations: Japan approved new history books in 2001, resulting in controversies within and outside Japan. Textbook authors claimed that students learn too much about Japanese wartime atrocities and not enough about the positive aspects of Japan's cultural heritage. The revised version was hugely successful. China and South Korea, however, were enraged at the way, in their view, the books softened and glossed over Tokyo's bloody conquest of much of Southeast Asia in the first half of the twentieth century (Nelson, 2002). These international examples point to the reality that local school politics and policies are related to the complex connections and disconnects between cultural values, such as nationalism and economic competition. The complexity of interrelations and paradoxes between governance arenas embedded with hegemonic values, assumptions, and silences highlights the difficulty involved in creating policies that are attentive to the needs of children.

Unanticipated Consequences and Hidden Goals

> The final results of political action often, no, even regularly, stand in completely inadequate and often ever paradoxical relation to its original meaning." (Weber, 1947, p. 117)

Policymakers frequently lament, "That is not what I meant at all!" So much happens in political tradeoffs when policies are formulated! Then, when a policy becomes law, procedures and regulations are created by agencies (e.g., the state department of education), sometimes altering intentions, creating timelines, guidelines, and models to follow. Then, policies are implemented through an array of mechanisms, agencies, and professionals, all of whom will lay their own meanings and needs on the policy. (See Chapter 2 to review the literature on implementation, and Chapter 3 to review the politics of knowledge.)

The "ecology-of-games" metaphor provides a way of understanding the messes and the disconnects that policies create. This metaphor is based on ecological perspectives that seek to understand the organic relationships between individuals who make, interpret, and implement policy. It suggests that policy making is a set of complex games played by policy makers and interest groups at various levels of policy making. Policy is then conceived of "as a chain of decisions stretching from the statehouse to the classroom . . . a byproduct of all those games" (Firestone, 1989a). This perspective highlights "the messiness and discontinuities in the policy process, the variety of games played by different people for different reasons and the loose linkages between those separate games" (Firestone, 1989a, p. 23). This section examines the various games decision makers play when creating policies and that lead to unintended consequences.

One example of this phenomenon serves to illustrate. A major component of the federally created Individuals with Disabilities Education Act (IDEA) contains a provision requiring children with disabilities to be educated in a "least restrictive environment," meaning that children should be mainstreamed into regular education classrooms when possible. The reality, though, is that implementation of this provision depends on numerous factors. Of particular consequence is that IDEA is not fully funded at the federal level. As mentioned in Chapter 7, often states and local districts must come up with the extra funding to implement IDEA. It can be more cost effective to group children in special education settings, so without financial support it can often be difficult to implement mainstreaming, which is more costly. In their study of six states, Hasazi and co-workers (1994) found that implementation of the "least restrictive environment" provision varied greatly across states and depended on contextual factors such as additional state and local funds, organization of state and local educational systems, support of local advocacy groups, knowledge of state-level administrators and staff in state departments of education, differing values and knowledge of staff and administrators, and differences in political cultures with the states. Not only are policy issues interconnected across levels, they are also shaped by cultures and knowledge that may vary across levels.

At times, analysis of the realities of policy implementation and policy effects raise critical questions about the original policy intentions. Suppose a policy asserts goals to redistribute resources from one group to another, but years later that has not happened. A policy might have a stated goal to "empower and retain teachers," but, in reality, the policy actually lowers teacher morale and increases the number of teachers who elect to leave the profession. The first policy question asked might be, "What went wrong?" But the next question might be, "Was the policy actually set up with hidden policy intentions?" The latter question suggests that policy makers might be playing games with one another by responding to political pressures rather than being free to just focus on creating an ideal policy that represents teachers' needs. The Lived Realities on the next page explores how policies aimed at addressing perceived needs are embedded within assumptions that actually get in the way of addressing the "problem" the policy originally intended to solve.

In the case of the AEP policy in Texas, the original legislative intent did not call for *de facto* racial segregation, nor did it assert an intention to give administrators power to send to AEP students who were guilty of not turning in their homework (sometimes be-

Lived Realities: Alternative Education in Texas

The Texas Education Code, in the 1984 school reform, allows for removal of serious juvenile offenders from the classroom, out of concern for the safety of teachers and students. Representative Alvin Granoff felt the old practice of expelling students for three days just gave them an unsupervised street furlough, so, convinced by a study of a Florida program, he persuaded the legislature to create alternative education programs. Students would have special attention and low teacher/pupil ratios, and all districts had to develop an Alternative Education Program (AEP). Over the years, the Department of Education created guidelines with mandates and definitions of who must be removed from the classroom, but permitted schools to place students in AEPs at their own discretion, based on their own code of conduct, with short- or long-term placements.

As a result, districts may make subjective judgments of behavior and assign students to their AEP for felonies but also for misbehavior such as copying the work of other students, unexcused tardiness, horseplay, or noncompliant behavior on the school bus.

In her analysis of the implementation of AEPs, Reyes (2002) showed that (1) AEPs segregate at-risk students, who are usually Latinos, African American, Native Americans, and poor Whites (mostly boys) from the rest of the population; (2) with schools' funding determined by an official per-pupil count taken the last week of October, schools often tolerated misbehavior until then; (3) AEP administrators' budgets increased when their clientele increased; (4) administrators may be motivated to assign low-achieving students to AEP so their test scores will not pull down site and district scores and make the principal ineligible for the cash rewards for high quartile performance (AEPs are not accountable to the same academic standards); and (5) in the period between 1996 and 2000, only 25 percent of the placements in AEP were for criminal behavior; thus, most were done at some administrator's discretion.

cause they cannot read). It was created before administrators had such clear incentives to remove academic underachievers. Ryan's story at the start of this chapter shows that the needs of each child should be weighed when making policy decisions, such as placing a child in an AEP. While this decision might have kept Ryan in school, in the case of the Texas AEP, placements reflected larger issues of economic and racial bias, which lead to segregation.

Cross-Purposes, Stupidity, and Contradictions

National policy making is inevitably a process of *bricolage:* a matter of borrowing and copying bits and pieces of ideas from elsewhere, drawing upon and amending locally tried and tested approaches, cannibalizing theories, research, trends and fashions and not infrequently flailing around for anything at all that looks as though it might work. Most policies are ramshackle, compromise, hit and miss affairs, that are reworked, tinkered with, nuanced and inflected thorough complex process of influence, text production, dissemination and ultimately, re-creation in contexts of practice.[2] (Ball, 1998, p. 126)

Policy gets ridiculous at times. So do policy makers and politicians. Malapropisms slip out of their mouths, allowing a little humor to lighten policy analysis. Boston Mayor Thomas

Menino once told a group of principals they should install *mental* detectors in schools, and former Vice President Dan Quayle, speaking against daycare, said, "Republicans understand the importance of bondage between a mother and a child" (Fussell, 2002).

On a more serious note, power plays to exercise political control over the direction and content of debate and discussion, or controlling arenas in which policy is discussed, are ridiculous but common. Consider the following incident in May 2001. The Massachusetts Department of Education forced the organizers of an education conference for teachers to cancel their planned keynote speaker. The speaker was to be Alfie Kohn, a prominent testing critic. Officials felt that Kohn was inappropriate for the conference because they assumed that his speech would be critical of the Massachusetts Comprehensive Assessment System (MCAS) tests. Kohn responded to the controversy by acknowledging the seriousness of the power play: "The same undemocratic sensibility that imposes high-stakes testing also acts to suppress dissenting views" (Walker, 2001, p. B1). The ACLU responded to the incident by suing the state for a violation of free speech (Weber, 2001). Such an incident is a highly visible example of the web of power controlling discourse at all levels of school politics. When policy hits the street level, it is implemented in the midst of political values–conflict laden contexts.

Furthermore, policies often create effects that are quite the opposite of their original intentions. An array of accountability policies seek to set higher standards and challenge school districts, educators, and students to work harder and achieve higher test scores. But some of these policies have greatly undermined teaching. For example, McNeil (1987) documented how the policies for improving teaching and learning by standardizing teacher performance demoralized teachers who, before being affected by the policy, had been highly creative and dedicated to their magnet school curriculum and students. Standardization can harm teachers' sense of professionalism and pride in their work.

Legislatures, trying to recruit new talented teachers, created policies for lateral entry into the teaching profession. These policies allowed people with college degrees and experience in another profession to take provisional teaching jobs, with some quick training for managing curriculum, children, and the work of teachers. Such policies spread through policy networks in many states, often with the cooperation of higher education institutions that provided quick training. Similarly, some states are considering policies for boosting the chances of teacher assistants to get trained and certified as teachers. Such policies do expand the pool of candidates for teaching. However, experienced teachers, teachers who spent the money and years going through the coursework and internship prescribed in traditional teacher education, who often spent their own money and vacation time for required professional development, and who, for years, took pride their own initiative, creativity, and membership in a profession with standards for entry, now feel insulted by lateral entry policies that seem to belittle their years of efforts.

Falling through the Cracks.   Every parent and teacher can cite incidents in which something important is ignored, lost, forgotten, or misplaced, and they explode with anger at the person they blame. More often, though, that person has been acting as a street-level bureaucrat, doing what they can with limited resources and in situations in which they believe there is little hope or reward for dealing thoroughly with the situation. The results are sometimes tragic when, for example, school counselors fail to notice or report evidence of a child suffering from abuse or when children's potential for advanced-placement classes are missed because of the color of their skin. Looking beyond the failure of the bureaucrats or educators who lost or ignored or forgot, we can almost always map backward to policy failure. Usually, mapping backward, we find mandates that educators must comply with without adequate funding, training, technology, or time. Often, we find situations in which policies and programs conflict with one another, causing confusion and inconsistency in interpretation, and creating huge areas of policy inattention. The following Lived Realities provides an example of these types of conflicting policies and programs.

Lived Realities: Going Home

After a successful administrator career, culminating in the superintendency of a good-sized suburban school district, Sam Bellows decided to spend his last working years near his birthplace. When the tiny superintendency in his hometown, Bridgetown, opened up, he grabbed the position and the town grabbed him. But he went prepared for harsh realities. He had escaped rural poverty when his basketball scholarship allowed him to attend college but had fond memories and also guilt about leaving behind the people who had had so much faith in him.

Bridgetown contained many of the problems and challenges outlined in *Why Rural Matters: The Need for Every State to Take Action on Rural Education* (Rural School and Community Trust, 1999). This work suggested the model of a "rural urgency gauge" based on variables such as the numbers of teachers teaching out-of-field, poverty rates, transportation costs, access to special education, access to technology, and number of households without high school diplomas. The report noted that deficiencies in these needs were often lost in the political shuffle of state politics, in which urban districts with outspoken legislators and coalitions of big-city lobbyists are heard but the special needs of rural communities are ignored. Sam's fellow superintendents teased him, saying, "So, now you can add to their problems, Sam, going there and giving them the problem of an over-the-hill semi-retired leader!" Although he knew they were joking, he took that as an "I'll show them" challenge, determined to create rural alliances that would have the force of getting more political clout. Too many Bridgetown kids were falling through the cracks, and his main job now would be to make sure politicians heard about them.

Sam Bellows' story is not the only policy issue fraught with contradictions. For example, accountability standards are designed to bring all students to a minimum standard of performance, with exceptions being made to accommodate students with exceptional learning disabilities. Yet the *inclusion* of students with disabilities into the classroom also places them into the main testing pool, disavowing their testing exemptions. The social value of inclusion is undermined by the necessity to include special students scores in the school report. School-based committees must decide where the greatest value lies—in the student with a disability or in the school's reputation as reported in the newspaper.

Why would anyone create education policies that erect incentives for districts to discourage students from higher aspirations? Yet this is going on. The following Lived Realities shows the sometimes paradoxical relationship between the intent of the policy and its unintended consequences.

Lived Realities: Incentives to Discourage Student Aspiration

In Johnston, North Carolina, in 2002, fewer than half of the seniors were taking the SAT, a decline from earlier years. The decline in participation brought an increase in the average SAT score for Johnston, so that by 2001 the district had an SAT average higher than the state average. District administrators said they were trying to make sure students who take the SAT are well prepared. But they also acknowledged they felt pressure to raise the system's average SAT score. The school board chair spoke of being under the gun from the public and from local industry. The superintendent said, "When you start to put emphasis on a number, people start to change the way they do things. . . . You want to be very careful, because you don't want to be seen as raising scores by discouraging kids from taking it." In fact, students may take SAT preparation classes for credit, and guidance counselors urge students to take tutorials. Still, more students are being encouraged to start at a community college, then transfer. Such an approach avoids the cost, trauma, and reporting of SAT performance (Sung, 2002).

Political pressure to raise achievement led to an "unintended consequence" of overemphasizing SAT scores as *the* measure of achievement. In Johnston's case, this emphasis raised the district's SAT scores but did so at the expense of limiting students' aspirations. With the vast array of policies and politics that influence schools, many often work at cross-purposes.

Interrelationships among Organizations and Interest Groups

With the multiple organizations and agencies that can have an impact on a child's education, it is crucial to understand how they relate to one another and the games they play to protect and serve their own interests. Business interest groups and private foundations, the legal system, and an array of social service agencies all can have an impact on a school's ability to serve its students.

Business Interest Groups and Foundations

A Nation at Risk (1983) was actually targeted to an audience of business leaders and emphasized students as raw materials. It questioned whether the national investment in the human capital developed by our educational systems was a cost-effective investment. Such business-oriented language legitimated business influence in educational decision making. Since that time, in powerful ways, the assumptions and values and needs of business leaders have become the grounding of education policy making. The following kinds of problems have been defined in specific ways because of these dominant assumptions:

- Viewing immigrants' children as costly and demanding
- Focusing on the "fourth R"—readiness for work—as a major goal of education

- Blaming low-income children and their parents for low school performance
- Criticizing vocational education
- Viewing technology as the solution for educational problems (Ray & Mickelson, 1990)

In *The Education-Industrial Complex,* Brightman and Gutmore (2002) raise ethical questions and concerns that businesses will control technology in the classroom, will target marketing to children, and that schools will be willing servants in this partnership. For example, companies like IBM, Apple, and Microsoft compete to place their products in schools, which essentially serve as advertisers of their products.

Bracey, in *The War against America's Public Schools: Privatizing Schools, Commercializing Education* (2002), suggests that schools are being pushed to serve business values. Historically, schools adopted the factory model in education policy. Public schools began to accept the assumptions that high productivity and efficient management of resources were the basis for structuring education programs. He demonstrates ways in which the *Nation at Risk* and TIMMS comparisons with other countries have been used to generate arguments for choice policies of all types, especially charter schools and vouchers, which, in turn, are becoming an "education industry" that can make money and get Wall Street attention. Besides private schools, Education Management Organizations (EMOs) (private, for-profit companies that manage public schools) are commanding some portion of the direction and funds for schooling. The National School Boards Association's 1995 analysis showed that saving money is the most oft-cited reason for districts' use of private companies, and that contracts for instructional programs were mostly for dealing with at-risk children, special education, and technology. Bracey critiques the major players in the business of managing entire schools and large portions of districts, including Edison, Nobel, Tesseract, Educational Alternative, Inc., and Beacon Education Management and Corporate Family Solutions/Bright Horizons (which started with the help of ex-Tennessee Governor Lamar Alexander and Bob Keeshan, a.k.a. Captain Kangaroo). He ends with the story of the student who got suspended from school for dramatically showing off a Pepsi t-shirt when his school was entertaining Coke executives during Coke in Education Day at Greenbrier High School, 130 miles west of Coke's Atlanta headquarters.

The dramatic increase in business inroads into the classroom and public debate triggered a U.S. GAO report and attempts at federal, state, and local levels to regulate the activities. The GAO identified product sales, direct advertising, indirect advertising, and market research as the main commercial activities carried out, and worried about children being forced to view ads, having unhealthful food and drinks marketed, and having their privacy invaded (Larsen, 2002).

Making the influence of business into a politics research question, McDaniel and Miskel (2002) analyzed, over a five-year period, the degree of influence a Michigan state business group had on state education reform policy. They found that business groups were effective at influencing education reform. Their work suggests that business interest groups are becoming increasingly influential in creating state policy, and groups such as the Business Roundtable have extended their reach to federal legislation as well.

Another way that businesses can influence education policy is through an array of foundations. Some are clearly aligned with Republicans or Democrats, and others try to be attuned more to policy issues than to partisan political alignments. The Fordham Foundation and the Heritage Foundation, in 2002, were arguing in Congress for laws allowing the private sector to step in when districts do not give parents options to get their children out of poor schools, reopening the Republican support for voucher policies.

As partners, as innovators, as powerful framers of issues, and as contractors, schools and businesses are intertwined. Writing checks and philanthropy has been a way corporations make financial contributions directly to local school systems. Corporations get tax deductions and good public relations as well as the opportunity to steer schools in directions they favor. As stimulators of organizational change, corporations fund targeted efforts for specific purposes, such as increasing math skills, by fostering collaborative projects (McGuire, 1990). Business leaders become policy reformers at times, taking charge of defining issues and identifying solutions. The Conference Board and the Committee for Economic Development (with its report called *Investing in Our Children*) represent the efforts of national business collaboratives targeted at suggesting ways to fix the education system. The Business Roundtable commands so much attention from education policy makers that it can be called a policy maker itself. Similarly, state-level business pressures for reform include using political influence to move reform proposals through legislatures, with proposals for early childhood education, class-size reduction, and restructuring sometimes presenting entire reform packages to legislatures and boards (McGuire, 1990).

From newspaper headlines, research studies, and looking at the actual work of school administrators, we can see the influence of funding contexts on education. Dominant policy discourses assume that school leaders' jobs include the work of raising funds by directing programs to the biases and desires of corporations. One recent study showed how this fund raising shapes educational priorities in both private and public schools. Private schools have been influenced by the lure of foundation funding for scholarships for minority students while, at the same time, public schools have been working hard to develop distinctive market niches and choice for attracting parents (St. John & Ridenour, 2001). In West Virginia, the Education Alliance is a catalyst for business and community involvement whose funding includes mini-grants for teachers' innovations, programs for promoting student health, for technology integration, and so on. A 1992 review promoted partnerships between schools and the private sector as a way of preventing the increased taxes and service cuts (Anna, 1992).

Courts

Rearing its powerful head when things go wrong, the court system can be a back-up policy arena for education. By their nature, courts are reactive, called in for strict interpretations of policy or for alleged violations of federal or state constitutions and laws. They are, at least, always in the back of the minds of policy makers who are wondering if a proposed policy might violate the Constitution or of practitioners who are deciding on a course of action and wondering if the action would violate a law. Policy makers pass legislation sometimes knowing that it might be tested in court. Examples include legislation allowing vouchers, school prayer and moments of silence, and mandatory school uniforms.

Courts become policy makers and make policy when legislative and executive policy makers do not respond to citizens' complaints. One famous example came in the 1974 *Lau v. Nichols* Supreme Court (1974) decision that determined that San Francisco was wrong when it denied provision of English language instruction to the 1,800 students of Chinese ancestry who did not speak English. Even with equal facilities and books provided, "students who do not understand English are effectively foreclosed from any meaningful education." This U.S. Supreme Court decision, though, emerged in the context of (1) the Bilingual Education Act of 1968, which provided federal funding for districts' bilingual education programs; (2) the 1970 Office of Civil Rights determination that the "sink or swim" language policy did not provide a viable alternative for language development; and (3) the lower courts having denied the parents' appeal. Language policy controversy certainly did not end. Many studies, lobbies, court cases, state variations of policies and programs for Limited English Proficiency (LEP) students, and clamor from the margins advocated for continuing protection of language-minority rights. Policy proposals to make English the required and only acceptable language in this country continue to emerge. They demonstrate that policy, whether made by the supreme court of the land or by a school principal, is not set in stone. Policy making is a continuous process and must be seen as a complex one, requiring constant attention (Reyes & Rorrer, 2001).

Nevertheless, the courts become policy monitors at times. The long history of desegregation, with many iterations of court review and monitoring of districts' plans and implementation, includes examples in which judges were, in effect, creating the district plans through their strict scrutiny and specific demands. The courts can intervene in policy decisions concerning an array of issues, such as vouchers, religion in schools, and segregation. The following Lived Realities highlights how legal decisions may not resolve deeper issues embedded in a case but instead may focus on tangential issues. In this case, the court case focused on whether a school should be allowed to suspend a student for posting satanic material on the Web.

Lived Realities: Satan's Mission

> A Michigan high school student was suspended from school for developing a website that school officials said was created to "intimidate and threaten" other students. The website, entitled "Satan's Web Page," suggested that to follow Satan's mission, visitors to the website should commit murder in order to enjoy watching someone die. Once a victim was selected, the website suggested first stabbing them, then setting them on fire while they are still alive, and then finally throwing them off a cliff while they were still on fire. Although the ruling came after the suspended student had already graduated from a neighboring school district, a federal judge ruled that the Michigan school district should not have suspended the student. The reasons given were that the student was not allowed to cross-examine witnesses at a hearing or to be represented by an attorney (*Raleigh News and Observer,* November 29, 2002).

The irony in this story is that the legal case was decided long after the student graduated from high school. Legal cases often take a substantial amount of time for resolution, and in the meantime, schools, teachers, administrators, students, parents, and interested parties are left hanging for resolution. The vignette also raises questions concerning the role schools should play in policing students' use of the Internet. In this case, clearly the school felt obligated to punish the student for the website's attempt to incite violence. As in many of these legal cases, there are no easy answers or quick solutions; rather, decisions require careful review of the case at hand and an understanding of existing legal precedents.

Making Connections: Family-Centered Integrated Service Systems and Schools

"When one steps into a schoolhouse today, it does not take long to realize that the persistent life situations of many students and their families call for multiple-agency, multiple-profession response (drugs, suicide, AIDS, teenage pregnancy, violence, poverty, etc.)" (Corrigan 2001, p. 182). The narrative that opened this chapter highlighted these very same issues facing the students in the second grade classroom at Marcy elementary school.

The professionals providing services for families and children are often uncoordinated and dysfunctional. They agencies work independently and, at times, at cross purposes. If we go back to the Ryan example at the beginning of the chapter, we can explore just how disconnected these services can be. For example, to serve Ryan's needs, school officials, Ryan's mother, medical professionals, a police officer, Ryan's mother's employer, and local politicians would all need to collaborate.

Yet even attempts to coordinate services among different organization can be challenging. For example, Castella (2002) studied the creation of community-based violence-prevention programs and found that these efforts can be stalled by inadequate funding, power struggles over turf, and a deficit model of the youth that shapes interactions with students. Rather than helping students turn away from violence, these collaborative programs can serve as watchdogs that seek to identify problem students for incarceration. Castella suggests that partnerships can link the school, community, and the judiciary in a triad that is "a racist and bureaucratic trap for young people" (2002, pp. 369–370). To avoid this trap, Castella suggests that collaborations will need to "be part of a larger systemic reworking of police departments, schools, social services, and city funding methods" (2002, p. 370).

Policy makers, recognizing this, are calling for interprofessional collaboration. Increasingly, education, social work, and healthcare professionals see the need for the development of family centered, community-based, culturally competent, high-quality integrated services, with families participating in their creation (Corrigan & Bishop, 1997). However, this requires a transformed paradigm for collaborative practice. It requires that training and licensing agencies like traditional departments in universities and field sites reconfigure their requirements. It requires that federal, state, and local funding streams create wider, more flexible categories for agencies. It requires sharing of information among agencies, even though clients' confidentiality must be protected. Perhaps the most basic challenge is "to get wealthy suburbanites to take seriously the problems of the community they may have fled or to get a small rural community to admit that it has hungry and homeless children and families who are in need of services" (Corrigan, 2001, p. 188).

"The rationale for collaboration is rooted in the premise that children bring more than educational needs to the classroom" (Corrigan, 2001, p. 177). Collaboration is "like a marriage," requiring building trust and confidence, giving up old ways of doing things, and overcoming jealousies, competitions, and biases. Pediatricians and social workers appear to be taking the lead in integrating service systems. To serve students like Ryan, policies and leaders are needed that connect schools, communities, and an array of public and private services for struggling students, parents, and communities.

Summary

As we have shown, classroom issues are deeply affected by policy decisions and "games" played in all arenas of policy making, from the macro arena of international policy to federal, state, district, and micro arenas, and by forces outside of educational institutions. Together, these interconnections, disconnects, and paradoxes of policy and politics targeted at schooling make up the complexity of the educational policy web. Throughout this book, we have provided information and examples of traditional ways of analyzing politics and policy, and we have critiqued them, offering theories, methodologies, strategies, and examples that provide alternative lenses. We have highlighted throughout, but especially in this chapter, the following:

- Conflicts and paradoxes in policies
- Contradictions/stupidities/layers
- Dominance/hegemony and discourses of derision
- The needs/insights of marginalized groups
- The way in which policies affecting schools and children are layered
- How the oft-used market models are insufficient for education
- The importance of contextual realities

Given these complexities, this book has highlighted and shown you how to analyze the powers and processes affecting schools. Being able to critique inequities embedded in policy formation and implementation provides an avenue through which to see the possibilities for educators to engage in re-framing, to interrupt the politics of domination, and to work for policies that fit with the lived realities encountered in real schools. Therefore, it is critical to propose new models for leadership for politics and policy that engage alternative values bases and new approaches to democracy, community, and diversity.

The next and final chapter offers theories, models, examples, and strategies for educational leaders who will be policy advocates and who will work toward effective participation in political arenas in which they can re-frame policies for education.

Exercises for Critically Examining Intertwined Policies, Pendulum Shifts, and Interconnections _____

1. Review the vignette on Harriett Stone and Ryan Franklin. Then identify two to three challenges faced by educators and draw diagrams of the array of forces, agencies, policies, politics, and contingencies that limit the chance of "doing good." Examples might come from adolescent pregnancy, children of immigrant families, kids with HIV, kids in homeless families, gifted and talented kids, and so on. Identify a point on the diagram at which a change

would make a great deal of difference (and debate in class whether, and how, one could get such a change to be made).

2. Give two examples of policy paradoxes or contradictions in which one policy or program (education-related) takes you in a direction that confuses another policy or program regulations or goals.

3. Give two examples of ways in which policies affecting children in schools are intertwined with policies and programs and agencies that aren't specifically about schools but nevertheless affect children's schooling.

4. Give two examples of the intertwining of federal, state, local, and judicial policies affecting education.

5. Review the Lived Realities on Sam Bellows and search for statistics on the differences in resources and outcomes between rural schools and others. Identify class members who went to rural schools and have them compare their memories of school resources with the resources available in the schools of class members with more affluent districts and/or those who attended private and parochial schools.

6. Examine websites, starting with the Business Roundtable's and others, then go to the critiques available from the Center for the Analysis of Commercialism in Education at www.uwm.edu/Dept/CACE. Construct a class debate, with one side presenting arguments in favor of different degrees of business involvement and another side presenting reasons to keep business and schools separate.

7. Examine the websites of five foundations whose priorities relate to school-age children and schools. Analyze their goals statements, the projects they fund, their histories, and other such clues to generate speculations about ways they could influence what school leaders think and do.

8. Generate a list of examples of incidents, issues, and needs that have "fallen through the cracks" and map backward to policy causes for the failure. Then draft memos to policy makers, describing the situation and recommending specific changes (capacity-building, budget, monitoring, revised policy, brand new policy, politicking from the margin, policy advocacy coalition, etc.) and strategies for collaboration aimed at making it happen. (The policy maker may be at any level of governance that is appropriate, given your analysis of "the cracks").

Notes

1. From J. Anyon. *Ghetto Schooling: A Political Economy of Urban Educational Reform.* Copyright 1997 by Teachers College Press. Used by permission.
2. From S. J. Ball. Big Policies/Small World: An Introduction to International Perspectives in Education Policy. *Comparative Education*, vol. 34, no. 2, pp. 119–130, 1998. Used by permission of Taylor & Francis Ltd. http://tandf.co.uk/journals.

10

Strategies for Policy Advocates

Guiding Questions _____

- How can one motivate and support educators' skills and dispositions toward political engagement and policy innovation?
- How can one handle social justice dilemmas in the contexts of the day-to-day activities, people, power dynamics, and structures of politics and with the constraining realities of education policy?
- How can one engage in power centers and politics from the margins simultaneously?
- How can one take activist stances and keep their job?
- How can one identify the best strategies that lead to creative, appropriate, and pragmatic policies for children and families?
- What models and examples provide approaches to leadership, politics, research, and policy analysis that can empower educators and redefine and re-frame policies?
- Given lived realities, what strategies and networks can be developed to build social capital for educational policies that promote equity through schooling?

Engaging Political Arenas

The traditional advice given to leaders who do not comply with the preferences of the powerful at the expense of doing what is right is, "Keep your bags packed." People leave jobs, professions, and positions when they become terribly frustrated or discouraged, feel unappreciated, or feel that political compromises are just too much to take. In these situations, those that leave often do so because they feel they cannot speak up, demand change, or make any difference. Other people use their voices to articulate their needs. Sometimes they achieve change, but sometimes they are attacked and even forced out of their positions for making waves. Still others show loyalty; feeling a sense of fealty to their organization and colleagues, they stay, continue working quietly, making do, and compromising. All of these choices have some negative consequences, but they do not necessarily change the status quo. Seeing responses to these kinds of situations as forms of resistance and agency is useful for understanding how to resist and respond to these situations (see Hirschman, 1970, for useful thoughts about exit, voice, and loyalty). This chapter focuses on ways of engaging political arenas, developing personal platforms, taking stands, and developing a sense of what needs to be done—and doing that effectively. The following Lived Realities highlights many of the challenges raised in this chapter.

Lived Realties: Mr. Venable Speaks Truth to Power

Every year Mr. Venable came up short. As Assistant Superintendent in a rural county, Mr. Venable's tasks in recruiting and retaining good teachers were set up for failure, and the state board policies were making it worse. So he composed a tough speech for the next Board meeting agenda item, "Teacher Retention." He rehearsed his speech with his wife, who tried to be supportive but thought to herself, "Time to assemble the packing boxes again." Particularly, she worried about these phrases of his speech:

"You cannot expect people like me to work magic without resources. Even when I can recruit teachers, I can't keep them happy when they cannot support their family or pay off their student loans. But salary is just one facet of the problem. Many dehumanizing policies are driving teachers out of the profession. You cannot expect these teachers to stay excited and challenged when the state curriculum guides and the end-of-year high-stakes testing regimes drive good teachers crazy."

Mrs. Venable thought the Board would accept his diatribes against the federal government, about unfunded mandates, about how wealthier parents will be able to use public funds and "drive their BMWs to take their priviledged kids to their chosen school."

But she tried, to no avail, to get him to moderate these dares: "If you dare to take a real look, come to my district and try to do my job. You will see why we have so many educators giving up and leaving the profession. If you dare, start creating policies that support educators and children whose parents subsist on limited resources. If you dare, search for ways to listen intently to the earnest pleas from loyal educators like me, and search for creative ways to make policy differently.

On the big day, Mr. Venable's daring speech not only got applause, he revived the sense of idealism he'd had so many years ago as one of those newbie teachers.

Historians of social movements have shown how difficult it is to make changes happen in the face of powerful oppression or indifference (Goodwyn, 1976, 1991; Scott, 1990). Mr. Venable was courageous, and his actions must be valued as a first step. As public intellectual Vaclav Havel notes,

This official interpretation consequently merges with reality. A general and all-embracing lie begins to predominate; people begin adapting to it, and everyone in some part of their lives compromises with the lie or coexists with it. Under these conditions, to assert the truth, to behave authentically by breaking through the all-englobing web of lies—in spite of everything, including the risk that one might find oneself up against the whole world—is an act of political importance. (quoted in Scott, 1990, p. 206)

Although Mr. Venable's desire to take a stand was honorable, he could have been more effective if he had built on his speech by creating strategies aligned with others, capitalizing on existing social movements, and developing strategies that took into account the intricacies of local, state, and national politics. Simply using the models from Chapter 1 and thinking about the best timing and key connections to people with power and influence would have helped. Being able to cite statistics and background research would have added a powerful dimension to his plea. This chapter provides models for acts of political importance.

Being Politically Wise and Strategic

What's an educator to do, given the pressure to work with powerful constituents, the need to maintain a status with political actors, and the pressure to think and talk with the values and words of the dominant discourse? How can an educator take assertive, effective, and powerful stances? How can he alter dominant discourses when he ignores the voices and needs from the margins, listening so attentively to the demands of business, postsecondary institutions, and the military while the realities and needs of children and teachers are ignored? People in educational leadership positions often enact certain roles:

- The diplomat/negotiators, who anticipate problems and conflicts, then talk in ways that ease the conflicts and create compromise settlements
- The political strategists, who identify powerful forces and assemble their positions and stances in such a way as to maximize their own ability to work in that context
- The executives, who command respect by asserting their expertise and declare that they are apolitical, neutral CEOs who use research and data to make decisions, unshaped by pressures from powerful constituents.

Of course, many construct some combination of these modes of operation. These roles are adaptations of a rational-political model of reality that enable educational leaders to maintain their status. Unfortunately, in many situations these modes leave the leader stuck with compromises, with shoving conflicts under the rug, with limited capacity for reaching out to those from the margins, and with a continuous pattern of acceding to the demands of those who have power.

Chapters 1 through 3 reviewed traditional and alternative lenses for analyzing policy and politics. Chapters 4 through 9 explored what is known about politics and policy when looking at the complexity and interconnectedness of activity in policy worlds from micro/site to global perspectives. Stone's problem definition model in Table 10.1 shows two discrete ways of viewing how policy problems are defined. The contrast between the rational-analytical model and the polis model highlights the limitations and naïveté in rational decision-making assumptions.

Table 10.1 displays how choices for rational analysis, while traditional, do not fit with political realities. Traditional functionalist leadership models echo the rational-analytical models and assume a neutral political reality. The rational-analytical model assumes a perfect world in which special interests, shifting values, and cultural differences are insignificant or nonexistent. Throughout the book, we have shown how traditional

TABLE 10.1   *Decision-Analysis Strategies of Problem Definition*

Rational-Analytical Model	Polis Model
State goals/objectives explicitly and precisely.	State goals ambiguously and possibly keep some goals secret or hidden.
Adhere to the same goal throughout the analysis and decision-making process	Be prepared to shift goals and redefine goals as the political situation dictates.
Try to imagine and consider as many alternatives as possible.	Keep undesirable alternatives off the agenda by not mentioning them.
	Make your preferred alternative appear to be the only feasible or possible one.
	Focus on one part of the causal chain and ignore others that would require politically difficult or costly policy actions.
Define each alternative clearly as a distinct course of action.	Use rhetorical devices to blend alternatives; don't appear to make a clear decision that could trigger strong opposition.
Evaluate the costs and benefits of each course of action as accurately and completely as possible.	Select from the infinite range of consequences only those whose costs and benefits will make your preferred course of action look "best."
Choose the course of action that will maximize total welfare as defined by your objective.	Choose the course of action that hurts powerful constituents the least, but portray your decision as creating maximum social good for a broad public.

Source: Table: Decision-Analysis Strategies of Problem Definitions", from POLICY PARADOX: The Art of Political Decision Making by Deborah Stone. Copyright © 1997, 1988 by Deborah Stone. Used by permission of W. W. Norton & Company, Inc.

lenses such as these, while describing a manageable and orderly world, often miss the lived realities, the marginalized, the silenced, and the oppressed.

Stone's polis model, however, *is* politically strategic. It recognizes that policy problems are defined within a constantly shifting political context. For example, Ortiz and Ortiz (1993) examined how the decision making of female Hispanic superintendents could be politicized due to assumptions about their how their race and gender shape their decision making. Specifically, they found that when a female Hispanic superintendent was hired for symbolic reasons (e.g., she was assumed to represent Hispanic interests) due to racial tensions, her leadership decisions were likely to be politicized. Any attempts at rational decision making were viewed by constituents as suspect, as "just politics." Such research highlights how a leaders' skin color or gender can have an impact on how decision making is perceived. Political realities such as these highlight the need for savvy political leaders to understand the strategies used by the powerful to shape policy issues. Given this context, how can educational researchers and leaders seek to re-frame policy to fit with their sense of professionalism, the lived realities of schools, or the needs of children, families, and teachers? To do this, policy analysis and leadership models are needed that offer new approaches to political engagement.

Several alternative models of praxis (the integration of theory and practice) are available that suggest strategies for policy advocacy designed to support social justice:

- Alternative perspectives and models for leadership that seek to support social justice and egalitarian conceptions of democracy
- Utilizing policy methodology that provides a way to re-frame questions to incorporate the voices and perspectives of those forgotten in policy debates
- Activist educator platforms wherein individuals refuse to live within the dictates of professional socialization and become actively involved in change-oriented political activities
- Formation of alliances, creation of networks, and construction of cohort training for building educational leaders who can and will build advocacy coalitions in support of children, families, and educators

The next sections provide an array of alternative models for leadership aimed at supporting social justice and also an array of strategies for using that leadership to re-frame policy questions.

Politicians, leaders and educators need to recognize when it is time to re-frame. When the situation has changed tremendously (e.g., the economic system or the demographics of clientele have changed), when a way of doing things just keeps on not working (e.g., vocational education), and when marginal voices have been ignored in previous policy formulation. One examination of school-to-work policies shows how the traditional underpinnings and assumptions about vocational education have resulted in persistent waste and negative outcomes (Crowson, Wong, & Aypay, 2000). It shows how a change in views of the purpose of K–12 education as preparation for college holds promise for re-framing vocational education. They lay out a new logic—the idea of making education the center of community revitalization, or enterprise schooling. In this new vision, the local school is a fully active player in a network of public/private community institutions, such as banks and other businesses, and activist and volunteer organizations. In these new networks, students would learn marketable skills needed in the immediate neighborhood and, at the same time, learn to contribute and invest as citizens with social responsibility and relationships. Students would develop new zones of influence and a sense of empowerment regarding their community and have a chance to be employed while contributing to needed services. Such re-framing requires re-framed approaches to educators' political involvement.

Models for Leadership and Political Involvement

Given all this focus on politics and policy, one might ask which model of leadership works well. The cynical answer is whichever gets the job! Traditional assumptions support leaders functioning with a model of bureaucratic management. Such leaders emphasize maintenance of routine and order, organization for efficient use of resources and accomplishment of tasks, and high productivity. Such a model dominates the thinking of many boards, community leaders, and politicians. Such a model is also given legitimacy by traditional politics. This functionalist model asserts that the expertise of the administrator gives her authority to make hierarchical governance decisions. While decisions might have a differential impact on subordinates, decisions are assumed to be values-neutral. This functionalist model dominates traditional administrator training through managerial professionalism. The foundational ideology claims of this model assume that efficient management strategies can solve any problem and that practices appropriate for for-profit businesses are also appropriate for education and social services.

Such a model might work if schools were apolitical and if their products were ball bearings or widgets. However, schooling is a social-political process and schools are places where both the product and the process are people—staff and students. Commanding the right to make decisions because of expertise tends to undermine democracy and exclude insights from others' lived realities.

What is needed are models of leadership that incorporate the reality that educators are professionals with exclusive knowledge and practice, a need and a right to exercise control over their occupation, and ethical concerns for their clients. In other words, educators need to be seen as having expertise, autonomy, and altruism. The models need to help us look at the educators who, working with such sociopolitical realities, bring together alliances and networks for collective action to improve circumstances for children and for teachers, that is, models that promote activist professionalism (Sachs, 2000). The models need to emphasize the care, relationships, emotional connections, and even spiritual mission of educators' work (Beatty, 2000). Fortunately, such models exist and can help to organize and frame the daily work of many educational leaders. They can help to re-frame the policies affecting schools. And they can help a leader construct a platform, a stance, and strategies for being policy advocates *as* educational leaders.

Social Justice Advocacy Leadership

Threads from emerging theories serve to create a new way of viewing leadership that incorporates advocacy and social justice; we entitle this social justice advocacy leadership (SJAL). What follows presents the thinking behind theories that, forged together, provide the basis for this new approach to educational leadership. Five discrete leadership perspectives inform SJAL: critical pluralist, transformational, moral/ethical, feminist, and spiritual/cultural.

Critical Pluralist.   The critical pluralist model is based on the idea that leadership should encourage democratic participation. Leadership should foster participation and input to ensure that policy decisions and reforms are operating from a pluralistic base of support. The pluralist ideal is a worthy goal, but the danger is that democratic representation does not ensure an equitable process or outcome. In Chapter 4, Scheurich and Imber (1991) examined how a district's attempt to embrace a cultural pluralist model—aimed at getting all segments of the community on committees—ultimately failed. Decisions were made that still favored affluent Whites and were made without Black participation. Scheurich and Imber (1991) found that while the policy aimed at diverse representation, the decision-making process was not open to these token diverse perspectives. When minority members of a policy committee tried to voice their opinions, their perspectives were not acknowledged or discussed by other members of the committee. Consequently, the minority members elected to not participate in the policy process. Norms structured interaction in such a way that it did not support inclusion. The critical frameworks applied to the case point to the need to address the persistence of the historical power relations and embedded assumptions that elites need to make decisions. Just embracing a critical pluralist framework will not ensure participatory decision making when disenfranchisement is subtle. Marginalized voices can be silenced and excluded despite rhetoric to the contrary.

Transformative Leadership. Transformative leadership builds on Freire's (1970) belief in the need for pedagogy that empowers and emancipates through education, in awakening a critical consciousness for social transformation that comes from people seeing societal, political, and economic contradictions and taking action against oppressive elements. It "is deeply rooted in moral and ethical values in a social context" (Shields, 2003, p. 22). Such leaders work toward organizational and social change, starting with conversations and dialogue, reaching to the core beliefs of educators, families, and society (Corson, 2000). They engage in dialogue about difference, deficit thinking, and other difficult issues. (This is not to be confused with transformational leadership, which works with the collective interests of an organization.) Transformative educational leadership centers on a pedagogy of social justice, in which educators and students engage in discourse about others' "foreign" meanings, dissonance, excuses, and blame for education's failures. This form of leadership utilizes an empowerment framework and takes responsibility for overcoming the societal silences about social injustices (Astin & Astin, 2000; MacKinnon, 2000; Shields, 2003). From this perspective, educators, then, become activists, not merely managers of the status quo (Brown & Anfara, 2002).

Moral and Ethical Leadership. Moral and ethical leadership recognizes schools as organizations for nurturing and developing children (Paul et al., 1997; Purpel, 1999; Sergiovanni, 1992; Shapiro & Stefkovich, 2001; Starratt, 1996). Moral and ethical leadership is grounded in deep philosophical questions about the purpose of education and schools. It centers on the belief that leaders need to ask ethical and moral questions when making decisions. Two books, *What's Worth Fighting for in Your School?* (Fullan & Hargreaves, 1996) and *What's Worth Fighting for out There?* (Hargreaves & Fullan, 1998) are excellent examples of this perspective. They seek to support educational leaders speaking up and becoming instigators of more radical and challenging activism as they enact their moral and ethical leadership.

Specifically, Hargreaves and Fullan (1998) suggest that four moral purposes of schools need attention: to love and care, to empower, to serve, and to learn. First, for students to fully develop intellectually and socially, they need to develop relationships in which they feel cared for and loved. Second, one of the most basic components of schooling and family life should be service to others. Third, the authors note that a commitment to empower the school community as a whole is central to creating an equitable community. Finally, the moral purpose to learn implies the need to transform teaching in such a way that it is engaging to all students, not simply a select few. Hargreaves and Fullan (1998) suggest that moral leadership that is focused on these four essential purposes requires both a passionate desire and a hopeful outlook in order to sustain vision and advocacy in difficult or challenging times. Thus, moral leadership creates a vision of schooling that is not tied exclusively to test scores and academic achievement but also to values for developing a sense of self-worth and community connections among faculty, staff, and students.

Feminist "Caring" Leadership.   Feminist leadership is inclusive and facilitative, eschewing domination and valuing relationships, promoting a sense of family and community, and evincing a willingness to work holistically for the development and nurturance of others. The ethic of care, for example, provides philosophical grounding for re-framing school policies and structures to downplay competition and to better create caring relationships (Noddings, 1984, 1992). Utilizing the metaphor of the home, Noddings suggests that our schools should provide shelter, a sense of place and belonging, a protected space for development of self and identity, an adequate supply of material resources, and at least one adult giving attentive love and guidance. This supportive "home" environment provides the opportunity for students to feel wanted and secure in their particular cultural setting. It is the "fundamental and complex enterprise of establishing and maintaining a home that supports the growth of all of its members" (Noddings, 2002, p. 301). In this context, individuals would not stand by and allow people to harm themselves, and they would not define *care* only in terms of personal virtues. Instead, they would "offer positive incentives in the form of realized expectations for behavior that promotes the mutual good . . . to create a world in which it is both possible and attractive to be good" (p. 302). Noddings suggests that for adults in the caring professions (e.g., teaching, social work, and nursing), inflexible policies, homogenous standards, and zero tolerance rules and penalties would not exist. Rather, professionals would be able to respond with care to those who ask for or need it and seek to find a way to ensure that their needs are met. In order to meet these needs, caring professionals would create effective programs and services to meet them, much like nurturing collaborative families do, rather than create dehumanizing bureaucracies.

Spiritual/Cultural Leadership.   Spiritual/cultural leadership is derived from examinations of Black female educational leaders who exhibit qualities like authenticity, care, sisterhood, and an obligation to one's own people. These leaders are willing to be activists, to go into unsafe terrain and ambiguous situations, and they are antiinstitutional. Spiritual/cultural leaders rely on "godtalk" and "womanist" orientations that are deeply spiritual and grounded in the female African American experience. This perspective reframes issues such as the obsession with the achievement gap and test scores so that a value is also placed on the need for children to be able to have a soulful, meaningful existence. It suggests that the well-being of teachers and children has to be the highest priority, because without this sense of security, the education process is without passion and meaning (hooks, 1994).

This form of leadership focuses on coalition and network building designed to nurture collective critical resistance (K. Murtadha, personal communication, November 16, 2002). African American women in leadership positions draw on profound historical traditions of inner spiritual strength as well as an activist ethic of risk/urgency (Murtadha-Watts, 1999, pp. 155–156). The lives of the women profiled by Ah Nee-Benham and Cooper

(1998) exhibit determination, courage, and compassion driven by their own sense of equity and justice, grounded in their experiences as minorities, and focused on helping children overcome obstacles.

In summary, social justice advocacy leadership (SJAL) builds on each leadership perspective outlined. Where these leadership styles converge is in their commitment to social justice. The critical pluralist model highlights the need to seek authentic democratic representation in decision making and policy, because numbers alone do not ensure "active" participation or that all voices are heard and valued. The transformative model examines the need for leaders to share power and encourage dialogue about inequities and silences, in order to encourage and value the agency of all involved in school. Moral and ethical leadership focuses on the need for leaders to be mindful of the larger social justice contexts in which schools are embedded. This perspective focuses attention on nurturing social and emotional skills as well as academic skills. Feminist "caring" leadership focuses on re-visioning the ways schools are structured so that the children, adolescents, and adults who inhabit them feel cared for. This "caring" emphasis suggests that leaders need to acknowledge that human beings have a right to feel supported and nurtured. Finally, spiritual/cultural leadership highlights the racial lenses that have shaped previous leadership models. It suggests that the spirituality and cultural histories of African American women provide much to learn about the need for leaders to be advocates. Taken together, these perspectives can be used to envision SJA leaders who ensure participation, act ethically, transform inequitable relations, care for the individuals they lead, and value cultural differences.

Chapter 3 presented alterative lenses for analyzing power and politics and policy, including cultural production via counternarratives and counterpublics. These alternative discourses often highlight unmet needs and the unintended consequences of policy. Combining these alternative lenses with the approaches to leadership presented in this chapter, SJA leaders can journey to uncomfortable contexts to engage with the purpose of understanding the desires and needs of those at the margins. In doing so, they can re-frame educational policy proposals in ways that fit with lived realities and will be supported by diverse communities, and that will present powerful challenges to dominant discourses. Furthermore, such journeys can amass social capital through enhanced networks of relationships built on trust and common values.

SJAL is useful for re-visioning the way educators work inside and outside of schools. These leaders seek to collaborate with communities, interest groups, and social movements and to act with passion and joy in an environment of trust and mutual respect, valuing the expertise of all parties involved (Sachs, 2000). Such leadership leads to partnerships for advocacy, garnering intellectual and political resources, including, for example, unions and wider social movements (e.g., civil rights, peace). Advocate leaders work with the system but also, at times, attack it. As Sachs (2000) says, "Disruption and advocacy are complementary strategies" (p. 88). SJAL works at shared inquiry to understand and improve practice, engaging in practitioner research and playing roles such as "critical friend" or "resource person." SJAL involves authentic engagement with the community and appreciation of diversity, quite different from the public relations, functionalist, ISLLC-relevant, bureaucratic style of management, or even the polis model, which leaves educational leaders compromised.

Read the following Lived Realities and ponder whether collaborating might have happened if the district superintendent had used SJA model of leadership instead of bureaucratic management and functionalism.

Lived Realities: "NAACP Chief Convicted in School Protest"

The local newspaper's report of the conviction for second-degree trespassing came after the judge rejected the argument that the loud protest chant was an exercise of free speech. The Reverend Curtis Gatewood had tried to persuade shoppers to boycott a local mall as a way to pressure the Durham, North Carolina, school board to fire the superintendent. The Durham community is racially segregated and has historically not been as effective with its Black students as it has with its White students. Test score results indicate that there is an "achievement gap" between White and Black students. At an open board meeting, Gatewood's group failed to obey the board chair's order to quiet down. They verbally continued to demand better treatment of a Black principal as well as other demands. At Gatewood's sentencing, supporters cried out, "That judge is trying to silence the whole community!" (Bickley, 2002).

The superintendent could have seen this protest as an opportunity to bring marginalized voices to the table. Instead of acknowledging Gatewood's concerns, the superintendent chose to silence him, and thus the concerns of members of the African American community and the NAACP he represented. SJAL would have required that the superintendent acknowledge and value Gatewood's perspective. The superintendent could have viewed Gatewood as an asset, someone with resources and connections to the African American community. Adding Gatewood's, and hence the NAACP's perspective, to the discussion could have helped the district leadership understand the cultural and community needs of the students not being served by the district. Such leadership usually comes from challengers from the margin. What if politically astute and courageous educational leaders engaged the ideas, rather than resisted and controlled the forum?

Developing a Platform and Articulating a Stance

What do you believe in? Policy advocates need to be able to develop and identify their own core values and reasons for being educators. Additionally, this requires determining how to position yourself, your policy, or your research strategically for leadership positions and identifying the ways of engaging politically when faced with challenges and dilemmas. The Lived Realities on the next page provides an example of a dilemma one principal faced, and where an advocacy policy audit might be used.

In this Lived Realities, clearly Moran has not taken the time to think through and articulate what her values and beliefs are on the issue of accountability. The next section explores the specifics of how to develop a personal platform and articulate a stance.

Lived Realities: Both Arguments Sound Good

As a school principal, Leticia Moran knew that she should take a position on the conflicting positions she read in the Sunday newspaper's editorial pages. In "Accountability Remains Essential," after providing a brief history of North Carolina's ABCs program for measuring how every school performs, the past chair of North Carolina Citizens for Business and Industry, asserted the following:

- "I believe supporting higher standards is one of the most important competitive actions . . . business executives can take."
- "Ensuring that our young people are prepared for the work force is a priority issue facing business and industry today."
- "In the business world, we have little choice but to monitor our progress against projected results and actual returns."
- "If education doesn't measure its most important product—student learning and achievement—how can it ever hope to improve?"

Leiticia had to agree but continued, reading the next opinion piece by the executive director of the North Carolina Justice and Community Development Center, "Manipulation Rules the System." She read Malhoit's debunking of the state board and the state superintendent's assertions that the problems in the state's testing program were minor technical errors. He argued that the program has "deliberately and systematically changed the culture in our public schools" because it

- empowers "a small group of education bureaucrats, operating in secret . . . to manipulate test results to achieve any number of social or education ends";
- "devalues imagination and creativity while rewarding memorization"; and
- values numbers over human differences and diminishes the role that teachers play in the learning process by encouraging "teaching to the test."

This executive director poignantly described parents, teachers, and children's dilemmas and stresses attributed to testing policies: pressure, fear of failure, stigma, and classrooms "permeated" by testing issues. Leticia had overheard snippets of similar talk in her staff room. The editorials would surely be brought up at the faculty meeting tomorrow. She wished she knew a good way to identify the pros and cons of each argument so she could seem leader-like tomorrow.

Guidelines for Platform Development

Developing your own political platform and value system requires a willingness to explore your biases and assumptions. It involves self-reflection about your set of values that may be tied to a specific set of religious/moral, ethical, or spiritual beliefs. This is an intensely personal process that is also tied to individual and collective identities and is bound up with history, culture, experience, and reflection. Being a policy advocate requires identifying core values and reasons for advocacy. It requires figuring out how to engage politically when faced with challenges/dilemmas. English (2003) provides one example of how a researcher/practitioner might establish a set of principals to guide action. In this case, he builds on postmodernist notions about truth and social justice to articulate what he calls the postmodernist's pledge, a set of belief statements designed to guide research on and the practice of educational administration. He suggests that to support social justice one needs to acknowledge the following (adapted from English, 2003):

- Multiple truths emanate from multiple experiences.
- Scientific knowledge should not be privileged above all other forms of knowledge.
- Truths are only temporary understandings and, as such, are likely to change over and over again.
- Humans beings have a right to exercise choice over their personhoods (e.g., in their outlook on life, sexual orientation, thought processes).
- Multiple "truths" emanating from human diversity should be celebrated and supported instead of seen as threatening to authority or governance.

In addition, English (2003) identifies several assumptions that work against social justice:

- Thinking that there is one "right way" to think anything, do anything, or search for anything. Dogma in any form, including a "knowledge base," is a challenge to deep questioning.
- Ignoring contextual variation by reducing complex social interactions to simple axioms, rules, or laws, such as "best practices," by which everyone must abide.
- Perspectives that silence, subordinate, or marginalize oppositional views.
- "Any doctrine or set of beliefs which is not open to an examination of its presuppositions and/or assumptions . . . in short, all forms of tyranny which demand unquestioned obedience or allegiance, or which require of me to suspend judgment and rest affirmation on somebody's word or good intentions." (English, 2003, p. 244)

English's pledge is based on postmodernist assumptions that value multiple perspectives, and acknowledges that values can serve as a guide when making decisions. Your values may be different—perhaps radically so—or you may value certain precepts more highly than English does, but however you proceed, you should at least begin from a clear understanding of the values on which you base your actions.

Central to their decision to give up the federal funds was a desire to do what was best for their schools, teachers, students, staff, and communities. Rather than simply react to federal guidelines and policy decisions, they decided to proactively assess the implications of the policy for their own schools. Comparing their vision of what they thought their schools and students needed with the federal policy directives, they saw gaps between their needs and the realities of the policy. Not all schools have the luxury of taking this type of stand. However, by taking an SJA approach, schools can see NCLBA as yet another example of policy that, while well intentioned, may not mesh with the realities of particular districts, schools, teachers, or students.

Lived Realities: Taking a Stand against Federal Intrusion

While the No Child Left Behind Act (NCLBA) garnered strong support in Congress and among business leaders, many states, districts, and schools struggled to understand and interpret its possible impact. While the aphorism, "no child left behind," conjures up images of a policy whose goal it is to ensure that all children are successful, the reality of the policy is far more complex. As a component of Title I of ESEA, the policy is actually targeted at schools that receive federal funding based on the numbers of students they have living in poverty. Thus, in some schools Title I funds are a relatively small component of its annual budget, yet all schools receiving federal funding must abide by the testing standards set forth by the policy, regardless of the amount of funds received. Four schools in Vermont— Hazen Union, Bellows Falls Middle School, Mount Anthony Middle School, and Mount Anthony High School—elected not to accept federal funding. Vermont, a small and primarily rural state, has a large number of smaller community schools with small numbers of children.

The leaders in each of the schools decided to take a stand. Rather than blindly follow federal regulations, they carefully conducted their own cost–benefit analysis (see Chapter 2) of what they would gain in federal funding versus what they would have to give up in terms of control of the curriculum, bureaucratic red tape, stress, and strain. Four school leaders, in consultation with district leaders, felt that the costs of taking federal funds was simply too great. Guidelines and accountability measures at the state and district levels were actually more sophisticated and held their students to a higher standard then the federal guidelines and standardized measures of assessment. Given the small size and limited resources of their schools, local school leaders felt that NCLBA would actually get in the way of their ability to help the children in their district (Walsh, 2003).

For school leaders, the arrival of a new policy for the school, district, or community is an opportunity to think about how to proactively and strategically work with or around it to achieve goals, rather than simply react to it.

Advocacy Policy Analysis

With these models for thinking about SJA, how, then, can one "do" politics and policy in a way that values marginalized groups? What are the right questions and methods to use? Again, the cynical answer is whatever gets the job, tenure, the grant, and/or the contract. The purpose of much traditional political work and policy analysis is to provide answers to the questions posed by those entrusted to make decisions. Questions that tend to be asked by the powerful are: Does this program produce the results we want (e.g., reduce the achievement gap)? Which alternative strategies (e.g., recruiting and retaining teachers) have the greatest impact? Rational decision making makes sense if the decision makers are really terrific question-framers and if decision-making arenas are open to all, regardless of their power and status. However, that is not the case, as educators and scholars have seen. For example, deep questions about how schools produce inequality and reproduce social in-

justice in the larger social order, or how schools can empower students to be full participants in democratic society, do not get asked. Waters (1998) says, "For the most part . . .
[school] reform efforts have been driven by what Barth (1986) calls perseverance of list
logic and what Giroux (1998) has called the ideology of the quick fix" (p. 2). Decision makers ask questions about how to fix bits and pieces and make small reforms using lists of
what should be reformed, but often don't get to asking deeper questions that underlie wider
visions of what schools should do. Fortunately, alternative models for policy analysis and
political leadership exist, an can be used by educational leaders taking charge of re-framing questions and re-creating modes of governance.

As mentioned in Chapter 4, sociocultural analysis conceptualizes policy itself as a
complex social practice, "an ongoing process of normative cultural production constituted
by diverse actors across diverse social and institutional contexts" (Levinson & Sutton,
2001, p. 1). It recognizes policy as a practice of power and seeks to understand the meaning of policy in practice. It recognizes not only policy enacted by elites, but also policy as
practiced, and even spontaneously and unofficially created, in normative but unauthorized
social practices. Its strength and validation come from analysis of official policy implementation, which has continuously demonstrated that powerful but unofficial practices and
norms blunt the effect of official policy intentions. Sociocultural analysis is also particularly useful for viewing the formulation of policy in official arenas as continuous, ongoing
social practice (and so no policy is done or complete and no powerful official has the final
say). Finally, its strength lies in the use of the term *policy appropriation* to highlight the reality that every actor (from senator to school maintenance worker) creates her own meaning, and thus appropriates any policy, usually to fit within her biases, needs, values, and
motivations.

A common thread in an array of emerging alternative approaches to policy analysis
is the acknowledgement of differing values and cultural experiences. As an analyst of politics and policy, one must not only determine one's own underlying values, but also account
for the range of values and biases held by the people who care about and will be affected
by any policy.

Discourse studies view policy making as "a constant discursive struggle over the criteria of social classification, the boundaries of problem categories, the intersubjective interpretation of common experiences, the conceptual framing of problems, and the
definitions of ideas that guide the ways people create the shared meanings which motivate
them to act" (Fischer & Forrester, 1993, pp. 1–2). Thus, policy analysts and planners attend
closely to policy language and to how policy "problems" are defined within a given a specific historical context. Thus, any analysis is partial and determined by those who create it.
Fischer and Forrester continue, "Policy and planning arguments are practical productions
. . . making claims that can be criticized by others or can subtly shape their attention to issues at hand" (p. 3). The political conditions in which policy analysts work affect problem
definitions; analysts know what to mention and what not to say, given the political setting.
By not questioning dominant assumptions embedded in policies, policy analysts, by default, support these assumptions. Yet policy analysts can also choose to question and challenge the assumptions that undergird policies, and can thus re-frame ways of constructing
policy. The very words used in analysis arguments can be powerful instruments. They can
create "democratic talk," and they can create "civic discovery" (p. 7).

As mentioned in Chapter 3, in narrative policy analysis, stories play an important role in making the argument to sway decisions. According to Kaplan (1993), "The narrative structure, with its organized beginning, middle, and end, requires the establishment of a readable, coherent plot" (p. 172) that integrates the multiple and scattered events and disparate perspectives into a whole. Kaplan continues, "Narratives are useful for policy and planning because they force the analyst to weave together a variety of factors and come to conclusions that flow naturally out of these factors . . . they create a tapestry that is both lovely and useful and that helps make sense of complex situations occurring within an environment of conflicting values" (p. 176). This approach to policy analysis veers considerably from rational planning and cold, hard cost–benefit analysis in its final presentation, but its strengths include that it communicates well and it fits with the way politicians often sway their audiences. The danger with narrative is that it can always exclude as well as include.

Recognizing how people are silenced and how deep questions are thrust aside and turned into non-events, critical policy researchers deliberately confront issues of institutionalized power, democracy, and inequity in educational programs and reforms efforts (Waters, 1998). "Critical" policy analysis recognizes that, because of unequal power relations, policies and institutions have, through cumulative history, created practices that provide opportunity and privilege for some and exclude and discriminate against others. Thus, the ultimate measure of a policy or plan is whether it facilitates democratic and emancipatory practice and aims and results in reducing oppressive forces. Critical policy studies, then, aim to uncover and lay bare any such potential in proposed policies. Further, policy analysis should identify alternatives that reconstruct institutions in ways that are inclusive, empowering, and equitable.

Recall from Chapter 3 that feminist critical policy analysis recognizes how gender and sexuality figure into power relations, thus creating and continuing institutionalized traditions that discriminate against women and girls. Such policy analysis lays bare the ways in which policies and programs have the effect of excluding or discouraging women and girls (e.g., from sports competition, from being superintendents). More subtly, such analysis identifies ways in which women's voices, values, and needs have not been incorporated into the framing of programs and policies.

Examples of each of these perspectives are threaded throughout this book. These perspectives provide a foundation for creating very different stances for educational leaders' analysis of political situations and very different approaches to politics and policy research, all aimed at supporting social justice.

Social Justice Advocacy Policy Research and Action

Educators' active involvement in politics and policy can lead to re-framing and re-visioning policies. In partnerships between researchers and educators, policy research involves cycles of collaborative problem or question finding, data collection and analysis, recommendations for change interventions, immediate evaluations, and then new recommendations. Educators' involvement with questions and problems generated in the real-world setting can lead to policies and programs framed to meet immediate needs, unlike many policies and programs framed in faraway policy arenas.

The following example demonstrates how collaborative policy research can create constructive solutions in politically and racially charged situations. Beginning with an understanding of the increasing gap between White and African American students, a gap that increased as students moved up in the district's grades, the Newton, Massachusetts, superintendent created an antiracist intervention. Pooling resources with six other suburban districts and a university-based consultant, he went to work. This move had major political implications, especially because he and all the other superintendents and most of the other administrators and teachers across the district were White, and were hesitant to speak about racial issues. Through a self-designed thirty-six-hour, semester-long professional development course, delivered by a biracial team, participants created a shared language for talking about the ways racism operates and how "only those who are actively antiracist" (Blumer & Tatum, 1999, p. 239) can interrupt the cycle of oppression. Designers and participants also connected racism "to other isms (sexism, class-ism, heterosexism, anti-Semitism, etc.)" (p. 260).

Another approach to re-visioning politics is recognizing and benefiting from educators as activists. School governance hierarchies dictate that political and policy action must take place in legitimized arenas such as school board meetings, and according to rituals and rules of order. Teacher training and teacher culture often suppresses teachers' sense of themselves as politically engaged citizens. However, some educators persist in their involvement in social movements, both within education circles and within the wider world. As educators they may, for example, join wider social action committees against high-stakes testing or in favor of enforcement of Title IX, seeing these as extensions of their educator role. They also may be involved in political actions such as demonstrations, petitions, guerilla theater, and publications. Educators may sponsor or participate in activities for eliminating world hunger or in favor of world peace, gay and lesbian rights, environmental preservation, democratic freedom at home or abroad, and other such causes, simply because they wish to be active citizens supporting what they value. This political activity can, in some cases, be viewed by others as inappropriate and may jeopardize educators' careers. Still, a re-visioned politics of education can explore ways to invite and support energized, politically attuned activist educators.

Purposeful Journeys to Margins and Centers

Why would researchers be interested in or care about embedding policy formulation in considerations derived from the lived realities of marginalized groups? How can one know to connect or reconnect with educators' ideals and the passion for improvement, helping, and social justice? How can one know the need to get people at the centers of power to use counternarratives and to help create alternative policy analyses? Principals, researchers, professors, policy makers, superintendents, and teachers need understandings and strategies. To even envision these needs, they must *see* and *feel* politics from the margin. They must envision ways to *move*, to travel to those margins shown in the advocacy policy analysis framework (Figure 10.1) and to use the awareness of unmet needs, lived realities, and counternarratives to present possibilities for re-framing policy. They need to envision ways to move these stories to the center of that model, to present alternative discourses that effectively and powerfully re-vision policy deliberations at the center. They must view the

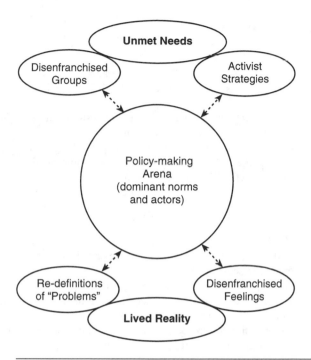

FIGURE 10.1 *Advocacy Politics*

politics of the margins as viable, powerful, legitimate politics—as part and parcel of the policy world.

The central argument of this book is that what researchers and leaders *can* do is journey among multiple communities (Figure 10.1), to be affected and shaped by diverse groups' worldviews. Although you may not be able to change the entire world, it is possible to make your part of the world more humane and equitable by seeking to understand the lives and experiences of others.

> We can change how we live: our habits, our neighborhoods, our circumstances, our political activities, our relationships. If the relationships and situations that we live with on a day-to-day basis allow us to rest comfortably in the knowledge that works for us, we will not see any reason to change or to inquire into other lives. (Thompson, 1998, p. 544)

With Thompson's thoughts in mind, leadership and policy research therefore should include purposeful intellectual journeys through outsider-within experiences (Collins, 1998, p. 233). Collins challenges researchers (and practitioners and policy makers) to search for justice and to promote agency. Viewing truth as "a process negotiated in outsider-within places, as compared to finished product" (p. 232), Collins implies that intellectual work requires journeys to the margins and borderlands.

Policy advocacy should include experiences in collaboration with other researchers, policy actors, and practitioners, and especially with people who are constructing counternarratives and are engaged in counterpublic social movements. Table 10.2 proposes

TABLE 10.2   *Strategies for Policy Advocacy*

Possibilities for Approaches to Research

- Critical policy evaluations to understand where the social programs aimed at the range of "at-risk" or dropped-out students have missed the meanings and realities of their expected clientele
- Narrative inquiry to understand counterpublic challenges (e.g., the stories of the choices of parents who place their children in charter, private, and home schools)
- Research agendas using discourse analysis to identify the ways powerful gatekeepers legitimize and delegitimize challengers and effective strategies of counterpublics who permeate the boundaries and create effective political action
- Collaborative policy analyses engaging counterpublics and eliciting counternarratives
- Collaborative action research

Possibilities for Research and Action

- Collaborative narratives of education activists, highlighting the connections they found or created to enable them to engage in social justice pursuits
- Participatory action research projects in which researchers, educators, school site councils, and parent groups move from rhetoric about schools as democratic communities and high expectations for all students into reality, with specific actions
- Coursework and in-service preparation to provide educators with skills for demanding that social justice issues be at the forefront of educational policy creation
- Creating roles, structures, and budgets for identifying policy re-framing opportunities and seeking counternarratives and counterpublics

Actions in Practice or Policy

- Devising departmental conversations among colleagues, beginning with personal experiences with systems of domination so faculties can examine their own biases as a precursor to infusing social justice ideals into the curriculum
- Devising "Daily Dilemmas Dialogues" with school participants, a time set aside as a community or family, aimed at bringing to the surface the unsolved issues and unresolved emotions, unmet desires or imaginings from the school day, and then creating relationships to address needs
- Devising selection criteria and methods for assessing educational leaders' commitment and abilities for developing caring communities and fighting for social justice

Reconceptualization

- Experimenting with devising labels and names for enabling policy discourse about repressed issues (e.g., enabling students to talk about their need for belonging rather than just talking about good test scores)
- Re-framing the rebellions and refusals of those concerned with social justice issues as productive and healthy challenges to support school change
- Engaging with the feminist critique of education policy to elicit the missed opportunities for alternative models of leadership, collaborative pedagogies, and schooling to incorporate the content relegated to the private sphere (emotion, child nurturance, sexuality, relationships of care, etc.)

---

routes for research designed to encompass marginalized policy issues and provides experiences for powerful possibilities of policy re-framing. It also provides examples of policy advocacy aimed at connecting marginalized voices to the center of policy making.

Getting Real

"That's all fine in a book," you may be saying, "but what about in the real world? How do I make these things happen?" To help you understand SJA in practice, this section provides examples of real educators taking charge in politicized situations. Specifically, this section examines scholar-leaders who have taken an activist/interventionist stance in their leadership, scholarship, or both, and in doing so, successfully shifted or refocused policy issues.

As mentioned in Chapter 7, Vermont's Senator Jim Jeffords took a stand on the need for the federal government to fund special education and was thereby willing to relinquish the power that Republican party membership gave him in order to do so (Jeffords, 2001). Yet his advocacy for full federal funding of special education through IDEA continues.

For an international example, another politician dared to stand firm for educational equity policies, even when it could mean losing constituents' votes. With all her political connections as member of Parliament in Victoria, Australia, Lorraine Elliott could have maintained her powerful position by backing off on her commitment to gender equity in education. Her sponsors strongly urged her to drop the gender equity agenda because equity values were being pushed aside in Parliament in a wave of economic rationalism. Instead, she worked outside traditional governmental channels to garner support for gender equity. She met with a range of gender equity activists, helped develop coalitions of teacher union activists, and used her insider information to help them find money, strategies, and rhetoric that would support continuing governmental work toward gender equity. In the Australian state of Victoria, as a result, the hard-won policies for gender equity could be maintained as long as someone like Lorraine Elliott worked this kind of insider-outsider strategy. (See the section in Chapter 8 about this Australian research and also Marshall, 2000a).

Deborah Meier (Meier, 1995, 2002) has been a role model for many aspiring advocacy leaders. As the principal leader of Central Park East in Harlem, Meier transformed a failing high-poverty school in New York City into a success story. At the heart of her advocacy for school transformation was the notion that students need to be nurtured and challenged intellectually. In her memoir, *The Power of Their Ideas* (1995), Meier suggests that the creativity, curiosity, and ability of children and youth need to be nurtured in schools. Central to her philosophy and advocacy is that

> there's a radical—and wonderful—new idea here—the idea that every citizen is capable of the kind of intellectual competence previously attained by only a small minority. It was only after I had begun to teach, that public rhetoric gave even lip service to the notion that all children could and should be inventors of their own theories, critics of other people's ideas, analyzers of evidence, and makers of their own personal marks on this most complex world. It's an idea with revolutionary implications. If we take it seriously. (p. 4)

Meier's work with Central Park East is a testament to the power of her ideas and vision. The school is actually a collection of four schools—three elementary schools and a secondary school woven together into a community. Starting out as an elementary school in 1974, Central Park East expanded to create two additional elementary schools because of increased demand. Then in 1985, the school expanded to create a secondary school. Central to what drives the schools is a progressive pedagogy that challenges students to be inquirers, a caring school culture and community-oriented organizational structure, and high expectations for student performance centered on higher order thinking. Although the majority of students are African American and Latino and lower income or poor, 85 percent of the first seven classes of the elementary school (1977–1984), against expectation, went on to receive high school diplomas, and 11 percent received GEDs. These numbers continued to improve between 1991 and 1995, with 90 percent of graduates going on to graduate from college. What these numbers reveal is that the students who are traditionally expected to fail succeed at Central Park East.

Another example is Principal Author Perkins, whose leadership is a "spiritual calling" in Peoria, Illinois. She fights for "her children" who live in a public housing project. School staff members describe her as caring, strong, and supportive. Her school was considered failing when she assumed the helm as principal. Unwilling to see children as unsuccessful, she pushed her staff and local community to improve their expectations of themselves and the students. Although twelve of thirty-seven schools in her district are on the academic watch list, hers is not one of them. An array of programs—phonemic awareness, after-school literacy through computers, school uniforms, engaged learning, a comprehensive educational component for family members, a violence-prevention program, and the like—are part of the reason. Perkins works tirelessly to bring additional funds and resources into the school. She sees herself as a mentor and role model for her students, their families, and her staff. Many on staff tell stories about how parents take increasingly better care of their children and of themselves (Lyman, 2002). Perkins' success where previous failure had loomed serves as a testament to the power of taking a stand for children and their communities.

Scholars' re-framings can grapple with very real quandaries. As mentioned in Chapter 3, Joseph Kahne (1994) re-framed tracking policy around democratic ideals. He suggested that traditional tracking works against democracy by separating students and not properly preparing lower tracked students to participate in democracy. Students in the lower tracks are often assumed to be intellectually inferior; thus, the education they often receive is more didactic and less critical. Kahne argues that separating students by race and social class works against democracy. Instead, he offers a vision of schooling in which the role of school is to prepare students to participate in democracy. He criticizes tracking policies for working against democratic ideals. He suggests that all policies should be assessed for whether they support the creation of democratic communities in schools. His democratic re-framing of policy pays attention to the process of education and offers an alternative to policies that focus exclusively on outcomes and individualized student achievement.

Specific tools and strategies can help. Equity audits are tools for leaders to self-assess whether their school or district is equitable in its treatment of children (developed by Skrla et al., 2004). Utilizing systematic data collection and review, these audits spotlight students whose voices and needs are not being served by districts. For example, data collection centers around twelve indicators that are grouped into three themes: teacher-quality equity (e.g., education, experience, mobility, and teachers without proper certification or training), programmatic equity (special education, gifted and talented, bilingual education, and student discipline), and achievement equity (state achievement results, dropout rates, high school graduation tracks, and SAT/ACT/AP results). Conducting an equity audit requires looking at each indicator to see whether certain groups of students (by quantifiable indicators such as gender, race, ethnicity, and income) are over- or underrepresented in the types of teachers they see, programs they are in, or their categories of achievement. Equity audits can help a leader identify areas in need of improvement and issues that need to be addressed. For example, it can help identify whether certain types of students (e.g., White and middle-class students) are identified as gifted while larger numbers of low-income minority students are placed in remedial education. This identification of inequity can serve as a starting point for activism targeted at transforming policy and practice.

Each of the scholar-leaders profiled in this section took a stand and were willing to take career risks in order to champion causes in support of social justice. Their stories show that change is possible in schooling, research, and politics. Though activism is often thought of as public picketing and strikes, SJAL or activist research may be more understated, behind the scenes, and subtle (Bell, 1995). But as all of these examples have shown, changing policy and practice begins with taking a stand.

Policy Advocacy Coalitions

The advocacy coalition framework, mentioned in Chapter 1, is designed to focus on the process of policy change over time in a particular social context, by understanding how groups work together to redirect or support policy. This section highlights several advocacy coalitions working in various policy arenas to create educational change. Not all of these groups are aimed at social justice; some are actually focused on narrower interpretations of the purpose of education.

School Reform via Community Advocacy

Started in 1982, the Algebra Project (2004) is an example of a grassroots change program that developed into an advocacy coalition that has cross-state implications. The project was begun by a parent, Bob Moses, who was concerned about the math education received by his child. Building on his work as a community organizer in Mississippi in the 1960s who encouraged Blacks to vote, he developed a grassroots algebra project that involved community members in understanding the importance of learning algebra. The program is centered on posing questions such as why it is important to study algebra and why every middle school student needs algebra in order to gain access to college preparatory courses. Central to the program is using algebra to encourage minority and low-income students to think about attending college (Moses, 1994).

The Harvey Milk School in New York City was created to be a nurturing and supportive environment for gay and lesbian youth. Founded by the Hetrick-Martin Institute, the school was named after Harvey Milk, an activist for gay rights and the first openly gay elected public official in California. Milk was assassinated in 1978. While initially started with private funds, the school successfully advocated to gain accreditation for and funding from the New York Department of Education (Harvey Milk School, 2003) so that it would have legitimacy and be able to serve more students in need.

Just as advocacy coalitions have developed to create safe havens for teens who challenge the norms and to encourage community involvement in education, there have also been effective advocacy coalitions designed to censor curricula and "stop the spread of homosexuality" (Opfer, 2000, p. 86). Specifically, religious groups have been affective at challenging curriculum that does not fit conservative Christian values. For example, attempts to teach evolution have often met deep resistance, as have sex education curricula or programs such as outcomes-based education (Lugg, 2000; Provenzo & McClosky, 2000). Many of these groups see curricula as a direct and threatening challenge to their entire belief systems. Yet, at the same time, these groups place a high value on moral and individual responsibility. Some believe that these groups are not as monolithic or "extreme" as they have been made out to be by the media or by progressive groups (Opfer, 1999). The focus on academic standards may actually be as problematic for religious groups as it is for progressive education groups, because it displaces a concern for teaching ethics and morality (Herrington, 2000).

Strange Bedfellows

Dissatisfaction with public education has given rise to coalitions between strange bedfellows, such as progressive educators and religious conservatives. Home schooling groups, such as the Alliance for the Separation of Church and State (2003), find themselves in alliance with conservative religious groups, such as Citizens for Excellence in Education (CEE) (a division of the National Association for Christian Educators). These groups share a common concern against government intrusion into education. Additionally, conservative religious groups such as CEE also find themselves allied with groups such as the Black Alliance for Educational Options (2003) in favor of school choice and vouchers.

The National Coalition of Women and Girls in Education (NCWGE) (2003) was established in 1975 to support Title IX. This coalition is made up of more than fifty organizations committed to supporting Title IX, including the American Academy for the Advancement of Science, the American Association of School Administrators, the American Association of University Women, the American Civil Liberties Union, the American Federation of Teachers (AFT), the Association of American Colleges and Universities, the Girl Scouts of America, the National Council on Negro Women, and the Young Women's Christian Association. This coalition was called into action in 2003, when a national commission was created to rethink Title IX. The secretary of education at the time, Rod Paige, created the Commission on Opportunity in Athletics to look into Title IX provisions. The commission report suggested drastic changes to Title IX that would greatly lessen its impact. NCWGE's response was to recruit an additional fifty organizations, and together the coalition of one hundred organizations launched a massive campaign in Congress that included a large letter-writing effort across party lines. NCWGE's campaign was successful, and Title IX was protected from any changes.

Another advocacy coalition has been quietly working toward higher standards and national accountability. As mentioned, business leaders have been working for the past few decades to reform public education. Powerful networks such as the Business Round Table, led by CEOs of Fortune 500 companies, have been pushing for educational reform that focuses on basic skills (reading, math) as measured through standardized testing (Business Roundtable, 2002). Many of these leaders feel that standardized test scores are a cost-effective way to hold schools accountable for student learning. These advocacy coalitions have been successful at both national and state levels, as evidenced through the identification of high-stakes accountability programs as *the* way to reform public education (McDaniel & Miskel, 2002; Reyes, Wagstaff, & Fusarelli, 1999).

Coalitions Aimed at Interagency Collaboration

The Children's Defense Fund (CDF) (2003), under the direction of Marion Wright Edelman (1992), is a nonprofit organization dedicated to advocating for children, particularly those who are poor, minority, and/or disabled. CDF takes a multipronged approach to its advocacy, from commissioning research reports that look into the education and health of children to grassroots programs aimed at developing advocacy within the Black community. For example, one of CDF's primary advocacy coalition programs is its Black Community Crusade for Children (BCCC). BCCC brings together African American policy makers, community leaders, educators, and clergy to develop financial support for projects in Cincinnati and Columbus, Ohio. In these cities, the projects seek to build community, interracial and intergenerational communication, interdisciplinary networking, and intergenerational mentoring.

The United Nations Development Fund for Women (UNIFEM) (2003) focuses on global efforts to achieve gender equity. One of the main roles of the organization is to conduct research and to support the capacity of groups working for gender equity within certain countries and cross-nationally. Their report *Progress of the World's Women 2002: Volume 2: Gender Equality and the Millennium Development Goals* (2003) cites troubling data that, globally, many poor women are less secure than previously and that gender inequity is actually on the rise. UNIFEM operates as a central resource for information on the global status of women and supports international and national efforts to improve the status of women by helping to network organizations, conduct research, and place gender equity issues into international policy discussions.

Building Advocacy Coalitions

Given that politics are messy, interconnected, and fraught with inequity, how would you go about forming advocacy coalitions in order to create policies that acknowledge critical perspectives? Building on critical pedagogy, Wink (1999) suggests a practical process for creating advocacy strategies and policies that involves "starting with a mess," that is, starting with a contradiction or paradox. Once you have established what the policy mess is, move to learn more about it, imagine alternative strategies, and think about possible roadblocks to your strategies. Having taken possible obstacles into account, prepare an action plan and a way to evaluate the action, draft a statement of commitment for the project, and then start the process all over again and define the "new mess." The specific questions to ask during this process are outlined in Table 10.3.

TABLE 10.3 *Starting with a Mess*

I. Start with a mess (problem, paradox, contradiction, difficult situation).
   Define it. Name it.
II. Learn more about it.
   How can we learn more about this?
   Who knows what about this?
   How will we share information with the group?
III. Imagine alternative strategies.
   List all of the ideas that might work. Think wildly and passionately.
   Dream. Think utopias.
   Collectively, choose an approach.
IV. Prepare.
   What are the roadblocks? How can we prepare for them?
   What new problems might this approach create? What are the possible directions for
   new problems? What could go wrong? What role might others play if we decide to try
   to change this?
V. Create an action plan and evaluation.
   Create a time line and plan of action.
   Do it; fix it. Do it; fix it.
VI. Write a commitment statement.
   We commit to . . .
   I commit to . . .
   Members of the group share personal commitment statements and agree to use their
   own expertise to help fix the mess.
VII. Begin again.
   Redefine and rename the new mess.

Source: From Joan Wink *Critical Pedagogy* © 2000. Published by Allyn and Bacon, Boston, MA. Copyright © 2000 by Pearson Education. Reprinted by permission of the publisher.

What is critical about this process is acknowledging that it *is* a process. It may have a clear beginning, but it may not have a neat and tidy end. The change process is continual and ever changing. While "starting with a mess" suggests a way to develop a strategy for change, it does not provide a way of critically assessing the process and outcome.

Coming back close to home, the following Lived Realities reveals details of a recent example of politically astute, coalition-building SAJL that started with just such a "mess."

Lived Realities: Walking the Tightrope of State Control

Trenton, New Jersey, designated an "Abbott" district—one of thirty struggling districts slated for state takeover following a Supreme Court decree that found that the schools needed additional resources and monitoring—clearly had to come up with new ways of doing things. The actions of Trenton's leadership were not typical responses to state control:

- They hired a new superintendent, Dr. James "Torch" Lytle, in 1998 and, in collaboration with diverse power bases in Trenton, created a "can-do" image, rhetoric, and stratagem.
- They held televised open "fishbowl" meetings, which were attended by employees, the general public, and city council and school board members, and their division heads explained budgets to the superintendent.
- They created before- and after-school programs, and a dropout recovery program and recruitment from street corners.
- They hired mostly minority administrators.
- They had the superintendent step in briefly for a non-cooperative principal.
- They dared to adopt deficit budgets, taking the chance that appeals filed to the courts and state Department of Education (DOE) would force full funding.
- They used universities and foundations to create district training for leadership development, technology, budgeting, and formative evaluation, thus re-focusing ineffective training from the state.
- They dared to remove three of the twenty-three district's minority principals (in a district that is 95 percent minority), drawing accusations of racial profiling.

Working alone, Torch would have put himself on the tightrope of the middle manager who, despite wavering state resources, must work around state's policy makers demands. However, by creating coalitions based on diverse bases of power within and outside the school system, he multiplied the sources of support for daring, risky, and different strategies. By 2002, data revealed that this atypical and risk-taking behavior was paying off both in school improvement and in political support.

The superintendent's and community coalitions' actions were derived not only from years of experience with urban school administration, but also from theory and research. Sensing that an underfunded and high-turnover DOE staff would be of little use, and that state and even court mandates for funding reforms to meet equity goals could not be relied on, they built their own sources of expertise. Lytle and other district and city politicians used insights from theory and research, building on the following strategies and theoretical lenses:

- Leadership for organizational change, particularly school-level change (Fullan, 1991; Senge, 1990)
- The dynamics of disruptive change (Christianen & Overdorf, 2000)
- Diffused and distributed leadership for building a deep sense of community
- "Sensor" skills used to collect and interpret soft data, and the use of it in daring and personalized ways
- Learning organizations (Senge; 1990)
- Openly available data and inquiry-based decision making
- Partnering with community
- Constant vigilance over symbols-management for creating meaning and moral purpose, seeing this as the center of change efforts (Fullan, 1991)

Recognizing 1998 Trenton as a case of "disruptive change," Dr. Lytle knew that successful organizations are good at responding to evolutionary changes in their markets, so he collaborated to create new markets, with feeder programs into the elementary schools (getting families at-

(continued)

Lived Realities   Continued

tuned to them rather than to charters) and with dropout recovery programs that helped triple graduation rates. Recognizing that top-down leadership and expertise would not meet the crisis, he collaborated in courses with principals that led to shared understandings about change, thus creating a learning-to-learn organization. And, recognizing that parents and the community want their children to become responsible, self-supporting adults much more than they want rises in aggregate test scores, he enabled others to center all change efforts around this as the moral purpose of reform.

Political frameworks were useful for recognizing the power vacuums created by the Abbott decision and by the DOE incapacities as great opportunities to dare new politics. Lytle could parse through the dilemmas that created the tightrope he was walking to see that standards-based reform focused on school sites and that states' monitoring of sites' scores had dramatically altered the roles of local boards and superintendents. Finally, this superintendent and the power brokers in the community were able to recognize that politics-as-usual would not work. Disruption of dysfunctional power bases, creation of new alliances, capacity-building implementation strategies, and a willingness to defy assumptive world rules that dug deeper holes, Trenton's new politics were clearly re-framed and re-visioned.

Theory and political analysis provided insights in the preceding Lived Realities, but decisions were also guided by SJAL. Theory, a well-developed political platform, and an orientation to seek and create power bases to facilitate and support strategies that maximize talents, expertise, and powers from both inside and outside "the system" can really guide action in such politics and governance quagmires—and create openings and policy windows for social justice leadership.

Advocacy Policy Audit

Once you have developed a platform, defined the "mess," and engaged in policy advocacy, how would you judge the degree to which a given set of actions and/or personal platform supports social justice? The notion of doing an advocacy policy audit builds on Collins' theoretical treatise on Black feminist thought (1990; 1998), Skrla, Scheurich, Garcia, and Nolly's (2005) notion of equity audits, and Patton's (2002) development of critical change criteria. Auditing policy advocacy requires a willingness to look for discontinuities, silences, and paradoxes. The following questions provide a way of reflecting on and critically analyzing a policy, political strategy, or your own practice,

1. Does it increase consciousness about social justice?
2. Does it apply fairly to all students? (Examine your data to see whether some groups are represented more than others in specific programs or achievement groups.)
3. Does it speak truth to people about the reality of their lives?
4. Does it equip people to resist oppression?
5. Does it move people to action?

6. Does it identify inequities and injustice?
7. Does it represent the perspectives of the less powerful?
8. Does it make visible the ways in which those in power might benefit?
9. Does it engage those with less legitimated power in ways that are respectful and collaborative?
10. Does it build the capacity of those involved to take action?
11. Does it identify potential change strategies?
12. Does it value connections between theory and practice?
13. Does it acknowledge the context of history and values?
14. Does it identify strategies to engage the attention of those in power?

These questions provide one way of assessing the degree to which your platform and policies support social justice and critical perspectives. It is not exhaustive and cannot encompass all of the questions and contextual factors of a given policy or strategy that may need to be addressed. But it is a start, a spark for reflecting on whether your own intentions may have created unintended consequences that need to be addressed so that you can continue to advocate equitably for policies that encompass the needs and realities of children, families, and communities.

Summary

This book has explored multiple ways of interpreting and analyzing policy. Policy advocacy requires that leaders, policy makers, and scholars learn to journey from our centers of privilege to visit multiple communities. It takes courage to go into uncertain, uncomfortable, and challenging terrain. Often it requires confronting blindness and privilege in the form of bias, misconceptions, and inequities. It requires daring to let go of the pretense that our policies and our research are value-free. It requires developing the "moral vision and ethical norms . . . to account for and transform existing forms of dogmatism, oppression, and despair" (Laible, 2000, p. 686). It requires embracing, as Laible asserts, "a loving epistemology," searching for an ethical, socially just, and widened way of knowing realities that consciously seeks out the voices and needs of the underrepresented and the marginal.

Exercises for Policy Advocacy

1. *Debate Mr. Venable's Actions.* Recall Mr. Venable's speech. Describe, in small groups or in a full class, the issues or situations in your career that have provoked you enough to speak truth to those in power. Discuss the feelings you had, ways you set up the situation to preserve your career, and good feelings or feelings of regret you have about what happened.

2. *Learn from an Educator Activist.* Identify someone who is an educator activist and interview her about how she manages to engage in political activism and social movements yet further her career. Ask her to talk about how being an educator affected the choices she made regarding her level of involvement, her level of visibility, and her choice of employment.

3. *Gatewood Discussion.* Recall the story of Reverend Curtis Gatewood. Then review functionalist and social justice advocacy (composed of

critical pluralist, transformative, moral and ethical, feminist caring, spiritual/cultural perspectives) leadership and conduct a class discussion centering on how each model would deal with Gatewood.

4. *Re-frame Policy.* In groups, identify current policies that are in need of re-framing to better benefit educators and children. First, identify the dominant assumptions that frame the current policy. Then generate alternative perspectives and note where counterpublics and counternarratives can contribute insights about what kinds of information could be useful for re-framing.

5. *Take a Journey.* Take a journey in search of marginalized voices. Conduct an equity audit on your school and reach out to the parents of children who seem disengaged. Ask them why they are not more involved and what the school could do to get them to participate more. Visit local community groups (homeless shelters, churches, religious organizations, neighborhood associations, outreach organizations) and get their perspective on what the issues are in your community. What do they think needs to happen to make the community more inclusive? Try to understand the issues and concerns of the groups that seem marginalized in your community.

6. *Identify Strategies for Advocacy.* Find one of these books—Alinsky's (1971) *Rules for Radicals,* Jansson's (2003) *Becoming an Effective Policy Advocate,* Shaw's (1996) *The Activist Handbook,* or Hergert, Phlegar, and Perez-Selles' (1991) *Kindle the Spark: An Action Guide for Schools Committed to the Success of Every Child*—and list the kind of advice and strategies it offers. Identify the key elements of the advice and strategies contained within the book, then generate a class discussion about whether (and why) the suggestions could work in your local educational context.

7. *Re-vision: Create an Innovative School.* Write a mission statement for a magnet or a charter school in which you articulate a model of leadership centering on alternative values such as an ethic of care, social justice, inclusiveness and diversity, and/or an egalitarian conception of democracy. Then generate plans for practical management—for example, public relations, student recruitment, budget, facilities, schedule and curriculum, and meeting state and federal requirements.

8. *Create an Advocacy Coalition for a Goodness Policy.* Plan a policy that addresses a policy "problem." Name it the "Goodness Policy." Lay out as many details as needed to ensure that the policy will be implemented and will have the intended outcomes. Then lay out details about how you will develop an advocacy coalition to support it in the relevant policy-making arenas. Be sure to assess who you are in the policy system so your proposal and strategies are attuned to your position.

Goodness Policy 1

The Policy
What is it?
Where does it come from?

What is the political context?
What kind of problem is it?
What kind of policy is it?
What could happen during implementation?
Who are you in this policy system?
What Can You Do?
Shape the original policy framing: heuresthetics
Use backward and forward mapping
Create scenarios
Appoint consiglieres
Remove redundancy and slack
Manage media
Reduce rhetoric
Shape attention
Set and manage the evaluation criteria
Keep evaluation criteria politically attuned
Promote phased implementation

9. *Create a Platform and Articulate Your Stance.* Look back at the section on developing a platform. Note English's postmodern pledge. Now think about what your own platform or stance

might be. What type of leader will you be? What do you value? Prepare a three-sentence speech about your stance. Then continue the speech, using the following prompts:

a. I will/will not get involved politically (describing situations).

b. I define politics as _____.

c. Education policy is best constructed through these kinds of processes: _____.

d. The most promising ways to study/analyze policy are _____.

e. For education, we need national, centralized education for these functions and no others.

f. Therefore, state government's education policy role should be to _____.

g. There's a tradition of localism—local control—for education policy. It should be for these issues or functions: _____.

h. District/local should leave to federal or state governments these functions regarding children's education: _____.

10. *Dream up Research Questions: An Exercise for Future Policy Researchers.* (You may change the focus by substituting, for example, language, child poverty, racial/ethic/religious tolerance for the word *gender*.) Suppose the International Institute for Support of Your Dream research sent you $2 million to design a study to identify how education policy regarding gender is made in eight countries. Based on what you know so far, you might start with these general purpose questions:

a. *Identifying the Historical/Cultural Influences.* When gender equity policy was enacted, how was the particular policy shaped by historical traditions for thinking and acting? What cultural assumptions are built into policy? More specifically, what cultural and policy history exists constrain that and shapes current formulation. (For example, historical agreements preferring local control of education will inhibit policy makers' generation of national policy initiatives. And cultural assumptions that men's vocations take precedence will inhibit policy makers' generation of vigor-

ous programs for girls that would take away from boys' advantage.)

b. *Identifying the Political Forces.* What created policy windows when gender equity policy proposals were enacted? What were the prevailing assumptive worlds? Who were the policy entrepreneurs? What coalitions were formed?

c. *Identifying the Policy Mechanisms and Variables.* What tools are chosen to achieve gender equity objectives? Tools range from exhortation and symbolic priority setting, to research and development, to regulatory and control measures, to incentives and disincentives (Majchrzak, 1984). How appropriate is the match between policy objective and policy tools?

d. *Developing a Gender Equity Inventory.* What is the range of ways for policy systems, education systems, and communities to affect gender equity? This study will identify the range of ways, developing an inventory—a listing of policy mechanisms, strategies, indicators, process measures, and outcome measures used for effecting gender equity in education. For example, the French strategy of creating a ministry of women's rights and the U.S. federal Title IX are examples of national policy efforts. British policies and programs are less evident, because, until recently, most policy development was left to local districts. By collecting program publications, evaluations, policy documents, and research on the array of policies in five countries, we will be able to provide a display of the range of policy approaches and an assessment of their effectiveness. From this display, further analysis of efficacy, cultural/political fit, cost–benefit estimates, and the like, can be developed in cross-national comparisons.

e. *Identifying Ideology, Theory, and Research Affecting Gender Equity.* What are the theoretical assumptions underlying policy? Are there theoretical shifts? Is there evidence of evolving feminist theories? Were there research studies and/or evaluations that affected policy? If so, how did these get translated and mobilized in the policy system? What in the policy system opened policy windows for these theoretical assumptions and values?

Critique your outline. Add to it, subtract from it. Write three to four paragraphs about the theories and the methodological approach(es) you will use in your research plan. Make a plan for how this research will be conducted. What eight countries will you study and why? How will you collect and analyze data? Make a budget. Make a time line. Will you have consultants? If so, what will be their qualifications? Write two paragraphs arguing the significance and utility of this research.

11. *An Exercise for Future Policy Advocates.* Collect key documents about your school or organization (e.g., requirements for admission, internships, courses, mission statements, faculty and student backgrounds, etc.) and analyze them. Identifying evidence of the degree and ways in which the program prepares educators to be effective policy advocates. Prepare interview questions for faculty, students, and graduates to elicit the same kind of evidence. Draw tentative findings and recommendations, as well as a list of continuing questions and methods to gather evidence for a more complete review and for a way to make effective use of these tentative findings and recommendations.

References

Abu-Haidar, S. (2001). *(Un)Silenced voices: A case study of three Latinas' successful negotiation of public deliberation about education.* Paper presented at the Annual Meeting of the American Educational Research Association, Seattle, WA.

Adkinson, J. A. (1982). *Local response to federal mandates: The implementation of Title IX.* Paper presented at the Annual Meeting of the American Educational Research Association, New York.

Adler, L. (1994) Introduction and overview. In L. Adler & S. Gardner (Eds.), *The politics of linking schools and social services* (pp. 1–16). Washington, D.C.: Falmer Press.

Adler, L., & Gardner, S. (Eds.). (1994). *The politics of linking schools and social services.* Washington, D.C.: Falmer Press.

Ah Nee-Bcnhan, M. K. P., & Cooper, C. E. (1998). *Let my spirit soar! Narratives of diverse women in school leadership.* Thousand Oaks, CA: Corwin Press.

Algebra Project (2004). The algebra project. Website. Retrieved December 12, 2003, from http://www.algebra.org/apinfo/origin2.html.

Alinsky, S. (1971). *Rules for radicals.* New York: Random House.

Alliance for the Separation of Church and State (2003). Website. Retrieved December 12, 2003, from http://www.sepschool.org/.

Allison, G. T. (1971). *Essence of decision: Explaining the Cuban missile crisis.* Boston: Little Brown.

Alston, J. (1999). Climbing hills and mountains: Black females making it to the superintendency. In C. Brunner (Ed.), *Sacred dreams: Women and the superintendency* (pp. 79–90). Albany: State University of New York Press.

Althusser, L. (1971). Ideology and ideological state apparatuses. In *Lenin and philosophy and other essays.* New York: Monthly Review Press.

American Association of University Women (1992). *How schools shortchange girls.* Washington, DC: AAUW, Educational Foundation.

American Association of University Women. (1994). *Elementary and secondary education act: Summary of gender equity provisions.* Paper presented at the American Association of University Women, Washington, DC.

American Educational Research Association (2002a). *Recommendation for the improvement of the federal Education Research Program.* Washington, DC: American Education Research Association.

American Educational Research Association (November 21, 2002b). *Press release: Societies raise concerns about document removal from U.S. Department of Education.* Website. Retrieved October 15, 2003, from http://www.aera.net/communications/news/021121.htm.

American School Board Journal. (1969). Get ready for a new force on the education scene: Mayors. *American School Board Journal, 157*(2), 28–29.

American School Board Journal. (2001). Education vital signs. *American School Boards Journal, 188*(12), 43–49.

Anderson, C. W. (1978). The logic of public problems: Evaluations in comparative policy research. In D. E. Ashford, *Comparing public policies: New concepts and methods.* Beverly Hills, CA: Sage.

Anderson, G. L. (1989). Critical ethnography in education: Origins, current status, and new directions. *Review of Educational Research, 59*(3), 249–270.

Anderson, G. L. (1990). Toward a critical constructivist approach to school administration: Invisibility, legitimation, and the study of non-events. *Educational Administration Quarterly, 26*(1), 38–59.

Anderson, G. L. (2004). Performing school reform in the age of the political spectacle. In B. Alexander, G. L. Anderson, & B. Gallegos (Eds.), *Performance theories in education: Power, pedagogy, and the politics of identity.* Mahwah, NJ: Lawrence Erlbaum.

Anderson, J. D. (1988). *The education of Blacks in the South, 1860–1935.* Chapel Hill: The University of North Carolina Press.

Andre-Bechely, L. (2003). Public school choice at the intersection of voluntary integration and not-so-good neighborhood schools: Lessons from parents' experiences. Unpublished manuscript.

Anna, D. (1992). *Public-private partnerships: The private sector and innovation in education.* Santa Monica, CA: Reason Foundation.

Anyon, J. (1997). *Ghetto schooling: A political economy of urban educational reform.* New York: Teachers College Press.

Anzaldua, G. (1987). *Borderlands: La frontera: The new mestiza.* San Francisco: Aunt Lute Books.

Apple, M. W. (1997). Justifying the conservative restoration: Morals, genders, and educational policy. *Educational Policy, 11*(2), 167–183.

Apple, M. W. (2000). Can critical pedagogies interrupt rightist policies? *Educational Theory, 50*(2), 229–225.

Arnot, M., & Weiler, K. (Eds.) (1993). *Feminism and social justice in education: International perspectives.* London: Falmer Press.

Astin, A. W., & Astin, H. S. (2000). *Leadership reconsidered: Engaging higher education in social change.* Battle Creek, MI: Kellogg Foundation.

Awbrey, M. (1995). Questions and answers: Administrator views of the uses and value of the standards. *Social Studies Review, 35*(1), 30–33

Bacharach, S. B., & Mundell, B. L. (1993). Organizational politics in schools: Micro, macro, and logics of action. *Educational Administration Quarterly, 29*(4), 423–452.

Baez, B., & Opfer, V. D. (2000). Ideology and educational policymaking: An analysis of the religious Right. *Educational Policy, 14*(4), 582–599.

Ball, S. (1987). *The micro-politics of the school: Towards a theory of school organization.* London: Methuen.

Ball, S. (Ed.). (1990a). *Foucault and education: Discipline and knowledges.* London: Routledge.

Ball, S. (1990b). *Politics and policy making in education: Explorations in policy sociology.* London: Routledge.

Ball, S. (1998). Big policies/small world: An introduction to international perspectives in education policy. *Comparative Education, 34*(2), 19–129.

Banfield, E. C., & Wilson, J. Q. (1963). *City politics.* Cambridge, MA: Harvard University Press.

Banks, J. (1995). The historical reconstruction of knowledge about race: Implications for transformative teaching. *Educational Researcher, 24*(2), 15–25.

Banks, J. A., & McGee Banks, C. A. (1997). Reforming schools in a democratic pluralistic society. *Educational Policy, 11*(2), 183–193.

Bardach, E. (1978). *The implementation game: What happens after a bill becomes a law.* Cambridge, MA: M.I.T. Press.

Barrett, S., & Hill, M. (1984). Policy, bargaining and structure in implementation theory: Towards an integrated perspective. *Policy and Politics, 12*(3), 219–240.

Barth, R. S. (1986). On sheep and goats and school reform. *Phi Delta Kappan, 68*(4), 293–296.

Basso, K. (1979). *Portraits of the whiteman.* Cambridge: Cambridge University Press.

Bauman, Z. (1992). *Intimations of postmodernity.* London: Routledge.

Baumgartner, F., & Jones, B. (2002). *Policy dynamics.* Chicago: University of Chicago Press.

Beatty, B. R. (2000). The emotions of educational leadership: Breaking the silence. *International Journal of Leadership in Education, 3*(4), 331–357.

Becker, H. (1986). Learning from other nations for educational reform in school and adult education. In T. N. Postlethwaite (Ed.), *International educational research: Papers in honor of Torsten Husen.* Oxford: Pergamon Press.

Beh, H. G., & Diamond, M. (2000). An emerging ethical and medical dilemma: Should physicians perform sex assignment surgery on infants with ambiguous genitalia? *Michigan Journal of Gender & Law, 7,* 1–63.

Benhabib, S. (1996). Toward a deliberate model of democratic legitimacy. In S. Benhabib (Ed.), *Democracy and difference: Contesting the boundaries of the political* (pp. 67–94). Princeton, NJ: Princeton University Press.

Bell, C. S. (1995). "If I weren't involved with schools, I might be radical": Gender consciousness in context. In D. M. Dunlap & P. A. Schmuck (Eds.), *Women leading education* (pp. 288–312). Albany: State University of New York Press.

Bell, C., & Chase, S. (1993). The underrepresentation of women in school leadership. In C. Marshall (Ed.), *The new politics of race and gender* (pp. 141–154). London: Falmer Press.

Bennett, C. J. (1991). What is policy convergence and what causes it? *British Journal of Political Science, 21*(2), 215–233.

Benveniste, L. (2000). Student assessment as a political construction: The case of Uruguay. *Education Policy Analysis Archives, 8*(32).

Berliner, D. C., & Biddle, B. J. (1997). *The manufactured crisis.* Reading, MA: Addison-Wesley Longman.

Berman, P., & McLaughlin, M. (1978). *Federal programs supporting educational changes, Vol. VIII: Implementing and sustaining innovation.* Santa Monica, CA: Rand Corporation.

Berne, R. (1995). Reinventing central office. *A primer for successful schools.* Chicago: Cross City Campaign for Urban School Reform.

Bickley, R. (2002). NAACP chief convicted in school protest. *City & State,* p. B1.

Bjork, L., & Lindle, J. C. (2001). Superintendents and interest groups. *Educational Policy, 15*(1), 76–91.

Black Alliance for Educational Options. (2003). Website. Retrieved December 13, 2003, from http://www.baeo.org/home/index.php.

Blackmore, J. (1989). Educational leadership: A feminist critique and reconstruction. In J. Smythe (Ed.), *Critical perspectives on educational leadership.* New York: Falmer Press.

Blackmore, J., Kenway, J., Willis, S., & Rennie, L. (1993). What's working for girls?: The reception of gender equity policy in two Australian schools. In C. Marshall (Ed.), *The new politics of race and gender* (pp. 183–202). London. Falmer Press.

Blasé, J., & Anderson, G. (1995). *The micropolitics of educational leadership: From control to empowerment.* New York: Teachers College Press.

Bloom, L. R. (1998). *Under the sign of hope: Feminist methodology and narrative interpretation.* Albany: State University of New York Press.

Blount, J. M. (1998). *Destined to rule the schools: Women and the superintendency, 1873–1995.* Albany: State University of New York Press.

Blumer, I., & Tatum, D. B. (1999). Creating a community of allies: How one school system attempted to create an anti-racist environment. *Leadership in Education, 2*(3); 255–267.

Board of Education of Westside Community Schools v. Mergens by and through Mergens, 496 US 226 (1990).

Bobrow, D. B., & Dryzek, J. S. (1987). *Policy analysis by design.* Pittsburgh, PA: University of Pittsburgh Press.

Boggs, C. (1976). *Gramsci's marxisms.* London: Pluto Press.

Bolman, L. G., & Deal, T. E. (1997). *Reframing organizations,* 2nd ed. San Francisco: Jossey-Bass.

Borja, R. R. (2002, February 6). Study: Urban school chiefs' tenure is 4.6 years. *Education Week, 21*(21), 5.

Borman, K., Castenell, L., & Gallagher, K. (1993). Business involvement in school reform: The rise of the Business Roundtable. In C. Marshall (Ed.), *The new politics of race and gender* (pp. 69–83). London: Falmer Press.

Bourdieu, P., & Passeron, C. (1977). *Reproduction in education, society and culture.* Beverly Hills, CA: Sage.

Bowles, S., & Gintis, H. (1976). *Schooling in capitalist America: Educational reform and the contradictions of economic life.* New York: Basic Books.

Boyd, W. L. (1974). The school superintendent: Educational statesman or political strategist? *Administrator's Notebook, 22*(9), 1–4.

Boyd, W. L. (1991, April). The power of paradigms: Reconceptualizing educational policy and management. Paper presented at the Twelfth National Graduate Student Seminar in Educational Administration, Chicago.

Boyd, W. L. (2000). The "R's of school reform" and the politics of reforming or replacing public schools. *Journal of Educational Change, 1,* 225–252.

Boyles, D. (1999). Perspectives on economics and education. [Review of the book *Schools for sale: Why free market policies won't improve America's schools, and what will]* *Educational Studies, 30*(2), 168–174.

Bracey, G. W. (1999, November 2). Poverty issues get short shrift. *USA Today,* A19.

Bracey, G. W. (2002). *The war against America's public schools: Privatizing schools, commercializing education.* Boston: Allyn and Bacon.

Brantlinger, E. A. (1985). Low-income parents' opinions about the social class composition of schools. *American Journal of Education, 93*(3), 389–408.

Brantlinger, E. A. (1993). *The politics of social class in secondary school: Views of affluent and impoverished youth.* New York: Teachers College Press.

Brightman, H., & Gutmore, D. (2002). The educational-industrial complex. *Educational Forum, 66*(4), 302–308.

Brody, C. M., Witherell, C., Donald, K., & Lundblad, R. (1991). Story and voice in the education of professionals. In C. Witherell & N. Noddings (Eds.), *Stories lives tell: Narrative and dialogue in education* (pp. 257–278). New York, NY: Teachers College Press.

Brown v. Board of Education, 347 US 483 (1954).

Brown, K. (2004). Leadership for social justice and equity: Weaving a transformative framework and pedagogy. *Education Administration Quarterly, 40*(1), 79–110.

Brown, K. M., & Anafara, V. A, Jr. (2002). The walls of division crumble as ears, mouths, minds and hearts open: A unified profession of middle-level administrators and teachers. *International Journal of Leadership in Education, 5*(1), 33–49.

Broz, A. N. (1998). *Nabozny v. Podlesny:* A teenager's struggle to end anti-gay violence in public schools. *Northwestern University Law Review, 92,* 750–778.

Brunner, C. (2003). Invisible, limited, and emerging discourse: Research practices that restrict and/or increase access for women and persons of color to the superintendency. *Journal of School Leadership, 12*(4), 428–450.

Brunner, C., Grogan, M., & Bjork, L. (2002). Shifts in the discourse defining the superintendency: Historical and current foundations of the position. In Murphy, J. (Ed.), *The educational leadership challenge: Re-*

defining leadership for the 21st century (pp. 211–238). Chicago: National Society for the Study of Education.

Bryant, T. J. (1999). May we teach tolerance? Establishing the parameters of academic freedom in pubic schools. *University of Pittsburgh Law Review, 60,* 579–639.

Bryk, A. S., Sebring, P. B., Kerbow, D., Rollow, S., & Easton, J. Q. (1998). *Charting Chicago school reform: Democratic localism as a lever for change.* Boulder, CO: Westview Press.

Burlington Free Press. (2003, May 20). Editorial: Arriving from Africa. Website. Retrieved December 9, 2003, from http://www.burlingtonfreepress.com/specialnews/bantu/edit2.htm.

Burrup, P. E., Brimley, V., Jr., & Garfield, R. R. (1999). *Financing education in a climate of change,* 8th ed. Boston: Allyn & Bacon.

Business Roundtable (2002). You'll be quizzed on the No Child Left Behind Law. Washington, DC: Business Roundtable. Retrieved December 16, 2003, from http://www.businessroundtable.org/pdf/826.pdf.

Butler, J. (1993). *Bodies that matter: On the discursive limits of sex.* New York: Routledge.

Callahan, R. E. (1962). *Education and the cult of efficiency: A study of the social forces that have shaped the administration of public schools.* Chicago: University of Chicago Press.

Callahan, R. E. (1967). *The superintendent of schools: An historical analysis, final report, S-212.* Washington, DC: US Office of Education, HEW.

Cambron-McCabe, N. (2004). Policy challenges confronting the preparation and development of school leaders: Implications for social justice. In C. Marshall & M. Oliva (Eds.) *Leadership for social justice: Making it happen.* Boston: Allyn & Bacon.

Campbell, J. C., Baskin, M. A., Baumgartner, F. R., & Halpern, H. P. (1989). Afterward on policy communities: A framework for comparative research. *Governance: An International Journal of Policy and Administration, 2*(1), 86–94.

Campbell, R. F., & Mazzoni, T. L., Jr., (1976). *State policy making for the public schools.* Berkeley, CA: McCutcheon.

Capper, C. A. (1988). *Students with severe disabilities in public schools: Policy in practice.* Nashville, TN: Vanderbilt University.

Carlson, D. (1993). The politics of educational policy: Urban school reform in unsettling times. *Educational Policy, 7*(2), 149–165.

Carnoy, M. (2002). Latin America: The new dependency and education reform. In H. Daun (Ed.), *Educational restructuring in the context of globalization and na-*

tional policy (pp. 289–322). New York: Routledge-Falmer.

Carspecken, P. F. (1996). *Critical ethnography in educational research: A theoretical and practical guide.* New York: Routledge.

Casella, R. (2002). Where policy meets the pavement: Stages of public involvement in the prevention of school violence. *International Journal of Qualitative Studies in Education, 15*(3), 349–372.

Casey, K. (1993). *I answer with my life: Life histories of women teachers working for social change.* New York: Routledge.

Center for Policy Research in Education. (1989). *Graduating from high school: New standards in the states.* CPRE Policy Briefs. New Brunswick, NJ: Rutgers University Press.

Chase, S. (1995). *Ambiguous empowerment: The work narratives of women school superintendents.* Amherst: University of Massachusetts Press.

Children's Defense Fund (2003). Website. Retrieved December 13, 2003, from http://www.childrensdefense.org/.

Christensen, C. M., & Overdorf, M. (2000). Meeting the challenge of disruptive innovation. *Harvard Business Review, 78*(2), 66–76.

Chubb, J. E., & Moe, T. M. (1990). *Politics, markets, and America's schools.* Washington, DC: Brookings Institution.

Cibulka, J. G. (1995). Policy analysis and the study of the politics of education. In J. D. Scribner & D. H. Layton (Eds.), *The study of educational politics* (pp. 105–125). Washington, DC: Falmer Press.

Cibulka, J. G. (2001a). The changing role of interest groups in education: Nationalization and the new politics of education productivity. *Educational Policy, 15*(1), 12–40.

Cibulka, J. G. (2001b). Old wine, new bottles. *Education Next, 1*(4), 28–35.

Citizens for Excellence in Education (2003). Website. Retrieved December 13, 2003, from http://www.pfaw.org/pfaw/general/default.aspx?oid=11396.

Clark, D. L., & Astuto, T. A. (1986). The significance and permanence of changes in federal education policy. *Educational Researcher, 15*(8), 4–13.

Clark, D. L., & Astuto, T. A. (1989). The disjunction of federal educational policy and national educational needs in the 1990s. *Politics of Education Association Yearbook, 4*(5), 11–25.

Clemons, R. S., & McBeth, M. K. (2001). Public policy praxis: Theory and pragmatism: A case approach. Upper Saddle River, NJ: Prentice Hall.

Clinton, B. (1992). The Clinton plan for excellence in education. *Phi Delta Kappan, 74*(2), 131, 134–138.

Clinton, H. R. (1996). *It takes a village: And other lessons children teach us.* New York: Simon and Schuster.

Cobb, R., & Elder, C. (1983). *Participation in American politics: The dynamics of agenda-building.* Baltimore, MD: Johns Hopkins University Press.

Cohen, M. D., March, J. G., & Olsen, J. P. (1972). A garbage can model of organizational choice. *Administrative Science Quarterly, 17,* 1–25.

Collins, P. H. (1990). *Black feminist thought: Knowledge, consciousness, and the politics of empowerment.* New York: Routledge.

Collins, P. H. (1998). *Fighting words: Black women & the search for justice.* Minneapolis: University of Minnesota Press.

Collins, P. H. (2000). *Black feminist thought: Knowledge, consciousness, and the politics of empowerment.* New York: Routledge. (Original work published 1990.)

Connell, R. W. (1996). Teaching the boys: New research on masculinity, and gender strategies for schools. *Teachers College Record, 98*(2), 206–235.

Conners, D. (1981). *Power and the polls: A community power structure and its implications for a school bond referendum.* American Educational Research Organization: Los Angeles.

Cooper, B. S., Fusarelli, L. D., & Randall, E. V. (2004). *Better policies, better schools: Theories and applications.* Boston: Pearson Education.

Cornbleth, C., & Waugh, D. (1995). *The great speckled bird: Multicultural politics and education policymaking.* New York: St. Martin's Press.

Corrigan, D. (2001). The changing role of schools and higher education institutions with respect to community-based interagency collaboration and interpersonal partnerships. *Peabody Journal of Education, 75*(3), 176–195.

Corrigan, D., & Bishop, K. K. (1997, July). Creating family-centered integrated service systems and interprofessional educational programs. *Social Work in Education, 19*(3), 149.

Corson, D. (1995). Ideology and distortion in the administration of outgroup interests. In D. Corson (Ed.), *Discourse and power in educational organizations* (pp. 87–110). Cresskill, NJ: Hampton Press.

Corson, D. (2000). Emancipatory leadership. *International Journal of Leadership in Education, 3*(2), 93–120.

Crain, R. L. (1968). *The politics of school desegregation: Comparative case studies of community structure and policymaking.* Chicago: Aldine.

Crotty, M. (1998). *The foundations of social research: Meaning and perspective in the research process.* Thousand Oaks, CA: Sage.

Crowson, R., Wong, K., & Apay, A. (2000). The quiet reform in American education: Policy issues and conceptual challenges in the school-to-work transition. *Educational Policy, 14*(2), 241–258.

Cuban, L. (2001). *Oversold and underused: Computers in the classroom.* Cambridge, MA: Harvard University Press.

Cubberly, E. P. (1929). *Public school administration.* Boston: Houghton Mifflin.

Czubaj, C. A. (1996). Maintaining teacher motivation. *Education, 116*(3), 372–379.

Dahl, R. A. (1961). *Who governs?: Democracy and power in an American city.* New Haven, CT: Yale University Press.

Dale, R. (1999). Specifying globalization effects on national policy: A focus on the mechanisms. *Journal of Education Policy, 14*(1), 1–17.

Daun, H. (Ed.). (2002). *Educational Restructuring in the Context of Globalization and National Policy.* New York: Routledge Falmer.

De Leon, P., & Resnick-Terry, P. (1999). Comparative policy analysis: Deja vu all over again. *Journal of Comparative Policy Analysis: Research and Practice, 1*(1), 9–22.

Derqui, J. M. G. (2001). Educational decentralization policies in Argentina and Brazil: Exploring the new trends. *Journal of Educational Policy, 16*(6), 561–583.

Dery, D. (1990). *Data and policy change: The fragility of data in the political context.* Boston: Kluwer Academic.

Dillard, C. B. (1995). Leading with her life: An African American feminist (re)interpretation of leadership for an urban high school principal. *Educational Administration Quarterly, 31*(4), 539–563.

Doherty, K. M., & Skinner, R. A. (2003, January 9). Quality counts: Introduction: State of the states. *Education Week.* Retrieved on December 18, 2003, from http://www.edweek.org/sreports/qc03/templates/article.cfm?slug=17sos.h22&keywords=accountability.

Dolan, K., & Ford, L. E. (1995). Women in the state legislatures: Feminist identity and legislative behaviors. *American Politics Quarterly, 23*(1), 96–108.

Drew, E. (1979). *Senator.* New York: Simon & Schuster.

Ducharme, E., & Agne, R. (1989). Professors of education: Uneasy residents of academe. In R. Wisniewski & E. Ducharme (Eds.), *The professors of teaching.* Albany: State University of New York Press.

Dura-Bellat, M. (2000). Social inequalities in the French education system: The joint effect of individual and contextual factors. *Journal of Educational Policy, 15*(1), 33–40.

Dye, T. R. (1992). *Understanding public policy* (7th ed.). Englewood Cliffs, NJ: Prentice Hall.

Dyer, C. (1999). Researching the implementation of educational policy: A backward mapping approach. *Comparative Education, 35*(1), 45–61.

Easton, D. (1965a). *A framework for political analysis.* Englewood Cliffs, NJ: Prentice Hall.

Easton, D. (1965b). *A systems analysis of political life.* New York: John Wiley.

Ebert, T. (1992). Political semiosis in/of American cultural studies. *American Journal of Semiotics, 8*(1/2), 113–135.

Edelman, M. (1977). *Political language: Words that succeed and policies that fail.* New York: Academic Press.

Edelman, M. (1988a). *Political language: Words that succeed and policies that fail.* New York: Academic Press.

Edelman, M. (1988b). *Constructing the political spectacle.* Chicago: University of Chicago Press.

Edelman, M. W. (1992). *The measure of our success: A letter to my children and yours.* Boston: Beacon Press.

Educational Testing Service (2002). *The twin challenges of mediocrity and inequality: Literacy in the U.S. from an international perspective.* Princeton, NJ: Educational Testing Service.

Eisenstein, H. (1993). A telling tale from the field. In J. Blackmore & J. Kenway (Eds.), *Gender matters in educational administration and policy* (pp. 1–8). London: Falmer Press.

Elazar, D. (1984). *American federalism: A view from the states.* New York: Harper and Row.

Elmore, R. F. (1978). Organizational models of social program implementation. *Pubic Policy, 26*(2), 185–228.

Elmore, R. F. (1979–1980). Backward mapping: Implementation and policy design. *Political Science Quarterly, 94*(4), 601–616.

Elshtain, J. B. (1997). *Real politics: At the center of everyday life.* Baltimore, MD: The Johns Hopkins University Press.

English, F. (1991). Visual traces in schools and the reproduction of social inequities. In K. M. Borman, P. Swami, & L. D. Wagstaff (Eds.), *Contemporary issues in U.S. education.* (pp. 84–104). Norwood, NJ: Ablex.

English, F. (2003). *The postmodern challenge to the theory and practice of educational administration.* Springfield, IL: Charles C Thomas.

Enslin, P., & Pendlebury, S. (2000). Looking others in the eye: Rights and gender in South African education policy. *Journal of Education Policy, 15*(4), 431–440.

Eulau, H., & Wahlke, J. (1978). *The politics of representation: Continuities in theory and research.* Beverly Hills, CA: Sage.

Ferguson, K. E. (1984). *The feminist case against bureaucracy.* Philadelphia: Temple University Press.

Feuerstein, A., & Opfer, V. D. (1998). School board chairmen and school superintendents: An analysis of perceptions concerning special interest groups and educational governance. *Journal of School Leadership, 8,* 373–398.

Fine, M. (1991). *Framing dropouts: Notes on the politics of an urban high school.* Albany: State University of New York Press.

Firestone, W. A. (1989a). Educational policy as an ecology of games. *Educational Researcher, 18*(7), 18–24.

Firestone, W. A. (1989b). Using reform: Conceptualizing district initiative. *Educational Evaluation and Policy Analysis, 11*(2), 151–164.

Firestone, W. A., & Fisler, J. L. (2002). Politics, community, and leadership in a school-university partnership. *Educational Administration Quarterly, 38*(4), 449–493.

Fischer, F. (1989). Beyond the rationality project: Policy analysis and the postpositivist challenge. *Policy Studies Journal, 17,* 941–951.

Fischer, F., & Forester, J. (1993). In F. Fischer & J. Forester, *The argumentative turn in policy analysis and planning* (pp. 1–17). Durham, NC: Duke University Press.

Fisher, J. (1993). *Out of the shadows: Women, resistance and politics in South America.* London: Latin American Bureau.

Fishkin, J. D. (1997). *Voice of the people: Public opinion and democracy.* New Haven, CT: Yale University Press.

Foley, D. E. (1996). The silent Indian as cultural production. In B. A. Levinson, D. E. Foley, and D. C. Holand (Eds.), *The cultural production of the educated person* (pp. 79–91). Albany: State University of New York Press.

Fordham, S. (1993). Those loud black girls: (Black) women, silence, and gender "passing in the academy. *Anthropology and Education Quarterly, 24*(1), 3–32.

Forester, J. (1993). *Critical theory, public policy, and planning practice: Toward a critical pragmatism.* Albany: State University of New York Press.

Forgione, P. D. (2000). Overwhelmed by assessment, but not the usual type. *The School Administrator.* Accessed 11/20/03 at http://www.aasa.org/publications/sa/2000_12/forgione.htm.

Forum on Child and Family Statistics. (2002). *America's children: Key national indicators of well-being*

2002. Washington, DC: Federal Interagency Forum on Child and Family Statistics.

Foucault, M. (1981). The order of discourse. In R. Young (Ed.), *Untying the text.* London: Routledge.

Fowler, F. C. (2000). *Policy studies for educational leaders: An introduction.* Upper Saddle River, NJ: Prentice Hall.

Frankerberg, E., Lee, C., & Orfield, G. (2003). *A multiracial society with segregated schools: are we losing the dream?* Cambridge, MA: Harvard Civil Rights Project.

Franstzich, S. E., & Percy, S. L. (1994). *American government: The political game.* Madison, WI: Brown & Benchmark.

Fraser, N. (1989). *Unruly practices: Power, discourse and gender in contemporary social theory.* Minneapolis: University of Minnesota Press.

Fraser, N. (1994). Rethinking the public sphere: A contribution to the critique of actually existing democracy. In C. Calhoun, *Habermas and the public sphere* (pp. 109–142). Cambridge, MA: MIT Press.

Fraser, N. (1997). *Justice interruptus: critical reflections on the "postsocialist" condition.* New York: Routledge.

Fraynd, D. J., & Capper, C. A. (2003). Do you have any idea who you just hired?!? A study of open and closeted sexual minority K–12 administrators. *Journal of School Leadership, 13*(1), 86–124.

Freedman, S. (1990). Weeding women out of "woman's true profession": The effects of the reforms on teaching and teachers. In J. Antler & S. K. Biklen (Eds.), *Changing education: Women as radicals and conservators* (pp. 239–256). Albany: State University of New York Press.

Freire, P. (1970). *Pedagogy of the oppressed.* New York: Herder and Herder.

Freire, P. (1985). *The politics of education.* South Hadley, MA: Bergin & Garvey.

Freire, P. (1993). *Pedagogy of the oppressed.* New York: Continuum.

Fritzberg, G. J. (2001). From rhetoric to reality: Opportunity-to-learn standards and the integrity of American public school reform. *Teacher Education Quarterly, 28*(1), 169–187.

Fuhrman, S. H., & Elmore, R. F. (1995). Ruling out rules: The evolution of deregulation in state education policy. *Teachers College Record, 97*(2), 279–310.

Fulcher, G. (1989). *Disabling policies? A comparative approach to education policy and disability.* New York: Routledge.

Fullan, M. (1991). *The new meaning of educational change.* London: Cassell.

Fullan, M., & Hargreaves, A. (1996). *What's worth fighting for in your school?* New York: Teachers College Press.

Fussell, J. A. (2002). Slip of the tongue tickles. *The News & Observer,* p. 7D.

Gaine, C. (1989). On getting equal opportunities policies—and keeping them. In M. Cole (Ed.), *Education for equality: Some guidance for good practice* (pp. 25–37). London: Routledge.

Garms, W., Guthrie, J., & Pierce, L. C. (1978). *School finance: The economics and politics of public education.* Englewood Cliffs, NJ: Prentice-Hall.

Gerstl-Pepin, C. I. (1998). *The prospects for democratic school reform: A critical examination of the A+ Schools Program.* Unpublished doctoral dissertation, University of North Carolina, Chapel Hill.

Gerstl-Pepin, C. I. (2002). Media (mis)representations of education in the 2000 presidential election. *Educational Policy, 16*(1), 37–55.

Gerstl-Pepin, C. I. (2003, April). *Native American mascots: Deconstructing racist and sexist policies.* Paper presentation at the American Educational Research Association, Chicago.

Gewirtz, S. (1998). Conceptualizing social justice in education: Mapping the territory. *Journal of Education Policy, 13*(4), 469–484.

Gewirtz, S., Ball, S., & Bowe, R. (1995). *Markets, choice and equity in education.* Buckingham, UK: Open University Press.

Gilliam, W. S., Ripple, C. H., Zigler, E. F., & Leiter, V. (2000). Evaluating child and family demonstration initiatives: Lessons from the Comprehensive Child Development Program. *Early Childhood Research Quarterly, 15*(1), 41–59.

Gilligan, C. (1982). *In a different voice: Psychological theory and women's development.* Cambridge, MA: Harvard University Press.

Gillon, S. M. (2000). *"That's not what we meant to do": Reform and its unintended consequences in twentieth-century America.* New York: W.W. Norton & Company.

Ginsberg, R. (1990). Boss Behrman reforms the schools: The 1912 New Orleans school reform. In D. N. Plank & R. Ginsberg (Eds.), *Southern cities, Southern schools: Public education in the urban south* (pp. 109–132). New York: Greenwood Press.

Giroux, H. A. (1998). Education incorporated? *Educational Leadership, 56*(2), 12–17.

Gitlin, A. (Ed.). (1994). *Power and method: Political activism and educational research.* New York: Routledge.

Gitlin, T. (1995). *The twilight of common dreams: Why America is wracked by culture wars.* New York: Henry Holt.

Glass, T., Bjork, L. B., Brunner, C. C., et al. (2000). *The 2000 study of the American superintendency: A look at the superintendent of education in the new millennium.* Paper presented at the American Association of School Administrators, Arlington, VA.

Goals 2000. (1994, January 26). *Raleigh News & Observer,* p. 9A.

Goertz, M. E., & Stiefel, L. (1998). School-level resource allocation in urban public schools. *Journal of Educational Finance, 23*(spring), 435–446.

Goldring, E. B., & Hausman, C.S. (1999). Reasons for prenatal choice of urban schools. *Education Policy, 14*(5), 469–490.

González, F. E. (1998). Formations of Mexicananess: Trenzas de identidades múliples. Growing up Mexicana: Braids of multiple identities. *Qualitative Studies in Education, 11*(1), 81–102.

Goodkind, J. R., & Foster-Fishman, P. G. (2002). Integrating diversity and fostering interdependence: Ecological lessons learned about refugee participation in multiethnic communities. *Journal of Community Psychology, 30*(4), 398–409.

Goodsell, C. T. (1990). Emerging issues in public administration. In N. B. Lynn & A. Wildavsky, *Public administration: The state of the discipline* (pp. 495–509). Chatham, NJ: Chatham House.

Goodwyn, L. (1976). *Democratic promise: The populist moment in America.* New York: Oxford University Press.

Goodwyn, L. (1991). *Breaking the barrier: The rise of solidarity in Poland.* New York: Oxford University Press.

Gough, N. (1999). Globalization and school curriculum change: Locating a transnational imaginary. *Education Policy, 14*(1), 73–84.

Green, P. C. III (1999). Can state constitutional provisions eliminate de facto segregation in the public schools? *Journal of Negro Education, 68*(2), 138–153.

Greene, K. R. (1992). Models of school board policymaking. *Educational Administration Quarterly, 28*(2), 220–236.

Greenstone, J. D., & Peterson, P. E. (1983). Inquiry and social function: Two views of educational practice and policy. In L. S. Shulman and G. Sykes (Eds.), *Handbook of teaching policy.* New York: Longman.

Griffith, A. I. (1992). Educational policy as text and action. *Educational Policy, 6*(4), 415–428.

Grissmer, D., Flanagan, A., Kawata, J., & Williamson, S. (2000). *Improving student achievement: What state NAEP test scores tell us.* Santa Monica, CA: Rand Corporation.

Grogan, M. (2000). The short tenure of a woman superintendent: A clash of gender and politics. *Journal of School Leadership, 10*(2), 104–130.

Grogan, M. (1999). A feminist poststructuralist account of collaboration: A model for the superintendency. In C. Brunner (Ed.), *Sacred dreams: Women and the superintendency* (pp. 141–161). Albany: State University of New York Press.

Gronn, P. C. (1983). Talk as the work: The accomplishment of school administration. *Administrative Science Quarterly, 28,* 1–21.

Guerra, P., Jackson, J., Madsen, C., Thompson, H. Y., Ward, J., et al. (1992). *Site-based management and special education: Theories, implications, and recommendations.* Paper presented at the University Council of Educational Administration, Minneapolis, MN.

Guthrie, J. W. (1993). Do America's schools need a "Dow Jones Index?" *Phi Delta Kappan, 74*(7), 523–529.

Gutmann, A. (1987). *Democratic education.* Princeton, NJ: Princeton University Press.

Habermas, J. (1975). *Legitimation crisis.* London: Heineman Educational Books.

Habermas, J. (1994). *The structural transformation of the public sphere: An inquiry into the category of bourgois society.* Cambridge, MA: MIT Press.

Hamann, E., & Lane, B. (2002). "We're from the state and we're here to help": State-level innovations in support of high school improvement. Accessed 11/24/03 at http://www.lab.brown.edu/pubs/csr/.

Hamann, E. T., & Lane, B. (2003). *How lessons are learned and applied at the SEA level: An anatomy of Maine's guidance of high school reform.* Paper presented at the annual meeting of the American Educational Research Association, New Orleans.

Hannaway, J. (1989). *Managers managing: The workings of an administrative system.* New York: Oxford University Press.

Hanson, E. M. (1979). *Educational administration and organizational behavior.* Boston: Allyn & Bacon.

Harding, S. (Ed.), (1987). *Feminism and methodology.* Bloomington: Indiana University Press.

Hargreaves, A. (1990, April). *Individualism and individuality: Reinterpreting the teacher culture.* Paper presented at the meeting of the American Educational Research Association, Boston.

Hargreaves, A., & Fullan, M. (1998). *What's worth fighting for out there?* New York: Teachers College Press.

Harvey Milk School. (2003). Website. Retrieved on December 13, 2003, from http://www.hmi.org/GeneralInfoAndDonations/QAndAsonHMHS/default.aspx.

Hasazi, S., Johnston, A. P., Liggett, A. M., & Schattman, R. A. (1994). A qualitative policy study of the least restrictive environment provision of the Individuals with Disabilities Education Act. *Exceptional Children, 60*(6), 491–507.

Heath, S. B., & McLaughlin, M. W. (Eds.). (1993). *Identity and inner-city youth: Beyond ethnicity and gender.* New York: Teachers College Press.

Heidenheimer, A. J., Heclo, H., & Adams, C. T. (1990). *Comparative public policy.* New York, NY: St. Martin's Press.

Heineman, R. A., Bluhm, W. T., Peterson, S. A., & Kearny, E. N. (1997). *The world of the policy analyst: Rationality, values, and politics* (2nd ed.). Chatham, NJ: Chatham House.

Henry, M., Lingard, B., Rizvi, F., & Taylor, S. (1999). Working with/against globalization in education. *Education Policy, 14*(1), 85–97.

Hergert, L. F., Phlegar, J. M., & Pereze Seles, M. E. (1991). *Kindle the spark: An action guide for schools committed to the success of every child.* Andover, MA: The Regional Laboratory for Educational Improvement of the Northeast and Islands.

Herrington, C. D. (2000). Religion, public schools, and hyper-pluralism: Is there a new religious war? *Educational Policy, 14*(5), 548–563).

Hess, F. M. (2002). *Revolution at the margins: The impact of competition on urban school systems.* Washington, DC: Brookings Institution Press.

Hess, F. M., & Leal, D. L. (2001). The opportunity to engage: How race, class, and institutions structure access to educational deliberation. *Educational Policy, 15*(3), 474–490.

Hess, G. A. (1999). Understanding achievement (and other) changes under Chicago school reform. *Educational Evaluation and Policy Analysis, 21*(1), 67–83.

Hildegartner, S., & Bosk, C. (1988). The rise and fall of social problems: A public arenas model. *American Journal of Sociology, 94*(1), 215–228.

Hirschman, A. O. (1970). Exit, voice and loyalty: Responses to decline in firms, organizations, and states. Cambridge, MA: Harvard University Press.

hooks, b. (1984). *Feminist theory from margin to center.* Boston: South End Press.

hooks, b. (1989). *Talking back: Thinking feminist, thinking black.* Boston: South End Press.

hooks, b. (1994). *Teaching to transgress: Education as the practice of freedom.* New York: Routledge.

hooks, b. (1996). *Reel to real: Race, sex, and class at the movies.* New York: Routledge.

Hollingsworth, S. (1997). Feminist praxis as the basis for teacher education: A critical challenge. In C. Marshall (Ed.), *Feminist critical policy analysis: A perspective from primary and secondary schooling* (pp. 165–182). London: Falmer Press.

House, E. R. (1998). *Schools for sale: Why free market policies won't Improve America's schools, and what will.* New York: Teachers College Press.

Hoyle, E. (1999). The two faces of micropolitics. *School Leadership & Management, 19*(2), 213–222.

Hunter, F. (1953). *Community, power, structure: A study of decision makers.* Chapel Hill: University of North Carolina Press.

Hutmacher, W., Cochrane, D., & Bottani, N. (Eds.). (2001). *In pursuit of equity in education: Using international indicators to compare equity policies.* Boston: Kluwer Academic.

Iannaconne, L., & Lutz, F. W. (1970). *Politics, power and policy: The governing of local school districts.* Columbus, OH: Charles E. Merrill.

Iannaccone, L. (1975). *Educational policy systems.* Fort Lauderdale, FL: Nova University Press.

Iannacone, L., & Lutz, F. W. (1995). The crucible for democracy: The local arena. In J. D. Scribner & D. H. Layton, *The study of educational politics, the 1994 commemorative yearbook of the Politics of Education Association.* Philadelphia: Falmer Press.

Jackson, B. (1999). Getting inside history—against all odds: African-American women school superintendents. In C. Brunner (Ed.), *Sacred dreams: Women and the superintendency* (pp. 141–161). Albany: State University of New York Press

Jackson, D. (2002/2003, winter). McDonalds or IBM? Rethinking schools, 17(2). Website. Retrieved 12/13/02 from http://www.rethinkingschools.org/archive/17_02/IBM172.shtml.

Jansson, B. S. (2003). *Becoming and effective policy advocate: From policy practice to social justice.* Pacific Grove, CA: Brooks/Cole/Thomson Learning.

Jeffords, J. M. (2001). *My declaration of independence.* New York: Simon & Schuster.

Jennings, M. K., & Zeigler, H. (1970). *Response styles and politics: The case of school boards.* Paper presented at the meeting of the American Educational Research Association, Minneapolis, MN.

Jones, R. (2000). The new minority to protect under Title IX. *The Education Digest, 65*(8), 20–26.

Jordan, G. (1981). Iron triangles, wooly corporatism and elastic nets: Images of the policy process. *Journal of American Public Policy, 1,* 95–123.

Kaestle, C. F., & Smith, M. S. (1982). The federal role in elementary and secondary education, 1940–1980. *Harvard Education Review, 52*(4).

Kahne, J. (1994). Democratic communities, equity, and excellence: A Deweyan reframing of educational policy analysis. *Educational Evaluation and Policy Analysis, 16*(3), 233–248.

Kalodner, H. I. (1990). Overview of judical activism in educational litigation. In B. Flicker (Ed.), *Justice and school systems: The role of the courts in educational litigation* (pp. 3–22). Philadelphia: Temple University Press.

Kanter, R. M. (1977). *Men and women of the corporation.* New York: Basic Books.

Kaplan, T. J. (1993). Reading policy narratives: Beginnings, middles, and ends. In F. Fischer & J. Forester (Eds.), *The argumentative turn in policy analysis and planning* (pp. 167–185). Durham, NC: Duke University Press.

Kathlene, L. (1990). A new approach to understanding the impact of gender on the legislative process. In J. M. Nielson (Ed.), *Feminist research methods: Exemplary readings in the social sciences,* (pp. 238–260). Boulder, CO: Westview Press.

Katz, M., & Fine, M. (1997). Poking around: Outsiders view Chicago school reform. *Teachers College Record, 99*(1), 117–158.

Kaul, C. (2002). *Statistical handbook on the world's children.* Westport, CT: Oryx Press.

Kelly, G. P., & Elliot, C. M. (1982). *Women's education in the third world: Comparative perspectives.* Albany: State University of New York Press.

Kenway, J., & Fitzclarence, L. (1997). Masculinity, violence and schooling: Challenging "poisonous pedagogies." *Gender and Education, 9*(1), 117–133.

Kerr, C. (1983). *The future of industrial societies: Convergence or continuing diversity?* Cambridge, MA: Harvard University Press.

Kinchloe, J., & McLaren, P. (1994). Rethinking critical theory and qualitative research. In N. K. Denzin & Y. S. Lincoln (Eds.), *Handbook of qualitative research* (pp. 138–157). Thousand Oaks, CA: Sage.

King, A. (1981). What do elections decide? In D. Butler, H. R. Penniman, & A. Ranney (Eds.), *Democracy at the polls: A comparative study of competitive national elections* (pp. 293–324). Washington, DC: American Enterprise Institute.

King, R. A., Swanson, A. D., & Sweetland, S. R. (2003) *School finance: Achieving high standards with equity and efficiency.* Boston: Allyn & Bacon.

Kingdon, J. W. (1984). *Agendas, alternatives, and public policies.* New York: HarperCollins.

Kingdon, J. W. (2003). *Agendas, alternatives, and public policies* (2nd ed.). New York: Longman.

Koppich, J. (1994). The politics of policy making for children. In L. Adler & S. Gardner (Eds.). *The politics of linking schools and social services* (pp. 51–62). Washington, DC: Falmer Press.

Koretz, D., McCaffrey, D., & Sullivan, T. (2001, September 14). Local flexibility within an accountability system. *Educational Policy Analysis Archives, 9*(44). From http://olam.ed.asu.edu/epaa/v9n44 .html.

Krashen, S. D. (1999). *Condemned without a trial: Bogus arguments against bilingual education.* Portsmouth, NH: Heinemann.

Labaree, D. F. (1997). Public goods, private goods: The American struggle over educational goals. *American Educational Research Journal, 34*(1), 39–81.

Ladd, H. F. (1998). *Local government tax and land use policies in the United States.* Northampton, MA: Edward Elgar.

Ladson-Billings, G. (1994). *The dreamkeepers: Successful teachers of African American children.* San Francisco: Jossey-Bass.

Ladson-Billings, G., & Tate, W. F. IV. (1995). Toward a critical race theory of education. *Teachers College Record, 97*(1), 47–69.

Laible, J. (1997). Feminist analysis of sexual harassment policy: A critique of the ideal of community. In C. Marshall, *Feminist critical policy analysis: A perspective from primary and secondary schooling* (pp. 201–215). London: Falmer Press.

Laible, J. (2000). Loving epistemology: What I hold critical in my life, faith, and profession. *International Journal of Qualitative Studies in Education, 13*(6). 683–692.

LaMagdeleine, D. (1992). "Deseg" talk: Educational policymakers' divergent assumptions in "two towns". *Educational Administration Quarterly, 28*(4), 473–503.

Lamont, M., & Lareau, A. (1988). Cultural capital: Allusions, gaps, and glissandos in recent theoretical developments. *Sociological Theory, 6*(2), 153–168.

Larson, C. L. (1997). Is the land of Oz an alien nation? A sociopolitical study of school community conflict. *Educational Administration Quarterly, 33*(3), 312–350.

Larson, C. L., & Ovando, C. J. (2000). *The color of bureaucracy: The politics of equity in multicultural school communities.* Belmont, CA: Wadsworth.

Larson, K. (2002). *Commercialism in schools.* Eugene: University of Oregon Press.

Lather, P. (1991). *Getting smart: Feminist research and pedagogy with/in the postmodern.* London: Routledge.

Lau v. Nichols, 414 US 563 (1974).

Lee, J. (2001). School reform initiatives as balancing acts: Policy variation and educational convergences among Japan, Korea, England and the United States. *Education Policy Analysis Archives, 9*(13). Retrieved at http://epaa.asu.edu/epaa/v9n13.html.

Leithwood, K. (2001). School leadership in the context of accountability policies. *International Journal of Leadership in Education, 4*(3), 217–235.

Levin, B. (2000). *Conceptualizing the process of education reform from an international perspective.* Paper presented at the American Educational Research Association, New Orleans.

Levin, H. M. (2000). A comprehensive framework for evaluating educational vouchers. *Educational Evaluation and Policy Analysis, 24*(3), 159–174.

Levinson, B. A., & Holland, D. (1996). The cultural production of the educated person: An introduction. In B. A. Levinson, D. E. Foley, & D. C. Holland (Eds.), *The cultural production of the educated person* (pp. 1–56). Albany: State University of New York Press.

Levinson, B. A. U., & Sutton, M. (2001). Introduction: Policy as/in practice—A sociocultural approach to the study of educational policy. In M. Sutton & B. A. U. Levinson (Eds.), *Policy as practice: Toward a comparative sociocultural analysis of educational policy.* Westport, CT: Ablex.

Lewis, A. C. (2002). New ESEA extends choice to school officials. *Phi Delta Kappan, 83*(6), 423–425.

Lieberman, M. (1997). The teacher unions. New York: The Free Press.

Lindblom, C. E. (1959). The science of muddling through. *Public Administration Review, 19,* 79–88.

Lindblom, C. E., & Cohen, D. K. (1979). Useable knowledge: Social science and social problem solving. New Haven, CT: Yale University Press.

Lipka, J. (2002). *Schooling for self-determination: Research on the effects of including native language and culture in the schools.* Washington, D.C.: Office of Educational Research and Improvement.

Lipman, P. (1998). *Race, class and power in school restructuring.* Albany: State University of New York Press.

Lopez. G. R. (2003). The (racially-neutral) politics of education: The need for a critical race theory perspective. *Educational Administration Quarterly, 39*(1), 68–94.

Lopez, G. R., Scribner, J. D., & Mahitivanichcha, K. (2001). Redefining parental involvement: Lessons from high-performing migrant-impacted schools. *American Educational Research Journal, 38*(2), 253–288.

Lorde, A. (2001). Our difference is our strength. In B. Ryan (Ed.). *Identity politics and the women's movement* (pp. 315–319). New York: New York University Press.

Lugg, C. (2003). Sissies, faggots, lezzies and dykes: Gender, sexual orientation and a new politics of education? *Educational Administration Quarterly, 39*(1), 95–134.

Lugg, C. A. (1996). *For God and country: Conservatism and American school policy.* New York: Peter Lang.

Lugg, C. A. (1998). The religious right and public education: The paranoid politics of homophobia. *Educational Policy, 12*(3), 267–283.

Lugg, C. A. (2000). Reading, writing, and reconstructionism: The Christian right and the politics of public education. *Eduational Policy, 14*(5), 622–637.

Lugg, C. A. (2001). The Christian right: A cultivated collection of interest groups. *Educational Policy, 15*(1), 41–57.

Lusi, S. F., (1997). *The role of state departments of education in complex education reform.* New York: Teachers College Press.

Lutz, F. W. (1996). Vulnerability of the vulnerability thesis. *Peabody Journal of Education, 71*(2), 24–40.

Lyman, L. L. (2002, November 1). *Leading a high poverty school: Case study of a principal.* Paper presented at the University Council of Educational Administration, Pittsburgh, PA.

Lytle, J. (2001). Emergent governance models for public schools and school districts: The case of New Jersey, of Urban districts in New Jersey, and the challenges of being an urban district superintendent in New Jersey. CEIC Review. Philadelphia: Temple University Laboratory for Student Success.

MacGillivray, I. K. (2000). Educational equity for gay, lesbian, bisexual, transgendered, and queer/questioning students: The demands of democracy and social justice for America's schools. *Education and Urban Society, 32*(3), 303–323.

Mackinac Center for Public Policy. (1998). *Collective bargaining: Bringing education to the table.* Michigan: Munk, L. R. G.

MacKinnon, C. (1982). Feminism, marxism, method and the state. In N. Keohane, M. Z. Rosaldo, & B. C. Gelpi (Eds.), *Feminist theory: A critique of ideology* (pp. 1–30). Chicago: University of Chicago Press.

MacKinnon, C. (1989). *Toward a feminist theory of state.* Cambridge, MA: Harvard University Press.

MacKinnon, D. (2000). Equity, leadership, and schooling. *Exceptionality Education Canada, 10*(1&2), 5–21.

Majchrzak, A. (1984). *Methods for policy research.* Beverly Hills, CA: Sage.

Malen, B. (1994). The micropolitics of education: Mapping the multiple dimensions of power relations in school polities. In J. D. Scribner, & D. H. Layton, (Eds.), *The study of educational politics: Politics of education association yearbook.* Bristol, PA: Taylor & Frances.

Malen, B., & Knapp, M. (1997). Rethinking the multiple perspectives approach to education policy analysis: Implications for policy-practice connections. *Journal of Education Policy, 12*(5), 419–445.

Malen, B., & Ogawa, R. T. (1988). Professional-patron influence on site-based governance councils: A confounding case study. *Educational Evaluation and Policy Analysis, 10*(4), 251–270.

Malen, B., Ogawa, R. T., & Krantz, J. (1990). What do we know about school-based management? A case study of the literature—A call for research. In W. H. Clune & J. F. Witte (Eds.), *Choice and control in American education. Volume 2: The practice of choice, decentralization and school restructuring* (pp. 289–341). London: Falmer Press.

Mann, D., & Shakeshaft, C. (2003, January). In god we trust: All others bring data. *School Business Affairs* (www.asbointl.org).

Mansbridge, J. J. (1980). *Beyond adversary democracy.* New York: Basic Books.

Mapp, A. J., Jr. (1991). *Thomas Jefferson: Passionate pilgrim.* Lanham, MD: Madison Books.

Margonis, F. (1992). The cooptation of "at risk": Paradoxes of policy criticism. *Teachers College Record, 94*(2), 343–364.

Marshall, C. (1991). Educational policy dilemmas: Can we have control and quality and choice and democracy and equity? In K. Borman, P. Swami, & L. Wagstaff (Eds.), *Contemporary issues in U.S. education* (pp. 1–21). Norwood, NJ: Ablex.

Marshall, C. (1993a). The new politics of race and gender. In C. Marshall (Ed.), *The new politics of race and gender.* London: Falmer.

Marshall, C. (1993b). Politics of denial: Gender and race issues in administration. In C. Marshall (Ed.), *The new politics of race and gender.* London: Falmer.

Marshall, C. (Ed.). (1997a). *Feminist critical policy analysis: A perspective from primary and secondary schooling.* London: Falmer Press.

Marshall, C. (1997b). Undomesticated gender policy. In B. Bank & P. Hall (Eds.), *Gender, equity, and schooling: Policy and practice* (pp. 63–91). New York: Garland.

Marshall, C. (1999). Teacher's Unions' Activism for Gender Equity Policy in the United States, Australia, and Canada. Paper presented at the American Educational Research Association, Montreal, Canada.

Marshall, C. (2000a). Policy mechanisms for gender equity in Australia. *Educational Policy, 14*(3), 357–384.

Marshall, C. (2000b). Policy as discourse: Negotiating gender equity. *Journal of Education Policy, 5*(2), 125–156.

Marshall, C. (2002). Teacher unions and gender equity policy for education. *Educational Policy, 16*(5), 707–730.

Marshall, C., & Anderson, G. (1995). Rethinking the private and public spheres: Feminist and cultural studies perspectives on the politics of education. In J. Scribner & D. Layton (Eds.), *The study of educational politics.* London: Falmer Press.

Marshall, C. & McCarthy, M. (2002). School leadership reforms: Filtering social justice through dominant discourses. *Journal of School Leadership, 12,* 480–502.

Marshall, C., & Mitchell, D. (1991). The assumptive worlds of fledgling administrators. *Education and Urban Society, 23*(4), 396–415.

Marshall, C., Mitchell, D., & Wirt, F. (1989). *Culture and education policy in the American states.* London: Falmer Press.

Marshall, C., Oliva, M., Gerstl-Pepin, C., et al. (2001). *Administration and social justice policy in seven states.* Symposium conducted at the meeting of the American Educational Research Association, Seattle.

Marshall, C., & Patterson, J. (2002). Confounded Policies: Implementing Site-Based Management and Special Education and Policy Reforms. *Educational Policy, 16*(3), 351–386.

Marshall, C., & Scribner, J. D. (1991). Its all political: Inquiry into the micropolitics of education. *Education and Urban Society, 23*(4), 347–355.

Marshall, C., & Ward, M. (in press). Policymakers' perceptions of social justice training for leadership. *Journal of School Leadership.*

Martin, J. R. (1994). *Changing the educational landscape: Philosophy, women and curriculum.* New York: Routledge.

Masse, L. N., & Barnett, W. S. (2002). A benefit-cost analysis of the Abecedarian early childhood intervention. In H. M. Levin & P. J. McEwan (Eds.), *Cost-effectiveness and educational policy: 2002 yearbook of the American Education Finance Association.* Larchmont, NY: Eye On Education.

Matsuda, M. J., Lawrence, C., Delgado, R., & Williams-Crenshaw, K. (1993). *Words that wound: Critical race theory, assaultive speech, and the First Amendment.* San Francisco: Westview Press.

Mawhinney, H. B. (1993). An advocacy coalition approach to change in Canadian education. In P. A. Sabatier & H. C. Jenkins-Smith (Eds.), *Policy change and learning: An advocacy approach* (pp. 59–82). Boulder, CO: Westview Press.

Mawhinney, H. B. (1997). Institutionalizing women's voices, not their echoes, through feminist policy analysis of difference. In C. Marshall (Ed.), *Feminist critical policy analysis: A perspective from primary schooling* (Vol. II, pp. 216–238). London: Falmer Press.

Mawhinney, H. B. (1999). Reappraisal: The problems and prospects of studying the micropolitics of leadership in reforming schools. *School Leadership & Management, 19*(2), 159–170.

Mazurek, K., Winzer, M. A., & Majorek, C. (Eds.). (2000). *Education in a global society: A comparative perspective.* Boston: Allyn and Bacon.

Mazzoni, T. L. (1991). Analyzing state school policy making: An arena model. *Educational Evaluation and Policy Analysis, 13*(2), 115–138.

McCarthy, M. M., & Kuh, G. D. (1997). *Continuity and change: The educational leadership professoriate.* Columbia, MO: The University Council for Educational Administration.

McCarty, D. J., & Ramsey, C. E. (1971). *The school managers Westport,* CT: Greenwood.

McDaniel, J., & Miskel, C. (2002). Stakeholder salience: Business and educational policy. *Teachers College Record, 104*(2), 325–356.

McDonnell, L. M., & Elmore, R. F. (1991). Getting the job done: Alternative policy instruments. In A. R. Odden (Ed.), *Education policy implementation* (pp. 157–183). Albany: State University of New York Press.

McGivney, J. H., & Haught, J. M. (1972). The politics of education: A view from the perspective of the central office staff. *Educational Administration Quarterly, 8*(3), 18–38.

McGuire, K. (1990). Business involvement in education in the 1990s. In D. E. Mitchell & M. E. Goertz (Eds.), *Education politics for the new century* (pp. 107–117). New York: Falmer Press.

McIntosh, P. (1988). *White privilege and male privilege: A personal account of coming to see correspondences through work in women's studies.* Wellesley, MA: Wellesley College Center for Research on Women.

McLaren, P., & Farahmandpur, R. (2001). Teaching against globalization and the new imperialism: Toward a revolutionary pedagogy. *Journal of Teacher Education, 52*(2), 136–150.

McLaughlin, M. W. (1987). Learning from experience: Lessons from policy implementation. *Educational Evaluation and Policy Analysis, 9*(2), 171–178.

McLaughlin, M. W. (1990). The Rand change agent study revisited: Macro perspectives and micro realities. *Educational Researcher, 19*(9), 11–16.

McLaughlin, M., Henderson, K., & Rhim, L. M. (1997). *Reform for all? General and special education reforms in five local school districts.* Paper presented at the American Educational Research Association, Chicago.

McNeil, L. M. (1987). Exit, voice and community: Magnet teachers' responses to standardization. *Journal of Education Policy, 1*(1), 93–113.

McNeil, P. (2003). Rethinking high school: The next frontier for state policymakers. Queenstown, MD: The Aspen Institute Program on Education in a Changing Society. Accessed November 24, 2003, at http://www.aspeninstitute.org/Programt2.asp?i=92.

McRobbie, A. (1991). Feminism and youth culture: From "Jackie" to just *seventeen.* Boston: Unwin Hyman.

Meadmore, P. (2001). "Free, compulsory and secular?" The re-invention of Australian public education. *Journal of Educational Policy, 16*(2), 113–125.

Meier, D. (1995). *The power of their ideas: Lessons for America from a small school in Harlem.* Boston: Beacon Press.

Meier, D. (2002). *In schools we trust: Creating communities of learning in an era of testing and standardization.* Boston: Beacon Press.

Mertz, C., & Furman, G. (1997). *Community and schools: Promise and paradox.* New York: Teachers College Press.

Mills, C. W. (1956). *The power elite.* New York: Oxford University Press.

Milstein, M. M., & Jennings, R. (1973). *Educational policy-making and the state legislature: The New York experience.* New York: Praeger.

Minogue, M. (1983). Theory and practice in public policy and administration. *Policy and Politics, 11*(1), 63–85.

Mitchell, D. E., & Boyd, W. L. (2001). Curriculum politics in global perspective. *Educational Policy, 15*(1), 58–75.

Moe, T. M. (1980). *The organization of interests: Incentives and the internal dynamics of politics and interest groups.* Chicago: University of Chicago Press.

Mora, J. K. (2002). Caught in a policy web: The impact of education reform on Latino education. *Journal of Latinos in Education, 1*(1), 29–44.

Morales-Gomez, D. A., & Torres, C. A. (1992). Introduction: Education and development in Latin America. In D. A. Morales-Gomez & C. A. Torres, *Education, policy and social change: Experiences from Latin America* (pp. 1–22). Westport, CT: Praeger.

Moses, M. (2000). Why bilingual education policy is needed: A philosophical response to critics. *Bilingual Research Journal, 24*(4), 333–354.

Moses, M. (2002). *Embracing race: Why we need a race conscious policy.* New York: Teachers College Press.

Moses, R. P. (1994). Remarks on the struggle for citizenship and math/sciences literacy, *Journal of Mathematical Behavior 13,* 107–111.

Mouffe, C. (Ed.). (1992). *Dimensions of radical democracy: Pluralism, citizenship, community.* New York: Verso.

Mouffe, C., & LeClau, E. (1985). *Hegemony and socialist strategy: Toward a radical democratic politics.* New York: Verso.

Mungazi, D. A. (1993). *Educational policy and national character: Africa, Japan, the United States, and the Soviet Union.* New York: Praeger.

Munk, L. G. (1998). *Collective bargaining: Bringing education to the table.* Midland, MI: Mackinac Center for Public Policy.

Murphy, J. T. (1973a). *Grease the squeaky wheel: A report on the implementation of Title V or the Elementary and Secondary Education Act of 1965, grants to strengthen state departments of education.* Cambridge, MA: Harvard Graduate School of Education, Center for Educational Policy Research.

Murphy, J. T. (1973b). Title V of ESEA: The impact of discretionary funds on state education bureaucracies. *Harvard Educational Review, 43*(3), 362–385.

Murtadha-Watts, K. (1999). Spirited sisters: Spirituality and the activism of African American women in educational leadership. In L. Fenwick (Ed.) *School leadership: Expanding the horizons of the mind and the spirit.* Lancaster, PA: Technomic.

Murtadha-Watts, K. (2001). Multicultural curriculum and academic performance: African American women leaders negotiating school reform. In M. Sutton & B. A. U. Levinson (Eds.), *Policy as practice: Toward a comparative sociocultural analysis of educational policy* (pp. 103–122). Westport, CT: Ablex.

Naradowski, M., & Andrada, M. (2001). The privatization of education in Argentina. *Journal of Educational Policy, 16*(6), 585–595.

National Coalition of Women and Girls in Education (2003). Website. Retrieved December 13, 2003, from http://www.ncwge.org/.

National Commission on Excellence in Education. (1983). *A nation at risk.* Washington, DC: National Commission on Excellence in Education.

Nearing, S. (1967). *The new education.* New York: Arno Press.

Nelson, J. K. (2002). Tempest in a textbook: A report on the new middle-school history textbook in Japan. *Critical Asian Studies, 34*(1), 129–148.

Noblit, G. (1999). The possibilities of postcritical ethnographies: An introduction to this issue. *Educational Foundations, 13*(1), 3–6.

Noblit, G., Berry, B., & Dempsey, V. (1991). Political responses to reform: A comparative case study. *Education and Urban Society, 23*(4), 379–395.

Noddings, N. (1984). *Caring.* New York: Teachers College Press.

Noddings, N. (1992). *The challenge to care in schools: An alternative approach to education.* New York: Teachers College Press.

Noddings, N. (2002). *Starting at home: Caring and social policy.* Berkeley: University of California Press.

Nowakowski, J., & First, P. F. (1989). A study of school board minutes: Records of reform. *Education Evaluation and Policy Analysis, 11*(4), 389–404.

Nuttall, D. (1994). Choosing indicators. In Centre for Educational Research and Innovation (Ed.), *Making education count: Developing & using international indicators* (pp. 79–96). Paris: Organisation for Economic Co-operation and Development.

Oakes, J. (1985). *Keeping track: How schools structure inequality.* New Haven, CT: Yale University Press.

Oakes, J., & Lipton, M. (1999). *Teaching to change the world.* Boston: McGraw-Hill.

Oberschall, A. (1993). *Social movements, ideologies, interests, and identities.* London: Transaction.

Odden, A. R. (1991a). New patterns of educational policy implementation and challenge of the 1990s. In A. R. Odden, *Education policy implementation.* Albany: State University of New York Press.

Odden, A. R. (1991b). The evolution of education policy implementation. In A. R. Odden, *Education policy implementation.* Albany: State University of New York Press.

Odden, A.R. (Ed.). (1991c). *Education policy implementation.* New York: State University of New York Press.

Office of Educational Research and Improvement. (2000). *The state of charter schools, 2000: National study of charter schools, fourth-year report.* Washington, DC: U.S. Department of Education.

Ogbu, J. (1994). Race stratification in the United States: Why inequality persists. *Teachers College Record, 96*(2), 264–299.

O'Leary, M., Kellaghan, T., Madaus, G. F., & Beaton, A. E. (2000, August 21). Consistency of findings across international surveys of mathematics and science achievement: A comparison of IAEP2 and TIMSS. *Educational Policy Analysis Archives, 8*(43). From http://olam.ed.asu.edu/epaa/v8n43.html.

Olson, M., Jr. (1965). *The logic of collective action.* Cambridge, MA: Harvard University Press.

Omni, M., & Winant, H. (1993). On the theoretical concept of race. In C. McCarthy & W. Crichlow (Eds.), *Race, identity and representation in education* (pp. 3–10). New York: Routledge.

Opatow, S. (1991). Adolescent peer conflicts: Implications for students and for schools. *Education and Urban Society, 23*(4), 416–441.

Opfer, V. D. (2000). Paranoid politics, extremism, and the religious right: A case of mistaken identity. In S. Talburt & S. R. Steinberg (Eds.), *Thinking queer: Sexuality, culture, and education* (pp. 85–103). New York: Peter Lang.

Opfer, V. D. (2001a). Beyond self-interest: Educational interest groups and congressional influences. *Educational Policy, 15*(1), 135–152.

Opfer, V. D. (2001b). Charter schools and the panoptic effect of accountability. *Education and Urban Society, 33*(2), 201–215.

Opfer, V. D. (2002). The politics of elections and education: A question of influence. In V. D. Opfer & K. Wong (Eds.), *Electoral outcomes and education policy: The Politics of Education Association Yearbook, 2001.* New York: Corwin Press.

Opfer, A. D., & Denmark, V. (2002). Sorting out a sense of place: School and school board relationships in the midst of school-based decision making. *Peabody Journal of Education, 76*(2), 102–118.

Orfield, F. (with Schley, S., Glass, D., & Reardon, S.) (1994). The growth of segregation in American schools: Changing patterns of separation and poverty since 1968. *Equity & Excellence in Education, 27*(1), 5–8.

Ortiz, F. I. (1982). *Career patterns in education: Women, men and minorities in school administration.* New York: Praeger.

Ortiz, F. I., & Marshall, C. (1988). Women in educational administration. In N. J. Boyan (Ed.), *Handbook of research on educational administration* (pp. 123–142). New York: Longman.

Ortiz, F., & Ortiz, D. (1992). Politicizing executive action: The case of Hispanic female superintendents. In C. Marshall, *The new politics of race and gender.* Washington, DC: Falmer Press.

Ortiz, A. A., & Yates, J. R. (1983). Incidence of exceptionality among Hispanics: Implications for manpower planning. *NABE Journal, 7,* 41–54.

Paige, R. (2002). An overview of America's education agenda. *Phi Delta Kappan, 83*(9), 703–713.

Pateman, C., & Gross, E. (Eds.). (1987). *Feminist challenges: Social and political theory.* Boston: Northeastern University Press.

Patton, M. Q. (2002). *Qualitative research and evaluation methods,* (3rd ed.). New York: Longman.

Paul, J. L., Berger, N. H., Osnes, P. G., Martinez, Y. G., & Morse, W. C. (1997). *Ethics and decisionmaking in local schools: inclusion, policy, and reform.* Baltimore, MD: Paul H. Brooks.

Pedahzur, A. (2001). The paradox of civic education in non-liberal democracies: The case of Israel. *Journal of Educational Policy, 16*(5), 413–430.

Pedraza, P. (2002). Participatory action research in education: The national Latino/a education research agenda project. *Journal of Latinos in Education, 1*(1), 45–48.

People for the American Way (2003). Website. Retrieved December 13, 2003, from http://www.pfaw.org/pfaw/general/default.aspx?oid=11396.

Peters, B.G. (1999). *American public policy: Promise and performance* (5th ed.) New York: Seven Bridges Press.

Peterson, P., Rabe, B., & Wong, K. (1986). *When federalism works.* Washington, DC: Brookings Institute.

Pewewardy, C. (1998). Our children can't wait: Recapturing the essence of indigenous schools in the United States. *Cultural Survival Quarterly, 22*(1), 29–34.

Pewewardy, C. D. (1994). Culturally responsive pedagogy in action: An American Indian magnet school. In E. Hollins, J. E. King, & W. C. Haymon (Eds.), *Teaching diverse populations: Forumulating a knowledge base.* Buffalo: State University of New York Press.

Phillips, A. (1993). *Democracy and difference.* University Park: The Pennsylvania State University Press.

Pillow, W. (1997). Decentering silences/troubling irony: Teen pregnancy's challenge to policy analysis. In C. Marshall (Ed.), *Critical policy analysis: Dismantling the master's house I* (pp. 134–152). London: Falmer.

Pincus, F. L. (2000). Discrimination comes in many forms: Individual, institutional, and structural. In M. Adams et al. (Eds.), *Readings for diversity and social justice* (pp. 31–35). New York: Routledge.

Pizzarro, M. (1998). "Chicana/o Power!" Epistemology and methodology for social justice and empowerment in chicana/o communities. *Qualitative Studies in Education, 11*(1), 57–80.

Placier, M. (1996). The cycle of student labels in education: The cases of culturally deprived/disadvantaged and at risk. *Educational Administration Quarterly, 32*(2), 236–270.

Placier, M., Hall, P. M., McKendall, S. B., & Cockrell, K. S. (2000). Policy as the transformation of intentions: Making multicultural education policy. *Educational Policy, 14*(2), 259–289.

Placier, M., Walker, M., & Foster, B. (2002). Writing the "show-me" standards: Teacher professionalism and political control in the U.S. state curriculum policy. *Curriculum Inquiry, 32*(3), pp. 281–310.

Polsby, N. (1984). *Political innovation in America.* New Haven, CT: Yale University Press.

Pressman, J. L., & Wildavsky, A. (1973). *Implementation.* Berkeley: University of California Press.

Pride, R. A. (1995). How activists and media frame social problems: Critical events versus performance trends for schools. *Political Communication, 12,* 5–26.

Prosise, R., & Himes, L. (2002). The collective bargaining tightrope. *The School Administrator, 59*(6), 18–22.

Prost, A. (2000). The creation of the baccalaureate professional: A case study of decision making in French education. *Journal of Educational Policy, 15*(1), 19–31.

Provenzo, E. F., Jr., & McCloskey, G. N. (2000). Religion and public education: An introduction to the special issue. *Educational Policy, 14*(5), 541–547.

Purpel, D.E. (1999). *Moral outrage in education.* New York: Peter Lang.

Quantz, R. A. (1992). On critical ethnography (with some postmodern considerations). In M. D. LeCompte, W. L. Millroy, & J. Preissle (Eds.), *The handbook of qualitative research in education* (pp. 447–505). New York: Academic Press.

Quiroz, P. A. (2001). Beyond educational policy: Bilingual teachers and the social construction of teaching "science" for understanding. In M. Sutton & B. A. U. Levinson (Eds.), *Policy as practice: Toward a comparative sociocultural analysis of educational policy* (pp. 167–192). Westport, CT: Ablex.

Raab, C. (1982). *Elite interviewing as a tool for political research: The case of Scottish educational policy-making.* Presented at the European Consortium for Political Research, University of Nijmegen, Nijmegen, the Netherlands.

Raab, C. (1994). Where are we now: Reflections on the sociology of education policy. In D. H. B. Troyna, *Researching education policy: Ethical and methodological issues* (pp. 17–30). London: Falmer.

Rajput, J. S., & Walia, K. (2001). Reforms in teacher education in India. *Journal of Educational Change, 2*(3), 239–256.

Rapp, D. (2002). Social justice and the importance of rebellious, oppositional imaginations. *Journal of School Leadership, 12,* 226–245.

Ravitch, D. (1983). *The troubled crusade: American education, 1945–1980.* New York: Basic Books.

Rawls, J. (1971). *A theory of justice.* Cambridge, MA: Harvard University Press.

Reed, L. R. (1998). Power, pedagogy and persuasion: Schooling masculinities in the secondary school classroom. *Journal of Education Policy, 13*(4), 501–517.

Rein, M. (1983). Value-critical policy analysis. In D. Callahan & B. Jennings (Eds.), *Ethics, the social sciences and policy analysis.* New York: Plenum Press.

Research Policy Notes. (2003, February/March/April). *Learning from international studies? Better hurry.* OIA Info Memo (p. 11). Washington, DC: American Educational Research Association.

Reyes, A. (2002, November 2). *Alternative education: The criminalization of student behavior.* Paper presented at the University Council of Educational Administration, Pittsburgh, PA.

Reyes, P., & Rorrer, A. (2001). US school reform policy, state accountability systems, and the limited English proficient student. *Journal of Educational Policy, 16*(2), 163–178.

Reyes, P., Wagstaff, L. H., & Fusarelli, L. (1999). Delta forces: The changing fabric of American society and education. In J. Murphy & K. S. Louis (Eds.), *Handbook of research on educational administration* (pp. 183–201). San Francisco: Jossey-Bass.

Rhodes, R. A. W., & Marsh, D.(Eds.). (1992). *Policy networks in British government.* Oxford: Clarendon Press.

Rippa, S. A. (1992). *Education in a free society: An American history.* New York: Longman.

Robson, R. (2001). Our children: Kids of queer parents & parents & kids who are queer: Looking at sexual minority rights from a different perspective. *Albany Law Review, 64,* 915–948.

Roe, E. M. (1989). Narrative analysis for the policy analyst: A case study of the 1980–1982 medfly controversy in California. *Journal of Policy Analysis and Management, 8*(2), 251–273.

Roe, E. (1994). *Narrative policy analysis.* Durham, NC: Duke University Press.

Rorrer, A. (2002). Educational leadership and institutional capacity for equity. *UCEA Review, 43*(3), 1–5.

Rose, R. (1993). *Lesson-drawing in public policy: A guide to learning across time and space.* Chatham, NJ: Chatham House.

Rural Schools and Community Trust. (1999). Why rural matters: The need for every state to take action on rural education. Retrieved May 5, 2003, from http://www.ruraledu.org/newsroom/wrm_new.htm.

Rumbaut, R. G., & Cornelius, W. A. (Eds.). (1995). *California's immigrant children: Theory, research, and implications for educational policy.* San Diego, CA: Center for U.S.-Mexico Studies, University of California.

Rury, J.L. (2002). Democracy's high school? Social change and American secondary education in the post-Conant era. *American Educational Research Journal, 39*(2), 307–336.

Rusch, E. (1998). *Barriers to excellence: The culture of silence in school systems.* Paper presented to the University Council of Educational Administration, St. Louis, MO.

Ryan, B. (2001). Identity politics: The past, the present, and the future. In B. Ryan (Ed.), *Identity politics and the women's movement* (pp. 315–319). New York: New York University Press.

Ryan, J.E. (1999). The influence of race in school finance reform. *Michigan Law Review, 98*(432), 432–481.

Sabatier, P. A., & Jenkins-Smith, H. C. (1993). *Policy change and learning: An advocacy coalition approach.* Boulder, CO: Westview Press.

Sachs, J. (2000). The activist professional. *Journal of Educational Change, 1,* 77–95.

Sachs, J., & Blackmore, J. (1998). You never show you can't cope: Women in school leadership roles managing their emotions. *Gender & Education, 10*(3), 265–280.

Sacken, D. M., & Medina, M. J. (1990). Investigating the context of state-level policy formation: A case study of Arizona's bilingual education legislation. *Educational Evaluation and Policy Analysis, 12*(4), 389–402.

Sadker, M., Sadker, D., & Steindem, J. (1989). Gender equity and educational reform. *Educational Leadership, 46*(6), 44–47.

Samoff, J. (1999). Institutionalizing international influence. In R. F. Arnove & C. A. Torres, *Comparative education: The dialectic of the global and the local* (pp. 51–89). Lanham, MD: Rowman and Littlefield.

Saward, M. (1992). The civil nuclear network in Britain. In R. A. W. Rhodes & D. Marsh (Eds.), *Policy networks in British government.* Oxford: Clarendon Press.

Schemo, J. (2002). GOP forsees expansion of themes on education. Raleigh, North Carolina, *News and Observer,* November 10, p. 22A.

Schattschneider, E. E. (1960). *The semi-sovereign people: A realists view of democracy in America.* New York: Holt, Rinehart & Winston.

Scheurich, J. J. (1994). Policy archeology: A new policy studies methodology. *Education Policy, 9*(4), 297–316.

Scheurich, J. J. (1998). The grave dangers in the discourse on democracy. *International Journal of Leadership in Education, 1*(1), 55–60.

Scheurich, J. J., & Imber, M. (1991). Educational reforms can reproduce societal inequities: A case study. *Educational Administration Quarterly, 27*(3), 297–320.

Scheurich, J. J., & Young, M. D. (1997). Coloring epistemologies: Are our research epistemologies racially biased? *Educational Researcher, 26*(4), 4–16.

Schneider, A. L., & Ingram, H. (1997). *Policy design for democracy.* Lawrence: University of Kansas Press.

Schram, S. F. (1995). Against policy analysis: Critical reason and poststructural resistance. *Policy Sciences, 28*(4), 375–384.

Scott, C., Stone, B., & Dinham, S. (2001). "I love teaching but . . . ." International patterns of teacher discontent. *Education Policy Analysis Archives, 9*(28).

Scott, J. C. (1990). *Domination and the arts of resistance: Hidden transcripts.* New Haven, CT: Yale University Press.

Scribner, J. D., & Layton, D. H. (Eds.). (1995). *The study of educational politics: The 1994 commemorative Yearbook of the Politics of Education Association (1969–1994).* London: Falmer Press.

Sederberg, C.H., & Clark, S. (1990). Motivation and organizational incentives for high vitality teachers: A qualitative perspective. *Journal of Research and Development in Education, 24*(1), 6–13.

Segal, L. (1997). The pitfalls of political decentralization and proposals for reform: The case of New York City public schools. *Public Administration Review, 57*(2), 141–149.

Seidman, S. (1994). Queer-ing sociology, sociologizing queer theory: An introduction. *Sociological Theory, 12*(2), 166–177.

Senge, P. M. (1990). *The fifth discipline: The art and practice of the learning organization.* New York: Doubleday.

Sergiovanni, T.J. (1992). *Moral leadership: Getting to the heart of school improvement.* San Francisco: Jossey-Bass.

Shapiro, S. (1990). *Between capitalism and democracy: Educational policy and the crisis of the welfare state.* New York: Bergin & Garvey.

Shapiro, I., & Greenstein, R. (1999). The widening income gulf. Center on Budget and Policy Priorities. Retrieved December 3, 2003; from http://www.cbpp.org/9-4-99tax-rep.htm.

Shapiro, J. P., & Stefkovich, J. A. (2001). *Ethical decision making in education: Applying theoretical perspectives to complex dilemmas.* Mahwah, NJ: Lawrence Erlbaum.

Shaw, J. (1995). *Education, gender and anxiety.* London: Taylor and Francis.

Shaw, K. M. (2004). Using feminist critical policy analysis in the realm of higher education: The case of welfare reform as gendered educational policy. *Journal of Higher Education, 75*(1), 56–79.

Shaw, R. (1996). *The activist's handbook, A primer for the 1990s and beyond.* Berkeley: University of California Press.

Shields, C. (2004). Overcoming the pathologies of silence: Social justice and academic excellence. *Education Administration Quarterly, 40*(1), 111–134.

Shields, P., & Knapp, M. (1997). The promise and limits of school-based reform. *Phi Delta Kappan, 79*(4), 288–294.

Shimizu, K. (2001). The pendulum of reform: Educational change in Japan for the 1990s onward. *Journal of Educational Change, 2*(3), 193–205.

Sikes, M. (1995). From metaphoric landscapes to social reform: A case for holistic curricula. *Arts Education Policy Review, 96*(4), 26–31.

Skrla, L., Reyes, P., & Scheurich, J. J. (2000). Sexism, silence, and solutions: Women superintendents speak up and speak out. *Education Administration Quarterly, 36*(1), 44–75.

Skrla, L., Scheurich, J. J., Garcia, J., & Nolly, G. (2004). Equity audits: A practical leadership tool for developing equitable and excellent schools. *Educational Administration Quarterly, 40*(1), 135–163.

Smith, L. T. (1999). *Decolonizing methodologies: Research and indigenous peoples.* New York: Zed Books Ltd.

Smith, M. L., Heinecke, W., Noble, A. J. (1999). Assessment policy and political spectacle. *Teachers College Record, 101*(2), 157–191.

Snyder, H. N. (2000). *Sexual assault of young children as reported to law enforcement: Victim, incident, and offender characteristics.* Washington, D.C.: Bureau of Justice Statistics, U.S. Department of Justice.

Song, M., & Miskel, C. G. (2003). *What are the influentials? A cross-state social network analysis of the reading policy domain.* Paper presented at the annual meeting of the Amercian Educational Research Association, Chicago.

Spring, J. (1998). *Conflicts of interest: The politics of American education.* Boston: McGraw-Hill.

Spring, J. (2001). *Conflict of interests: The politics of American education* (4th ed.). Boston: McGraw-Hill.

Sproull, L. S. (1981). Response to regulation: An organizational process framework. *Administration and Society, 12*(4), 447–470.

Starratt, R. J. (1996). *Transforming educational administration: Meaning, community, and excellence.* New York: McGraw-Hill.

Stein, N. (1993). It happens here too: Sexual harassment and child abuse in elementary and secondary schools. In S. K. Biklen and D. Pollard (Eds.), *National Society for the Study of Education Yearbook 1993: Gender and education.* Chicago: University of Chicago Press.

Stephens, D. (1984). President Carter, the Congress, and NEA: Creating the Department of Education. *Political Science Quarterly, 98*(4), 641–663.

St. John, E., & Ridenour, C. (2001). *School leadership in a market setting: The influence of private scholarships on educational leadership in urban schools.* Bloomington: Indiana University Press.

St. Pierre, R., Goodson, B., Layzer, J., & Bernstein, L. (1994). *National impact of the comprehensive child development program.* Cambridge, MA: Abt Associates.

Stone, D. (1997). *Policy paradox: The art of political decision making.* New York: W. W. Norton & Company.

Stout, R. T., Tallerico, M., & Paredes-Scribner, K. (1995). Values: The "what?" of the politics of education. In

J. D. Scribner & D. H. Layton (Eds.) *The study of educational politics* (pp. 5–20). Washington, DC: Falmer Press.

Stromquist, N. P. (1995). *Romancing the state: Gender and power in education.* Paper presented at the Comparative and International Educational Society annual conference, Boston.

Stromquist, N., & Monkman, K. (2000). Defining globalization and assessing its implications on knowledge and education. In N. Stromquist & K. Monkman (Eds.), *Globalization and education: Integration and contestation across cultures* (pp. 3–25). Boulder, CO: Rowman and Littlefield.

Stroufe, G. E. (1995). Politics of education at the federal level. In J. D. Scribner & D. H. Layton (Eds.), *The study of educational politics* (pp. 75–88). London: Falmer Press.

Student's Rights Violated, Judge Says. (2002). *The News & Observer,* p. 12A.

Suarez-Orozco, M. M. (1998). State terrors: Immigrants and refugees in the post-national space. In Y. Zou & E. T. Trueba (Eds.). *Ethnic identity and power: Cultural contexts of political action in school and society* (pp. 283–320). New York: State University of New York Press.

Sung, E. (2002). Some steered from SAT. *The News & Observer,* p. A1.

Swadener, B. B., & Lubeck, S. (Eds.). (1995). *Children and families "at promise": Deconstructing the discourse of risk.* Albany: State University of New York Press.

Talburt, S. (1999). Open secrets and problems of queer ethnography: Readings from a religious studies classroom. *International Journal of Qualitative Studies in Education, 12*(5), 525–539.

Tallerico, M. (1989). The dynamics of superintendent-school board relationships: A continuing challenge. *Urban Education, 24*(2), 215–232.

Taylor, A. (2001). "Fellow travelers" and "true believers": A case study of religion and politics in Alberta schools. *Journal of Educational Policy, 16*(1), 15–37.

Taylor, S. (1997). Critical policy analysis: Exploring contexts, texts and consequences. *Discourse: Studies in the Cultural Politics of Education, 18*(1), 23–35.

Taylor, S., Rizvi, F., Lingard, B., & Henry, M. (1997). *Educational policy and the politics of change.* New York: Routledge.

Thompson, A. (1998). Not the color purple: Black feminist lessons for educational caring. *Harvard Educational Review, 68*(4), 522–554.

Thrupp, M. (2001). Education policy and social class in England and New Zealand. *Journal of Educational Policy, 16*(4), 297–314.

Torrez, N.M. (2001). Incoherent English immersion and California Proposition 227. *The Urban Review, 33*(3), 207–220.

Townsend, R. G. (1990). Toward a broader micropolitics of schools. *Curriculum Inquiry, 20*(2), 205–225.

Trend, D. (1997). *Cultural democracy: Politics, media, new technology.* Albany, NY: SUNY.

Trinh, M. T. (1989).*Women, native, other: Writing postcoloniality and feminism.* Bloomington: Indiana University Press.

Truman, D. B. (1951). *The governmental process: Political interests and public opinion.* New York: Alfred A. Knopf.

Tyack, D. (1992). Restructuring in historical perspective: Tinkering toward utopia. *Teachers College Record, 92*(2), 170–191.

Tyack, D., & Hansot, E. (1982). *Managers of virtue: Public school leadership in America, 1890–1980.* New York: Basic Books.

UNIFEM: The United Nations Development Fund for Women. (2003). Website. Retrieved on December 12, 2003, from http://www.unifem.undp.org/newsroom/index.html.

U.S. Department of Education. (2002). National Center for Education Statistics: Statistics of State School Systems; Revenues and expenditures for public elementary and secondary education; and Common core of data survey, Table 156: Revenues for public elementary and secondary school, by source of funds: 1919–2000. Retrieved May 25, 2004, from http://www.nces.ed.gov/programs/digest/do2/index.asp.

Van Meter, D. S., & Van Horn, C. E. (1975). The policy implementation process, a conceptual framework. *Administration and Society, 6*(4), 445–488.

Verba, S., & Nie, N. H. (1972). *Participation in America: Political democracy and social equality.* New York: Harper and Row.

Villenas, S. (1996). Chicana ethnographer: Identity, marginalization, and co-optation in the field. *Harvard Educational Review, 66*(4), 711–731.

Villenas, S. (2001). Latina mothers and small-town racisms: Creating narratives of dignity and moral education in North Carolina. *Anthropology and Education Quarterly, 32*(1), 3–28.

Vinovskis, M. A. (1999). *History and educational policymaking.* New Haven, CT: Yale University Press.

Vogler, K. E. (2002). Ruling out rules: The impact of high-stakes, test-mandated student performance assessment on teachers' instructional practices. *Education, 123*(1), 39–55.

Wagstaff, L., & Gallagher, K. S. (1992). Schools, families, and communities: Idealized images of new realities. In *Educational leadership and the changing contexts of families, communities, and schools, Part II* (pp. 91–117). 89th Yearbook of the Study of Education. Chicago: University of Chicago Press.

Walker, A. (2001, May 14). MCAS critic is silenced. *Boston Globe,* Metro/Region, p. B1.

Walker, E. M. (2003). Devolving authority. *Education Policy Analysis Archives, 10*(33). Website. Retrieved May 24, 2004, from http://epaa.asu.edu/epaa/v1On33.html.

Walsh, M. (2003). Four Vermont schools opt out of federal program. *Burlington Free Press,* pp. A1, A5.

Waters, G. A. (1998). Critical evaluation for education reform. *Educational Policy Analysis, 6*(20), 17.

Watts, T. G. (1989). Electoral structure and opportunities for blacks to achieve school board office in North Carolina. Unpublished doctoral dissertation.

Weatherford, J. M. (1981). *Tribes on the hill.* New York: Rawson, Wade.

Weatherly, R., & Lipsky, M. (1977). Street level bureaucrats and institutional innovation: Implementing special education reform. *Harvard Educational Review, 47*(2), 171–197.

Weber, D. (2001, December 14). State Ed Dept. Sued for Halting Anti-MCAS Speaker. *Boston Herald,* News, p. 22.

Weber, M. (1947). *The theory of social and economic organization.* Glencoe, IL: Free Press.

Weick, K. E. (1976). Educational organizations as loosely coupled systems. *Administrative Science Quarterly, 21,* 1–18.

Weiler, K. (1993). Feminism and the struggle for a democratic education: A view from the states. In M. Arnot & K. Weiler (Eds.), *Feminism and social justice in education: International perspectives.* Bristol, PA: Falmer Press.

Weimer, D. L., & Vining, A. R. (1989). *Policy analysis: Concepts and practice.* Englewood Cliffs, NJ: Prentice Hall.

Weiss, C. H. (1989). Congressional committees as uses of analysis. *Journal of Policy Analysis and Management, 8*(3), 425.

Welner, K.G., & Oakes, J. (2000). *Navigating the politics of detracking: Leadership strategies.* Arlington Heights, IL: Skylight Professional Development.

Westbury, I. (1992). Comparing American and Japanese achievement: Is the United States really a low achiever? *Educational Researcher, 21*(5), 18–24.

White, L.E. (2001). Raced histories, mother friendships, and the power of care: Conversations with women in Project Head Start. *Chicago-Kent Law Review* (76 Chi.-Kent. L. Rev. 1569). Downloaded June 23, 2003, from http://web.lexis-nexis.com/universe/printdoc.

Whitty, G., Power, S., & Halpin, D. (1998). *Devolution and choice in education: The school, the state, and the market.* Birmingham, UK: Open University Press.

Willis, P. (1997). *Learning to labor.* Westmead, England: Saxon House.

Willower, D. (1991). Micropolitics and the sociology of school organizations. *Education and Urban Society, 23*(4), 442–454.

Wink, J. (1999). *Critical pedagogy: Notes from the real world.* New York: Longman.

Wirt, F. M., & Kirst, M. W. (1992). *Schools in conflict.* Berkeley, CA: McCutchan.

Wirth, A. G. (1990). The violation of people at work in schools. In W. E. Eaton. (Ed.), *Shaping the superintendency: A reexamination of Callahan and the cult of efficiency.* New York: Teachers College Press.

Witherell, C., & Noddings, N. (Eds.). (1991). *Stories lives tell: Narrative and dialogue in education.* New York: Teachers College Press.

Wong, K. (1999). *Funding public schools: Politics and policies.* Lawrence: University of Kansas Press.

Wong, P. L., & Balestino, R. (2001). Prioritizing the education of marginalized young people in Brazil: A collaborative approach. *Journal of Educational Policy, 16*(6), 597–618.

Woolcock, M. (1998). Social capital and economic development: Toward a theoretical synthesis and policy framework. *Theory and Society, 27*(2), 151–208.

Young, I. M. (1990). *Justice and the politics of difference.* Princeton, NJ: Princeton University Press.

Young, K. (1977). "Values" in the policy process. *Policy and Politics, 5*(3), 1–22.

Zimmerman, J. (2002). *Whose America? Culture wars in the public schools.* Cambridge, MA: Harvard University Press.

Zou, Y., & Trueba, E. T. (Eds.). (1998). *Ethnic identity and power: Cultural contexts of political action in school and society.* Albany: State University of New York Press.

Index